Johnny Deadline, Reporter

JOHNNY

The Best of

BOB

DEADLINE, REPORTER

GREENE

Nelson-Hall nh Chicago

Library of Congress Cataloging in Publication Data

Greene, Bob.
  Johnny Deadline, reporter.

  I. Title.
AC8.G8318   081   76-6932
ISBN 0-88229-361-3

Grateful acknowledgment is made for permission to reprint lyrics from the following songs:

"The Night Chicago Died," copyright 1974 by Intune Ltd., London, England.

"Mrs. Robinson," copyright 1968 by Paul Simon.

"The Ballad of Bobby Greene," copyright 1975 by August Day Music Inc.

For Susan, of course

Contents

Foreword

Newspaper columnists, like cartoonists, tend to get hooked on "style." Not only is it fun to be recognized, but it gives you something to fall back on. When ideas fail, you can always be your cute self.

The danger, of course, is that "style" tends to take over. Eventually, as with a character actor, the writer's personality tends to dominate the story he's trying to tell.

So far in his bright career, Bob Greene has avoided this. What makes him really special, in my opinion, is that it is obvious from his choice of subjects that he feels deeply about them—while managing not to inject himself into their scenes.

Greene gently leads his reader up to the person he's describing, makes sure the two have met, and leaves them alone. Almost never using tape, and discreetly and unobtrusively making notes, Greene gets it all and gets it right.

In this collection of columns there is a devastating story of Judge Julius Hoffman watching a TV dramatization of himself presiding over the Chicago 7 trial. The reporter resists satirizing the old man. He lets Hoffman render his own verdict.

Bob handles sentimental stuff in an offhand way that has you reaching for the Kleenex before you know you've been had. He tells of a young woman who's lived a hard life and discovers her father after 27 years, and he tells of a black teenager who is paralyzed by a stranger's bullet. He makes what happens to them important to you, and he never gets between you and them.

And that is the ultimate in style.

BILL MAULDIN

Introduction

Most of the stories in this collection were written with one eye on the clock. They cover a period ranging from the beginning to the middle of the 1970s. Looking back over the pieces now, as this book is prepared to go to press, I am tempted to change them—smooth them out, update the opinions, delete some of the naivetes that inevitably appear.

But I don't think I'll do that. The stories will stand as they were written—as deadline pieces, as journalism produced on the run, usually for consumption the next morning. Taken as a whole, I hope they say something about what has been going on in our country during this particular and unique time in history. They are a very personal look, to be sure—but having been there myself, I hope I am able to convey to you what it was like.

"Johnny Deadline" started as a joke around the office—the kind of perfect newspaper name for a speeded-up kid reporter racing all over town all day long, trying to find something that will get him a byline in the next edition. It became sort of a jesting persona, but all of a sudden I began to realize that it stands for something somewhat serious, too: for a certain period in my life, a period that has been fun and exciting and even thrilling, but which nevertheless has a duration that is anything but certain. Doing this kind of work is a young man's game, and I feel lucky that I have been allowed to play it.

Chicago is the perfect town for it. I have a feeling that the young Ben Hecht understood the Johnny Deadline feeling, too, and that he felt just as fortunate to have had his crack at it before he became too old to take the risk of embarrassing himself at times. Because if there's anything that these pieces are, they're headlong jumps at the news, and when you do that, you run the daily risk of failing big. It's hard to make a quiet mistake in front of a million or so readers.

What I do is write a daily column for the *Chicago Sun-Times*. The editors of the paper, for some secret reason that I hope to be let in on some day, decided in 1971 to give me a free run at the town. The ideas, the assignments, the research, the reporting, and the execution are my own, and seldom do my bosses interfere. Often I can sense a gnashing of teeth coming from the front office, but hardly ever has the gnashing become any more than that, and I can't imagine a better group of men to work for.

The column, as you know if you read it regularly, and as you will find out if you are seeing it here for the first time, has no specific focus. I have one guideline: if it interests me, I go out and write about it. I am often asked how I get a new idea every day, and the answer is, I don't know. My backlog of columns is zero. When I wake up in the morning, there is nothing to fall back on, no rainy-day column to pull out of a bottom drawer. My days are spent looking for something that somebody out there might want to read about. My deadline is in the early evening. Every night at 11 o'clock, when the three-star edition begins to come off the presses, I'm on the telephone to Max Limanowski, the young city desk assistant who mans the telephones, to see how the column made out, where it was played and what the headline writers put on top of it. Max and I have a kind of verbal shorthand. "City desk," he'll answer. "Paper up?" I'll say. "Yep," he'll say, and then give me the specifics. Only then do I give a thought to what might be in store for the next day.

There are two questions that I get asked most often: "Doesn't the pace wear you out?" and "Don't you feel that you're unbelievably lucky to have such a job?" The answer to both, of course, is yes. This kind of work turns you into a zombie, but for my money I'm the luckiest zombie in the world. Being allowed to go out and see whatever of life I choose and then getting paid to tell a city of people about it, and getting paid well on top of that—the Johnny Deadline days are going to be quite a thing to look back on. I'm glad it has happened so fast, because if I'd had the time to think about it, I never would have believed it.

Well, enough of this. Before we get into the book itself, I want to acknowledge the *Chicago Sun-Times,* in which the great majority of this material originally appeared, for permission to reprint it here. Thanks also to the following publications for their permission to reprint some of the pieces in the collection: *Newsweek, Harper's, Sport,* and *New Times.*

And finally, some thank yous to some people who have been so kind to me along the way. In Columbus, Mrs. Sara Amos, Don Weaver, Charles Egger, Jack Keller, Sam Perdue, Tom Keys and Kaye Kessler; in Evanston, George Heitz and the late Fred Whiting; in Chicago, Emmett Dedmon, Dick Trezevant, Jim Hoge, Ralph Otwell, Jim Peneff, Dick Takeuchi and Joe Reilly. Special thanks go to three men who first provided inspiration and peerless examples from afar, and later personal kindness and encouragement from up-close: Jimmy Breslin, Larry L. King, and Jack Griffin.

BOB GREENE
Chicago, September, 1975

1
ON THE
STREET

This chapter begins with a young mother hacked to death on a sunny afternoon in a Chicago park, and it ends with a girl singing a private, cryptic tune on a sidewalk outside a funeral home. These columns are street reporting, in the sense that to get them, I had to go out into the city and look. Most aren't as gruesome as the first—the night backstage at a performance of the Joffrey Ballet was a far more pleasant way to spend a few hours than examining the spot where Mrs. Judith Ott was murdered—but in each of the pieces the intention was to take the reader along, to put him on the street with the reporter and to let him see how it was at a particular hour on a particular day in a particular city.

Murder on a Summer Afternoon

Murder in the afternoon. These are some of the sights and sounds and thoughts that come to you at a place of sudden death:

———There can be no more helpless feeling in the human experience than the one that shot through David Ott at 1:40 P.M. Monday, as he stood on a patch of grass holding his young son and listened to his wife's last wrenching scream come from inside that brown frame washroom over there, a pebble's fling away. "The husband was right here where you're standing now," says Paul V. McLaughlin, the weary-faced white-haired commander of the First Police District. "Right here. This close. Twenty, twenty-five feet away." From this distance, David Ott could have heard his wife if she had spoken to him in normal, conversational voice. He was close enough to count the slats on the side of the washroom, to read the signs that say the park closes at 11:00 P.M., and that there is a $200 fine for littering. Close enough to discern the pattern of the wire in the mesh windows of the little building. But unable to do anything for the wife who was dying within easy distance of his voice.

———People are used to the idea of murder. The place of the killing is directly next to Lake Shore Drive, and so each car in the long southbound line has to pass by the washroom. "Let's go, let's go, let's go," the traffic cops keep calling between bursts of their whistles, and when the motorists ask, "What's going on?" and are told, "A lady was murdered," the response is usually "Oh, really." And then a turn to the other passengers in the car, and a repetition of the phrase: "A lady was murdered." No crowd of any size forms behind the police lines. No crowd, even in Grant Park; even on a hot summer day; even in the middle of the afternoon.

———Five minutes after the act of random horror, a murder site becomes the safest place in the city. It is almost as if by gorging the tiny area with uniformed patrolmen and brown-suited detectives and crime lab photographers and newspaper reporters and television and radio correspondents, we are proving to ourselves how easily a place can be made secure and normal. But ten minutes ago, none of these people were here; just a man with an 8-inch knife, waiting in the women's washroom for someone to come in. Waiting for the one moment that will make him famous, talked about throughout the city.

——There is a crushed, 16-ounce Schlitz beer can half-covered with dirt near the washroom. This is the kind of detail that you notice only at a time like this. Normally, you would not even notice the corner, would not even notice that there is a public washroom here. But noticing details is a kind of catharsis; it is a temporary way of avoiding the reality of the situation, the blunt, simple reality of what happened in there. So you notice the beer can; you notice the neat piles of tree limbs that have just been pruned by park workers; you notice the bare dirt patch in the middle of the grass; you notice the stubby chimney atop the washroom; you notice that the number of the blue-and-white police squadrol at the end of the path is 6178. These are easier thoughts to deal with than the thought that a young life that existed ten minutes ago exists no more.

——"This is what happens when you take away the death penalty," says a man watching from behind the restraining ropes. "Now maybe people will complain about security in the park," says another man. But neither man's ideas have anything to do with the truth of what happened on this piece of land on this day. Strict laws and swarms of security guards cannot prevent a man from watching a restroom until he sees that he can sneak inside, and then waiting until he can kill.

——"The way it looks now, with the repeated stab wounds, it's an entirely different kind of crime. There were no stab wounds in the other ones." Commander McLaughlin talking again, down-playing the thought that this day's killer of Judith Elaine Ott is also responsible for the three other murders in Grant Park in the past year.

——This is the part of Chicago that the city government wants people to see. The skinny facade along the lakefront. The long stretch of park. The Art Institute across the way. The sailboats in the marina on the other side of Lake Shore Drive. The Prudential

Building and the new Standard Oil Building over to the right. This is the part of the city that Chicago is proud of. The part of the city that is pointed out to tourists and visitors. Like David and Judith Ott and their baby son Aaron, travelers on their way west, who had a few hours to waste between trains.

——A few blocks away, in the police headquarters building at 11th and State, David Ott is sitting in a small room telling the investigators what he remembers about the 30 seconds that have crushed his personal universe. His baby is crying, and the baby's voice fills the adjacent waiting room every time the door is opened for a policeman to go in or out. For the rest of his life, David Ott will be asking himself why he and his wife had to decide to walk in the park, why they had to decide to turn this way instead of that way, why they had to decide to stop at this particular washroom, at the corner of Jackson and Lake Shore Drive. In the headquarters of the Chicago police, a place he never thought he would ever be, David Ott is now talking about it for the first time.

——They have not cleaned the blood out of the washroom yet. But other than that, it is over. Judith Ott is dead. David Ott is telling his story to the police. A suspect is in custody. The park is quiet again. A passerby who has been watching the death scene turns around, and looks out at the lake. "What a beautiful day," he says. . . .

Celebration of Leavings

It is supposed to be a night for noise and laughter and forgetting the bad things that have come in the 12 months before. It is supposed to be nonstop whisky talk, and wishes for only the finest of luck in the days to come. And for most people, at ten minutes until midnight on the eve of the new year, it was like that.

But there are others. At ten minutes until midnight on the last day of the year, James L. Dickston took a cracked plastic plate and scraped the remains of a cheeseburger and french fries from it. The mess plopped into a rubber-rimmed hole, where it joined the leavings of an entire evening of cheap meals.

"Jimmy, you falling asleep in there, or what?" came the voice from the other side of the high counter. "We need some forks out here, hurry it up, will you?"

So James L. Dickston wiped his hands on the front of his dirty apron. He turned around and picked up a basket full of silverware, and he carried it out to the front of the restaurant.

There weren't many people in the place. A coffee shop on North Broadway is no place to spend New Year's Eve, and most of the customers were men sitting by themselves and reading the newspaper. Dickston didn't even look at them as he handed the utensils to the counterman, then turned and walked back into the kitchen.

James L. Dickston is a bus boy, although that is a misnomer. For he is 47 years old, a black man who came to Chicago from Mississippi 35 years ago. His job in life is to take the plates as they come into the kitchen, and to remove the leftovers of the meal from them. Then he hands the plates to another man, this one really no more than a teenager, who washes them and dries them and stacks them so they can be used again.

Dickston does this every night, and New Year's Eve was just another shift for him. He would work until the end of his eight hours, and then he would take the L to his home on the South Side, and then he would sleep until it was time to come back for the next shift.

There was a clock in the kitchen, but it had broken some time ago, at 7:42 on some forgotten morning or evening. Dickston was not wearing a watch, so unless someone told him, he would not know when midnight came.

The younger man did not have any dishes to soap up at the moment, so he called over to Dickston. "Some party we having tonight, huh Jimmy?" he said with a laugh.

Dickston looked up, but did not smile. "One night's like another," he said. Dickston has a slight speech impediment, causing the words to run into each other, but the younger man understood him.

"My girl don't believe that," the younger man said. "She don't like sitting by herself on New Year's Eve."

Dickston shrugged, "Just another night," he said. "I'm too old to start worrying about finding a woman to wait up past midnight for me."

Out front, one of the men at the counter was listening to a transistor radio. The station was playing hit songs from the year just past. The disk jockey interrupted in the middle of a song.

"We've got just about 15 seconds left to go," came the tinny voice from the radio. "Make that 10 . . . 5, 4, 3, 2 . . . Happy New Year, everybody!"

All over town they were singing and kissing each other and ordering one more drink. If James L. Dickston was aware that the new year had begun, he wasn't showing it.

He knocked a piece of toast from a dirty plate and methodically passed the plate over to the young man who washed the dishes. When someone came into the kitchen to shake Dickston's hand and wish him a good new year, he looked surprised.

"I'm not one to celebrate much," said James L. Dickston, a small part of a big city on a noisy night, waiting for the end of his eight-hour shift.

Bikers for Christ

I was walking to work Monday when I was confronted by three of the dirtiest, smelliest, most menacing-looking motorcycle hoods I had ever seen. My first instinct was to run. My second was to apologize for being alive. My third was to hand over my wallet and

say thank you. Before I could act, though, the gang members began
to talk to me.

"God loves you," said the first biker.

"Look to Christ," said the second biker.

"Without Christ, life is nothing," said the third biker.

This was an original prelude to a chain-whipping, I thought. I
decided to wait for my stomping like a man.

"Relax," said the first gang member. "We are Christ's Patrol."
All three of them shook hands with me.

"Uh . . . you mean you're not a motorcycle gang?" I said.

"Yes, we are a gang," said one of the members. "We are a gang
for Jesus."

The threesome introduced themselves. They were Phillip
(Blade) Smith (the nickname came from his dexterity with a knife),
Robert (Blacky) Munroe, and Jimmy (Simon) Bullard. They said
that their gang was based in California and admitted that most
people who see them assume that they are "a hell-raising, terroriz-
ing group of guys." They looked at one another and giggled.

"The moral fiber of our nation is collapsing every day," said
Blacky.

"America is in severe shape morally," said Blade.

"Like Sodom and Gomorrah," said Simon.

Blade said that Christ's Patrol has more than 500 members and
that the three of them were in Chicago to recruit new believers from
local motorcycle gangs. He said that they also were trying to
convince young people to attend a June rally sponsored by something called the "Youth Crusade for America."

They postured in their cruddy leather jackets, chains, denims
and beards as they told me of their mission for righteousness.

"What you're saying is disgusting," I said. "If there's one thing
we decent Americans have always been able to depend on, it's the
thought that motorcycle thugs like you are villainous, degenerate
outlaws. Now you're trying to take even that away from us. What is
happening to our country? You ought to be ashamed of yourselves."

Blacky moved toward me quickly and jammed a hand into his
pocket. I recoiled in terror.

"Be cool," Blacky said. "I was just reaching for this." He
handed me a miniature Bible.

"I was in gangs in Detroit since I was a teenager," Blacky said. "I rode with the Unforgiven Few. I was a heavy drinker, a fighter. Then I saw the Lord. It changed me. I've only been riding with Christ's Patrol for a month, but I am a new man. Oh, yeah. I am super-happy. I have so much happiness." He stared at me, and I found myself nodding in agreement.

"A lot of the other gangs don't like us," said Blade, who says he is a reverend, too. "They don't want the word to get out that we are converting their member bikers to Christ. They think that the goody-goody image will hurt them. But it's spreading like wildfire."

He said that one gang leader in California had become so infuriated with the Gospel as preached by this Jesus gang that the biker had pulled out a switchblade knife and held it to Blade's throat.

"I just kept telling him that Christ loved them and died for their sins," Blade said. "He started to thrust his knife toward my throat time after time, but he couldn't make himself do it. Jesus had reached him."

"They must confess their sins," Blacky said. "If they confess, then they will be comforted."

Blade said, "The Bible says, 'I become all things to all men, that I may in some way win some.' That's Paul the apostle."

"It is the Lord's way," Blacky said.

"Oh, stop it," I said.

Blade said he was trying to line up a business deal with Pat Boone.

"Pat Boone?" I said.

"He's terrific," Blade said.

"He's great," Simon said.

"I've always liked him," Blacky said.

"A beautiful person," Blade said.

Blade, Simon, and Blacky told a few stories about their pasts, including duties with gang "execution committees" and fights with daggers, pliers, clubs, and the like.

Then they said they had to be going. They had parked a few streets over and were worried about the police.

"We don't want any parking tickets in Chicago," Blade said.

"Christ is the answer," said Blacky.

Taking Note of Tony

When a man is very old, and he has no money and no family and very few friends, death holds a special terror. The prospect of one's body lying forgotten in a strange funeral home, with no one to care or come pay respects, is a final humiliation that even in a life of loneliness is difficult to accept. So when Tony Nawrot, a 72-year-old man who lived by himself in a first-floor rear flat at 1108 N. Hermitage and who could neither read nor write, died last week, it was with the certain knowledge that he would leave no trace of his life behind him.

Tony never considered himself to be anything special, and this morning is the first time his name ever appeared in a newspaper. He was only 5 feet tall, and never weighed more than 120 pounds. The other people in the neighborhood knew him by sight, and some knew his first name, but not many have noticed that he is no longer there. There are many like Tony; they die every day, and no one takes note of another old man gone.

"Tony wanted a kitten," said Joe Masbaum. Joe is young, a 29-year-old who lives in the apartment building next door to the place Tony lived, and who took a liking to the old man and treated him kindly. "I had a mother cat and four kittens, and Tony came up to me one day and said, 'Could I have one, please? I have nothing, and I would like to have one of the kittens to come live with me. It would mean a great deal to me if you possibly had an extra kitten you could give me.' "

There were others who also had asked for the kittens, so Joe asked Tony to wait for a day or two. When Joe went to ask Tony if he still wanted the kitten, the old man said that perhaps a puppy would be better for him. He would like to have a puppy if he could.

So one day Joe decided to take Tony on a little trip. Tony spent most of his days just sitting inside, and Joe thought it would be nice to let him get off the block for a few hours. The young man took the old man to Navy Pier, to sit in the sun and look at the lake.

"We had a nice time," Joe said. "Tony got a little sad. He told me that he wished he could find some odd job that he could do for five or ten hours a week, just so he could feel he was worth something to somebody. I didn't know what to say to him. So I told him that maybe we could go fishing some time. On the way back to his apartment, I stopped the car at the Anti-Cruelty Society. I thought I would buy Tony a pet. You should have seen him looking at the animals. He was so happy to be around them. He was just crazy about them. He wanted this miniature German shepherd, but Tony was kind of weak, and the dog kept jumping and knocking him over, so we decided it was best not to buy it. I took him home without a pet."

Most of Tony's days were spent in the apartment of a 60-year-old widow who lived upstairs in the same building. The woman's apartment faced the street, which Tony's did not, and he would welcome the chance to sit in front of her window and look out at Hermitage Avenue. It was not much of a view—just other old apartment buildings—but it was better than what he had in his own apartment.

"He never went anywhere, hardly," the widow said. "He would just look out that window. He didn't have anything to do at night, of course. So about seven o'clock every evening, I'd say, 'Well, I'll see you in the morning, Tony.' And then he would go downstairs to his own place. He didn't have a TV. Just a radio. And he would listen to the radio until he fell asleep."

When Tony died, the police called the Malec & Sons Funeral Home at 834 N. Ashland, which buries many of the people from the neighborhood. They came and got the body and then waited for the inevitable period of time that passes between the day an impoverished old man with no relatives dies, and the day the public aid authorities approve payment for a simple funeral.

The only people Tony really knew, the widow and Joe Masbaum, thought they should do something. So the widow bought a new pair of brown pants, and a gold short-sleeved shirt. Joe selected one of his own neckties, one that was not so youthful and stylish-looking that it would seem foolish on Tony, and he took the clothing over to the funeral home and asked that Tony be buried in it, so that he would look nice.

On Monday, the word came through that Tony could be buried with public funds. "We're trying to set up a time for it now," said a man from the funeral home. "We're trying to locate some people to come to the funeral. We haven't been able to reach anyone, not yet. It happens a lot this way in this neighborhood. So many older people who came to America from Europe, with no relatives and no will."

The funeral will take place this week. "I suppose there will just be the two of us there," said Joe Masbaum, the 29-year-old who took Tony to the lake. "Just me and the widow lady from Tony's building." Joe said that he hopes Tony will look presentable in the new shirt and pants and tie. He said that he had checked to see if the old man needed new shoes to be buried in, and that he had found out that Tony's feet were so small that he had died wearing a pair of children's shoes, size eight children's shoes. . . .

Homicide Cop

"It makes you wonder what's happened to our concept of the value of a human life," Joe Di Leonardi said. "We'll go out on a homicide investigation, to a house where there's just been a murder, the wife has shot the husband. And so we'll walk into the living room . . . and the husband's dead body will be on the living room floor, and the wife will be sitting there watching a television program! We'll ask her what happened, and she'll start talking about the TV show. She'll tell us what's happened on the program."

Di Leonardi is the commander of the Chicago Police Department's homicide section. His task is a grisly one. Last year the city set a record, with 970 murders. Di Leonardi took over the homicide section in December; his job is not to prevent murders—it is to solve them after they've been committed. But he sees violent death on a more regular basis than almost any other man in the

United States, and he can't avoid having some thoughts about what is going on.

"I don't want to sound corny, and I know that a lot of people do a lot of talking about the moral decay of our society," Di Leonardi, 42, said. "But homicide detectives see the end result. The murderers are getting younger. A 14-year-old who kills . . . I don't know. When I was growing up, there was warmth and compassion in the house. There was laughter, too, but there was a sense of discipline. Even when I was in the service, when I'd be out on a pass at four in the morning, I could hear my mother's voice saying, 'Joe, get home,' and I'd go back to the barracks.

"Now so many young kids have absolutely no concept of what it is to have that kind of love in the home. When I was the head of the gang crimes unit, I'd see young men who had been involved with the gangs, and I would talk to them in the office and really chastise them quite severely. The next week, they'd be back, saying, 'Can we just sit down and talk, Joe?' These kids are so hungry to know what it means to have a parent who takes an interest in them that any adult who takes the time to talk to them becomes a father figure." (Di Leonardi and his wife have no children of their own and have been trying to adopt, but so far have been frustrated by delays at several adoption agencies.)

Lately, Di Leonardi has been going into Loop movie theaters to sample some of the ultraviolent films now being exhibited. "I literally feel sick some of the time," he said. "The police will be portrayed as pigs right in the opening scene. The hero will be a guy who shoots people and then walks away with the big car and the beautiful girl—he never goes to jail. The audience cheers. There's already a pattern developing: in a lot of our robbery homicides, the young robbers will come into a store and use the exact language they picked up in a robbery scene in a movie theater. The exact wording, all the way down to using the name of the movie hero.

"People look at the murder statistics, and they turn to the police, but what can we do? We're police officers, we can't change the society around. We talk about how we have to get rid of the handguns, but that doesn't seem to do any good. Yeah, we had 970 murders in Chicago last year, and do you know how many of those people would still be alive if there weren't any handguns around?

Seven hundred. That's right. Seven hundred. In this country there is now one murder committed every 27 minutes. That's how far things have gone."

Di Leonardi knows the figures by heart. In 1940, there were 232 homicides in Chicago. In 1945, 213. In 1950, 257. In 1955, 292. In 1960, 372. In 1965, 395, And then came the beginning of the mounting horror, year by year: 510, 552, 647, 715, 810, 824, 711, 864—and 970. Still, though, he says he has not become calloused by it.

"You can't be hardened and be a homicide investigator," he said. "Not when you're dealing with life and death. You have to sit with the family of a murder victim and show compassion. You really feel for them. And then you go out and you start looking for the killer. You have to get your adrenalin going, and if you're too hardened, you can't do it."

Nevertheless, Di Leonardi has noticed a change in himself, and he is a little worried about it. In the summer of 1971 he was a sergeant, a detective with Area 6 homicide. At that time he was the subject of a profile written by *Sun-Times* reporter Bob Olmstead, who wanted to see what life was like for a homicide investigator. "I've never met a real mean person," Di Leonardi said at the time.

Wednesday Di Leonardi admitted that he has changed his mind. "Up until a couple of years ago, I really believed that murderers were not mean people, that they were involved in one-time acts committed in the heat of passion. I could understand that. I could deal with it.

"But now? I see meanness. I see one brother shooting the other because he won't sing 'Happy Birthday' to him. I see girls shooting each other over cigaret butts. I'm seeing fewer murders done in the heat of passion and more being done just for kicks, for the spontaneous thrill. I'm seeing very young killers who have absolutely no remorse when we catch them. I see people killing for fun. Killing for fun."

Backstage at the Joffrey

Twenty minutes until curtain. Out front, the Auditorium Theater is filling up with patrons for whom it will be one special night. Back here, it is a day at the office. Robert Joffrey, the head of the ballet company that bears his name, is nose to nose with Jeffrey Hughes, one of his dancers. Joffrey is wearing a dark blazer and gray slacks; Hughes is dressed to dance. Joffrey is leading Hughes through a troublesome routine one more time. "Hold," Joffrey says. "Hoooolllld."

The 40 members of the Joffrey touring company are here for the third time of the day. In the morning there had been a class. In the afternoon there had been a rehearsal. Now it is nearing show time. "There is no problem getting them here on time," says a man who travels with the troupe. "The problem is keeping them away. Some of them are back here at the crack of dawn, trying to get in."

Up two flights of iron stairs, Pamela Nearhoof is wandering in a communal dressing room, wearing a yellow sweater. She is scheduled to dance twice tonight, but she will not. She has the flu; this morning the doctor told her not to dance. So she will skip *Monotones,* but she will dance the third ballet, *Deuce Coupe II,* anyway. No one else in the company can do her part, and if she will not go on, *Deuce Coupe II* cannot be presented.

"It's OK," Miss Nearhoof says. "Two years ago I had a 108-degree temperature, and I went on, and by the time I came off, I was fine. I'll do *Deuce Coupe* because it's more move-y than *Monotones.* If I blew something in *Monotones,* they'd see it in the audience. On *Deuce Coupe,* they won't.

Downstairs, it is starting. *Kettentanz,* the first ballet of the evening, is on. The dancers appear weightless and floating out beneath the stage lights. The moment they enter the wings their smiles disappear. They are panting and perspiring and gasping for air; they tug at elastic. The backstage area smells like a gymnasium.

The dancers sit on folding chairs and rub sandpaper over the bottoms of their pink shoes.

The union men working the lights are wearing flannel lumberjack shirts and Concerts West T-shirts. They are paid by the hour, whether the job is a circus or a rock concert or the Joffrey Ballet. Their instructions come from a little PA box, carrying the whispering voice of an unseen master out in the house: "This is a warning on light three . . . OK, three, go, 10-9-8-7-6-5-4-3-2-1, follow spot three, 10-9-8. . . ."

Three dancers pay no attention to the ballet on stage, or to the electricians in the wings. They are Adix Carman, Michael Tipton, and Richard Colton. They are working by themselves at an exercise barre that is hidden behind the last black backdrop. On the floor is a cassette tape recorder; the machine is turned to a low volume, so as not to interfere with the music of the orchestra. The voice coming from the machine is that of Maggie Black, the New York teacher of the three men; she is running them through their moves half a continent away.

To the audience, the Joffrey is pure artistry, but to the traveling company there are real-world logistics to deal with. Donna Cowen, wearing a bathrobe over her dancing clothes to fight the Chicago wind coming through the stage door, is looking at a notice on the backstage bulletin board:

"For each day that we are in Chicago, you will receive $1.80 for transportation between hotels and theater. This will allow each of you four round trips, via public transportation; or if you travel in groups of four or more, it can cover taxi rides. This money will appear all together on the check of the second week here."

There are other such notices, but the one that is read the most thoroughly is typed all in capital letters, on long, yellow legal sheets. Each night Robert Joffrey watches from the back of the house, and breathes his comments about the performance to his secretary, Karen Bohner, who later transfers the criticism to the legal sheets. The next morning, the sheets are on the board, more important to the company than any reviews that appear in the newspapers: "BOB THOMAS BRING THE ARMS TO THE WAIST ON TIME." . . . "KEVIN WAIT UNTIL REBECCA LOOKS BACK TO YOU BEFORE YOU RUN ON." . . . KEVIN PUT BECKY DOWN MUCH MORE SOFTLY ON ALL THE LIFTS."

The first ballet is over, the second is starting; new dancers take to the stage, winded dancers watch now from the wings. Pamela Nearhoof, still in her yellow sweater, is in the wings, also; she will watch the dance she has given up for tonight.

A stagehand approaches her and gives her a small tin of Chicken-of-the-Sea tuna.

"Thanks, John," she says.

"It's the last can," he says.

"I guess I'll eat it before I go on," she says. "Or I won't make it through."

Miss Nearhoof returns up the stairs to the dressing room. *Monotones* ends, and the frenzied applause from the audience brings a curiously distant, bloodless echo backstage. A uniformed usher is walking across the stage to present a bouquet of flowers to Ann Marie De Angelo, who has danced in place of Miss Nearhoof; just out of sight, stagehands wait with mops and brooms, and as soon as the curtain has dropped they hurry forth to remove the perspiration and resin, and make the stage floor new again for *Deuce Coupe II.*

The *Deuce Coupe II* dancers straggle out behind the fallen curtain and limber up one more time. Out in the lobby, the 15-minute intermission is ending, and the lights are flashing on and off to signal the audience back to their seats.

Two women are rolling like puppies on the stage floor, drawing laughter from the others as they loosen up. A stage manager with a clipboard checks the names; "Ann Marie?" the stage manager calls.

"Yeah," calls the dancer. "I'm here."

"All right," the stage manager says. "Will you kill our work lights, please?"

The backstage lights go off. The murmur from the audience comes through the curtains, and then the music is playing and the curtain is going up and the audience is applauding again.

Pamela Nearhoof, now in her dancing clothes, is on the stage. If she is sick, she is not showing it. She is at work now, doing her job, a dancer on the road. She is like the rest of them: she has realized her dream; she is in the Joffrey; she is a professional. She is 18 years old. . . .

Old Friends

At five o'clock in the morning, there is no real reason for a pedestrian to pay attention to the traffic signals. The city is quiet, and there are few cars on even the biggest streets. But on this morning, the two old friends were waiting on Michigan Avenue for the "walk" light to flash on, even though there was not an auto in sight for blocks.

It was cold and dark and the wind was up, and it would have made sense for them to hurry across against the light to get to wherever they were going, and find some warmth inside. But still they waited, until the light changed on the empty street, and then they started.

One of them, the taller one, walked with a heavy limp. His friend helped, holding onto an arm to lend support as they slowly crossed. They both wore wide-brimmed hats, the old kind with big, dark bands, and they must have been close to 70.

When they had arrived on the other side, it turned out that they weren't heading for anyplace in particular, after all. "Where would you like to go?" the tall man with the limp said.

"Oh, I don't care," said his friend. "Maybe we could go look at the lake. If you're not too tired."

"We only get the chance to do this once a year," said the tall one. "I have all next year to get over being tired. Let's go."

Theirs is a different kind of Christmas story. The tall man's name is Curtis. His friend's name is Davidson. Many years ago, when they were young, Mr. Curtis and Mr. Davidson went to Northwestern University, in Evanston. They were roommates then.

After they graduated, Mr. Curtis moved to Cleveland, and Mr. Davidson moved to Los Angeles. They were both married, and in the 1950s, both their wives died. They both live alone now, retired and in less than perfect health. But every December, they come back to Chicago to be with each other for a few short days and to try to remember about being young.

They rent a hotel room, and they talk. They take a cab to Evanston and walk around the campus. They visit the places in Chicago where they used to hang out 50 years ago. But more and more, they are finding that the old places are not only gone, but that no one even remembers them.

They started the 5:00 A.M. walks a couple of years ago, when Mr. Curtis' leg got especially painful. "We don't like to be any trouble," he said. "When we come here, it's the Christmas-shopping season, and it seems that two old men dragging around just get in everyone's way. There's no reason for us to be out and about during the business hours, anyway. We don't know anyone but each other anymore. So we can see what we want to see now, before anyone's up, and we can talk and take our time."

They walked past the Drake Hotel and through the little park, on their way to the Oak Street Beach. A lone police car passed by them. The cop saw Mr. Curtis limping and Mr. Davidson helping him along. He slowed the squad car, figured it was a couple of harmless old drunks on their way home and drove on his way.

"We might as well sit and watch until the sun comes up," Mr. Davidson said. They went down by the sand and took a bench and pulled their coats up to ward off the cold.

They talked of many things, of young ladies and friends now dead, of nights in spring and blizzarding winters in Evanston. They laughed a lot, and tried to remember exactly when they started to meet in Chicago in December, and could not remember.

They talked of going back to their homes for another year, and Mr. Curtis said, "But we'll be right back here next December."

Mr. Davidson put his hand on his friend's shoulder. "You know, one of these years, there'll just be one of us left to come to Chicago," he said.

"I know," said Mr. Curtis. "I know."

The two old friends sat and watched the lake until the sun was all the way up. The traffic on Lake Shore Drive had begun to get heavy as they started back for their hotel, slowly, the one helping the other.

Luh Cloooooob

I was reading one of the gossip columns the other day, and I ran across an item that said an exclusive new private club was opening that would "guarantee to bring the chic back to Chicago." The place was called Le Club. I had just been thinking about how the chic had mysteriously vanished from my life, and so I made a mental note to drop by and check Le Club out.

I ran into a problem immediately when I found out that Le Club was open only from 11:00 P.M. to 4:00 A.M. So I set an alarm, and in the middle of the night I brushed my teeth and set off for Le Club, which is located at One East Scott.

Within minutes after my arrival, I found myself sitting in a zebra-lined booth with Walter Holmes, the man who told the gossip columnists that he would bring the chic back. Walter Holmes is the director of Le Club; he is a fashion designer from England, and he talks in a voice somewhere between Arthur Treacher and Sally Quinn.

"We are sitting in what normally would be called a banquette," Walter informed me. "But a banquette seems to me to be so . . . conventionny, so wedding party-ish. And a booth, to me, says, 'cafeteria.' I prefer to call this a 'wombette.' "

"A wombette," I said.

"Yes," Walter said. "Wombette. Like a womb, that is warm and envelops you. Womb, with an e-t-t-e on the end."

I sensed that it was time to get down to business. "I heard that Le Club was only going to allow 300 members to join," I said, and before I could finish the sentence, I noticed a flash of pure pain come across Walter's face. He had seemed to suffer the seizure at the approximate moment I had said the phrase "Le Club," the second word of which I had pronounced as if it were a wooden instrument with which you would bash someone in the back of the head.

"We do not say 'club,' " Walter corrected me. "We say, 'Luh Clooooob.' "

"Ah," I said. "Luh Clooooob." Walter nodded approval.

"Some say that if a person does not know how to pronounce Luh Clooooob properly, then that person need not even attempt to get past the door here, Robert," Walter said.

We laughed heartily.

"Well, anyway," I continued, "I heard that membership in Luh Clooooob is going to be very restricted. How come?"

Walter stared deep into my eyes. "Chic finds chic," he said. "Birds of a feather fly together. One cannot just throw Luh Clooooob open to the public. Otherwise, the chic would be offended. I would be offended. Do you understand, Robert?" Walter's continued predilection for calling me Robert marked the first time in ten years than anyone, man, woman, or child, had called me anything other than "Greene," and his civility was beginning to bring tears to my eyes.

"I hate to ask you this, Walter," I said. "But could you define 'chic' for me a little bit?"

"I would be glad to," Walter said. He paused for dramatic effect. I leaned forward in the wombette. "Chic is not being aware of being chic," Walter said.

"Well, of course," I said.

"Luh Clooooob is for our own type of people," Walter continued. "We must limit it to 300 Chicagoans and 100 international members. The names are submitted for membership by personal friends of mine, and by our membership committee. The membership committee consists of 20 people, of social and professional prominence. It is a secret committee. The members do not wish their identities to be known, for obvious reasons."

I winked conspiratorially.

"This came about because of a real need," Walter said. "Everyone I know kept saying, 'There's no place to go. There's no place to go. There's no place to go.' And then one day I realized that there was no place for me to go, either. So we began Luh Clooooob. I designed all of the clothing for the men on our staff. On opening night we all wore dinner suits designed by me, made of silk and wool, with satin lapels."

I asked about the international members.

"We will accept 100 people from outside Chicago," Walter said. "Just last night we took one. His name was Renaldo, I forget his last name, he was from Bogota. He was a friend of Suzanne Falk, who you probably know."

"Suzanne," I said.

"And then William and Jonna Wood-Prince called the other night. They wanted to bring over 20 people who were in town from London," Walter said. "They had an unbelievable time."

Walter sipped from his glass of white wine. "When I first came to Chicago from London in 1965, I expected to see people with straw between their teeth," he said. "But instead, I have found elegant and attractive people. Michigan Avenue is one of the most beautiful shopping areas in the world. People who know me say, 'I don't consider Walter Holmes funny. I consider Walter Holmes fun. Where Walter is, that is where the fun is going to be.' And Robert, from now on I am going to be at Luh Cloooooob."

I asked if Walter did not feel a twinge of guilt, allowing only 300 Chicagoans to share his fun, and shutting out some four million others.

"Yes, it is true," he said. "I do feel guilt. I don't like the idea of having to exclude those four million people from Luh Clooooob. But what can I do? I simply don't know them."

A Suburb's Quiet Horror

Five in the family, dead. It happened up there, in that red-brick, ranch-style house. The neighbors are starting to come around. Ropes in the neighborhood, blocking off the lawns. Strange afternoon in Park Ridge. The chat is of multiple murders.

"Is Lynda one of them?" The questioner is Gayle Kreft. Gayle is 15, a freshman at Maine Township East High School. Gayle has just walked over from her own house, and she is wearing faded jeans and a denim jacket with a silver star design on the back. "Lynda's a weird one," Gayle says, present tense. "She's not like the rest of us, you know? We like to party every night. She just sits at home. She's a tomboy. She dresses real straight."

There is a gas-powered air pump clattering outside the front door of the death house, part of the firemen's equipment. The visitors automatically raise their voices to talk above the machine sound. They are waiting to see some bodies.

". . . arms tied behind her," the coroner's man is saying, standing in the driveway of the death house. He is giving out the early details of the death of the Raymond A. Fuchs family, and his voice heightens and then disappears, leaving grotesque phrases in the air. ". . . tied to a sink in the basement," the coroner's man says, ". . . knife found floating in the water." The children of the neighborhood press close, trying to get some of this for themselves. ". . . an animal found dead, too," the coroner's man says.

No tears for the Fuchs family. Not this afternoon, outside the death house. It is growing chilly, and the drizzle is turning into a hard rain, but the crowd does not diminish. Not mourners, not yet. Five dead in Park Ridge, and it provides an eerie fascination to break the quiet of the last days of spring. The dark green trees in front of the house sag with the weight of the droplets, and the curious visitors stare, dry-eyed.

"I hardly ever saw him, except when he was walking their dog," Debi Gustafson says. Debi is 18, wearing a halter top, and standing in the garage of her house, just down the block from the death house. "I'm talking about Jeff," she says. "He was the one who was my age. He was real smart. He never did anything. No class in the way he dressed, you know what I mean? I don't even hang out around Park Ridge, myself. My friends are in the city."

The bodies are still inside the house, the four of them that are left. One—the one they found upstairs—was taken away hours ago. But the final four—the four that were wrapped in blankets, down in the basement, with the heads and faces covered with towels—they still have to be carried out. An ambulance is waiting in the driveway. In the yard against the trunk of one of the Fuchs' trees, an empty Dunkin' Donuts carton brims over with coffee and Coca-Cola cups and tissue-paper doughnut wrappers, the flotsam of the people come to call on the afternoon of death.

"Remember how Jeff always carried a briefcase in school?" says a boy pressing against the police ropes.

"Weird," says a friend.

The bodies are coming through the garage, carried by firemen and policemen, moving with deliberation, a slow-motion movie. The first body is in a long, heavy, shiny green bag. The men in uniform turn sideways so that they can edge between the cars in the garage, a gray Oldsmobile and a gold Dodge, consecutive license plates, NH2527 and NH2528. The bag is shoved into the back of the red-and-white ambulance. Now the second body, in a second green bag. The ambulance pulls noiselessly away. Two bodies still left.

"Help me, I think I'm fallin', in love with you . . . ," Joni Mitchell sings, her voice lifting tinnily out of a transistor radio carried by a boy on a bicycle with raised handlebars.

"I don't know why they can't tell us how long the bodies have been dead," a reporter complains mildly. "They should know just by the odor. I know plenty of firemen who can come close to getting it exactly, just from their experience."

The men from the board-up company have arrived, and they are banging big plywood sheets over the front windows, where the firemen had knocked out the panes to clear the smoke. As the workmen construct the temporary closure, the ambulance returns. Time for the final bodies.

These two are brought out in a hurry, this time in bags of black vinyl-like material. They are placed in the ambulance one immediately after the other, and then they are gone, the last of the Fuchs family taken from their home.

Gayle Kreft is still watching. "It's kind of a neat day," she says. "Nothing like this ever happens around here. Another block and it could have been us." Next fall she will be a sophomore. Quiet horror on a strange suburban afternoon. . . .

Last Broadcast

Maybe there were 50 people present on the night they took Jack Eigen's broadcast away. The people milled around the long, narrow WMAQ radio studio, placed Styrofoam cups of coffee on the red and yellow plastic chairs and waited for the last show to begin. Friends of a radio star with three hours left in the string.

They used to call Eigen arrogant and abrasive and egotistical, and some hated him. But that was 20 years ago, when late-night radio shows were big business and were beamed from nightclubs, the sound racing through the blackness of the early morning to towns all over the country. Jack Eigen was a big shot back then, a comer, and people talked about his show-business interviews the next morning. Even if they despised him, they listened, they caught Eigen's show from the Chez Paree.

You could not hate Jack Eigen at 9:45 last Saturday night. With 15 minutes until he was to begin his final show, he sat in his bare, tiny office, drummed his fingers on the desk and waited. He did not look tough or wise-mouthed or mean; he looked like a tired, beaten little 58-year-old man who was about to lose the only thing that has mattered to him for the last 20 years.

"The phone's been ringing all night," Eigen said, but at this moment the phone was tauntingly silent on the desk. "I don't know what I'll do, exactly. We're going to open the house in Florida, but if the right opportunity comes in Chicago . . . well, I think we'll take a long vacation first, and see what happens."

Then he went into the studio and the people applauded. They were his friends, who did not want him to be alone on this, the last night. People used to pack into the nightclub to see Eigen, but in the years since he was moved into the little radio studio, away from the noise and the crowds, only a handful showed up each night. The friends wanted it to sound like the old days on this night; they wanted it to sound like fun.

"Thank you, no, no, please, that's enough," Eigen said into the microphone. But at the same time he was motioning to them for more applause. "No please," he said, still motioning, and they kept clapping.

"This is the broadcast," Eigen said. "I know that's a strange way to open a show, but that's the way I opened 20 years ago at the Chez Paree. You know, it was the late Fred Allen who told me, 'Jack, if you can get 50 per cent of the audience for you and 50 agin you, you've got it made.' Well, tonight will be another broadcast."

The problem now is not getting half the audience for and half against; it is getting them to care or listen at all. It is so much easier to watch the images on the television screen late at night, to see the celebrities. The magic of making a man a part of people's lives solely on the basis of hearing his voice every night seems to be gone. Eigen was the first to do the now standard talk-show routine; he introduced it at the Copacabana in New York. But that was a long time ago, when a radio chatter show could be considered stylish.

"My God," whispered one man in the audience. "Where are the press agents? Eigen supported those guys for 20 years. Where are they tonight?"

The man was right. A few PR men were there—Sherman Wolf, and Benny Dunn from *Playboy,* and maybe a couple of others—but on the last night, knowing Eigen could not help them promote their products and their celebrities anymore, most of the press agents managed to find important business elsewhere.

Jimmy Byrne was there, an old gentleman who had been in the audience at the Eigen broadcast at least four nights a week for the past 20 years. He was there the first night at the Chez Paree in 1951, and he was there this night, and he seemed to show how the voice of a radio broadcaster could take some of the loneliness out of people's lives. He said he was not sure what he was going to do after the last show.

"For the last week," Eigen said into the microphone, "my girl Friday has been my wife Dorothy. Saves me money that way."

Of course. It had to end that way. In the glamour days, when everyone knew Eigen, gorgeous models connived and dealed to become his "girl Friday" and get their names on the air, to become known in the 38 states where Eigen claimed to be heard. But Eigen could not help any starlets any more, and on the last night his wife fetched his coffee and waited for it to end.

He interviewed his last guests, and talked about the old shows.

He talked about how he had once, as a joke, mentioned a phony gathering in the lobby of the Hotel Croydon, and the next morning the Croydon's lobby was packed, and the hotel took out 13 weeks of advertising. But tonight there were embarrassingly few commercials as Eigen talked about his favorite interviews of the past.

At one point he played the "Jack-Jack-Jack" musical opening from the Chez Paree show, and part of one of his old monologues, and for a moment you could imagine the excitement and the mystique. But the day for that kind of thing will never come back, and maybe the radio station had no other choice than to take the show away from Eigen.

At the very end Eigen said: "May you all live as long as you want and never want as long as you live." The tough guy cried halfway through the sentence, and the words didn't even sound corny, just terribly sad.

Pawnshop Christmas

The other side of Christmas:

"Hello, what's your trouble?" asks Sidney Swesnik, the pawnbroker.

"You know better than I do," says the customer. The customer is a black man in a black suit. He is standing in front of Swesnik's cage holding a brown paper bag which has been folded around a large, rectangular object.

"What do you need from me?" asks Swesnik.

The customer unfolds the bag and reaches inside. He comes out with a black-and-silver portable radio. "I need $10," the customer says.

"I give you $10 for it last time?" asks Swesnik.

"Ten last time," says the customer.

"All right. Ten," says Swesnik.

"I could use $15," says the customer. "It's Christmas."

Swesnik shakes his head. "I wish I could do it," he says. "But I have to give you $10 for it. I want to make it easier for you to get it back."

The customer does not speak. Instead, he merely shoves his radio through the opening at the top of Swesnik's cage. Swesnik hands the customer a $10 bill and a pink form to fill out. "Merry Christmas," says Swesnik.

"Merry Christmas," says the customer, already turning to leave the shop.

It has been like this all day long. A few blocks away, over at Field's and Carson's and Wieboldt's, the State Street shoppers are making their last-minute purchases. Here in the little pawnshop owned by Sidney Swesnik and his brother Joe, the holiday story is different. The Swesniks have seen it before. Every winter, in the days just before Christmas, it begins anew.

"These people want to have a nice Christmas, too," Sidney Swesnik says. "They want to buy presents for their children, too. Two or three days before Christmas, they begin to realize that if they're going to have any money, they're going to have to pawn."

The pawnshop is at 18 W. Van Buren, beneath the L tracks. The business was started in 1910, by the Swesniks' father. "It was all my father knew how to do," Joe Swesnik says. "Now, if you wanted to go into this business today, you wouldn't be in your right mind. Sidney and I are in the business, so we'll stay in it. It's done."

There is a blue cardboard sign tacked above the Swesniks' cage: "Merry Christmas and a Happy New Year." Beneath the sign is another one, in red neon: "Loan Department." There are a few strands of silver tinsel hanging near the ceiling.

Sidney Swesnik opens up his book of receipts and goes over the items that have been pawned in the last two days: "Diamond ring. Radio. Watch. Medallion. Ring. Fur jacket. Jewelry. Camera. Bracelet. Ring. Watch. TV. Clarinet."

He keeps reading aloud, and already the line at his cage is growing longer. There is a young man with a flute, a fine silver instrument for which Sidney Swesnik loans $40. "Merry Christmas, man," says the young customer before leaving. "I suppose he's a musician," Swesnik says, putting the flute on a shelf. "He's been here before. I never asked him for an audition."

There are more: a man with a battered typewriter, a man with a pair of binoculars that he says was given to him by his father, and a man with a wedding band. Sidney and Joe Swesnik do not talk much. They examine each item; Sidney bangs on the typewriter's keys, making sure that the machine is not broken. When they make their offers, the offers are taken; the customers do not seem to have the heart to bargain.

The dark comes early. Up by the fluorescent lights, the sheets of sticky yellow paper carry their load of flies and night insects, dead since summer. "It will be like this right up until closing time Christmas Eve," Joe Swesnik says. "You think you have troubles, then you see the next man, and you thank the Lord for your blessings."

Another customer has entered the store. He is a big, elderly man, and he approaches the cage and stands silently.

"Hello, Lopez," Joe Swesnik says.

The customer reaches down and, without looking, removes a gold watch from his left wrist.

"Ten dollars," says Joe Swesnik.

The customer still does not speak. But he hands over his watch, still not looking down, and accepts his money.

"Merry Christmas," says Joe Swesnik, knowing that there will be no answer. . . .

Glutton

It's the same stomach-turning story, night after night. I'm sitting in the city room, finishing up the next morning's column, and I look up toward the front of the room, and there is Bill Cunniff, eating garbage. Bill Cunniff is a copyboy, and his eating habits can be described in two words: "foul" and "constant." Never, during his eight-hour shifts, have I seen him without popcorn, peanuts, ice cream, greasy burgers, sweet-flavored soda pop, and other assorted slop, scarfing it down into the sludge-pit that is his innards.

"Cunniff," I said the other night, "you and I are going to take a trip in the morning. Be here at 11:00 A.M. sharp."

My plan was simple. This is the week that the National Restaurant Show has been in town, and I figured that it was time for someone other than Chicago's hookers to benefit from it. The National Restaurant Show, held at McCormick Place, consists of approximately 1,000 booths and exhibits, most of them featuring free foods of all kinds. The show is a free-loading glutton's delight.

There is one problem, though. The show is not open to the public; it is limited to delegates from the food industry, who tend to see so much of the stuff in the course of their everyday work that they have no desire to gobble up the samples at McCormick Place. Which is a good thing for them; the food on display there, consumed indiscriminately, is enough to kill a pig.

I planned to take Cunniff to the restaurant show. My purpose was twofold: (1) I figured that maybe he would be so grateful to me that he would quit spilling grape soda on my copy and dropping popcorn kernels between my typewriter keys; and (2) I figured that he would become so painfully, nauseatingly sick wolfing down all that food that he would see the light and change his revolting eating habits. Call me a reformer.

Cunniff showed up at the office right on time. He was dressed in his usual business attire, consisting of a green Oakland Athletics T-shirt turned inside out, a pair of ripped and faded jeans, and blue sneakers with no socks.

"I'm ready," he said.

We rode out to McCormick Place. If Cunniff felt uncomfortable among the restaurant executives in their snazzy summer suits, he hid his feelings very well. I took him to the press room. "This here is a member of the Fourth Estate," I said. The woman at the desk tilted her head and looked at Cunniff. Cunniff winked at her. She gave him a pass.

Within a minute we were on the first exhibit floor. Cunniff was gone in a flash. I found him at Booth 1727, run by Pfeiffer's Foods, of Buffalo. Cunniff grabbed a handful of lettuce and dunked it into a vat of Pfeiffer's Chunky Blue Cheese Dressing. "Not bad," he said, as the Pfeiffer's representatives stared at him.

But he was already gone. Off to Booth 1835, operated by the Golden Dipt Doughnut Company. "Nice and hot," Cunniff said through a mouthful of doughnut, as he moved quickly toward the Best Quality Breadstick Co. exhibit.

The next two hours were among the most astounding I expect to experience in my life. It comes back to me now only in episodic flashes: Cunniff at the Rotomation Inc. booth, informing the proprietor that the hamburger sandwich was "thick enough, but too greasy"; Cunniff at the Longacre Inc. exhibit, confessing that "I never liked chicken salad" even as he was swallowing a massive mouthful of chicken salad on a cracker; Cunniff at the Ardmore Farms display, downing a carton of fruit punch, licking his chops and saying, "Now that's pretty good"; Cunniff at the Diamond E Onion Ring pagoda, nodding sagely at the salesmen and saying, "Very good, a thick crust—I like it that way."

My notes are surely incomplete, for I could not keep up with Cunniff, but I show him stopping at more than 75 booths. The following words seem to be scrawled on my notepad: Sunflower nuts. Washington State potatoes. White cake with strawberry topping. Hot apple pie. Creme de menthe candy. Cocktail meatballs. Hires Root Beer. (Here my notes quote Cunniff as saying, "I dig root beer.") Minestrone soup. Chopped steak. Roast beef sandwich. Lemonade. Cheese sauce on crackers. Pitted California prunes. Pressed turkey. Mazzone Enterprises' pizza. Fried clams. This goes on and on.

And as this was happening, Cunniff was becoming a star. Word of his presence at the show spread. The regular delegates, who know enough to steer clear of all the food, began to gather and observe Cunniff. They began to take bets on when he would drop. A businessman asked him how he felt. "I feel wired," Cunniff said with a grin.

On only two occasions did it seem that Cunniff was weakening. Both proved to be false alarms. The first came after he had finished all of the food on the first level of McCormick Place, and we were riding the escalator up to Level Two. Cunniff fell in a heap and sat on the moving stairs, but in a few moments he looked up and said, "Just pacing myself."

The second false alarm came at the Granny Goose French Fries booth. A lovely blonde model named Lisa Miller had just handed Cunniff a sack of fries when suddenly he lunged for her, threw his arm over her shoulders and leaned against her. I thought that he was surely suffering some sort of gastrointestinal attack, but it turned out to be a simple case of teenage lust.

I began to feel ill. I do not remember whether it was during Cunniff's assault on the Italian ice dessert display or his ransacking of the General Mills brownies booth, but I started to be afflicted by a terrible ache deep in my gut. I began to perspire and experienced difficulty breathing. I had not eaten a thing at the restaurant show, but watching Cunniff had done me in. I felt the blood rushing out of my head and my stomach leaping toward my throat. "Out . . . air . . . please . . . leave," I gasped. I tugged at Cunniff's T-shirt. I tried to drag him toward the door.

"What's the rush?" Cunniff said.

"Please," I moaned.

Reluctantly, he left with me. That was an hour ago. I have now swallowed two rolls of Tums and am searching through a nauseous haze for the typewriter keys. Cunniff is not here. As soon as we got back to the office, he said he had to go over to Billy Goat's for a beer. He said he felt fine. Just a little thirsty.

The Singer

Encounter:

The funeral girl was singing, no words. Her voice was true, rising and falling in the dusk. The funeral home is on Erie, near State, and that is where she sang, on the sidewalk, her back against the wall.

She looked out at the street and played the tune with her voice. She wore no coat, even though it felt like the beginning of winter. She showed no reticence, to be offering this city serenade. There was mystery to her; her face was clear and bright, her voice alive. No druggie here, no street-corner drunk.

A passer-by stopped, and listened for a moment. He asked her what she was doing. "This is what I do," she said.

But why here? the passer-by said. Why outside the funeral home?

"This is what I do," she said, smiled and returned to her song.

The street was not full. Those who did come by, most of them, walked quickly and did not look. If the girl's song had a name, it was not a famous one. Her voice seemed to be following itself.

The passer-by stayed. The voice of the girl was hypnotic, and he watched and listened. He wanted to interrupt, to talk, but he hesitated to intrude. She paid him little notice.

Soon enough a crowd began to gather. The sight of the passer-by standing and watching was enough to take away the urban embarrassment; once the audience had started to form, an unspoken sanction had been granted. The funeral girl looked around the semicircle, and laughed for a moment. But she did not stop her song.

"Crazy," said a man at the back of the audience, and continued along his way. A number of the others left with him.

A young couple had stopped. When they saw the others begin to walk away, the wife pulled at the husband's wrist and whispered. He nodded, reached into his pocket, withdrew his wallet. He pulled out a bill. "Very nice," he said to the girl. "We like it very much." He extended his hand, and the money.

The funeral girl's smile cracked wider. As she sang, she shook her head from side to side. Her hands were folded in her lap, and she did not move them, did not reach for the money. In a few seconds the man put it back into his wallet, and left with his wife.

Full darkness had come, and still the girl did not stop. In another world, she would not have borne notice: a girl in the country, humming to pass the time, is an easy thought to deal with. The girl outside the funeral home on a cold Chicago night was not, for a number of reasons, and with the darkness her audience abandoned her.

So she was going only for the passer-by and two or three others when it ended—when the car arrived. The man at the wheel was at least 30 years older than the funeral girl, perhaps her father. He knew what he was looking for. He began to pull up toward the curb well before he could have seen her sitting back against the wall, and when she saw the car come to a stop, she ended her song.

She stood up and brushed off her pants. She smiled once again at the few who remained. The man in the car leaned across the front seat and threw open the door on the passenger side. The funeral girl walked toward the car. Then she turned back. "Thank you," she said to the passer-by, and kissed him on the cheek. She climbed into the car and kissed the cheek of the driver, also. City nights. . . .

2

HOURS TO REMEMBER

Some stories stay with you. The lead piece in this chapter, "It Took This Night to Make Us Know," was written in a hotel room near the Pentagon during the 1972 Nixon-McGovern campaign. I had already written a column for the next day and had ordered up a few room-service drinks, when I turned on the TV just in time to get the news of the murdered Israeli Olympians. I walked over to my portable typewriter and wrote "It Took This Night to Make Us Know" in less than ten minutes, then transmitted it to Chicago in place of the earlier column. It drew the largest response of any single piece of writing I have ever done—more than 5,000 letters. Even now not a week passes when I do not get a request for reprints or a random phone call asking to talk about the column.

The other stories in this chapter also seemed to touch certain chords in the readers. "Good-by, Phi Ep" is about the demise of my college fraternity, but judging from the reaction it elicited, it said something more about the end of an era. "Soul of a Bookseller," too. "A Thanksgiving Memory"—perhaps because holidays are often times of loneliness instead of joy—has become a favorite of many, or so I have been told, and the *Sun-Times* reprints it each Thanksgiving day.

Many readers have reported being moved emotionally by one or another of these pieces. "Death of a Newspaper" is the only column here that affected me the same way. For the first and only time, I felt myself fighting back tears after I finished it.

It Took This Night to Make Us Know

WASHINGTON—It is not supposed to be very strong in us, for we cannot remember. We are the young Jews, born after Hitler, and we have never considered the fact that we are Jewish to be a large part of our identity. A lot of us have not been near a temple in ten years, and we laugh along with the Jewish jokes to show that we are very cool about the whole thing. We are Americans, we have told ourselves, we do not go around calling ourselves Jews; that is for the elderly men with the tortured faces, the old Jews we feel a little embarrassed to be around. Let them recall the centuries of hurt, we think; it is over now, so let them recall those years while we live our good todays.

It is not supposed to be very strong in us, and yet I am sitting at a typewriter in a hotel room hundreds of miles from home trying to write a story about a presidential campaign, and I cannot do it. For the television has just got done telling the story, the story of how once again people who hate the Jews have knocked on a door in the middle of the night and done their killing, and I can think of nothing else. Now the lesson is being taught all over again: it is not up to us to decide how to treat our Jewishness. That was decided for us centuries ago.

It is not supposed to be very strong in us, because all the barriers are down now, and a hotel will not turn us away or a restaurant will not deny us a table if our name does not sound right. And yet when the killings began, they thought to get a young man named Mark Spitz out of Germany, because he may be the best swimmer in the world, but first of all he is a Jew, and no one wanted to think what might happen to him. Many of the people who thrilled as he won his gold medals were very surprised to find out now that Spitz is a Jew. Later they will say that of course it doesn't matter what his religion is. But Spitz knew that it mattered; we all knew that it mattered, and that it would be smarter for him to go.

It is not supposed to be very strong in us, and we have heard the term "six million Jews dead" so often that it is just an abstraction to us. And yet if the Dachau concentration camp, just a few miles from the Olympic site, was not enough to remind us, the killers in the Munich darkness made sure that we remembered. There is a hate for us that goes back centuries, and every time it seems to have weakened with the years there is another band of men ready to show us that the hate is still strong enough to make them kill in the night.

When the news was certain, when there was no question but that the young Jewish men were dead, I called some friends and we talked about it. They were thinking the same way I was. For all these years we have acted bored with the Jewish traditions, smirked at the ancient, detailed ceremonies, patronized the old ones who insisted on showing their link with the past.

And for us, it took this one night to make us know that maybe it will never go away. We are all Jews who were born into a world where money and education and parents who speak with no accent were part of the package, and that can fool you. But this is the oldest hate the world has ever seen, and 25 years of Jewish prosperity in the United States is hardly enough to erase it from the earth.

It is nothing that we young ones have ever talked much about, and there are not many words to tell it now. Words cannot tell it as well as the look we have seen for years in the faces of the oldest Jews, the look of deepest sorrow that has been there for as many centuries as the hate.

This time the look is there because of a group of Arab terrorists. But it goes so far beyond Middle Eastern politics; the look was there in this same Germany 30 years ago, it was there in Egypt centuries ago, it has been there in every place there have ever been Jews who were not wanted because they were Jews. And because there have been so many of these places, the look has been reborn and reborn and reborn.

There are young men who are dead this week who should be alive, and it would be a horrible thing no matter who they were. But of course they were Jews; the reason that they are dead is because they were Jews, and that is why on this night there are so many of us starting to realize for the first time what that means.

It is not supposed to be very strong in us, for we cannot remember. We grew up laughing at the solemn old Jewish phrases that sounded so mournful and outmoded and out of date in the second half of the twentieth century. Ancient, outmoded phrases from the temples, phrases like "Let my people go." Phrases that we chose to let mean nothing, because it is not supposed to be very strong in us.

Death of a Newspaper

In two hours the newspaper would be dead, but meanwhile there was an edition to get out. Chris Agrella, 53, rewriteman, sat at his desk by the window and jabbed at his typewriter. Working from notes, wire service copy, and clippings, he quickly put together his lead:

"The government today dropped an extortion charge against Alderman Paul T. Wigoda (49th Ward), which stemmed from accusations that he received a $50,000 payment for his influence in getting rezoning. . . ."

Agrella worked swiftly. In any other business which had announced weeks ago that it was folding, the employees would not be here in the final hours. But newspapermen are not businessmen; there was one last deadline coming up, and so the men and women who produced *Chicago Today* filled the city room. As soon as the three clocks within eyeshot of the reporters reached 1:30 P.M., *Chicago Today* would exist no more. Until then, Agrella and his colleagues were going to report the news.

Agrella's story would win no awards; he held no illusions about that. It was a standard piece of breaking news, the stuff of which papers are made, the staple of the trade. Agrella went to work for the Associated Press in 1941, and has been a newspaperman in Chicago ever since; he has written tens of thousands of stories just like the one in his typewriter on this final day. He has had his prizewinners, too, but stories like this one, routine news developing as a deadline approaches, are how he has made his living. He is known as one of the best.

Bob Smith, the newspaper's city editor, walked over to Agrella's desk. Smith, the sleeves of his blue shirt rolled up to his elbows, glanced at Agrella's copy. "This will be one of the last stories," Smith said to a reporter from across the street who had dropped in to say good-by. "Agrella's going to give me seven or eight grafs, and that'll be it. The paper's locked up. If nothing else breaks, this'll be the last story to come out of the city room."

Then Smith turned around to look at his other reporters. "Everybody get enough boxes?" he said.

Someone laughed shortly. All around the room, the reporters and copy editors and deskmen had cardboard crates stacked on top of their desks. They were moving out. Workmen strolled casually up and down the aisles, ripping out telephone connections, prying tables loose, measuring specifications for the next tenants. The newspaper people did not talk to the workmen; everyone had a job to do, and there was not much to say.

The copy desk had been taken away the day before. For some reason the movers were eager to get it out of there, and so the big horseshoe had been lifted into dollies and carted from the city room. Now the copy editors were reading stories for the last edition at a series of shoved-together tables. Some of them were wearing black armbands. They were cramped, and the jostling by the movers pushing through was annoying them, but they were getting the stories down to the composing room. There would be fresh news in the last paper. Marni Ziemer, a copygirl wearing bluejeans and a borrowed gray fedora with a makeshift press card in the band, waited to receive the pages from the slotman.

There is something about a city room, something about the jangling of a hundred telephones, and the shouts of a half-hundred reporters, and the constant motion around the desks and the rush for the fresh editions when they reach the front of the room and the beautiful humming clatter of a floorful of typewriters working at the same time—there is something about a city room that, if you have tasted it and loved it, you will never willingly walk away from. Which is why, even though no boss would complain, no publisher would balk if all these men and women were to chuck it all and depart the building right this minute, no one was leaving.

For one more edition Chicago was going to be the only great four-newspaper town left in America. No one was going to go out the door while that was still true. Smith stopped by the desk of one of his reporters, Pat Krochmal. "Are you going anywhere in the next half-hour?" he said.

She shook her head.

"Later on, are all of you going over to the Boul Mich?" Smith asked. "I'll be joining you."

The clock moved toward 1:30 P.M. A new workman appeared, unplugged an Associated Press wire machine, loaded it onto a cart, and wheeled it out of the room. Other workmen, carrying out a gray wooden table, found that it was too wide for the door; they broke the table apart with hammers, and then walked out with the splintered remnants.

On the floor of the city room, a green galley sheet lay face-up, bearing proofs of some of the last headlines: "Boston school buses get escort"; "Sirica shuns pardons, vows trial"; "The end of a colorful 93 years."

The room became almost silent. There were no tears; just faces quietly looking at each other, and at the clocks.

Just before 1:30, Johnrae Earl, the slotman on the copy desk, picked up the final piece of copy. "Boy!" he called. "Tube it!"

A copyboy named Ron Bobulsky appeared at Earl's side. He took the sheet of paper, and placed it into a pneumatic tube that led to the composing room.

There was no announcement. None was needed. One by one, the reporters began drifting away from their desks, and toward the city desk.

In one reporter's typewriter, a piece of copy paper remained in the carriage, the lower-case notes from this last day: "upheld two extortions, reversed one . . . in the edgewater property, there was no goods actually moved . . . tax charge remains . . . if they paid off to get rezoning, but nothing ever built, so no hobbs act." And then, at the bottom of the page, another typed notation: "the end is near."

Someone brought out a bottle of champagne, and handed it to Bob Smith. Smith set the bottle on top of the city desk, and tried for a moment to open it. "Here," he said, handing it back. "I'm no good at opening champagne." The phones were still ringing, but no one seemed to want to answer them.

Soul of a Bookseller

It was one of those small moments that come to you unex-pectedly, and stay with you as long as you live. The two of us were walking home from work, up Michigan Avenue, and we decided to stop and look for some books. It was just after 6:00 P.M. We figured that Stuart Brent's store still might be open.

A few paces in front of us a man was having the same idea. He walked to the front door of Brent's store, tried it, found that it was locked. He resumed his walk. Within a few seconds we, too, were passing the door, and there was Brent. He had heard the man shaking the door and had come to the front of the store to look. We kept going, but Brent motioned to us through the glass. He bent down to unlatch the lock by the floor. He opened the door.

"It's OK, if you're closed . . . ," one of us said.

"No, no, what a fortuitous moment," Brent said. "Come with me." He knelt again, relocked the door, then gestured for us to follow him toward the back of the store.

There he had a small table set up. It was covered with bills: bills that publishers had sent him, bills that he was preparing to send to his customers. There were books on the table, too, and a typewriter. Brent searched for a moment, then came up with a sheaf of papers, stapled together. He motioned for us to sit down and then, without any preface at all, he began to read aloud.

"My father's hands were a miracle of perfection," Brent read from his manuscript. His voice was loud and mellifluous, like an actor's, unashamed to be sounding alone in the store. "He could build a house singlehanded. He could give you a haircut and butcher a cow. . . . But it was not his genius as a craftsman which he passed on to me; it was his infatuation with reading."

Brent looked up from the page every few seconds, to be sure that he had our attention. He is 59 years old; he has been a seller of books for 30 years. His books are what he lives for. He is a rambling, difficult man, not one for a crowd. Those who like him think that he is a joyful eccentric; those who are made uncomfortable by him think that he hs half crazy. As he continued to read aloud, we saw that he had been writing this piece to explain his love of reading, his love of books.

"Often in the morning, my father would arise from bed an hour earlier than necessary to finish reading what he had started the night before, so he could go to work satisfied," Brent read. "It was a solitary addiction. He could not even discuss his reading with his near neighbors. Cohen, who lived on the right side of us, couldn't put two words together. Rosenberg, our neighbor on the opposite side, couldn't care less."

His words echoed through the empty store. Out on the street, we could see the people hurrying by, some stopping to look at the display in Brent's window. Here inside, the aisles were deserted, the books piled high everywhere you turned. Brent's is one of the country's finest bookstores; it is not a part of a chain, its inventory is not decided by computers or main offices. Brent alone is in charge of the selection.

In an age when reading seems threatened to become a lost pleasure, Brent is an oddity. The reading public for hard-bound books is small; a book can sell as few as 15,000 copies and become a nationwide best seller. A phonograph record, on the other hand, can sell a million copies and not be considered an unusually big success. Brent has chosen to cherish the written word, and to honor it.

We did not stir as he read. His manuscript was long; the minutes passed. It would have been unthinkable to move as if to leave, or to interrupt. We saw what was happening here. This man, sitting in his locked-up store surrounded by millions of words written by other people, had been busy trying to find words of his own, words to tell why he is who he is, and he was overjoyed to have an audience. He read on and on, telling how he had acquired his need to read from his father, and had never known any other life. Reflections of the dying sun came through the glass at the front of the store and fell across his books, and we, who otherwise would have been at home watching the televised news, were transfixed.

"I think of those days when my hair was long, and I wore the only pair of pants I had until they were in shreds," Brent read. "I used to sit in the classroom with my overcoat on so that the patches on my behind would not show, or stay in the library until closing time was called. Then I would go out into the solitary night, walking thoughtfully home. I didn't want money or success or recognition. I didn't want a single thing from anybody. I wanted only to be alone, to read, to think, to unfold."

He looked up. He was finished. He walked us to the front of the store, unlocked the door again to let us out.

"Thank you," he said.

Good-by, Phi Ep

It was just a little 4-inch item in the back of the newspaper, and you probably didn't even notice it as you flipped the page. But I looked at it, and I couldn't believe it. I read it five or six times, and then I put the paper down and looked at the wall and started to think.

> The Phi Epsilon Pi fraternity house at Northwestern University in Evanston will close because of a lack of membership. Steven Herrup, president of the fraternity, 576 Lincoln, Evanston, said only three members attended the meeting at which the decision was made two weeks ago.

OK, maybe no one should worry about something like that. Fraternities all over the country are shutting down, a sign of the continuing trend toward egalitarianism on the campuses. And that is probably a good thing, I suppose; more people have been hurt by the cruel system of fraternity rush than anyone will ever know.

Still, Phi Epsilon Pi was my fraternity at Northwestern, and when I graduated, it was one of the two or three strongest houses on campus. Now the paper said that it was dead. I had quit the house at the beginning of my junior year for a lot of reasons, some of them even altruistic and valid, but it was my fraternity, it was where my college friends ate and lived and it meant something to me.

It has only been in the last two or three years that most young men coming to college as freshmen have scorned the idea of joining a fraternity. In September, 1965, when I first came to Evanston, it still was the thing most everyone did.

They told us when they gave us the pins at the initiation ceremony that we would be Phi Eps for the rest of our lives, and we all laughed at that, the pledges and the actives, too. After all, you don't do *anything* for the rest of your life, and the thought of remembering or caring about a fraternity seemed pretty stupid. For us, at the time, it was just a place to watch TV, to take girls, to drink;

a convenience. We were 18 years old and it was a place that we could pretend we owned, our first home away from the houses we grew up in. That was all.

And yet when the newspaper said that Phi Ep was dead, I did not want to believe it. It couldn't die with no one knowing or caring about it, not after all the things we had done there. It couldn't.

We were all wearing coats and ties on that September morning in 1965. It still was three years away from a time when you came to campus in jeans. We were in the Tech Auditorium, and the dean of men was telling us to be very careful in choosing a fraternity. "Look around the house that you like the best," the dean said, "and then ask yourself, 'Are these the kinds of young men I would want to take home to meet my parents?' If you can say yes to that question, then that's probably the house for you."

This was at the convocation before we went out to look at the houses. All of us looked the same, in our blazers and gray slacks and Weejuns. There was one kid, a kid named Bert from upstate New York, who was in a green T-shirt and baggy pants because he didn't know about these things, and he didn't have any good clothes. But he was the only one, and we laughed at him and went out to pick our fraternities.

There were lunch dates and dinner dates and smoker dates. We were signed up at a different house for each date, every day of the week. There were the usual smiles and handshakes: "Where are you from?" "What school are you in?" "What's your major?" All the houses looked the same, but we knew which ones were best by the number of jocks in the receiving line and the freshman dorm rumors about which fraternities had the best reputations.

But it was easy for us Jews. In long ago days, Jewish freshmen were in bad shape because the big gentile houses wouldn't take them, and the few Jewish fraternities were not really any good. But by 1965 that had changed. Now a Jew could get into almost any house, but none of us really wanted to. There were three predominantly Jewish houses, and of them, the one to get into was Phi Epsilon Pi. While the other houses had members who resembled characters in old college football weekend movies, Phi Ep was the apotheosis of what the new college guy wanted. University rules prohibited women or liquor in living units, but at Phi Ep, the word was, girls and beer were up in the bedrooms every night, and no one did anything about it. The other places just hadn't figured out how far they could go yet.

The other houses bored us; they talked about "helping the brothers adjust to college life," but at Phi Ep the actives talked about getting us chicks tomorrow night. The big gentile houses were trying to get us to join, but we weren't interested. Hell, Phi Ep even had black members, and in 1965 we were breathless at the many wonderful implications of that.

So we walked in the front door of Phi Ep, and instead of stiffly formal guys with names like Ted Dawson welcoming us and escorting us to the dining room, we got Ronnie Joseph and Richie Abrahams, their ties loosened and Scotch on their breath, motioning us into the living room. Ronnie Joseph, the Olympic figure skating champion, and Richie Abrahams, the national butterfly swimming record holder! They motioned us in and there was a band—not a hired band, but three guys from the house, not playing dumb college songs, but playing the whole Beatles Help album, every cut, and sounding great. And the other guys in the house were sitting on the floor listening and smiling. Not like a phony adult cocktail party, like it had been at the other houses, but like the way we wanted to go to college, loose and laughing and dirty-mouthed. We were home.

To be sure, not all of the young Jews were home; most of them, as a matter of fact, ended up getting ignored and forgotten, like the hundreds of young men who don't make it in every house. And they wanted in so badly, but we didn't really notice them, not us cocky freshmen who could tell that we fit in, that we belonged here. We just knew about ourselves, and we knew that we were having a good time.

So they pledged us, 29 of us, including Jeff Buckner, a black football player from Akron whose hand we could slap, and Frank Digiansante, an Italian from Yonkers who was wanted at Phi Delt and SAE and Delt and all the traditional gentile houses, but who was cool enough to spot a winner. We thought that was great, too.

Me, I was playing it cautious. I had received my bid from Phi Ep, but I figured I'd wait a few days to make sure I really wanted it. I *hung around the Phi Ep house and watched all the other freshmen pledge, and I was almost sure, but I thought that as long as I had time, I'd take it. Until the third night of rush.*

That night, I was walking around the second floor of the house and out of a bedroom came Dick Werbel, one of the seniors. He had been missing all evening, I noticed. From the room came the sound of about three girls laughing. Werbel appeared very drunk.

"You ought to come in," Werbel said. "We're having a party."

Terrific, I said, let's go.

"Wait a minute, though," Werbel said. "You ain't pledged yet, officially, have you?"

No, I said, I was still thinking about it.

"Yeah, well you go pledge, and then you come up to the party," Werbel said.

Sold. I found the rush chairman and said I was ready to become a Phi Ep. He blew the air horn, and everyone gathered around and shook my hand and yelled. Then I went back up to Werbel's room. I knew I had made the right choice.

Later, on the last night of rush week, all the houses on campus had arranged to take their pledges out for a big party. We assumed that the same thing was in store for our freshman class.

So all 29 of us, new friends, showed up at the house and asked when we were going out.

"What, are you crazy?" some of the upperclassmen said. "We don't do that stuff. Look, you want to have a good time? There's another house down the row, and they're taking a bus downtown to see some stripper they've hired for the night. Tell 'em we said you were our pledges, they'll let you come. We got dates tonight, we don't have time to screw around with you gooks."

So we crashed the other fraternity's party, we 29 new Phi Eps, and we laughed all night long. By morning we were friends, and we were glad to be where we were.

Phi Ep dead? It couldn't be. So I went up to Evanston to find out what had happened.

John Borg was the first person I saw in the house. Borg was the houseman, a Swede who had been there for more than 20 years. He was sitting in the living room, which was a mess, and he smiled when he saw me.

"You came just in time," he said. "Next week, the university's coming in and closing the place down. They're going to remodel it during the summer and open it up as a dorm in the fall."

The living room was a shambles. We had always kept the house in disarray, but I wasn't ready for this. Someone had ripped up the piano, breaking most of the keys. There was scribbling on the walls. The curtains had been torn down. Garbage was all around.

"When they heard that it was official, that the place was closing, they started tearing up," Borg said.

In 1948 John Borg was married in the Phi Ep house. The members, a more conservative and quieter bunch in those days, attended the wedding in their best suits. They gave John a watch and a few hundred dollars. Then they abandoned the house for a week and let John have it to himself for his honeymoon.

"I'll never forget those boys," John Borg said. "I loved them. I couldn't have had a real wedding and a honeymoon, but they took care of it for me. I'll always feel like I'm a Phi Ep, too. What's happened now, with the house closing . . . it makes me feel sick."

There always had been destruction in the Phi Ep house. Every year the pledges would pull their "prank," pouring molasses all over the floors, flooding the hallways, overturning the actives' beds and dressers. It was maddening and infantile, but it was college, and we all did it. We had food fights, too, taking the garbage after dinner and hurling it at each other until it was stuck to the walls and ceilings and we were exhausted from laughter. John Borg would stalk out of the house in anger after each of these outbursts, but we would clean everything up ourselves, make it right again, and he would come back.

"I would never mind that," John Borg said. "After all, Phi Eps are crazy, everyone knows that. But this time, why bother to clean it up? No one cares any more. I'm one of the last Phi Eps, you know?"

Idella Sanford came up from the kitchen. A black woman from Kentucky, she has been the cook all these years.

"Last year they put me on the composite picture as their housemother," Idella said. "Right in the middle, my picture and the words 'Idella Sanford, housemother.' Then this year they put a picture of a dog in and called *that* the housemother, the bastards."

But we always went for Idella, she was hedonistic like the rest of us, and often she would go away for three or four days only to return with a cab driver or a wink and cook us dinner.

"But we always ate, didn't we?" Idella Sanford said. "You used to go to those Cubs games and drink beer all afternoon, and I always had your dinner warm for you, didn't I? Didn't I always save you some food and keep it from those other animals? We always ate, baby, drunk or sober."

Idella said this latest—this last—bunch of Phi Eps was impossible and that they were bad people and that is why the house was dead. But she always said that about every bunch of Phi Eps, and she never meant it.

"What ever happened to that friend of yours, that guy Monk?" Idella said. "I'll never forgive that dirty rat. I stole him a few steaks from the freezer one night, and he gave me a pint of gin in return. So I hadn't even opened the gin, that same night, and Monk comes storming into my room. He says he's got a date, and he needs just a little of the gin. He took it from me and he drank it all, and he never paid me back. I'll break his neck if I ever see him again."

John Borg and Idella Sanford talked together, but the house was empty; once in a while a young man would walk through, but it was so quiet, it wasn't like the Phi Ep that always was.

By the spring of 1967, the 29 of us thought we owned the campus. We had been through two years of Phi Ep. That year we were all living in the house, and we were contented.

We would pile on the little roof that extended over the front door and soak up the sun. None of us went to classes in the spring; we would put a record player by the window and play Sgt. Pepper's Lonely Hearts Club Band *over and over and over, all spring, letting "Lovely Rita" and "Lucy in the Sky With Diamonds" carry us toward summer.*

Some of the Phi Eps were smoking dope fairly regularly by then, but no one really worried about it. In other houses, strict rules had been passed saying none of that in the fraternity house. But we had talked about it and decided no one could catch us—it was just an extension of liquor and girls staying all night. Everything was cool, right?

A lot of us began to talk about the whole idea of fraternities, and we knew that, on principle, we didn't like it. The whole arbitrary selectivity rubbed against all the ideas we seemed to be developing, but we didn't think too much about it. Right or wrong, it was a place for us to live, and we liked each other. We were developing our own cliques, of course, but that didn't matter. We could stand to stay in the same house, and that was all that mattered.

We had our all-day party at a big resort in Wisconsin. Most of us went up the night before and made a three-day thing of it. The girls all seemed to want to go with us. The other fraternities still were stuck with the idea of making theirs a one-afternoon event because the dates had to be back by 2:00 A.M. Saturday. We gave it our usual treatment, i.e., just leave campus for the weekend and no sorority housemother is going to say anything. Only one year later, this would seem so mild as to be laughable, but in 1967 it was a problem, and we thought we were pretty gutsy for pulling it off.

We had it too good. We were sophomores in college, and we were already getting bored with the thing.

"I've got an idea," Harvey Miller said one afternoon. "I know about this house in Wilmette that we can rent cheap because they're going to tear it down in a few years. Why don't you and me and Monk and Max get it next year?"

I had been thinking of quitting the fraternity anyway, and moving to the old house seemed like it would be fun. After all, what did we need Phi Ep for? The house would always be there for us whether we were official members or not. No one would keep us out on a Friday night just because we weren't paying dues. Everything's cool, right?

So we moved to the big house in Wilmette. Monk and I quit the fraternity; Harvey and Max stayed in. It was the same with all of the 29; slowly many of the people in our class were dropping out. But you couldn't tell it to look around the house during the Super Bowl or on a weekend night. The faces were the same; Otto and Max and Skeeter and the rest were all there. The treasurer kept yelling that

the house was running out of money, but we didn't listen. We were
Phi Eps forever, weren't we? That didn't end just because we didn't
pay dues and didn't live in the house. We were having a good time.

John Borg and Idella Sanford didn't really have anything to do
for the rest of the afternoon. No one to clean up for, no one to cook
for. Then Steve Herrup came in.

Herrup is the last president of Phi Ep at Northwestern. He is a
good kid and a smart one. When he talks, he looks and sounds just
like we did when we were all Phi Eps; I suppose it has always been
like that.

"Sorry about the way the place looks," Herrup said. "It wasn't
really the people in the fraternity who did it. It was the boarders."

The boarders?

"Yeah," Herrup said. "Everyone refused to pay their dues at
the beginning of this year. We had no social program because who
the hell wants to go to dances and exchanges anymore? So we had
nothing planned, and everyone said if there's no program, then we
ain't paying. So we had no money to run the house. And everyone
was either living with chicks or in apartments of their own, and no
one was living in the house.

"You can see we had a problem," Herrup said. "So that we
started renting the empty rooms out to guys who weren't Phi Eps.
Just like a boarding house. Except they didn't care about the
house—I mean, they cared even less about keeping the place up than
we did—and the place started to fall apart. They were really bad
guys, too, and we didn't get along with them.

"So it ended up that everyone was walking around here mad all
the time, not talking to anyone," Herrup said. "Besides which, a lot
of the boarders were real dopers. You know, there were always
drugs around this house, but this year it was getting ridiculous. No
one cared any more. And when we decided that we had to close the
place, some of the boarders just ripped it up because they had
nothing else to do."

Herrup and Richard Brenner, another one of the last Phi Eps,
started walking around the house, showing me what it was like in its
last days. "Watch, here comes one now. One of the boarders,"
Herrup said. "Watch this."

A kid was walking up the stairs from the back door. "How are you," Herrup said.

The other kid looked at Herrup like he was crazy.

"See?" Herrup said. "Granted, Phi Eps never were very nice to each other. But that was because . . . well, you know, Phi Eps are like that. But it's different when you have a bunch of surly gooks running around the house, and you don't even know them, for Christ's sake. When it's like that, you might as well give up."

We went into the rooms upstairs where all of us used to live and none of us would live again. We sat around and talked, the three of us. Herrup and Brenner seemed sad that it was ending, but they were relieved, too.

"There's no reason to keep it alive," Brenner said. "It's just a headache all the time. It's fine for you to get nostalgic about it, but that's because you don't have to live with it."

I asked them about the possibility that, in a few years, people might want to get together and live in the house again. But the house would be gone, used by Northwestern as a dorm. Wouldn't it be worth keeping it open as Phi Ep just on the strength of the possibility that in time there might be people who want to do the fraternity thing again?

Herrup shook his head. "No, I don't think that's it," he said. "I think that before long, this is going to happen to just about all the houses here. Who needs a fraternity anymore? What can a fraternity do for you that you can't do for yourself these days?

"I think it's just like always," Herrup said. "I think this is a case of Phi Ep being three years ahead of every other house on campus."

In June of 1969, the 29 of us, now seniors, got together one last time. Many had quit the fraternity, had quit paying dues and eating in the house and living there. But we went to the senior banquet at the house, even those of us who weren't members, to laugh one more evening away and to say good-by.

We ate lobster and steak, and the room was full. There was our class, and the juniors and the sophomores and the freshmen. The younger ones were getting a kick out of our maudlin reminiscences. We seemed kind of young to be looking back, after all.

We looked at the underclassmen and saw our own faces, and it seemed that Phi Ep could never die. We knew there were financial troubles, and it was hard to find anyone who still believed in the concept of The Fraternity Way. But somehow that seemed unimportant when you looked around the room. It had always been this way, and it always would.

Late that evening, we all got up and made our senior speeches. It was one of the few traditions left; the coats and ties had been replaced by jeans and T-shirts, even at this final banquet, but we thought we ought to take this one damned step and make senior speeches like seniors had been doing forever.

Some of it got embarrassing, like when some of the stoned or drunk seniors attempted to get serious and talk about what the fraternity had meant to them. No Phi Ep ever got serious in public, and it seemed wrong.

Monk and I had come to the banquet because we knew we belonged there even though we hadn't been members for the last two years. We lived in an apartment in south Evanston, but that night we knew that we had to be at the house.

As the speeches were going on, the president of the house passed around wooden Phi Ep plaques. They went only to dues-paying members.

As Monk got up to make his speech, he tried to steal one of the plaques. "Hey," yelled one of the real members, "those are only for guys who are legitimate members."

So Monk got up to make his final speech. It was very short, only 14 words.

"I might not get a plaque," Monk said, "but I'm getting your goddamn lobster for free."

Now that was Phi Ep.

But it was dead, and Steve Herrup left me alone to walk around the house one last time. The water had backed up in the shower on the first floor, and the mirror was broken.

I went downstairs to the dining room. All the big composite photographs were on the wall, showing portraits of the members every year. I traced the fraternity from the mid-50s until 1971, the last composite.

You could see it change. First the crew cuts and skinny ties. Then JFK hair. Then Beatles and wide striped ties. Then mustaches and beards. Then work shirts and wide-brimmed hats and cigarets in the mouth.

They were going to store all the big composite pictures in the attic in case anyone ever wanted them. But no one ever would; it is all dead, and it will never mean anything to anyone.

Once, when I was a pledge, the actives lined us up in this room and made us do push-ups all night long. It was part of pledge training. They threw things at us and made us memorize the names of the founders of Phi Epsilon Pi. It was ignorant, and it deserves to die.

But there were the nights, too, when some of us couldn't sleep and we would come down here and talk. Some guys would play cards, and some of us would turn on the TV and just waste the night away. We could always sleep the next day; classes were not nearly as important as this. And in retrospect, they really weren't; this was the best of the college times.

They won't be doing that anymore when this is a dorm; the people will use it as a place to sleep, and that will be it. Their friendships will be formed elsewhere. This place will not be referred to as the Phi Ep house. It will be called 576 Lincoln Street, and when the people who live here graduate and go away from Northwestern, they will forget it, like freshmen forget their impersonal dormitories.

I went up and sat on that roof over the door where we used to take in the late spring sun. No one else was out there, of course; there were no more Phi Eps to talk to. So I sat there for a while, waiting for something, listening for something. But whatever I was waiting for never came. *Sgt. Pepper* is an old album, and Monk and Otto and Digiansante and Buckner all are somewhere else now, and they probably don't even know that Phi Ep is dead. After a long time, I got up and went back downstairs to say good-by to someone, anyone. But no one was there.

A Thanksgiving Memory

It was his first Thanksgiving away from home, and he thought it would be a good change, with the football games on television and none of the relatives to bother him and ask him how life in the big city was.

After all the years of dinners with the cousins and the aunts and uncles, he was looking forward to being by himself for once. This was just a couple of years ago, his first Thanksgiving out of college, and he was a reporter for a newspaper in an important city, and he didn't feel like going home.

So for the first time ever, he wouldn't be there. During the four college years, he had made the reservations so he could be in Ohio the day before, so he could be there and be bored on Thanksgiving night and wish he was back by himself. Not this time, though; this Thanksgiving would be just another day, which is how he wanted it.

So on Thanksgiving morning, he made the telephone call and told his family that yes, he was sorry he couldn't be there, too, and yes, he was missing them. But really he was happy that he wouldn't have to put up with it for once, and he sat back to ease it through the day.

He had bought some sliced turkey for dinner, which he thought was a nice irony. But about noon or a little after, he ate all the turkey up, and it was gone. And in the middle of the afternoon he was getting hungry and it was dark outside, and he didn't like being there so much anymore.

It was a one-room apartment in Rogers Park, what they call a modern studio. But all it was really was a 9-by-12 cubicle with white walls and a hallway leading off to a bathroom, for $135 a month. A 45-minute L ride away from the Loop, and by five o'clock he couldn't take it anymore. It hadn't got to the point where he wished he was with the uncles and the cousins, but this certainly wasn't the way he wanted to spend his Thanksgiving.

By six o'clock, he knew he would have to have something to eat.

He looked in the icebox, and all he had was a bottle of Spanada wine, bought for a buck a couple of days before. And in the cupboard there were two boxes of animal crackers, which made him laugh. He couldn't remember when he had bought those.

He knew that the grocery down the block usually stayed open until nine o'clock, so he walked down to get himself some hamburger for dinner. He was really hungry by now, and ready for a quick meal and then an attempt at sleep, even though he wasn't tired.

But when he got to the store, it was closed—closed since four o'clock because it was Thanksgiving Day. No food after all. There was no one on the street, and he started to walk. He walked for about an hour, and the snow had begun to come, and yes, he was lonely. He even thought about being home.

He started back for his one-room apartment, so he could pull his hide-a-bed out and try for sleep. He passed the grocery store again, and the girl was there.

She was alone, too. She was wanting to buy some food, and she was just finding out that she could not, because today the store was closed.

Her name, it seems now, was Janie. She was wearing baggy bluejeans and a pea jacket, and standing by the door of the closed store she looked sad and absolutely beautiful. He stopped to talk with her. This was her first Thanksgiving alone, too.

They stood in the snow for a while, and then they figured that this was silly. So they went up to his room for their Thanksgiving dinner.

It was a dinner of animal crackers and Spanada wine, and it was delicious. They ate it slowly, and they talked, and it was easier to smile than before.

She said that she had thought it would be easy to spend the day with herself, but when dinnertime came, she had felt the same sadness. And they both laughed because they were supposed to be old enough to stay above such feelings.

They laughed a lot that night, and the one room was warm and nice. And when the night was over, they both said that it was the best Thanksgiving they had ever had, and that they would like to see each other again. But they each knew it was a lie, although a lovely lie, and the girl named Janie went away, and now she is just a Thanksgiving memory.

It was only a couple of years ago. They never did see each other again. So he does not know what became of the girl named Janie, where she went or what she is doing. But it is Thanksgiving again, and he is hoping that she is having a happy one, maybe even the second best one ever.

3

I SAW A MAN, HE DANCED WITH HIS WIFE

One summer Sunday evening, with the newsroom almost deserted, I was hanging around the city desk when I heard Earl Moses, the night city editor, let out a short laugh and say, "Oh, God!" I didn't even have to ask him the details. He was looking at a fresh bulletin from the City News Bureau, and I knew that it had to be a story so horrible, and yet so full of the grisly and twisted humor unique to the town where we worked, that we had another "Chicago story" on our hands.

Technically, all news stories breaking in Chicago are "Chicago stories," but in the verbal shorthand of the city room we are only talking about the ones that make you listen to the facts, shake your head, and say "Jesus! Chicago!" An example: a west-bound bus on Madison Street skidded in the rain and rammed into a light post, doing serious damage to the bus and injuring 36 passengers. In the impact the fare box was thrown out onto the street. A passer-by, hearing the moans and cries of the passengers, looked down at the street, saw the coin box, and picked it up and walked away. And the driver of the bus—a woman, by chance—was trapped in her seat by the force of the accident. Someone approached her as if to unpin her, and instead walked off with her wallet.

That's a "Chicago story." So was the one that Earl Moses was "Oh God"ing about on that summer evening, and it turned into the lead column in this chapter, "Burning Love." The other pieces here all share that same thread. You wouldn't expect to find these things going on anyplace else, and you're half-appalled and half-delighted to know that in Chicago they're all a part of business as usual.

We have some Chicago politics here—"Grave Deliberations" is a report on a meeting of the Chicago City Council, and the two columns titled "The Mayor Speaks" are examples of a phenomenon you will encounter nowhere else. In both of these columns, Mayor Richard J. Daley is quoted verbatim—*exactly*. And for both of these columns, I was greeted with severe, even venomous criticism, both from members of the public and from City Hall. The unanimous tone of the complaints was "Print what the mayor means, not what he says." Only in Chicago can you get blasted for refusing to misquote a man.

Two other columns, "The Ride Down" and "The Governor Is Guilty," are on a somewhat more somber side of the political picture. Both are stories of men in high public office who are found putting the fix in, and who are caught here in the darkest moments of their lives, as juries of their peers file into courtrooms and start them on their way to prison. And of the other stories in this chapter, no matter what they say of the venality and greed of people, I can only think of the parting comment of Yellow Kid Weil, the greatest con artist of them all: "I was gleeful!"

Burning Love

Just an old-fashioned love story:

Maurice and Thomasine McClinton have been married for three years, but lately they have not been getting along so well. They separated several months ago, and have since been living apart.

McClinton, 30, of 6800 S. Dante, has been having other problems as well. Back in April he was sitting on a windowsill, passing the time of day. He leaned back, thinking he was on the first floor. He wasn't. Since that day he has been confined to a body cast that starts at his chest and runs down to his toes.

The cast makes him virtually immobile; he stays in his bed all day. He can move his arms, though, and when he received a letter over the weekend, he opened it and found that it was his disability check. He asked his brother, Horace, who lives across the hall from him, to go out and cash it.

Horace, 34, did. He brought his invalid brother back some money, plus a supply of food stamps.

Coincidentally, Maurice's estranged wife decided to pay a visit to her formerly beloved. She showed up at the apartment, and engaged in a few pleasantries. Then she got down to business. She said she would like part of that disability check.

What follows is an account, gleaned from the police and from Maurice and Horace, of what took place next.

Maurice reached over to his bedside table and gave Thomasine around $25 worth of food stamps. He said he did not want to give her any money. She left the apartment.

Thomasine, 22, had walked three or four blocks when she decided that she would rather have some money. She sent her five-year-old son back up to Maurice's sickroom. "Mama says she doesn't want stamps," the boy said. "She wants cab fare home."

Maurice said too bad. Food stamps or nothing.

The little boy relayed the message. Thomasine sent him back up again. Again, Maurice said he wasn't giving up any money.

This time Thomasine went up to the third-floor apartment herself. She tore the food stamps up and threw them in Maurice's face.

She left again. But she decided that still another trip was in order. She returned to Maurice's bedroom. She looked at her husband, helpless in his bed, and she did the only logical thing. She took a plastic hospital-type pitcher of ice water and threw it all over him. Then she left.

Maurice began to scream and shriek. Brother Horace ran into the apartment. He lifted Maurice onto a couch, dried him off, and changed the sheets.

Maurice was quite chagrined. "That woman threw cold water on me," he said.

Horace noted that this was evident. He carried his brother back to bed. They assumed that the tender series of encounters was over.

It wasn't.

Several hours later, Thomasine returned once again. She went directly to Maurice's sickroom.

Brother Horace, hearing Thomasine's voice, went across the hall to see what was up.

"Horace," Thomasine announced, "I would like to speak with Maurice. Would you please leave the room?"

"Uh-uh," Horace said. "No way. You threw water on him before."

Thomasine then went into a nearby bathroom. She was carrying a bag with her. When she came out of the bathroom, she was carrying something she had retrieved from the bag.

It was the obvious item you would want to bring to a sick friend who is unable to move: a can of lighter fluid.

"She tore the top off the can and started pouring the lighter fluid all over Maurice," Horace recalled later. "Just throwing it all over his body. On the skin, on the cast, everywhere."

Maurice reacted with some panic. "Horace, gas, gas!" he screamed.

Horace, who was standing on the other side of the room, had noticed. He was already moving toward Thomasine.

Thomasine, ready to add the finishing touch to the day's romantic interlude, had dreamed up a thoughtful finale. She had taken out a book of matches, and was preparing to light one.

"Horace, she's going to set me on fire!" Maurice cried.

"I can dig it," Horace said.

Horace, a 200-pound karate instructor, wrestled Thomasine across the hallway into his own apartment, and jammed her against a wall.

"Light all the matches you want now," he said. "I'm calling the police."

He did. The police came. Thomasine explained that she would have preferred cash to food stamps. All present agreed that she had every right to this preference. She was then charged with aggravated assault.

Horace returned to Maurice's apartment. He carried his brother to the couch again, washed him off again, changed the sheets again, carried him back to the bed again.

"Generally, I like women," Maurice said. "But I do not appreciate this kind of treatment."

Yellow Kid at 99

Joseph (Yellow Kid) Weil, reputed in his day to be the shrewdest, most money-hungry con man ever to work the streets of Chicago, looked out of a second-floor window of the nursing home where he lives, and waited for the afternoon to pass.

There had been a birthday party for The Kid the day before, but now it was over and he was not exactly exuberant about being 99 years old. There was a knock at The Kid's door. It was David Pliska, the assistant administrator of the home, and he was bearing two letters for The Kid, from people who had remembered.

"Joe," Pliska said, "I have some birthday cards here for you. Let me open them up." Pliska slit open the top of the first envelope.

"Much money in there?" The Kid said.

"No money, Joe," Pliska said. "Just a card."

The Kid turned away, not interested.

In his time, he bilked, swindled, cheated and conned his fellow citizens out of sums estimated at more than $10 million. He was world-famed as the best in his business, namely, deviously separating people from large amounts of their personal finances. But The Kid's ill-gotten gains are all gone, and his home today is the small room where he sat Monday, at the Lake Front Convalescent Center, 7618 N. Sheridan.

The Kid was wearing a formal blue suit jacket, a pair of shiny gray slacks, and a white hospital-type identification bracelet on his left wrist. Pliska opened the second birthday card for him, and then said, "Joe, this gentleman has come to talk to you."

"What gentleman?" The Kid said, and looked at a visitor. "You know what a gentleman is? A gentleman is just another name for a loafer. Go to work! Make a living, quit being a loafer!"

The visitor sat down on a bed, and asked The Kid if the age of the great con man is over.

"Hell, no!" The Kid said. "People are just as gullible as they ever were. The lure of money is an eternal enticement. If you can make a man believe that money is to be had, then you'll get him."

The visitor asked if the public today were not more wary of con games, less likely to fall for a flimflam man's fast-talking scheme.

"Wrong," said The Kid. "The right con man could come along today and take whoever and whatever he chose to swindle. There are new people to swindle. The old ones have died off, and there are new ones to take. But the con game is a lost art. I am the last of the Mohicans."

Did The Kid ever get the urge to go out on the street and try it again himself? the visitor asked.

"I have no need to make the money," The Kid said. "I've had the money. I went to wine parties. I bought my wife diamonds. I sent my two sons abroad to study. But now what would I use the money for?"

Was The Kid afraid that he might be too old to be a decent con man any more?

"Hell, no," he said. "My age would help me. It would help me convince people that I was harmless. I'd use it to my own advantage."

Was there a man ever born who could pull a swindle on The Kid?

"Hardly."

Did The Kid ever give anyone any money back?

"Never as much as I took."

Did The Kid mind being called a liar?

"You have to be a liar when you're swindling. A good liar."

Was there any way The Kid could be tricked into making a careless move?

"I could be lured by a beautiful woman."

The Yellow Kid's gaze returned to the window. "My wife is dead," he said. "My father is dead. My mother is dead. My daughter is dead. My sons are dead. I'm the only one left. I will tell you something very sad. I'm tired of living. There are no allurements for me. There's nothing for me but what you see me doing today. Sitting in a chair."

The Kid and the visitor looked out the window together for a few minutes, and then the visitor got up to leave. He had one last question: Did The Kid ever feel a sense of shame about anything that he had ever done?

"Never," said The Kid. "I was gleeful!"

Election Day

Oh! say, can you see,
by the dawn's early light . . .

Election day, the purest flower of American democracy, is scheduled to grace our town in just 48 hours. The common vote, that stirring monument to the principles of the Founding Fathers, is upon us again, and so it seemed appropriate to take an advance look at what this most patriotic of days will mean to us here in Chicago.

"From every indication we're getting, this is going to be the dirtiest one ever," said Thomas F. Roeser, a vote-fraud expert. "This city is no stranger to vicious, underhanded elections, but I've never seen warning signs as frightening and ominous as this year."

Roeser is chairman of Project LEAP (Legal Elections in All Precincts), an organization dedicated to combating crooked elections. Most U.S. cities have no need for such organizations. I asked Roeser to characterize the spirit of our city as it will be on election morn.

"It's warfare," he said. "It's blood."

I asked him if, for the benefit of the more guileless, open-hearted, hopeful believers in the free election process, he perhaps could use some other terms to describe election day.

"Yes, there are other terms," he said. "Brutal. Tense. Ugly. Hate-filled."

. . . What so proudly we hailed
at the twilight's last gleaming. . . .

I asked Roeser why Tuesday's election is likely to be worse than others in the recent past.

"In other parts of the country, a presidential election or a congressional election is the most important and vital," he said. "Not here. This time the mayor and the aldermen are up for election, which means it's going to get a lot rougher than in a presidential election."

I asked if there are any other factors involved.

"There is a general feeling that this is Mayor Daley's last hurrah," he said. "We've never seen pressure for fraud as great as the pressure being applied this year. All kinds of people are coming out of the woodwork. I am not overestimating how rugged this is going to be."

I asked for a rundown of which wards are going to experience the most cheating.

"There are so many," Roeser said. "But here's a partial list: 2, 5, 7, 8, 9, 16, 23, 26, 28, 29, 30, 31, 33, 35, 37, 41, 43, 44, 46, 47, 48, 49."

I asked Roeser if he had a word of advice for a civic-minded voter on the way to the polls Tuesday.

"Yes," he said. "First, try to wake up the cop asleep in the corner of the polling place. Then call the state's attorney."

> . . . *Whose broad stripes and bright stars,*
> *through the perilous fight,*
> *O'er the ramparts we watched,*
> *were so gallantly streaming. . . .*

"We're outnumbered from the start," Roeser said. "We have 1,700 election judges and 200 pollwatchers working through Project LEAP. That's to go head to head with 45,000 paid city employees, out piling up the vote.

"We'd need at least 45,000 ourselves to catch everything—the payoffs in the corner drugstore, or out on the street; the votes being cast in the names of dead people; the chain-ballot effect, where the vote is already cast before the voter goes into the booth; the precinct captains taking perfectly healthy people into the booth, claiming the voter is disabled and then casting the vote. And the senile, unfortunate men and women wheeled out of nursing homes and wheeled into a voting booth, where they don't even know where they are, so the captains can pull the levers."

> . . . *And the rockets' red glare,*
> *the bombs bursting in air,*

> *Gave proof through the night,*
> *that our flag was still there. . . .*

I asked Roeser what kinds of men and women become helpers in LEAP's campaign to stop fraud.

"Many of them don't return for the next election," he said. "I don't really blame them. It's a psychologically crushing experience, going up against the kind of tactics that we see. To be attacked, abused, shoved around. It's tough. By the end of the day, many of our workers are sick at heart."

I asked if he is hopeful that LEAP can keep the election clean.

"It's an impossible task," he said. "When poor people are being told that if they don't vote for the machine, they'll be taken off welfare, or that members of their family will lose their jobs, it's very hard."

I asked Roeser how he, himself, felt with election day drawing so near.

"I'm girding myself," he said. "It's kind of like anticipating the feeling of getting beaten up."

> *. . . Oh! say, does that*
> *star-spangled banner yet wave*
> *O'er the land of the free,*
> *and the home of the brave.*

I asked Roeser how a person voting for the first time in Chicago should prepare himself mentally for the election day.

"That person should imagine what it is like to stand on the side of a street while a full-scale riot is going on," Roeser said.

I asked if this was a very heartening way to talk to someone who is about to participate in the American democratic process.

"A first-time voter in Chicago shouldn't allow himself to be fooled," Roeser said. "He will not be participating in the democratic process. On election day in Chicago, there is no such thing as the democratic process."

Hijack Hijinks

Nobody ever accused Chicago's criminals of being overly smart, or of operating with excessive elan and finesse.

But on Monday, a gun-wielding thug set some sort of record for dumbness.

He tried to hijack a Chicago Transit Authority L train.

To be specific, he tried to hijack the Evanston Express.

Now, if you think about it, this is quite a trick. It does take a few minutes to figure out, however. When word first came to the newsroom that a hijacking was in progress aboard a CTA L train, there was a flurry of activity. It took perhaps two minutes before someone brought up the logical question:

"Where the hell does the guy think he's going to take it?"

A good point. Once the Evanston Express leaves Howard Street, there's no place it's going to end up except the Merchandise Mart. There are these tracks, see.

A quick call to CTA headquarters confirmed this assumption.

"We know they're not going to Cuba," a CTA spokesman said.

And indeed they didn't. According to CTA officials, Monday's aborted hijacking happened like this:

At 3:43 P.M., the Evanston Express train was traveling south toward the Loop. At that time of day the train stops at several L stations in Evanston, makes a final stop for passengers at Howard Street and then heads nonstop toward the Merchandise Mart.

Passengers on the Evanston Express must carry little slips of paper they are given at the time of boarding and display them to the conductor. If a passenger does not have the slip, called an "ID check," he must pay an additional fee.

The conductor on this train, Richard Kane, 22, who was hired by the CTA in June, was working his way down the aisles, collecting the slips of paper from those who had them and change from those who did not. Kane was in the lead car, where approximately 15 passengers were riding, when he asked a man for his ID check.

The man—described as being around 30 and wearing a yellow knit sweater—pulled out a gun, pointed it at Kane and yelled, "I don't have no ID check, and I'm not going to pay."

The gunman's ire can perhaps be excused. It was 87 degrees in Chicago at the time of his outburst and he was, after all, wearing that knit sweater on the L.

However, his lack of sartorial foresight did not change the fact that he was waving a gun around and that he had, in effect, taken over the car. He had hijacked himself an L train.

There was a moment of confused silence. Kane waited for instructions from the hijacker, knowing all the while that there weren't a whole lot of options open. Gun or no gun, that train was going to the Merchandise Mart.

Kane tried to explain this to the hijacker. To the hijacker this conceivably could have sounded like a trick on Kane's part; FBI sharpshooters dressed as airline catering employees have been known to sneak up on airplane hijackers, for instance, and because of this hijackers are not an especially trusting lot. But in this case it apparently began to dawn on the hijacker that perhaps he had not thought this caper out fully.

"Tell the motorman to stop the train!" the hijacker shouted. "I want off!"

One of the facts of life that regular L riders have to deal with is that it is difficult to leave a train at a random point on the tracks. One needs a station. This, too, belatedly occurred to the hijacker.

"Go to the next station," he yelled.

This presented a fresh dilemma for the conductor. As we have noted, the next station was all the way downtown at the Merchandise Mart; thus the reason for the "express" portion of the term "Evanston Express." A trip all the way downtown undoubtedly was a longer ride than the hijacker wished to take.

The train's motorman, Howard Stratton, 29, made a decision. He stopped the train at the Lawrence Avenue station and opened the doors. Since this was an unscheduled stop, there were several sets of tracks between the train and the station platform.

This did not faze the hijacker. Novels and motion pictures like *The Taking of Pelham One Two Three* are fine for fantasy, but the Evanston Express hijacker was beginning to realize that he really had no place to go with this train. He leaped out the door, scurried over the tracks, pulled himself up onto the platform, and disappeared from sight.

Conductor Kane, perhaps sensing that the hijacking had been somewhat lacking in traditional drama and suspense, looked around at the passengers. Then he yelled, "Everybody hit the floor!"

Some did.

But the hijacker was gone. The Evanston Express hijacking was over. Police were looking for the dumb desperado.

Paddy's Back

The rumor coming out of City Hall was unlikely, but intriguing. Usually reliable sources reported having seen Paddy Bauler, the legendary scoundrel and old-time alderman from the 43d Ward, lurking around the hallways.

There was no reason for him to be there. Bauler retired from the City Council in 1967, after 30 years as an alderman, and has been living in retirement in New Mexico. He is 85 years old now. He has become a part of Chicago history; it was Bauler who first uttered the famous phrase, "Chicago ain't ready for reform." There would be no plausible excuse for Bauler to stray from the warmth of New Mexico in the middle of the winter—but then, there is an election coming up in Chicago next week.

On a hunch, I called Bauler's old phone number, at the apartment above the saloon he used to run on North Avenue. A rheumy voice answered. I asked if Paddy Bauler was in town.

"Who the hell wants to know?" the voice said.

I introduced myself.

"This is Paddy Bauler," the voice said.

Uh . . . how are you doing?

"Doing the best I can," Bauler said.

And why are you in town?

"I came in to vote for Daley," Bauler said. "Why the hell do you think I'd be in town?"

You came all the way from New Mexico to vote for Mayor Daley?

"I had to go into the hospital for a checkup," Bauler said. "I told the doc, 'Doc, I'm all right. I got to get out of here so I can vote for an old pal.' "

Gee, you mean you've already made up your mind about how you'll vote? What about William Singer?

"Who?" Bauler said.

Singer. He's from the same ward you used to run.

"Oh, what the hell," Bauler said. "I never even met that guy in my life. I don't like him and I don't like any of them other eggheads. Eggheads! They've got holes in their shoes and holes in their heads. Singer thinks he's so smart. He's so dumb, he probably thinks the forest preserve is a new kind of jelly."

But Singer has been making some charges about corruption in Mayor Daley's administration . . .

"I never even heard of Singer," Bauler said. "What a phony. Daley's got the experience, just like I had the experience. I'd rather vote for old experience than a young phony. Daley's a good Chicago guy. Just like me."

What do you think of Dan Walker, the governor?

"I never even met that gabby bastard either," Bauler said. "I never met him, and I don't want to meet him, and I don't want no part of him. He ain't a regular."

Is there anything at all to Singer's charges that the Daley regime has been corrupt?

"Why can't those phonies live like we do?" Bauler said. "Singer's just out for his own self, just like everybody else, the big phony."

But is Daley corrupt?

Bauler did not seem to hear the question. Instead of answering, he began to sing in a high, quavering voice: "Chicago, Chicago, that toddlin' town. . . ."

Paddy, do you know anything about corruption in Daley's administration?

". . . Chicago, Chicago, I'll show you around. . . ."

All right, then. Do you expect a clean election next Tuesday?

"Clean?" Bauler said. "What the hell? I always ran a clean election. I washed my face, put on a new suit and changed my undies and socks. How clean do you want to be?"

Are you sure Daley needs your vote this time?

"This time!" Bauler said. "I never miss! You used to vote for any name they gave you. Daley needs every one of those votes. Every vote counts. I'll be out there early to vote for him."

How many times?

"Once," Bauler said. "One vote. There was a day, I used to have a little fun. They knew me even when I was wearing a fake mustache."

The rumor is that you were seen in City Hall this week.

"I was there," Bauler said. "I was so happy to see it again. City Hall is better than the White House. I was at that hall when they built it. Sometimes I didn't even know what payroll I was on."

Is Chicago ready for reform?

"Chicago?" Bauler said. "Christ! Who the hell would want to live here if it was? This is the big city, boy! This ain't Honolulu! Reform? It'll never be ready! Not as long as I'm alive!"

Grave Deliberations

The City Council on Wednesday decided to turn its attention and collective wisdom to one of the great social issues of our time: the role of a free press in an open society. The debate was decorous and solemn.

"An irresponsible reporter at a typewriter is more dangerous than a drunken doctor in an operating room," howled Alderman Roman C. Pucinski (41st), quoting from Scriptures.

At the front of the Council chambers, Alderman Clifford P. Kelley (20th) came walking past the desk of Alderman William Barnett (2d). Alderman Barnett's eyes lit up when he saw the dazzling plaid suit being worn by his colleague from the 20th Ward. Alderman Barnett reached up, took the rear flap of Alderman Kelley's suit jacket, and rubbed the material between his fingers, nodding in approval and letting out a low whistle.

"The man who has never looked into a newspaper is better informed than he who reads them," intoned Alderman Pucinski, a former *Sun-Times* reporter. "Inasmuch as he who knows nothing is nearer to the truth than he whose mind is filled with falsehoods and errors."

Alderman William S. Singer, the mayoral candidate from the 43d Ward, leaped to his feet and launched into a spirited defense of the press.

Alderman Terry M. Gabinski (32d) lumbered out from behind his desk and made for the door. "Hey, Fred!" he called to Alderman Fred B. Roti (1st), who waved a return greeting, but declined to join Alderman Gabinski in his exit.

Alderman Singer continued to support the working press.

"Ah," said Alderman Roti, gesturing toward the press section with a cigaret that was jammed between his thumb and first finger. "Singer's just hoping those guys'll give him some more support."

Alderman William Cousins, Jr., the anti-Machine alderman from the 8th Ward, rose to object to the resolution on the floor—a document that had been offered by Alderman Pucinski, and which praised Marshall Field, publisher of the *Sun-Times* and the *Daily News,* for his "courageous call for greater responsibility in reporting by the news media" and for Field's proposal that "an individual who feels he has been wrongly or unfairly treated in a story should be able to sue not just the media that printed—or broadcast—the story, but also the individual who wrote or reported the story."

Alderman Barnett turned his back on Cousins, dipped his hand into a box of rock candy on his desk, and ate a mouthful.

Alderman Edward R. Vrdolyak (10th) was recognized, and said, "Instead of suing individual reporters, we should go back to the art of dueling." There was general hilarity in the chambers.

Alderman Paul Wigoda (49th) left his desk, approached the press section, and struck up a conversation with several reporters.

"Hey!" said Alderman Roti. "Don't come over here and cop a plea, understand, Wigoda?"

"This is a high-level discussion, and I want to keep it at that level," said Alderman Pucinski.

Several aldermen pressed on in their endeavor to object to Alderman Pucinski's resolution, but were beginning to be drowned out by laughter and shouting.

Alderman Gabinski returned to the chambers. "You want a sandwich?" he yelled to Alderman Stanley Zydlo (26th). Alderman Zydlo nodded. Alderman Gabinski left the room again.

The question of reporters' personal net worths was brought up on the floor.

"They get a lot of free pencils," said Alderman Roti.

Alderman Gabinski reappeared, and called to Alderman Zydlo again. "Somebody already went out to get a sandwich for me," he shouted. "I'll give you half."

The debate was being overtaken by jeers and giggles. Alderman Barnett was slapping out a tune with his hand on the back of a chair. There was a call for a vote. The Pucinski resolution was adopted 33 to 9.

The Mayor Speaks: I

Mayor Daley responded Wednesday afternoon to charges that his son, John, is engaged to the daughter of a crime syndicate hoodlum.

Daley, in a City Hall press conference, was reacting to a story in the *Daily News* that said the son was to be wed to Mary Lou Briatta, identified by the *Daily News* as the daughter of Louis Briatta, who was characterized as "a Loop gambling boss for the mob."

Daley, entering a fifth-floor conference room, was asked what he thought of the disclosures.

"What disclosure, the announcement?" the mayor said. "Very happy, that he's marrying a young girl that is a fine Catholic Italian young girl that, a college graduate, a fine person that I met on various occasions. Why? Is anything wrong with her?"

A reporter referred to the *Daily News* story.

"I didn't see the *Daily News*," Daley said. "I don't read the *Daily News*."

Another reporter told Daley that the newspaper story had characterized his prospective in-law as an alleged Mafia boss.

"Well, they could say the same thing about your father," Daley said. "Sure. Yeah, but I mean, sure, well, yeah, I say, what a great example of Christian attitude of anyone and especially the exalted and multimillionaire editors, I hope any of those wouldn't take an occasion to mar the fine wedding of two young people on allegations and charges. I don't know whether, where's the evidence, what was he convicted of and when, would any of you men and women tell me, and where?

"I'm not saying, but it isn't easy to say your father or my father was a, I know all of my relatives weren't great people, one of them, I think there's a bounty on their head over in Ireland, and we all know that the Lord picked twelve, and one denied it, doubted Him, and one denied Him, and one betrayed Him, and He was the finest person that worked this earth, but dear, I think that two young couples entering into marriage both of them are fine Catholic young persons. I met her, she is a girl of great culture, and she's a, she does a lot of painting with her fine mother, and I hope they have a happy wedding."

A reporter asked if Daley had ever met the young woman's father.

"Have I met her father?" the mayor said. "I meet him in the, I ran the softball games and baseball games, I've always occasionally, and I'd meet him at the games when the youngsters would be trying to make members of the White Sox and Cubs."

Another reporter asked Daley about charges that Briatta had once taken the Fifth Amendment, presumably before either a U.S. Senate subcommittee or a federal grand jury.

"Well a lot of your people took the Fifth Amendment," Daley said. "Is there anything wrong with a man taking the Fifth Amendment? His constitutional rights? Have you read about some of your newspapermen taking the Fifth Amendment? The Fifth Amendment is a constitutional right that belongs to any individual, and there isn't any contrary to what exists, you're entitled to your constitutional rights and when you take it there should be no implication, because if it isn't there they should remove it!

"And a person has the right when he appears before an anti, prejudiced grand jury, read the history of the grand jury, read the exposé in Florida about what was said by the district attorney, and if any of you people knew, and you do, you get all of the secrecy of the grand jury to the newspapers, but no one else gets it. The grand jury should be opened up, in my opinion, ladies and gentlemen, and the woman and man that goes in there should have their own counsel, it shouldn't be a one-way proposition, because the grand jury was created at a time under the English law when they assembled the grand jury from people who witnessed the crime that was committed, it wasn't any secret proceeding and it wasn't run by any district attorney or any state's attorney saying to the grand jury, 'You have to do it for me, you have to indict these people, my reputation is on the line.'

"It takes a minute, ladies and gentlemen, to indict a man in the federal, and this is according to, and I don't rely on it, the *Daily News'* story of a few months ago, one minute, about the safety and the imprisonment of a person, is that our type of justice, no other circumstances, they run 'em through in almost production methods. That isn't. The grand jury should be substituted for a district attorney to present in open court before a judge that you're charged, with something, dear, you know in open court who's making the charges, and you don't have all this bickering and you don't have all this phony secrecy. . . . I've watched this from the days I was in law school, and I watched the abuse of what happened in the English law under the Lord Coke and all these tyrants that sat on the bench and that's what we see today with the abuse of the grand jury.

"Any other question? I hope you all attend the wedding and have a great time. . . ."

Daley was still talking, but he began to walk away from the microphones, and a reporter asked him to return to the podium.

"What are you doing?" Daley said. "Working for you? I'm tired of being a, you should put me on the payroll."

A reporter asked Daley if he considered the publicity about his son's wedding to be an invasion of privacy.

"The sons and daughters of a public official are never private," the mayor said. "And I don't mind what they say, my girls went to high school and the first time I ran, the newspapers said I would open up the houses of prostitution. I would turn the city over to drugs and thieves and tugs, and the little girls at school said to my daughter, when she come home crying, the other had some she didn't and then the two of them didn't cry, but they said all we know our daddy and they might say that he's going to turn the place over to prostitutes or they might say he's gonna turn it over to drug addicts, and gonna turn it over to tugs."

A reporter asked if Daley thought that the newspaper story was a low tactic.

"The lowest thing," Daley said. "Of course, there's never anything as low as a newspaper, or television."

The Mayor Speaks: II

Mayor Daley met the press Thursday to discuss matters of current interest. In the audience, along with the reporters, was Benjamin Adamowski, a man who once ran against Daley for mayor. City Hall records show that Mr. Adamowski did not win. Mr. Adamowski told newsmen that he is now an attorney for Burger King hamburgers, and that Burger King had given the city tickets to a circus, which was why he was present.

Mayor Daley said:

"If we're supposed to be the great society and the full society in the great country we can't keep telling kids coming out of college and high school there's no jobs, that's what I read too much and hear too much on radio and television, there's no jobs, there's always a job for a good man and a good woman and a good young man and I think very frankly not being critical of but suggesting to you we do it on a more, maybe there's television add on additional people, maybe there's newspapers, maybe the radio even to do anyone kind of work to orient a youngster into the great employment field and I think in addition to that we have to have sports and we have to have different things; we, Eddie has outlined, Eddie Kelly and Bob Ahrens and all that, we have to take care of our senior citizens and we are, we hope to have thousands of them with the help of Burger King, the generosity and kindness, we'll have more and more, we'll have senior citizens there every day, we'll have buses to bring 'em there, we meet them at the different locations . . . we have senior citizens in every church and every parish and every park and they're actually doing a great job.

"I hope you're all invited, you, and if you're interested in tickets I'll give you some of the tickets Burger King gave me. Bring your family down, it's a great thing to go to a circus. I don't think any of you are so kind of crass that you don't want to see a circus, or, what do you say?"

There was no answer from the reporters. Daley continued:

"Is there any questions on the circus or any other topic you have in mind?"

A woman reporter started to ask about Governor Walker's address to the Legislature.

"You goin' to the circus?" Daley said.

The woman said yes.

"Good. All right," Daley said.

A question was asked about budgetary problems. Daley said:

"You see, under the Constitution, gentlemen, and ladies, budget is prepared by the executive and submitted to the Legislature. I do that, I'm responsible to submit in the City Council and I've recommended cuts and I've recommended increases, so it's, I don't complicate the answer, I think that's the answer."

Daley was asked another question about his own city budget. He said:

"I thought that in times of economic crisis that's when the government should spend, and we've tried to spend more this year; you've noticed the bond issues to provide employment and to get the economy moving so that the private economy will start a pickup of some of this vast millions of people in our country, the 10 or 12 million that are unemployed.

"Government function is to do that, that's why I was astounded when the president vetoed a bill for five billion, six hundred million dollars on the grounds he must have some poor economic advisers that it was inflationary, but you do know that 50 per cent of it would come back in taxes to the government and the other 10 or 15 per cent would be a slowdown in unemployment compensation and the things the government is paying now, and were we told basically and fundamentally you have to spend money to make money?

"You can't, we can't ask the people of this country, 10 or 12 billion million people, wait until it bottoms out, it's comin' back now, the commerce commission enters a statement that the unemployment is still goin' up, and if government, I've always said that, now I might be wrong, and your have a right to your views, if the private industry doesn't provide a job for a man and woman that wants to work then the government shall.

". . . We could collect refuge three and four times a week we could clean the rivers, we could clean the parks, we could build buildings as they did under CCO a lot of time a few years ago, we could have all elements of our society engaged, and what happens there? When you pay 'em, they pay a tax back to the government, don't they? What's your tax? They pay 10, 15, 20 per cent and then they spend money when they have it, they buy Burger Kings, they buy potatoes, they buy meat, I, I don't understand myself, of course I'm not a great internationalist or a nationalist, I just try to have a local guy from the stockyards but I have some ideas."

Filthy Wimmen

Social progress just won't stand still. You take a few weeks off from the job, and when you come back you find out they've changed the whole town around on you. When I left for vacation, the downtown area was still dotted with the same wholesome, traditional mix of massage parlors, peep shows, and dirty book stores as always. But when I returned to the office the other day, I started hearing rumblings that there was a new civic cultural phenomenon in Chicago.

Oh, well. When you draw a salary, you go out on the street and you do your basic investigative journalism. So I walked over to 109 W. Hubbard, went inside, and said hello to the three young ladies on duty.

"Are you the filthy wimmen?" I inquired.

"We certainly are," said Cinder, the co-manager of the place.

"Is this really a dirty-talk parlor?" I followed up.

"First one in America," Cinder boasted.

"But what is it exactly that you do for a living?" I asked.

"We talk dirty to people," said Veronica, another of the demure hostesses.

"I take it this is not free," I said.

"Ten dollars for ten minutes of dirty talk," said Janice, the third coy lass.

On we charge into the '70s. The dirty-talk store, which is part of an operation called Just Filmz, is already catching on big. While I was in the establishment, a steady succession of gentlemen, many of them conservatively dressed business sorts, came in to look around. The premise of the quaint little shop is that the customer will tell his wildest sexual fantasies to one of the women on duty. Then the woman will escort him back to a viewing booth in the back of the store. The customer will enter the booth, and a door will close after him. A pornographic movie will begin to show in the booth. There is a small hole in one wall of the booth. Outside this little window, the woman will be standing, whispering a string of obscenities designed to appeal to the customer's stated fantasies. There is no physical contact, so all of this is legal. That First Amendment is a sly little devil.

"Doesn't it get tiring, talking dirty for ten minutes straight?" I asked.

"Sometimes I take a break, and just breathe real loudly for a minute or so," said Cinder, who said she was a graduate of Southern Illinois University and a former children's speech therapist.

"But why do people come in here?" I asked.

"It builds them up," said Veronica, who said she is a graduate of the Goodman Theatre school. "It's a fantastic ego boost for men. They have us say things to them that they don't hear at home."

"Have you ever thought about what would make a man want to pay a woman money so that he could hear her talk dirty through a hole in the wall?" I asked.

"Every culture has its sexual taboos," said Janice, a former cultural anthropologist who claims to have worked with Margaret Mead. "America has more than its share. All I know is, there's a big market for it. Business is good, and it's getting better."

Noting that I was an investigative reporter in pursuit of truth, the three young women offered to provide me with a sample dirty-talk session, administered by all three at once. They said that this triple-filth special was not one of their standard offerings, but that they were great admirers of a healthy and vigorous free press.

"First you have to tell us what your weirdest fantasy is," Veronica said.

"I don't know," I said. "I've been giving a lot of thought lately to moving to the suburbs, raising a nice family, and accepting a position of responsibility with the local PTA."

"God, that *is* twisted," Cinder said.

"Don't you have a kind of Greatest Hits performance?" I asked.

We went to the back of the store. They closed me in a hot little room about the size of a telephone booth. In a couple of seconds, a raunchy movie started flickering on one of the walls. Through the hole in the wall, a stream of suggestive, lewd banter filtered through, in three distinct voices, all having the approximate cadence of a Walter Jacobson commentary.

Those girls sure did have foul mouths. As a matter of fact, I'd have to go so far as to say they were generally nasty people. But I knew that I was taking that chance when I first moved to Chicago, that it was only a matter of time until I would find myself locked in a muggy closet with a stag movie while three immoral women spat obscenities through the wall at me.

As I left the dirty-talk parlor, Janice told me that she was thinking about going along with Margaret Mead on an anthropological expedition to the Galapagos Islands, and that there might be a few rooms left on the boat if I was interested. I said I would give it every consideration, but that right now I had to return to the city room, for I was a working man again. Nice to be back.

"Nurse Dunn Called the Ambulance!"

When I heard that five wrestling fans had been shot by a gunman during the matches at the International Amphitheatre over the weekend, I must admit that my first thoughts did not go to the victims. Rather, I found myself trying to guess what the reaction would be from Bob Luce, the famous wrestling promoter and TV wrestling show host. Luce, who speaks exclusively in a terrible yowl and reacts to the sight of bloodshed and violence much as a hungry pup reacts to raw steak, was the impresario of the ill-fated Saturday night wrestling card.

So I called Luce on Monday, and made arrangements to meet him at the Executive House bar. His period of mourning seemed to be over. At the appointed hour Luce was waiting for me, working on a glass of tomato juice and wearing a red plaid sport coat, a yellow-and-white striped shirt, and an orange, brown, blue and yellow floral-patterned tie. His shriek, while toned down perhaps a decibel or two from the volume utilized on his television show, was nevertheless the loudest noise in the barroom. He was kneeing the underside of the table, always a sure sign that he is ready to talk. He needed little prompting to begin his soliloquy.

"When Kennedy got shot it bothered me!" Luce hollered. "When Bobby Kennedy got shot it bothered me very much! When Martin Luther King got shot it struck me very bad! When Kennedy got shot it was in Dallas! There is wrestling in Dallas! But I didn't think about wrestling! I thought about Kennedy getting shot!"

I asked Luce if he could reconstruct the Amphitheatre shootings for me.

"It was a male from 38 to 40 from what the lieutenant of police told me!" Luce said. "He was firing from the balcony! He was shooting at the ring! He was trying to shoot the referee! He fired two shots! One went through a boy's neck! Then it grazed a woman's neck! Then it ricocheted off the ring! It hit a boy's arm from Wilmette! The second hit a woman's finger! She was waving! Then it lodged in a woman's chest! The people who were hit! Three white! One Spanish! One black! I get a very good cross-section!"

I asked if, from now on, wrestling fans would be frisked before coming into the arena.

"We're not going to frisk anybody!" Luce said. "We're going to look for the suspect! Frisking is not necessary! If they come in inebriated we give their money back! Gagne versus Bockwinkle! Heenan was on the apron! He is the manager! It's an isolated incident! Bill Kurtis said that had to make him laugh! But it's a true statement! It's a precedent in our business!

"My family sits at ringside! My daughters are 10 and 12! My wife! She's licensed to referee! Bernie Turovitz was at ringside! From Ben's Auto Sales! My TV sponsor! He had his wife and three daughters there! I would not let my beautiful daughters sit there if it was dangerous!

"We've had injuries before! A woman fell in the washroom! A couple of guys in a fight! The Bears get the same thing! The incidents crop up! The people I have working for me have drills for something of this nature! Nurse Dunn called the ambulance! She's a registered nurse! She works for me! She comes and leaves in a cab! She's treated bruises!"

I said that, even though no one had been killed in the weekend shooting incident, I was surprised that there would be no frisking in the future. I pointed out that frisking is done as a matter of course at rock concerts.

"They're not frisking for guns!" Luce said. "They're frisking for acid! They're frisking for marijuana! They're frisking for pills! They're frisking for pushers! Heenan's been hurt going into the ring! He's been hit over the head with a hammer!

"We aren't concerned! We are in the business! If you're a promoter and you have two beautiful daughters at ringside! I am not concerned! I put my daughters there! My business is wrestling! It's where one fella grabs another fella! It's like football! Gagne says it was one lunatic! I have had 296 shows in the Chicago area! I have had 156 shows in Chicago itself! No incident has even come close! Ask Frain! He said if you call him he'll tell you that no one uses more men! I am unprecedented! I used 103 ushers and 36 guards last weekend! That is unprecedented! I will do nothing different! We will have a composite picture! We will look for the fugitive!"

I asked Luce if he thought that the shooting incident would keep fans away from his wrestling cards.

"Even this shooter wasn't taking it out on his fellow fans!" Luce said. "He hit the fans by mistake! He was aiming at the ring! He was trying to hit the referee!

"This is not precedent-setting! These are all good people who were shot! They were enjoying themselves! There were 140 people at the Sirloin Room for dinner before the matches! It costs $10.95 for dinner! This was the Sirloin Room, not a lunatic fringe! Seaman Thomas was there! I was there!

"There is another card February seventh! The Ox against the Bruiser! Heenan is back in a tag match! The fringe fan may be deterred! Not the fan who wants to go! A car goes off the track and kills 14! He's back the next race! The wrestling fan is a pretty hearty fan! The Bruiser has no fear!"

The Toddlers Have Their Say

I am second to no one in my admiration for Roger Ebert, the *Sun Times'* Pulitzer Prize-winning movie critic. Having said that, I must admit that I was a bit skeptical about one of his recent reviews.

The movie in question was something called *Mandingo*. Ebert took the almost unprecedented step of giving it no stars on the four-star rating system. He called it "wretched trash . . . obscene . . .

nauseating. . . and excruciating to sit through in an audience made up largely of children, as I did last Saturday afternoon." Ebert graphically described the horrendous violence and explicit sex in the film, and although he is a prototypical civil libertarian, he called for censorship of the film as far as children are concerned.

It is not Ebert's evaluation of the picture that I object to. If he says it is trash, then I'm sure it's trash. Rather, I wondered about the last line in his review: "This is a film I felt soiled by, and if I'd been one of the kids in the audience, I'm sure I would have been terrified and grief-stricken."

Now, Ebert is a man of great sensitivity. But when he was a child growing up, he lived in the small town of Urbana. I'm sure that if he had seen *Mandingo* as a lad downstate, he might have been "terrified and grief-stricken." Chicago in 1975, however, is not Urbana in the 1950s, and I wondered if children growing up here really would have the reactions that Ebert feared for them. I wondered what the children in the theater would have said if he had asked them.

So I had an elementary school teacher of my acquaintance take a random survey. She teaches at a large, ethnically mixed Chicago elementary school in Area C on the city's North Side. (The policies and quirks of the Chicago Board of Education being what they are, the teacher requested that I not name the school, and that I use only the first names and last initials of the children, for fear of reprisals from her supervisors).

The children, who ranged from second to seventh grade, were asked to write about movies. Here are excerpts from their responses:

ROSA M.: "I saw *Mandingo*. That was really a good movie. The fights were good fights. Mandingo bit the guy on the chest and a whole lot of blood came out of him. I think you can learn lots of things from movies, and I would like to go see that movie again."

TYETA J.: "The kind of movies I like are either gory movies or love movies. My favorite part of a movie is when someone gets killed or torn to bits. The only thing I like in a movie is the bloody parts. I like very gory, gory movies."

JOSEPH M.: "I like movies that have killings and murders. My favorite part are the people who get murdered. I like violence and blood because it looks cool and bloody. Fighting in the movies are the best part, when they get killed or shot by guns or knives. I like to see bloody movies because they are always killing each other. I would like to see the movie *Mandingo* because the violence sounds good and the sex sounds good."

KIM W.: "I saw *Mandingo*. I like the movie because it was bloody and nasty. He took him in the boiling hot water and stabbed him with a rake. The white man drank booze and he told her to take her clothes off, and the white man told the black woman to take her clothes off." (Kim is a second-grader.)

DANIELLE W.: "I like bloody gory fighting movies. But why pay $2 to see *Mandingo* when you always see it in real life for free?"

MARK D.: "I think fighting is the best part of the movie because there is a lot of killing and blood and junk so I think it is the most coolest part of the movie."

GONZALO R.: "I like violence and blood movies. It gives me the creeps and tickles my stomach."

FLOYD M.: "I saw *Mandingo*. . . . They wanted to have fun with the girl. They asked her if she was a virgin. She said yes, so he took the other one and led her over to the bed and took off her clothes and started beating her with a strap. . . . I felt the movie was very entertaining. It was very bloody and horny."

DIRK J.: "The kind of movies I like are the ones that have a lot, and I mean a lot, of violence. I like to see violence and blood."

DAMAIN R.: "I like blood in the movies because it looks real. I like it when they start fighting and they start killing each other."

IRMA M.: "Bloody movies are good because they are exciting to me."

CHRIS N.: "The kind of movies I like are scary and gory movies with lots of blood. My favorite parts are the bloody parts when people get torn apart and it's real bloody."

DON W.: "I liked *Mandingo* very much. I liked when he boiled the guy in hot water, especially when the guy was making it with his girl. Then the white guy made it with the black girl. They beat them with a wooden stick until they bled to death. My favorite part was when they whipped a man to death."

There are more of these reviews, but you get the picture. I was going to show Ebert what the schoolchildren had written, but I decided against it. I was afraid that he would be terrified and grief-stricken.

Neistein's Concerto

Bernie Neistein awakened early on Sunday morning. This was going to be an important day in Neistein's life. Oh, not that he had been without honors before; Neistein once had the distinction of having his name mentioned in a famous book about Chicago, for instance. The book was called *Boss,* and the reason Neistein was mentioned was that the author felt it was essential to identify him as a front man for the Mafia. Neistein chooses to shrug off such things. But Sunday was different.

For his morning meal, Neistein fixed himself a breakfast of an 8-inch Queen Bin No. 3 cigar. He is a short, thick, gravel-voiced man of 58 who came out of the city's West Side and became one of its most clout-heavy machine politicians. He was the protege of the late Democratic kingmaker Al Horan and still is committeeman of the 29th Ward. The ward is in the festering slums of the city and is totally poor and black; Neistein represents it from his lavish Lake Shore Drive apartment in another, far-wealthier ward.

This is not supposed to happen, but Neistein does not spend many hours worrying about it. He is what you might call wise in the ways of the world. He spent 16 years in the state Legislature and was the first person to be indicted under the state's Ethics Law (he beat the rap); he carries himself with a combination of benevolent menace and absolute assuredness that comes from a lifetime of getting things done.

Neistein is one in a long line of behind-the-scenes power-wielders in this town who carry the reputation of being bad men to cross. When rural mothers and fathers are fearsome about their sons and daughters leaving the farm and coming to Chicago, because of some undefined but very real terror they harbor about what lurks in the big city, Bernie Neistein is what they have in mind.

In any other city, these factors might be presumed to perhaps work against a man, in terms of his associating with polite company. Not here. This is what Sunday was all about. Witness the elegant announcement in the newspaper last week: "Gold Coast Chamber Orchestra. Milton Preves directs this new group, with Bernard Neistein violin soloist, in repertory from Vivaldi to the present. At 3:30 P.M. Sunday, Thorne Hall, Chicago Campus of Northwestern University."

So, shortly after noon Sunday, Neistein strode onto the stage of Thorne Hall for one final run-through of his solo before the concert. He took his violin—a Dario Verne, made in Turin, Italy—from its case, and then the bow. Neistein has done all right for himself since leaving the West Side; the bow alone cost $6,000. When a visitor to the concert hall approached him and asked to talk, Neistein turned out to be gracious and receptive.

"I took violin lessons when I was eight years old, but then I quit," he said. "Then I went 46 years without a lesson. I still played, though. When I was in the state Senate, there'd be all of these late-night sessions. You know, deals being made on the CTA, the Park District, income taxes, the whole thing. So I would take out my violin and play, right there on the floor. Two years ago I began to take lessons again. The people who convinced me to start up again said that I was the second natural talent to come across their paths in the last 50 years. Today is my first concert."

The other members of the chamber orchestra began drifting onto the stage for the last-minute rehearsal. They carried their own violins, some of which bore famous names. Neistein looked around, and then whispered to his visitor:

"The biggest ripoff there is is on violins. I know. A label only costs a nickel. They can con you into thinking you got a Strad, whatever. They tried to rip me off. Not me."

The others in the orchestra were treating Neistein with some deference, and he accepted it well. "I told the mayor about my violin playing, and he said that he used to take violin lessons when he was a kid, too," Neistein said. "He said that we ought to start a duet called Daley and Neistein. I said, 'Uh-uh. Neistein and Daley. You ain't in my league yet.' "

One of the other violinists, a reverend named Edward McKenna, came onto the stage. "Hey, Father," Neistein called, full of good cheer. "You ready?"

The orchestra began its run-through. Neistein played beautifully. At times his violin sounded like an angel softly crying. He had a look of total peace on his face.

Neistein's teacher, George Perlman, was sitting in the audience watching the rehearsal. "He'll come into my studio, that big cigar entering the door before he does, and then he'll put the cigar in an ashtray, and a metamorphosis will take place," Perlman said. "From a very positive, powerful little politician, this man will turn into a sensitive, innocent, gentle creature. The moment he learns something he simply exudes gratefulness. I can't tell you how grateful this man is to learn violin.

"He becomes as simple and as unspoiled as a youngster. I see a working-out taking place. Something dormant, something that has been asleep in this man for all these years. . . . He has a desire to project something from within him, and the way he projects it is the violin."

The rehearsal ended, and the orchestra went backstage to wait for the audience to arrive. Neistein lit up a cigar and talked to the visitor. "I know what they write about me," he said. "I don't let it bother me. They've never proved a thing about me. They're jealous, they're angry because I can produce. In 1960? When Kennedy ran against Nixon? I brought in my ward 27,000 to 500 for Kennedy. They can say what they want. I don't worry. I'm very loyal to my friends. In my business you got no cans on the shelf to sell. All you got is your word and your loyalty."

The visitor asked Neistein why he played the violin.

"I'm doing something I love," he said. He put his hand on his heart. "It moves me in here. It's exhilarating. It's a stirring feeling."

And was he nervous about the concert, which would begin in a matter of minutes?

"I got confidence in what I do," he said. "It'll be all right. I have no doubts."

He went out and played, and at the end he was given a standing ovation. Among the men on their feet and shouting were George Dunne, the president of the Cook County Board; Marshall Korshak, the former city treasurer; Frank Sullivan, the mayor's press secretary, and a platoon of judges. These are not people who usually spend their Sunday afternoons going to see neighborhood orchestras. Perhaps it was an illusion, but Neistein seemed to blush as he heard the cheers.

The Ride Down

If only these stories could end like they do in the newspapers and on the ten o'clock news. Neat and clean and simple. "Barrett Found Guilty On All Counts," period. On to the next story. Walker Reveals Budget. Lindsay Won't Run. Yankees Swap Wives.

But of course, it can't happen like that. Nothing can be that final and bloodless. After the verdict had been read, after the hard news was official, after the bulletin was out that Edward J. Barrett's life had collapsed and that he had been found guilty of everything the government had charged him with, there was still one small matter to deal with. The matter of a 72-year-old man in his hour of shame, who at the moment was still in his seat at the defense table, his hands gripping both arms of the black leather chair. The news story was complete, and the spectators in the courtroom were already talking loudly about what had happened, as if the old man had automatically disappeared the moment he was found guilty. It would have been easier for everyone that way, but unfortunately

Barrett had not disappeared, he was still right here, and the problem at hand was to find a way to go home with some show of dignity, some attempt at pride.

You can snicker at that if you want to, because today is the day to self-righteously pile on the Eddie Barretts of our world. The jury found that he did indeed take a lot of bribe money during the years that he has been clerk of Cook County, and he can be sentenced to up to 80 years in prison for that. But Eddie Barrett is of another time, a time when power-wielding and fast dealing were a standard, dirty, expected part of Chicago politics. It was wrong, of course, and now that time is finally starting to show signs of ending. But even if you understood that, it was not hard to look at a sick, disgraced old pol and wish his exit could be a little more graceful, a little less filled with humiliation.

His eyes were dead. The federal judge who had tried the case, Richard B. Austin, had just told the jurors: "I doubt that there will be many who will disagree with your verdict," adding a final twist of the knife to Barrett's worst day. There was nothing to do but leave. He walked unsteadily to a cloakroom, across the room from the jury box. He and his lawyer, Tom Foran, looked for Barrett's overcoat, but for a moment could not find it among all the others hanging there.

"Come on, Ed," Foran said. "We can't lose a coat, too."

Barrett, in a very small voice, said: "I won't have much use for one now."

Foran went back into the courtroom, but Barrett went the other way. He walked down the 25th-floor corridor with an assistant, and there was no elevator waiting to take him downstairs. So he lingered until one came, and was forced back into the far right-hand corner of the elevator car by the crush of other people wanting to ride downstairs.

No one in the elevator was talking. Everyone knew that Barrett was in there, and to make idle conversation about anything but the verdict would have been transparent and useless. Someone could have brought up the trial, of course, and said something like, "Why didn't you ever take the stand?" or, "How do you feel?" But that was best left for the second-string TV reporters, the ones who had not been assigned to the courtroom, but to the first-floor doorways, and whose only hope of making the night's news would be to shout such things at Barrett when he arrived downstairs. It seemed a bit more human to let the man ride in silence and kind, although false, anonymity, just for these few seconds.

On the way downstairs the elevator stopped. A woman got on, and she knew many of the people who were aboard. Apparently she did not see Eddie Barrett, way in the back, because she began to talk in a loud, cheerful voice.

"I haven't heard about Linda Lovelace today," she said, and laughed. She was referring to the star of the film *Deep Throat,* and the question of whether it had yet been banned in Chicago again.

The man she was addressing, who knew that Barrett was there, gave a short, quiet answer.

"Have you seen the film yet?" the woman asked.

The man said that he had not.

"Oh, you should," the woman said. "It's really quite funny. You really should see it."

Barrett, his eyes still lifeless, looked briefly up in front of him to see what floor the elevator had reached. It stopped again, not yet having descended to the ground floor. A woman departed, and some bells sounded. "Those bells mean that 120 pounds just got off," another woman said after the doors had closed.

Elevator talk never works, and it certainly wasn't going to work with this load. The car stopped again, a man got on. The bells rang again. "And those bells mean that 150 pounds just got on," the bell woman said. And then the car was at the first floor.

There were no good-bys for Eddie Barrett. The people on the elevator parted so he could leave, and the TV shouters practiced their art. If Eddie Barrett answered them, his words were a whisper. No sound came from his lips. His path to the revolving doors was blocked, but at length he made it through.

It was windy outside the Federal Building. There was no limousine to take Barrett home. Just a dented Yellow Cab, hailed at random as it rumbled up Dearborn. He stopped and climbed into the back seat. Case closed. Guilty as charged.

The Governor Is Guilty

It has not happened yet. The jury knows, but he does not. Theodore Isaacs, 62 years old, is alone. He is walking down the deserted 25th-floor hallway of the Federal Building, and his footsteps are echoing like radiator pipes banging in an abandoned ballroom of an old hotel. The building is closed to the public; it is a legal holiday, and Isaacs is on his way to find out his fate.

"Are the others here yet?" he asks someone.

The answer is no. Otto Kerner, Isaacs' co-defendant, and the defense attorneys have not arrived on the floor. The telephone calls went out only 15 minutes or so ago, the calls saying that the jury has reached a decision.

Isaacs has been found guilty, but of course he does not know it yet, only the 12 jurors know it. The guilty verdict could mean a 73-year prison term for Isaacs. "The others must be held up somewhere, or something," he says.

Isaacs walks to the double doors of the courtroom. He is carrying his overcoat folded over his right arm. He reaches out to pull the doors open. They do not budge. They are locked. He stands in place for a moment, tries again. Then he walks away, ends up over by the wall. There is nowhere else for him to go. He crosses his arms and begins to wait.

Finally the doors are unlocked, Isaacs enters the courtroom and goes to the defense table. Otto Kerner comes in with his family and the defense attorneys. Kerner, former governor of Illinois, now on leave as a judge of the U.S. Court of Appeals, makes a steeple of his hands and places them in front of him, rests them on the shiny table.

He, too, has been found guilty; he, too, does not yet know it. His prison term could be 83 years. He and his friend Isaacs, a successful Chicago attorney and former state revenue director, do not speak, not even small talk. There is nothing left to say. The door through which the jury will enter is still closed.

James Thompson, the young U.S. attorney who prosecuted Kerner and Isaacs on the charge that they accepted bribes in the form of horse-racing stock during Kerner's term as governor, is ten feet away, at the government's table. He is facing away from Kerner and Isaacs, looking toward the empty jury box. One of his assistants says something to him, but he does not answer. Instead, he yawns.

Robert Phillips, a United States marshal, walks toward the spectator gallery. He tells the dozens of reporters that he does not want a stampede after the verdict is read. It is 11:10 A.M.

The minutes are dragging. For Kerner, a guilty verdict could mean the utter, heart-stabbing ruin of a life filled with words of praise and official certifications of honor. He does not look like a man who is afraid. He looks like he is posing for the engraved portrait on a $100 bill.

But Kerner is a man who knows how to behave in public; he has been appearing in public most of his life, and he is aware of the methods a man can use to hide the churnings that tear his insides apart.

And still the door where the jury will enter is shut. Kerner does not look out into the gallery. He knows that the people are staring at him; he chooses not to meet their eyes. It is like Rennie Davis, a defendant in another famous Chicago trial, told a reporter on the day he and his fellow Chicago 7 co-defendants were waiting at their table for their jury to come in: "They'll come in and give their verdict, and we'll be led away to jail, and you'll sit there and make your notes about what the expressions on our faces were and what kind of clothes we were wearing." Kerner knows how the game works; he will not waste any smiles on the people in the gallery, not on this day.

The jury door opens. But it is just a court official wheeling in a gray steel cart containing evidence and exhibits. He pushes the cart by one end, and it glides silently over the carpeting in the courtroom, until it ends up flush against a side wall, next to the still-empty jury box.

At 11:44 A.M. the jury comes in. Their path leads them directly past the end of the defense table. The jurors do not look at Kerner, and they do not look at Isaacs. No one in the room is speaking.

Within 60 seconds, Otto Kerner and Theodore Isaacs either

will be vindicated, or their lives will be forever horribly muti-
lated. Kerner leans back to wait. Isaacs looks over at the jury box.

Robert L. Taylor, the U.S. District Court judge from Knox-
ville who has tried the case, asks the jury if it has reached a decision.
William Michael, a brickmason from Riverdale who is jury fore-
man in this trial of a former governor and his trusted friend, says
the decision has been reached. He hands a white envelope to John
Booris, a court clerk.

Two sentences, and it is over. "We, the jury, find the defendant, Theodore Isaacs, guilty as charged in the indictment. We, the
jury, find the defendant, Otto Kerner, guilty as charged in the
indictment."

Paul Connolly, Kerner's attorney, reaches out a hand and lays
it on Kerner's arm. Kerner shows nothing. Neither does Isaacs.

Judge Taylor polls the jurors, one by one, to reconfirm their
decision. They he gives them some final instructions, asking them
not to discuss what went on in their deliberations. "The jury room is
a sacred place, a secret place," he says, and finally, across the room,
Otto Kerner has to bite down on his lips to stop the trembling.

The jury is led out. Kerner follows a few moments later,
through the same door. In the end, Theodore Isaacs is wandering
around the emptying courtroom, alone again. He is smiling at
people, who are avoiding his gaze in embarrassment. "I still can't
believe it," he says softly as he moves back and forth in the area next
to the defense table.

Downstairs, in the office of the United States attorney, James
Thompson's assistants are standing around their boss' desk,
laughing and smiling and congratulating each other. Light is
coming in through big windows in the corner office, flooding the
room with brightness, and it looks like the beginning of a long party.

There are no windows in the courtroom. "I still can't believe it,"
says Theodore Isaacs. But there is no one left to listen.

The In Crowd

America, relax. Everything is going to be all right. Wholesomeness, patriotism, and clean family values are back in style.

Evidence of this came in the form of the opening of a new private club in Chicago the other night. The club is called Zorine's, and you may have read about its first party in the newspapers the last few days. The party at Zorine's was well-attended by society figures and widely reported; the party embodied many of the facets of decadence, bisexual chic, and jaded glitter-foppery that first captured the public imagination in Nazi Germany.

Guests were greeted by naked twin boys, each painted silver and each with a jewel in his navel, waving feather fans. Behind a buffet table was a reclining woman painted silver, nude from the waist up, wearing a fishtail from the hips down. Each waiter was adorned in a glittery undershirt and single rhinestone earring in the shape of a Z. The doorman was a woman dressed in mesh hose.

All of which is cause for the rest of us to breathe a sigh of relief. Such unusual behavior as witnessed at Zorine's was considered sophisticated and chic in New York and Los Angeles five years ago. Playful decadence suddenly was the rage of East Coast and West Coast society. Serious thinkers began to ponder whether such a depraved atmosphere and ambiguous sexuality might signal the downfall of the nation.

But now the danger is over. As everyone knows, the only function served by the "society" crowd in Chicago is to act as a signal of what has gone out of fashion. By the time Chicago's self-appointed social leaders have read enough New York publications to realize what the fad is, the fad is over. New York society may have come over on the Mayflower, but Chicago society came on the Rock Island Line, and when Chicago's social lions—who made their entrance into society by dabbling in meat-packing plants, farm implements, and oat futures—decide that they are ready for silverchested fan boys and bare-breasted mermaids on the dining table, then we can all rest assured that decadence is dead.

Let us trace the path of the sophisticated-debauchery fad from its birth on the coasts several years ago to its death at Zorine's the other night. When New York's social leaders decided to adopt such dandyism and tame wickedness, it was being practiced and flaunted mainly by a group of people on the fringes of the rock scene, most of them teenagers, homosexuals, or drug addicts.

Well, time passed before the idea made it to Chicago. Among the glitter freaks from Chicago's decadent teenage rock crowd who showed up as guests at the Zorine's opening were James M. Rochford, superintendent of the Chicago Police Department; Philip W. K. Sweet, Jr., president of the Northern Trust Bank; William Wirtz, president of the Chicago Black Hawks; Potter Palmer, the current in a long line of Potter Palmers; and the wife of the chairman of the board of the Standard Oil Company of Indiana.

Further comment should be unnecessary. Of course, the affair at Zorine's will cause no change in attitude on the part of the normal people in Chicago toward the society crowd. The people of Chicago will react to the society figures in the same way they always have, which is to say they will laugh at them.

I did go to the trouble of contacting the one friend I have in Chicago who is from one of the city's oldest, wealthiest, most socially prominent families, and who I knew would not be caught dead at Zorine's. I asked him whether he had heard about the party.

"Yes, I heard about it, and I read about it," he said.

I asked him whether he had any comment about it.

"When Richard Speck kills the nurses, you don't have to comment on it," he said. "Just reporting the facts is enough. I'm embarrassed to see how many fools there are among the people who are supposed to be my friends."

After the opening-night party, Zorine's has been shut down so the final building and decorating of the interior can be completed and invitations for membership sent out. By the time the club opens for good later this year, though, the news that the Chicago social elite finally have caught on to glitter and glamorous decadence will have reached the coasts, and you won't be able to find a trace of depravity or chic sinfulness in all of New York or Los Angeles.

Already, the Chicago correspondent for *Women's Wear Daily* has filed a report on the party. When her story hits the streets in New York, there's going to be a run on milk, Walt Disney movies, and home Bible-study lessons like you've never seen in your life.

The Night Chicago Died?

Time for a little investigative reporting here. It seems that the Number One rock-and-roll record in Chicago, according to WLS Radio, is a song called "The Night Chicago Died." Performed by a British group called Paper Lace, the song purports to be the story of Chicago during the Al Capone era. The song begins:

Daddy was a cop
On the East Side of Chicago,
Back in the U.S.A.,
Back in the bad old days.

About 15 seconds into the record, the tale turns to what happened "in the heat of a summer night":

When a man named Al Capone,
Tried to make that town his own,
And he called his gang to war,
With the forces of the law.

The singers of Paper Lace recount "what a night it really was, what a fight it really was" during "a battle that rang through the streets of the old East Side." Apparently Capone's men were good shots, because, as the song relates:

There was shouting in the streets,
And the sound of running feet,
And I asked someone who said,
About a hundred cops are dead.

The song ends happily, however, as the "daddy" of the song, a Chicago policeman, arrives home safely to brush mama's tears away.

Not having been around during the Capone days, I decided to contact some men who are familiar with the era and read them the lyrics to the song to check its authenticity. Even though none of the experts contacted are connoisseurs of rock and roll, they agreed to listen. Here are their responses:

ART PETACQUE, famous crime reporter and untenured professor of sociology: "What the —— is this? What's this about the night Chicago died? Capone made Chicago happy. There was bootlegging, popping corks, whatever the —— dance was before the Charleston. And what's this about a hundred cops were dead? Capone owned the police department. A hundred cops were loaded, maybe, but not dead.

"The cops used to be paid so much per barrel for letting Capone's trucks of booze pass through their district. Capone's men killed a lot of people, but never a cop, as far as I know. He killed the cops with kindness, that's what he killed them with. They were paid off from the captains on down.

"The mother in the song is crying, is she? She's probably crying with joy in anticipation of her husband the cop coming home with extra cash for the baby's shoes."

BENNY BENTLEY, press agent and former prizefight promoter: "I am driving in my automobile the other day. I am listening to beautiful music on WNUS, and my daughter begins to punch the buttons. She gets Larry Lujack, and then WLS, and then WIND. She is punching every button, and on every station is this song about the night Chicago died. I listen to this song, and I tell my daughter, 'This song is a phony.' She says how could it be a phony, it's playing on the radio. She believes in the song. Who wrote this song, anyway? Was it a guy from Chicago?"

No, Benny is told, the songwriters were young Englishmen.

"Aha!" Benny cries, triumphant. "It figures! A guy in England does not know what goes on! London, Paris, England! A guy sits in England, he wants to write a song, so he pulls some clips! He watches an old movie! Now he writes a song! Now if he wrote a song like this . . ."

At this point Benny begins to sing: "Oh, George Washington, he died at the Valley Forge. . . ."

He stops his song, and continues in his normal speaking voice, which is only slightly less hurried than the speed of sound, and which, when Benny is walking over the Michigan Avenue bridge, can be heard at the Water Tower: "That song would be history! That song would be truth, because George Washington really did die at the Valley Forge! But not this song about Chicago dying.

"The idea of this! That Capone would take over the town in one night! He was already entrenched! He came here as a bouncer in a nightclub! The Four Deuces Club on Wabash Avenue!

"That song about Chicago could possibly be a hit in London. It could possibly be a hit in Paris. They would eat it up in Saigon. But in Chicago? Why, this song is not telling the truth! I am speechless!"

LEN O'CONNOR, television commentator and Chicago landmark: "First of all, if Capone's gang is fighting on the East Side of Chicago, who are they fighting, the fish? The East Side is the lake. And they're supposed to be fighting against the cops? Why should they fight against their friends? I don't even know how to answer a question about this song. Not only would I never buy the song, I would never be caught dead listening to it."

So there you have it. In consideration for the time they devoted to this survey, our three panelists are each being sent a copy of "Rikkie Don't Lose That Number," by Steely Dan, with the exception of Mr. Bentley, who instead has chosen a luncheon date with Neil Young during the upcoming Crosby, Stills, Nash, and Young concerts here.

Weird

The most talked-about movie in town these days is *Emmanuelle,* currently playing at the Michael Todd Theater. *Emmanuelle,* which had a black-tie opening here, is being billed as "the first X-rated film you can see without feeling guilty" and as "a beautifully photographed, lushly filmed celebration of erotica." In other words, a dirty movie that opens new frontiers for dirty movies.

But all of the praise for *Emmanuelle* has been written by publicists and critics who are not used to dealing with pornographic films, and whose experience is generally in the area of legitimate cinema. It seemed to me that to obtain a true evaluation of *Emmanuelle,* what was needed was not a film critic, but a scummy pervert who has wallowed in filth for so long that grimy degeneracy is his true home. I immediately got on the phone.

"Harold," I said, "how would you like to go to the movies?"

"Is it free?" said Weird Harold Rubin, the loathsome smut peddler who is the proprietor of Weird Harold's Adult Book Store, Massage Parlor, and Nude Modeling Studio.

"Absolutely," I said. "I need your professional evaluation of something."

So at midday on Monday, I arrived at the Michael Todd. Harold was waiting for me by the ticket booth. Even on crowded Dearborn Street at high noon Harold gave off the foul aura of a child molester hanging around a playground at dusk. Pedestrians were making a point to steer a wide path around him.

"I am always glad to be of assistance to a member of the Fourth Estate, our valiant free press," Harold said.

"Can it, Harold," I said. "My editors made it quite clear to me long ago that they disapprove heartily of any mention of your name in the column. The only reason I have turned to you now is that in the area of slime and vileness, you are without a doubt the local authority by many a mile."

"Thank you," Harold said. We entered the theater.

The main floor was packed. But this was not the tuxedo-and-evening-dress crowd that had received so much publicity on opening night; the patrons of this daytime showing of *Emmanuelle* were furtive and seemed a trifle nervous. More than 99 per cent of them were male, and if they were convinced that seeing the movie would not make them feel guilty, they were not so convinced that they could look one another in the eyes. The theater management helped preserve the mood of anonymity by keeping the lights turned off, even while the screen was blank.

First there was some loud rock music piped in, stolen off the radio (whoever made the tape forgot to switch it off in time, and half of the WLS jingle boomed through the theater), and then a pair of trailers for *The Towering Inferno* and *Earthquake* came onto the screen.

"How awful," Weird Harold said. "The way some people cash in on tragedy and violence."

Then *Emmanuelle* began. There were some establishing shots of the heroine of the movie driving through the teeming streets of Bangkok. She was fully clothed. The patrons watched expectantly, waiting for the scenes they had paid their money to see.

"This is terrible," Harold said. "It looks like Maxwell Street." Several members of the audience moved away from us.

The film progressed in a leisurely fashion. There was some nudity, but if the patrons had been expecting another *Deep Throat* or *Devil in Miss Jones,* it didn't look as if they were going to get it.

"Not much action here," Harold announced to the audience. "What is this, Walt Disney?"

Still, the crowd waited. But it soon became evident that *Emmanuelle* was what is referred to as "soft-core," as opposed to the "hard-core" pornography that has become commonplace in recent years.

"Something like this, you have to use your imagination," said Harold with undisguised scorn.

The dialogue was in French, which may have contributed to the fact that the next time I turned to Harold, he was asleep. I shook him awake and pointed to the screen, which featured the heroine floating down a jungle river in a gondola.

"I can see this on 'Passage to Adventure,' " Harold said.

Harold began to talk to the screen with more and more frequency. He muttered something about "consumer fraud," and at one point said, "This isn't even dirty. It does nothing to deserve its X rating." After another lukewarm love scene, Harold said, "If I snipped this movie up and put it in peep show machines, I'd go out of business."

On the screen the heroine said in French, "What do you want from me now?"

"What a stupid question!" Harold responded, causing more of the audience to leave our part of the theater.

During the love scene that is intended to be the climax of the movie, Harold could take no more. He exploded with the most savage criticism he could level at the film: "This thing doesn't even violate the Supreme Court guidelines on poor taste! This isn't even pornography!" He picked up his coat and made ready to leave.

He was shaking his head as we walked out the door and into the Loop. "I hope you didn't have to pay for those tickets," he said. "I've seen dirtier movies at a kiddie show."

I motioned to a line of customers, waiting to get in to see the movie. "Someone must like it," I said.

"That just shows you what is happening to our country," Harold said.

4

THINGS WE
SAID TODAY

One of the most gratifying things about writing a newspaper column is that if you are itching to say something, you don't have to wander down to the corner bar to seek out a tolerant ear—you've got the next edition as your outlet instead, and by morning no one is going to have any doubts about where you stand.

I never considered myself a politically-inclined person, at least not any more so than the next guy, but by October of 1973 I knew I could not, in good conscience, avoid writing "Time for You to Go." And when the anticipated flood of angry letters never materialized, I began to realize that Mr. Nixon's time really was up, and that now it was only a matter of when.

The other pieces in this chapter are also basically straight commentary, with the exception of the first column, which is an obituary for a man who probably would not have received one otherwise, and who I thought deserved to be remembered.

Requiem for a Disk Jockey

Someone called the other day to say that Jim Runyon had died. The news was about three weeks old, but I had not heard; no one writes obituaries for a disk jockey. Jim died in Cleveland, I heard, and as soon as I learned about it, I found it hard to think about anything else for the next few hours. I never knew Runyon, at least in the sense that I never met him or shook his hand, but I thought I should say something about his life, anyway.

I heard that he was 43 years old, and that cancer had done it to him. His name probably means something to some people in Chicago, because he played rock-and-roll records on WCFL here for a couple of years. But when I thought of Runyon, my mind went back to the summer of 1964, and I started hearing his voice again.

When you are 17 years old, and you are lucky enough not to have to worry about making money to give to your family, the summer has a kind of magic to it. It is a time to build memories, a time to give yourself the good old days that you will bore people with 40 years later. If you are lucky, you have not seen the bad side of life yet, and there will be no summers better than your 17th.

When you grow up in Ohio, you head to the northern part of the state in the summer, to hang around the lakes. There your time is spent drinking 3.2 beer that you're too young to buy for yourself, lying around in the sand next to Lake Erie, and talking nice to girls you will never see again. Most of your time is spent in a car, cruising with your friends, telling yourself that nothing is happening and that you're bored, but knowing inside that it may never be better for you.

And if you were 17 years old in 1964, the radio in the car was tuned to KYW, the strong-signal station in Cleveland.

Even now I can tell you who the voices on that station belonged to. Early in the morning it was two men who called themselves Martin and Howard. Before noon Jim Runyon took over and went until the middle of the afternoon. Then it was Jim Stagg until dinnertime, and then Jerry G until 10:00 at night. Jay Lawrence came on for the early-morning hours.

The voices narrated our lives. It was not important work they were doing; it was not dignified or historic. And yet they became a part of us. They would tell silly jokes and make senseless patter, and then they would play "Things We Said Today" by the Beatles, or "Time Is on My Side" by the Rolling Stones, or "Pretty Woman" by Roy Orbison, and they became as much a part of that summer for us as the people we met or the places we went. The KYW jocks may have been sitting up in their studio, in a tiny airless room, smoking cigarets and putting in their required hours, but we did not think about that; all we thought about was that we were living a special, easy time, and that the voices were a part of it.

This may not be the way things should be, but when I think back to that part of my life, I do not think about a schoolteacher I had, or a book I read, or a movie I saw. Instead, I think about cruising around the lakes in a steamy blue Ford with my friends, turning KYW up all the way and listening to the music and the jocks. We did not think in terms of anyone dying, not then; the idea of Jim Runyon, who called his show "The Runyon Room" and told us that he was "a Runyon named Jim," being dead was too distant to even cross our minds.

When I heard that he was dead, I instinctively started calling friends from that summer, telling them about it, asking if they remembered. They all did; summers like that do not disappear from the mind very quickly, and the voices of the long summer days, and of nights by the lake, have a tendency to stay in your ear.

I called Jim Stagg and Jerry G, too. They are in Chicago now. Stagg runs a talk show on WMAQ radio, and Jerry G, now a grown-up called Jerry G. Bishop, is with WFLD television. They said that the KYW crew had all drifted away from Cleveland. Runyon had come to WCFL here, and then had become tired of rock and roll and had gone to Boston to do other radio work. In the end, they said, Runyon ended up back in Cleveland. KYW had been sold twice, the call letters had changed twice, but when he died Runyon was back on the same spot on the Cleveland dial that he had been that summer.

Stagg and Bishop both told me that the KYW days had been special for them, too. But I could tell it was not the same for them as it had been for us. They were working at the time, earning a living, and we were not. We were just enjoying it and letting it into our lives, and that is better.

So Runyon's dead, and we're all getting a little older, and it certainly is not 1964 anymore. I just thought someone should say that there are people who remember.

Time for You to Go

Dear Mr. Nixon:

And so the game is finally up. Until now, until this present turn of events, there were people in the country who could still pretend that throughout history, presidential politics had always been like this. That yours was like any other presidency, and that your opponents were merely people with deep philosophical differences with yourself.

That has all disappeared now, of course. Your most recent actions were so repugnant to a sense of what is fair and decent, so cowardly even in the eyes of the citizens who had trusted you, that everything has finally been laid bare. With the forcing out of Mr. Cox, Mr. Richardson, and Mr. Ruckelshaus, the whole country is finally seeing the truth. You can no longer be a man pretending to "tough it out"; rather than being tough, you are now desperate, wildly so, and yours are the actions of a man with nowhere else to turn.

For years you had asked us to accept the radical, the vocally liberal, the anti-war as enemies of America. With great ease you moved the demarcation line toward the center—from Rennie Davis to Charles Goodell, to George McGovern, to Lowell Weicker.

For a long time, it worked. But no more. You are now asking the country to believe that Mr. Cox, Mr. Richardson, and Mr. Ruckelshaus are somehow foreign to what is right and just. But it will not work any longer, because everyone remembers that these were the men selected by you to find out what was foul in our 1973 America. Apparently they were finding out only too well.

The three of them, by refusing to be a part of your frantic scheme, have reminded the country what honor and patriotism are. The three of them are the type of men you used to embrace as your own kind of people, but thankfully for us all, they have shown us that they are not like you at all.

Who is left to defend your name? Haldeman and Ehrlichman and Mitchell are gone, their lives a disgrace. Agnew, the man you assigned to do the blame-pointing, is gone, a convicted felon. And now the three men brought in by you to give your name a veneer of cleanliness have left you, too, after seeing to what depths your fear would take you.

And you would make villains of these three men? It will work no longer. You pretend to be able to "take the heat," but instead you run and recklessly try, once again, to molest the meaning of justice in order to hide the truth about yourself. The tapes? They are not so important now. Who would believe the legitimacy of anything coming out of your office?

I hope you do not plan to depend on the support of the people you once called "Middle Americans," for by now they, too, know about you. They will not be fooled into thinking that Mr. Cox, Mr. Richardson, and Mr. Ruckelshaus somehow had the worst interests of the country in mind. I think the truest reaction I have heard came from a man who voted for you three times and who, until a few months ago, thought you were one of the great presidents in American history. That man read about what you had done this past weekend, and he said, "How do I tell my children what has happened to this country?"

There was a time when the idea of the presidency could be held up to schoolchildren as a stirring, hopeful, positive ideal. No more. There are actually children who think that all presidents are like you. It may take generations to show them they are wrong.

You have done quite enough. You have embarrassed and disgraced your country. You do not have the moral authority left to utter a credible sentence in your own behalf, much less speak for the nation. You ought to be ashamed of yourself, but clearly you are not. In the years to come, perhaps there will be time to analyze this, to assess the damage you have done, to study it and discuss it and decide what it has all meant. But that is for later. You can abolish a prosecutor, and seal up an attorney general's office, but you cannot abolish the people, you cannot seal up the mind of a country. Your country sees you as you are now. And now it is time for you to go.

Babylift

The so-called Operation Babylift out of Vietnam is being hailed as a wonderful and noble gesture on the part of the United States. It is not. Instead, it is an appalling continuation of the overwhelming American arrogance that has made Vietnam a tragedy for our country from the day we arrived there.

I realize that this is going to be an unpopular notion; judging by the wet-eyed reports from newscasters and reporters, the U.S.-sponsored flights of orphans from Saigon to the United States are widely being viewed as positive evidence of America's humanitarianism and decency. It is easy to get good press when you can use babies as props.

But before this goes too far, it is time to stop for a moment and admit the real thinking that lies behind the taking of babies out of Asia: the theory that the American way of life is the only good way of life on earth, and that we are doing the Vietnamese a favor by allowing them to try to be like us.

We went over there to win hearts and minds. We failed miserably. Now it seems that every person in Southeast Asia who is old enough to talk is busy proclaiming hatred for the United States. So what do we do? Still refusing to learn, we start grabbing the only

Asians who are too young to talk back to us, and we bring them over here and announce plans to make them American citizens.

No one could object to evacuation of the children from Saigon now that an attack on the city seems imminent. Throughout the history of warfare, efforts have been made to get children out of the line of fire until the danger has passed.

But this is different. We are not taking the babies to a safe zone until the threat of bombing is over. We are picking them up out of their homeland, and flying them halfway around the world to our own country, where we have determined that their new home should be.

It is a very easy and convenient way to alleviate American guilt over what has happened in Vietnam. To show an American president cradling a Vietnamese baby in his arms is to comfort a nation. But where was the concern for Asian infants when we were conducting saturation drops of fragment bombs all over the Vietnamese countryside? Where was the concern for Asian infants when we were dropping napalm as a matter of course?

On Monday the South Vietnamese tried to stop the taking of Asian babies out of Asia, but our own country protested, and so the flights were resumed. Will no one stop to ask what right we have to be doing this? Will no one stop to wonder how we are so sure that a Vietnamese child will be happier growing up in Illinois or Alabama than in Vietnam?

The news film has shown Vietnamese foster mothers weeping as planeloads of the babies lift off from Saigon. Can anyone blame the foster mothers? Our country is still so smugly confident that it knows best, that it has all the answers to the mysteries of life in Southeast Asia. We have been proven wrong again and again and again, and yet we will not stop.

It will be hard to blame the Vietnamese if they consider Operation Babylift to be nothing more than kidnaping. To say that we have homes and parents available for the Vietnamese children here in the United States is simply not enough. To say that Americans feel profound and genuine sympathy for the Vietnamese children is simply not enough. It is not our right to determine that the Vietnamese children will be happier as Americans.

Joseph H. Reid, executive director of the Child Welfare League of America, has addressed himself to this question. This is what he said: "Vietnamese, like all people, do not want to lose their children. All Vietnamese have a strong sense of family obligation, and they have shown themselves willing and capable of caring for their own children. Our great moral responsibility is to enable them, in their time of great tragedy, to do so. . . . Wouldn't it be far better for the children of Vietnam to be cared for in their own highly civilized culture—whether Communist or non-Communist—than to destroy that culture further by exporting tens of thousands of them to alien homes? Hundreds of thousands of Vietnamese men, women, and children have died during decades of war. Do we further deplete their population by 'rescuing' their children through flight to the U.S.?"

The unspoken thought behind the taking of the children from their homeland is that we are saving them from growing up under communism. But are we so certain that a Vietnamese child will be less able to adjust to a North Vietnamese government than to a foreign life in the United States? The war is a civil war, and there is no reason to believe that, in its aftermath, North Vietnamese soldiers would do purposeful harm to Vietnamese infants. My Lai was an American atrocity, not a Communist atrocity.

But we will not listen, of course. Instead we will bring planeload after planeload of Vietnamese children to the United States, where we will give them to American parents and change their names to American names. And they will grow up, outsiders in a land not their own, and as they approach adulthood they will read the history of what happened in the land where they were born. They will read of the American adventure in Vietnam, and they will wonder how it ever developed that they ended up here. But they will know the answer. They are here because they are the final chapter of an American blindness and an American shame that we still will not admit is real.

Airport

PHILADELPHIA—There are no answers to this. Now that it is with us, we probably will live with it forever. The line in the airport concourse is stretching for 30 feet, hardly moving, but everyone is waiting patiently. No one is angry. Up against the wall over there, a businessman is being frisked. He looks at his watch while it happens, wanting to be sure he does not miss his plane. No one glances back at him as they walk past.

Another man walks through a big metal-detecting shed. Apparently he does not pass the test, for he, too, is told to wait. A uniformed security policeman approaches, holding an electric cattleprod-like device with a long metal loop on the end. The security policeman sticks the device under the man's arms, between the man's legs, inside the man's suit jacket. No one stops to watch.

In the end it is not the big events of history by which we remember our times, not the presidential elections or World Series that we flash back to when we try to remember a time in our lives. Those are just guideposts. Rather, it is the little parts of life, the things we deal with every day without noticing or thinking, that come back to us later to remind us of what it was like.

And when we think back to this part of our times, the image that may haunt us most is that of an airport, any airport, and of citizens of the United States of America being frisked and searched and poked at and funneled through electric mazes. All of them presumed innocent, but all of them also suspected of the possibility of harboring a secret madness.

Of course it has to be this way. Of course, with things as sick as they are in the land, it is absolutely essential that this has happened. Of course, ugly as it is to watch and be a part of, there is no real alternative, and it must be done.

But knowing that does not make it any better. Finally we are beginning to realize that so many of our beliefs about the openness and warmth and fundamental goodness of this country are turning out to be myths. The new airport scenes say it for us: we are afraid of each other, we are terrified of the evil that may lie inside our neighbor's heart, we cannot afford to be trusting anymore. We do not and cannot accept the sanity of strangers on faith. We want everyone to be searched, including ourselves. It makes us feel better.

All the American children who are growing up now, who have yet to take their first airplane ride, will never know it was ever any other way. They will not know of the days when a person carried a shopping bag full of gifts onto an airplane with just a nod and a smile to the stewardess. They will not know of sitting in a departure area all day, without a ticket, just to watch the planes take off and land. They will not know of wandering around an airport as if it were a public library or a ballpark or an art museum, an open, cheerful place instead of a hall of suspicion and fear.

On TWA flights this month, one of the selections on the stereo headsets is a series of spoken-word essays from a new album by John Wayne titled *America, Why I Love Her.* Over a background of inspiring, patriotic music, Wayne talks about what he calls "the good things." He says, "We hear a lot about war, the hurricanes that hit our shore, but all that does is sing the blues about America. What about the good things, the men who love their wives and take their sons fishing?" He says, "In my son's eye, I spotted a gleam. 'I wanted to surprise you, dad—I'm on the football team.' " He says, "You ask why I love America; give me the time, and I'll explain. Have you seen a Kansas sunset, or a Louisiana rain? Have you strolled along a New York dock? Have you seen the mighty Tetons, have you watched an eagle soar?" But then the airplane's captain cuts in and says, "Sorry for that delay in taking off, but we had to wait a while due to airport security, which unfortunately is all too necessary these days."

It would be so nice if John Wayne's America were the real America anymore. But it isn't, and pretending that the most striking thing about the United States is still its open skies and beautiful scenery just isn't enough, not in a time of grayness and distrust and fear of noises behind you on the street, or of packages in the hand of the man behind you in the airport ticket line.

If the mighty Tetons and the soaring eagle are the symbols of John Wayne's America, then the terrible, necessary scene inside the airports is the truest symbol of the new America. Strangers searching through our bags and feeling at our clothing do not seem to bother us much; that kind of privacy is just another principle that we have had to give up, another trade made inevitable to deal with the terrors of our time.

"Hey, Jim," one security guard in Philadelphia's airport called loudly across the concourse to another. "Give me a hand here, will you? This fellow says he's wearing a leg brace."

The man with the leg brace stood very still. He was about 35, thin, wearing an olive business suit. The guards knelt on the floor in the middle of the concourse and felt his legs. The fact that he had a handicap was hidden pretty well; it wasn't until the guards pressed the cloth in that the shape of a metal brace became obvious. If he was hurt that the other people in the airport now knew that he could not walk without support, his face did not show it. The others hurried past him as the guards continued to feel at his legs. It probably will never be any other way in America, never again.

Blaming LBJ

It was a time for our viciousness. We were a whole generation, we who were in college during the years of Lyndon Johnson, and we could never forgive him for the fact that he was not John Kennedy. It did not occur to us, in those years when the country was just beginning to fall apart, that the problems might have run deeper than any one man.

No, we did not want to think about that. The nation was in love with us, everyone wanted to be young just like we were, and we did not have time to go into things too deeply. "Hey, hey, LBJ, how many babies did you kill today?" we chanted, and no one told us to shut up. Soon every college freshman who was eight weeks out of high school found it very comfortable to sit around and talk about how the President of the United States was a happy murderer.

It was so easy for us. Things had just begun to turn, the way we live had just started to go sour, and it was so simple to blame it all on Johnson. He was not hip and he looked physically clumsy, especially after Kennedy. We did not like this; it displeased us. So it started on the campuses, the hatred for Lyndon Johnson that was to spread over the land and, in the end, to break his heart.

We, of course, did not choose to recognize that the man had a heart. We were ready to ignore the steps he had taken to further civil rights; we were kind of bored with that, anyway; it was going out of fashion. We could ignore the compassion he was showing for the powerless, and the things he was trying to do to help keep the country together. Vietnam was enough for us, and we used it well.

We used it so well. We were so thrilled that we were right and he was wrong, that we were almost happy to see the battle lines forming, to see the whole country choosing sides and squaring off one against another. There was no need to talk to each other about it; each of us had plenty of company on our own side, more than enough company to keep us comfortable and convinced that we were 100 per cent correct. And right out in front, a clear shot for everyone to blame the troubles on, was Lyndon Johnson.

When was it that we discovered that Vietnam was only the beginning of our agony? That somewhere along the road, our meanness and hatred had triumphed over everything else, and that the war had become just another one of the terrible plagues that are poisoning us all? That while we were so eagerly slashing away at Lyndon Johnson, the problem had become ourselves?

Certainly the realization did not come until we had shamed Lyndon Johnson out of the White House and, as a replacement, ushered Richard Nixon in. But still the war would not stop, and we slowly came to the recognition that perhaps it was stronger than even the strongest of men, perhaps it was not fair to judge a man's whole being on the basis of that war alone.

Johnson was gone by then, though, back in Texas, away from us. If we had been mistaken in making him pay the price for the horrible convulsions of an entire nation, it was a little too late for apologies. He had been our president at the time of a national collapse of the spirit, and he had paid. It was too hard for us to blame ourselves, and it was no great chore to turn on him.

There was much that he did wrong, and many things that should not have been. But in the end, the most lasting thing about these years since 1963 will be the dark unhappiness of America, and we made sure that Lyndon Johnson understood that unhappiness, that he understood it very well indeed.

All for Nothing

These are the hours we knew might someday come. Those who opposed the war from the beginning and those who supported it until the end all knew. And now that it is becoming truth, now that the television news programs are full of film documenting the Communist take-over of massive stretches of South Vietnam, the time has come to admit it, once and forever: it was all for nothing.

In a period of eight years, 56,400 American men died in Vietnam. Many of those lives ended in the central highlands, in the 27,000 square miles that fell so easily in recent days. The American lives were spent to hold on to those miles; here at home, during the U.S. military involvement, strident voices pleaded on both sides, saying that the miles were not worth it, saying that the miles were. Now the miles have been lost.

It is easy to let the statistics deaden the impact of what this means. The numbers always were so staggering that they threatened to defy comprehension; there was a time, for instance, when the United States was spending $2 billion a month in South Vietnam. But the war was not about miles, and the war was not about dollars.

Here at the *Sun-Times,* in the reference library, there are 11 fat yellow envelopes, all bulging to overflowing with clippings about young men from the Chicago area who were sent to Vietnam and who were shipped home dead. You can dump the envelopes onto your desk and form an obscene paper mountain composed of the stories of men whose dreams died in an instant in Asia.

Time has passed; if you pick up a handful of the death stories, and begin to try and find the families of the men who died, you discover that many of the parents are dead now themselves, many of the widows have moved or remarried. But if you keep calling, you will find that there are men and women who have been watching the news reports of the loss of South Vietnam with more than a passing interest.

You can make a call to the 5200 block of South Monitor and talk to Mrs. Mary Palcowski.

"I watch the films on TV, and it makes me feel cold all over," Mrs. Palcowski will say. Her son, Richard, was killed in Da Nang in September, 1970. "My son just died for nothing at all.

"Before last week, at least I felt that he died so that other boys might be saved. But now I know that I shouldn't fool myself. Richard and 50,000 other boys all died for nothing at all. My wish was to go to Vietnam someday and see the place where my son died. Now I don't think I'll ever get the chance to go. When the reports come on TV, I see them begin, and then I walk away."

You can make a call to the suburb of Streamwood and talk to Cecelia Dassie. Her brother, Fernando S. Figueroa, died in 1972 after his helicopter was shot down near Hue.

"It hurts quite a bit for me to hear the news," the sister will tell you. "It's such a shame, all of that death for nothing. My personal opinion of the war doesn't matter. My brother thought that he was over there to do some good. He was discharged once, but he re-enlisted. He was wrong, wasn't he? He was supposed to be over there to keep the land from the Communists, and now it's been taken over by the Communists, hasn't it? I don't really understand."

You can make a call to the 3800 block of North Oakley.

"Yes, I have been seeing it," Mrs. Leona Woehrl will tell you. "And it was all worthless. He gave up his life for nothing." Mrs. Woehrl's son, Michael, died near the Cambodian border.

"This just cheapens his life," his mother will say. "What's the use?"

Her voice will break, and all these years later, she will begin to weep and say, "He served his country, and it didn't mean anything.

He was a nice boy, a mild boy. He never should have been there. His life is nothing now."

You can make a call to the suburb of Burnham. Mrs. Raymond Jamrock's son Philip was a tank commander in Vietnam when he died.

"He was such a full-of-life kid," Mrs. Jamrock will say. "It hurts me to think about what's going on over there now and what it means about what Philip died for. When the news comes on television, I walk out of the room. I make myself a cup of coffee and wait until the news is over."

In 1965 Walt W. Rostow, adviser to Lyndon Johnson, said, "The Viet Cong are going to collapse within weeks. Not months, but weeks."

You could call the families of all the local men who died in Vietnam in the years since 1965, but it would take you months. Not weeks, but months. You could call them in search of a legacy, if you wanted, but you would fail. This war left no legacy at all. Only death without meaning.

5
RICH AND FAMOUS

Writing about celebrities is a tricky business. On the one hand you have the credo of the late sportswriter Jimmy Cannon, who, speaking to author Jerome Holtzman in the book *No Cheering in the Press Box,* said: "I remember when [another sportswriter] said what a great life he'd led and how fortunate he was that he had met all the great athletes of his time. I think the great athletes are fortunate that they met me."

It's not hard to see Cannon's message: stand in awe of someone you're trying to write about and you might as well give up before you sit down at the typewriter. On the other hand, if you approach a story with the idea that the subject is merely someone for you to jab at and ridicule and eventually knock down—all because that subject happens to have achieved some degree of fame in life—then you're not much better off.

The stories in this chapter are about people who are rich, or famous, or often both. In a few cases I know that I violated my own vague set of ethics. There was no way that I was going to approach

Uri Geller with respect and deference, and there was also no way I was going to approach Joe DiMaggio with a jaundiced or cynical eye. But on all of them I tried to do the only worthwhile thing a writer can do for his readers, which is to give a decent sense of what it was like to be there.

So in this chapter you'll be there for a week-long stay at Hugh Hefner's Playboy Mansion, and you'll be there on the road with Howard Cosell (during a time when he fancied himself a candidate for the United States Senate), and you'll be there flat on your stomach in a rural field with Rod Stewart, the rock star.

If I had to choose one profile to keep in my personal collection, it would be the first one, "Judge Hoffman Remembers." It was written in July, 1975, more than five years after the end of the Chicago 7 Conspiracy Trial. I know that I will be thinking about that night for a long time to come.

Judge Hoffman Remembers

The listing on the television page had been brief. "Eight P.M., Channel 11," it had said. "Hollywood TV Theater. Chicago Conspiracy Trial. A dramatization using actual trial transcripts of the 1969 trial in which a group of political activists known as the Chicago 7 were accused of conspiracy."

The program, a two-and-one-half-hour re-creation of the trial featuring professional actors in a realistic courtroom setting, was being aired as a network presentation of the Public Broadcasting Service. All around the United States, viewers were settling down in front of their television sets to experience once again the notorious trial that has become a part of American history.

Many thousands of those viewers were watching in Chicago, on the local public television station. And of those thousands, one was sitting in Room 251 of the Drake Hotel. Outside the hotel room's windows, an endless stream of white headlights moved steadily southward on Lake Shore Drive, then turned with the curve of the lake and disappeared to the east. Inside the room, Julius J. Hoffman, 80 years old, his chin resting in the palm of his right hand, stared at the screen of a Zenith Chromacolor set. The red armchair in which he sat had been pulled across the low-pile yellow carpeting so that it was closer to the set. On the television the actor portraying the trial judge was reprimanding the defendants, saying sharply: "Please don't raise your voice to me. I don't like it."

In the hotel room, Julius Hoffman chuckled softly. He gestured toward the screen. "Tough guy, that judge," he said.

At first he had decided against watching the television show. "That trial was five years ago," he said on the day before it was to be broadcast. "I have put it aside altogether. No, I think I'll let it pass. That was just one criminal trial, one trial among the many I have presided over. I read in the newspaper where this television show was going to be a re-enactment of 'the greatest political trial in American history.' Why, on my court calendar, there are only two kinds of trials: criminal and civil. There is no such thing as a 'political trial.' This was a criminal trial, that's all it was to me. Do you know, I have sent more syndicate criminals to the penitentiary than probably any other judge in the country. But people aren't interested in hearing about Mr. Teetz Battaglia. They're more interested in hearing about what Mr. Kunstler referred to as a political trial."

No, he had said, he would let the evening pass without watching the program. But then he had changed his mind. "I don't suppose I can be accused of being excessively modest," he had said. "Everyone likes to be noticed. Maybe I would like to see it after all." His wife had been ill for some time, and he did not want to disturb her by watching the program at home. So he had arranged to take the hotel room for part of the evening and watch the drama based on the most famous trial he had ever presided over.

He came to the room at 7:45 P.M. He was dressed, as usual, impeccably. He wore a perfectly tailored gray glen-plaid vested suit, with highly polished black shoes, a white shirt, red-and-yellow striped tie, and gold jewelry. He is on senior status in the federal judiciary now, and he is not seen around town as much as in the past. He has a reduced caseload, and most evenings he spends at home with his wife. But he looked exactly as he had five years ago, during the four and one-half months of the trial that made him a national symbol.

"Is the set working?" he said. "I took pains to see what the competition is, by the way. There's not much on tonight on the other channels. I think we'll have a pretty respectable audience."

On the screen, the dramatized trial was beginning. Hoffman took his seat, and fixed his eyes on the television set. Random sounds from the cool summer night came through the window, but as the courtroom proceedings started to unfold before Hoffman, everything else became forgotten.

The defendants, and their lawyers, and the prosecutors, and of course the trial judge were introduced, one by one. The camera panned in on the actor portraying Judge Hoffman. In the hotel room Hoffman showed no reaction, other than a rapid tapping of his right foot on the carpeting. It took no more than a few minutes before all of the heat and anger and electrical fury of the trial became real again, the days that divided a nation and made Julius Hoffman one of the most controversial and emotion-stirring figures of his time.

The actor playing the part of defense attorney William Kunstler approached the lectern before the television judge's bench and began the first of his many arguments with the video Hoffman.

"Too young," said the real Julius Hoffman. "That's a bad makeup job. Kunstler is a much older man than that."

And when the actor portraying the judge began his reply, Hoffman leaned forward in the hotel room, watching very closely.

"Well, I suppose you have to take into consideration that he's an actor," Hoffman said. "I understand that he's one of the great actors of the theater. He seems to be making an effort to be exceedingly correct. He's doing a pretty good job . . . not as good as Hoffman, mind you, but pretty good anyway."

And then something very strange began to happen. As the trial progressed, and Hoffman became more involved in it, he began to laugh softly. It was not a harsh, malicious laugh, but rather the private laugh of a man who is enjoying a solitary secret that no one else will be allowed to know about. The first time he did it was when the actor portraying Bobby Seale came onto the screen.

The black actor stared directly into the camera. He was trying to create the effect of glaring at the actor judge, but in this room he was eye-to-eye with the real Hoffman. The actor said, "I think there is a lot of racism involved, myself . . . that racist, that fascist. . . . Look, old man, if you keep up denying me my constitutional rights, you are being exposed to the public and the world that you do not care about people's constitutional rights to defend themselves."

And Julius Hoffman, on the second floor of the Drake Hotel, chuckled.

He did it again when the man portraying Jerry Rubin berated the television judge. And again when the man acting the part of David Dellinger leaped to his feet in protest. It was becoming increasingly clear that whatever passions had once raged inside Julius Hoffman concerning these defendants and this case now were replaced with a starkly different emotion. It seemed to verge on a staggering kind of nostalgia. The actor playing Abbie Hoffman screamed, "Your idea of justice is the only obscenity in this room. . . . This ain't the Standard Club. . . . How's your war stock doing, Julie?"

And the real-life Julius Hoffman, five years later, laughed quietly again, and said, "He's a funny man, that Abbie. He used to wear his hair in a bun in the back. Tied it in a ribbon. We were very close. He used to call me 'Julie.' Not my Christian name, 'Julius,' but 'Julie.' "

When the television David Dellinger, in a burst of anguished emotion, stood up from the defense table and said, "I feel that you are a man who has had too much power over the lives of too many people for too many years," and compared the judge to King George III, Hoffman turned to the other person in the hotel room and said, "You may genuflect to me before I leave. In the courtroom on Monday, people can call me 'Georgie.' Not 'Julie,' but 'Georgie.' "

It went on like this throughout the program. Hoffman appeared to be highly entertained by the presentation. If he was having any thoughts that perhaps, around the country, other viewers were raging against him and believing that he had destroyed the concept of justice, he was hiding those thoughts very well.

His mood varied only once. That was when the actor portraying William Kunstler began to deliver his famous, emotional speech accusing the judge of disgracing the law. "I am going to turn back to my seat with the realization that everything I have learned throughout my life has come to naught," the actor said, "that there is no meaning in this court, and there is no law in this court, and these men are going to jail by virtue of a legal lynching, and that your honor is wholly responsible for that. . . ."

Julius Hoffman turned to the person who was watching the program with him. Hoffman was not smiling; he produced, from an inside pocket of his suit jacket, a typed manuscript.

"I've put some thoughts together," Hoffman said. "Maybe you can find an idea or two in here."

The manuscript was four pages long. The first paragraph read:

"Judge Julius J. Hoffman has struck a stronger blow at crime than all the study commissions combined in his courageous sentencing of the infamous Chicago 7 and their lawyers for contempt of court. Judge Hoffman's ordeal in court at the hands of these leftist radicals and revolutionaries. . . ."

On the television, the actor playing Kunstler was continuing with his address. In the Drake Hotel Julius Hoffman said:

"You know, one of the causes of crime is that there are lawyers standing in the wings who are willing to do what lawyers like Kunstler did. . . . You notice, I stopped this kind of behavior. No matter what happened in the higher courts, we stopped this kind of disruption. You haven't seen it since, and that was a result of this trial. I think the Movement has definitely died down. It hasn't disappeared, but you don't hear of it anymore. On the campuses they're behaving normally now."

Hoffman looked at the television Kunstler again.

"Fools," Hoffman said. "Freaks. To me . . . you know, I don't call a man a freak because of his principles. That's his First Amendment right. But to behave as Kunstler did in that courtroom . . ."

In a moment he was back to his earlier mood. The actor playing

Abbie Hoffman was shouting insults at the television Julius Hoffman, and the real Julius Hoffman laughed and said, "He plays this part all right."

Soon the program was over. A new show appeared on the screen. Hoffman stood up to leave.

"They can call me an old bastard if they want," he said. "Some people think I'm the greatest trial judge in the country. People I respect. Others think I'm a rotten judge; they have the same opinion that these fellows had of me. Franklin Delano Roosevelt, he was elected to the highest office in the land four times, and now you hardly ever hear his name. I like to be talked about. I think I'll get a pretty good obituary, don't you?"

He straightened his suit jacket. "All this time later, and there is never a social occasion I attend that this funny trial doesn't come up," he said. He walked toward the door, opened it, and headed slowly down the hotel corridor, going home.

Hef's

My first secret fantasy in this life started when I was ten years old and used to sneak into my father's shirt drawer. Under a pile of white shirts I would find his latest copy of *Playboy*. In the late '50s, in Columbus, Ohio, you couldn't buy the magazine over the counter at most stores, and no family would think of keeping a copy out on a living room table. I would take my father's copy into my room, lock the door, and stay for hours. The naked girls were fine, they were great, but that wasn't the fantasy. The fantasy was much bigger than that. What I really wanted to do was to grow up, get myself to Chicago, and live in Hef's pad.

God, what a life! *Playboy* would run all these stories about the parties Hugh Hefner gave for his celebrity friends in his mansion in Chicago. Every issue for years, it seemed, had full-color shots of that dark living room with the suit of armor in the corner and the LeRoy Neiman paintings on the walls; and the steam room with the girls sitting there with towels around their bottoms; and the firepole with cool-looking men wearing Italian suits and holding their drinks in one hand while sliding down to yet another level; and spiral staircases where people would kind of lounge around and make brilliant small talk.

Most of all I would think of something the caption writers called Woo Grotto, which was a small cranny of the swimming pool that seemed private, but that was actually visible through a trap door in a little room in the mansion, so that Hef and his fun-loving pals could peek at what was going on down there. Or so I recall.

Wherever I went during the years that followed, however much I was enjoying myself, I understood implicitly that they were having a better time at the Playboy Mansion. During high school, when my 16-year-old friends and I would get older guys to buy us six-packs of beer and we would drive off to drink it in someone's back seat, my thoughts were on the mansion. I knew that Hef was in the living room with some Bunny or Playmate, doing the frug while he clamped down on his pipe and butlers circulated with drinks. And in college, while the Revolution was forming in the fraternities and dorms, I was thinking of the mansion on a Saturday night, with girls stretched out and cuddled up in armchairs while Hefner had private showings of movies I would like to see.

It was also in college that I first read the Playboy Philosophy. This was Hefner's rambling, dull explanation of the changes in morality taking place in the country. The philosophy ran on for thousands upon thousands of words, but what it came down to was this: if something feels good and doesn't really hurt anybody, then go ahead and do it.

I had never read any philosophy before, but to a college freshman, the Playboy Philosophy didn't sound so bad.

At the time it was considered pretty daring stuff, and I dimly remember Hefner printing a load of letters in the magazine from clergymen and theologians and the like, saying Hefner had a point.

And then of course came the explosion of the late '60s in the way people lived in America.

By the beginning of the '70s no one talked about the Playboy Philosophy anymore. That is because the Playboy Philosophy had become the American way of life. If you don't believe that, consider the fact that, in the spring of 1968, it was front-page news all over the country when a male college student and a female college student in New York admitted they were sharing an apartment. In the years since then, we have come to the point where Linda Lovelace can tour America's talk-show circuit on the strength of how good she is with her mouth, and where the women on Michigan Avenue in the summertime often approach the state of undress that was pictured in Hefner's magazine in the early days.

Sometime between then and now, the philosophy of *Playboy* magazine stopped being a point of national controversy and began being the way we live. You don't buy *Playboy* under the counter anymore. It sells more copies than *Time,* or *Newsweek,* or the *Atlantic,* or *Harper's,* or *Rolling Stone*—seven million copies every issue.

During the years of *Playboy*'s growth, though, the revolution in sexuality and morality in the country ended any reason for a ten-year-old to sneak into his father's shirt drawer in order to fantasize about living at Hefner's. You don't have to go to a mansion on North State Parkway in Chicago to live a life where feeling good is reason enough to do what you want to do. You can do that in any high school in the country now.

So when I read somewhere that *Playboy* was about to celebrate its 20th anniversary of publishing, I decided to satisfy a curiosity that had started 15 years ago. I would live in Hef's pad. What better setting for thinking about the Playboy Philosophy, 20 years after Hefner had come up with it?

I made a phone call and inquired about living in the mansion for a week or so, and it didn't take long for an affirmative answer to be returned. Easy as that. They said to just let them know when I would like to check in.

I arrived on a Sunday afternoon. A butler let me in. We walked upstairs. The living room was empty. Hefner and most of his staff at the mansion keep night hours, and 3:00 P.M. was too early for them to be stirring. In preparation for a buffet that evening, a platoon of waiters and butlers was forming in a side room. One waiter was looking at the latest issue of *Oui,* Hefner's new magazine, and pointed to a picture of a man and woman in a difficult-to-achieve sexual position. "Would you look at that!" the waiter said. "Whooooo!" Another waiter turned to him and said, "That's for younger men."

I was shown to my room, which was just off the living room. Called the Blue Room, it was comparable in size to a room in a nice hotel, and done all in blue. After the butler had given me the key and had left, I started to look around. I walked into the bathroom, only to find three women in bathrobes. "We thought we heard someone come in there," one of them said.

The tallest of the women, a blonde, was a prospective Playmate of the Month, and it turned out that she was staying in the Red Room, right next door to the Blue Room, and that we shared the bathroom. The other two women had stayed with her the night before. We all allowed as to how it was nice to know each other.

I walked around the mansion. Early years of reading *Playboy* had left a lasting impression. In every room—the swimming pool room, the steambath room, the underwater bar, the winding staircases—I felt as if I had spent hours there before. Perhaps because the house had been photographed so much, it actually seemed small to me, almost like a movie set of the Playboy Mansion. I kept waiting to see a part of the house that I had never seen in the magazine, but there was no such area. I sat by the swimming pool for 45 minutes. No one appeared.

That evening, *Westworld* was shown on a full-width screen in the living room. Several of the 25 or so Bunnies who pay $50 a month to live in a dormitory section of the mansion came to see the movie.

When it was over, a Bunny named Joyce asked if I would like to see a bar where the Bunnies go on nights they don't work at the Chicago Playboy Club. I said sure, and we took a cab to a place called The Bistro. The Bistro is a gay bar that features a dance floor and music. "Hey," I said to Joyce, "there's guys dancing with guys in here." "You're very observant," she said.

I asked why Bunnies liked to go to The Bistro, and she said that it was a place where they could relax and have a drink and listen to music without worrying about men hitting on them and grabbing at them and trying to pick them up. "We get enough of that all the time," Joyce said. "In here, you usually don't have to deal with that."

We didn't stay long. As we were walking back to the mansion, we talked about the changes in American culture in the years since Hugh Hefner started his magazine. Joyce is in her early 20s; she had been a child when Hefner was designing the pages of Vol. 1, No. 1 of *Playboy*.

Now, in 1973, she was living in his house. She is a striking-looking girl with a perfect body that she shows off to her best advantage. I said that so much of what we had seen in the past hour could be traced back to Hefner—her, for instance, a young woman physically beautiful and thus drawn, naturally enough, to a job as a Playboy Bunny; and the homosexual bar where we had just been, a place that would only have been whispered about 20 years ago, but now, in the age of anything's OK, a well-known, legitimate, hip, popular spot in downtown Chicago; and Rush Street, where we were now walking, with its singles out for the one-night stands that had become an acceptable part of being unattached and alone in the modern city.

We talked about this for a while, and about how it all seems natural anymore, but that it grew in a climate that was mainly nurtured by one man, Hugh Hefner. And we agreed that it did seem a little strange to be going back to Hefner's home in light of all these thoughts—that it was odd, when you thought about it, to realize that the man who started the loosening of sexual attitudes in America was in fact still fairly young himself, and still living in Chicago.

When we got to the mansion we walked into the living room. The movie screen had been rolled up. The guests had gone home. And there was Hefner, wearing green pajamas. A song by the Carpenters was on the stereo. It was not yet midnight. Hefner was with his girl friend, Karen Christy, and two of his associates in Playboy Enterprises. While the wicked city did its stuff outside, Hefner was here with three friends. They were sitting around a Monopoly board, and Hefner was rolling the dice. He looked like a suburban father killing time, waiting for his teenage daughter to come home from a date.

The Monopoly routine was not unusual, I found out. Hefner divides his time between the mansion in Chicago and another one in California, and most of his late evenings are devoted to playing Monopoly or backgammon with friends.

One night I sat in on the game. "New Hampshire!" Hefner shouted as someone's token landed on his property and he was able to collect a new pile of play money. "That's $200," he said to the rival player, who was being slow to pay off.

Maybe because of Hefner's close identity with his magazine, to me he always has been kind of a lecherous uncle figure, and I found it impossible to dislike him. He has been criticized for his glorification of material possessions, and for his, quote, treatment of women as sexual objects, unquote. But he has never hidden his liking for a certain style of life, and if he is ostentatious and showy about it at times, well, there have been a lot of people just like me who grew up getting a kick out of Hefner's fantasy life. Besides, allowances should be made for special cases, and Hugh Hefner happens to be the Citizen goddamn Kane of our age, and his mansion happens to be San Simeon.

Among the things he has done, in an era of electronic communications, is to prove once again that the printed page is capable not only of being immensely profitable, but also of creating an image, an aura, that can be presented in no other way. Hefner knows that the printed page can act as a medium of suggestion, a seductive invitation to a way of life, that breeds most heartily in the imagination. Television cannot do that; it is too graphic, too stark. Say the word "Playboy," and a picture of a whole way of living forms in the mind of just about every person in America. The printed page has done that. Say the words "Tonight Show," or "Wide World of Sports," or whatever, and the image is much more limited. Hefner understands why.

"Come on," Hefner said to Karen Christy, "get your mind on the game. It's your turn to roll." While she rolled the dice, Hefner studied a list he had compiled of all properties on the Monopoly board—which ones are the most profitable, which ones are likely to be a waste of money. The board itself was somewhat different from most Monopoly boards. Instead of standard tokens, each person played with a ceramic figure sculptured to look just like the player; a stack of these personalized tokens was kept by Hefner for friends who frequently played. And instead of standard hotel pieces, Hefner's board featured models of his Playboy Plaza in Miami Beach.

The stereo clicked off. Hefner walked over and punched two buttons. He has a huge collection of records to choose from, but insisted on playing the same two albums over and over. One was a collection of old ballads by Harry Nilsson, the other a collection of old ballads by Peggy Lee. He never seemed to tire of these two records. "Maybe I'm right, and maybe I'm wrong . . . ," Hefner sang along with Nilsson. "You can love me like I am, or good-by . . . ," Hefner sang with Peggy Lee. As he sang and played Monopoly, he drank an endless supply of Pepsi Cola. As soon as he had finished half a bottle, he would ring for a butler to bring a fresh one.

He examined his supply of paper money. "You can't lose too much in Monopoly," he said. "That's one of the nice things about this game."

Hefner was deadly serious about winning the game. He prided himself on being the household champion. At one point Victor Lownes, who runs Playboy's operations in Europe for Hefner, looked as if he were going to dominate this particular contest. Lownes, in Chicago on business, was staying in a guest room at the mansion. As he acquired yet another property on the board, Hefner turned to him. "The lock on your room and the outside lock on the house will be changed," Hefner said.

It was getting late. Watching the game was kind of a kick for awhile, but before long it became immensely boring, especially when it became obvious that this was what Hefner would be doing for the rest of the night, probably until dawn. I thought of all the cars in all the small towns of America, with the famous rabbit decal stuck to the back windows, and the young men behind the wheels looking for action, for good times and fast women.

"Maybe I'm right, and maybe I'm wrong . . .", Hefner sang along with Nilsson.

There was a rustling over in the corner of the living room. An unlikely scenario was unfolding. Hefner's dog was unquestionably trying to form a sexual union with Hefner's cat.

"Now look at that," Hefner said. "This *is* a house of love."

The thing about living in the mansion, I discovered after the first few days, is that you soon learn that there is no good reason to leave, ever. Each guest room has a room-service menu so comprehensive, so enticing, that it is possible to do nothing but plan your days around the next meal. With the staff of butlers and waiters and maids actually there on a genuine 24-hour basis, it is as easy to have a steak and a milkshake at 4:00 A.M., and then to go for a swim and have a few drinks, as it is at 2:00 P.M., or 7:00 P.M.

The movies are the usual way of passing idle hours in the mansion. In the living room there is an oversized card file, and in the file is a list of the motion pictures that Hefner has on hand. There are hundreds, and they are all good—*The Godfather, Casablanca, The Graduate, Goldfinger*—and all you have to do is tell a butler what you'd like to see, and within five minutes the projector in the living room is set up, the screen is lowered, the lights are switched off, and you are watching.

For me, the hardest thing was to get used to dealing with butlers on those terms. While I was staying at the mansion, I usually got the urge to see a movie somewhere in the middle of the night, and my natural inclination is not to bother other people at so late an hour. But the all-night crew would *rather* be doing something—the alternative for them is to sit around until dawn looking at old copies of *Playboy*—so they welcomed the chance to show a movie, just to break the boredom.

The other time-killer is the game room, just off the swimming pool. Here Hefner has installed bank upon bank of pinball machines, electronic tennis machines, shooting-gallery machines, electric hockey machines. All of them are wired for free play.

On my first day in the mansion, I spent about five minutes in the game room before becoming restless. But by the end of the week, I could spend two or three hours at a shot there, drinking vodka and trying to better my record scores on each machine. Once you realize there is no reason to rush around, that the services of the mansion are there for you all day and all night, and that it is unnecessary to hurry or rush or glance at your watch in order to meet some schedule that doesn't exist, it becomes very easy to play the pins for a couple of hours, or to order up three movies in a row.

Life in the house isn't an orgy day-and-night; rather, it is just so pleasant and easy in a low-key way that it provides a hypnotic kind of soothing pleasure that becomes increasingly magnetic. Little things: your shirts are dirty, you go out to play the pins and take a swim, and when you come back to your room, the shirts have been laundered and hung in the closet. Each edition of the newspapers appears regularly in the living room and the breakfast area where the Bunnies take their meals, and where you can go for a snack if you are tired of room service. The telephone rings, and a voice tells you that a buffet will be served in the living room at 7:00 P.M., if you would like to attend.

It doesn't take long before you begin to make excuses to avoid going outside the mansion. It is all just so much *easier* there. Have to meet someone for an appointment? Call them and tell them to meet you at the mansion instead. They'll be there.

It is not surprising that, among the people who live in the mansion, stories have arisen concerning the evil things that can befall you if you go outside. The Bunnies talk about the time that Victor Lownes went to Old Town and was mugged; he learned his lesson, and now whenever he is in Chicago, he seldom leaves the house. Johnny Crawford, the star of *The Naked Ape,* a Playboy movie production, was staying in the house while I was there, and he told me that he had gone outside, and that a drunk on the street had harassed him and the Bunny he was with. He learned his lesson, too; he would think twice before going outside again.

One morning I went to the breakfast-room area and ordered eggs. Thirty minutes later they had not come, which seemed odd because I was the only person at the table, so I asked a waiter what the delay was.

"The boss woke up and was hungry," he said. "When he orders, everything else stops."

I checked this out later. It was true: when Hefner places a food order, everything else is scrapped. One man cracks the eggs, another puts bread in the toaster, another greases the frying pan. Every butler, cook, and waiter is put to work on the order, so that Hefner receives his food quickly.

"We try to anticipate," one of the waiters told me. "If we know that Hefner is up, and we get a feeling that he's getting hungry, we make up a whole batch of the things he likes to eat and hope he chooses one of them. That way, it's ready as soon as he calls."

Over the years hundreds, probably thousands, of famous people have stayed at the mansion at Hefner's invitation. But Hefner has chosen to commemorate only one of these visits. In the game room is a framed poster. It features a drawing of an airplane with a familiar lapping tongue logo on the tail. There are five signatures on the poster: Charlie Watts, Keith Richards, Mick Taylor, Bill Wyman. And, over to the left: "To Hugh Hefner, for his warm hospitality—from Mick Jagger and the Stones."

One night, after watching Hefner play backgammon with Victor Lownes for an hour or so, I went to my room to go to bed. It was about 1:00 A.M., and Hefner was drinking his Pepsi and singing along with Nilsson on the stereo. The next morning, at 10:30, I walked through the living room on my way to order breakfast. Hefner and Lownes were still at it, still sitting in the same chairs. Hefner was drinking his Pepsi and singing along with Nilsson on the stereo.

On another evening Hefner had a screening of the movie *Cops and Robbers.* Only a dozen or so people were in the living room for the picture. Hefner was in his pajamas, his girl friend Karen in a bathrobe.

When the movie ended, Hefner began discussing its merits. Because he tends to become the center of attention when he is out and about in the mansion, everyone in the room looked at him and listened. Then, in the middle of a sentence, he began to nuzzle Karen, and within a minute, was laughingly simulating what used to be referred to, in the days before Hugh Hefner, as an "unnatural act."

The other people in the living room fell silent. Despite all the connotations of unrestricted sex attached to the word "Playboy," it was still slightly awkward to be sitting in the living room watching Hefner play with his girl friend.

Finally Gene Siskel, the movie critic for the *Chicago Tribune* and a friend of Hefner's, broke the quiet. He motioned at Hefner and said, "Take pornography away from people, and see what happens? They go wild."

In the middle of my week at the mansion, Hefner announced that he would be flying to the California mansion. He said he would be leaving the next afternoon and asked if I would like to come along.

I had to say no, because I had commitments in Chicago that I could not postpone. And it was just as well; California would undoubtedly be fun, but this way I would have the Chicago mansion to myself, which wouldn't be all that bad either.

The evening after Hefner left, I took a slow walk around the house. In the game room I noticed that several scoreboards were attached to the wall, posting Hefner's all-time best efforts on the pinball machines. I stopped at each of the bars throughout the house and poured myself a fresh drink whenever I needed one. I walked down a corridor to Hefner's bowling alley, punched a button to turn on the automatic pinsetting machine, and bowled until I tired of it.

I had no idea what time it was, but by this point in the week it didn't matter. I took my drink to the underwater bar and leaned back on a padded deck next to a big window that looked into the pool. On the walls were large color transparencies of past Playmates.

I attempted to do some serious thinking about What It All Meant, as that was ostensibly why I had come to the mansion. Several times during the week I had begun to try such thinking, but every time I had put it off for a few hours. My original theory, before I had come to the mansion, was that the Playboy Philosophy, 20 years later, was an anachronism—that Hefner was living in a self-contained harem based on the principle of easy pleasure when, in reality, he didn't have to, when he could have the same thing just by going out on the street, just like anyone else.

But that theory didn't seem quite right. The whole idea of the Playboy Mansion as a harem isn't even right. Yes, Hefner has the 25

Bunnies living in the house, and they are around all the time. But that idea, to the millions of American men who know about it through the magazine, is far more exciting in the imagination than it is in reality.

It's not that "the mansion is more sexless than a convent," as one writer put it. That isn't true, either. Rather a house with 25 attractive young girls in it is no more a monolithic entity than the 25 Bunnies; they are all different, and they are all there for different reasons, and most of them have been living there for so long that they don't even consider it unusual that their home is the Playboy Mansion. A few are so shy that they hesitate to ring the waiter to bring lunch, and instead wait for someone else to come in and beckon the waiter. Others more perfectly fit the image of the Bunny as a free-and-easy woman. (One Bunny was at breakfast one morning looking through an advance copy of a new issue of *Playboy*. She stopped at a survey of sexual activities among Americans, running her finger down the list of practices as if she were looking for something in particular. Finally she found it. "All RIGHT!" she said. "Anal intercourse.")

So it's nice that the girls are around, and maybe, in an earlier year of *Playboy*'s history, it was even a great turn-on. But if that were the only reason for the mansion's existence, then my original theory would be right. Life in the mansion would indeed be an anachronism, if it depended on the availability of 25 women for its lure. If that were the only criterion, then Hefner would not have a monopoly on his particular way of life.

That is not the case, of course. The appeal of the Playboy Mansion comes from the one thing that Hefner has been able to give himself that is so rare in America these days—a way to lock out the troubles. In that mansion Hugh Hefner has devised a little world that is carefree and completely self-contained. There are people paid to make sure that the master of the house never wants for anything. In the United States in the '70s, it is often true that nothing works anymore. In the Playboy Mansion, everything works, always. There are electricians and technicians in the house around the clock to fix up anything that should go wrong—to replace the bulb in the movie projector, to repair the knob on the electronic tennis game, to secure the beaded curtains by the swimming pool. There are plain-clothes guards posted around the house to make sure that no one gets in who is not wanted. There are men assigned to keeping Hefner's movies and records up to date. There are butlers whose duty is to make sure the master's supply of Pepsi never dwindles below the danger point. Everything has been thought of.

For years, Hefner has been criticized for living this way. The Playboy way of life, epitomized by Hefner's personal way of life, has been called shallow and meaningless and plastic. But almost all the people who scorn Hefner, who mock his values and the way he chooses to live, are people whom Hefner has never met, and will never know. Hefner has done the one thing that sounds so simple: he has thought about the way he would like to live and then has gone ahead and lived that way.

My last night in the Playboy Mansion, I went into the living room and asked one of the butlers to show me a movie print of the first "Frank Sinatra: A Man and His Music" television special. Another butler brought me some drinks while I was watching Sinatra sing, and then I asked to see *Midnight Cowboy,* and while that was showing I had dinner.

When the movies were over, I looked around the room. Here it was, Hefner's house. There were the LeRoy Neiman paintings, and there was the suit of armor, and over there was the spiral staircase leading down to the swimming pool. Some of the Bunnies were just beginning to come in from work, and they were sitting around the living room with nothing to do on a Saturday night. I gave some thought to those days of sneaking *Playboy* out of my father's shirt drawer, and then a butler came up and asked me if I would like another drink. I laughed out loud; this was just crazy, and too funny. Hefner was out of town, and I had the run of the mansion. Too much.

In the morning I got out of bed early, packed my bag, gave the key to my room back to a butler, and left. I didn't even stay for breakfast. As I walked out the front gate, a middle-aged man and woman were stopped on the sidewalk, looking at the house. The man asked me if this wasn't Hugh Hefner's Playboy Mansion, and I said it sure was. He rolled his eyes. I winked at him. I thought about hailing a cab, but I walked home instead.

Man from the Moon

He could not have known it would turn out this way. He was the ninth man off the plane. The American Airlines Astrojet had just arrived from Washington, and he hesitated for a second as he walked into the O'Hare terminal. He seemed to be waiting for someone to come to him, to pick him out of the crowd. But no one came. He stood still for a moment. Even the three people who had come to Gate H-2 to greet him did not know his face.

In the history of the human race, there have been 12 men who have walked upon the surface of the moon, and he is one of them. The crowd in the airport shoved past him, and he turned to a clerk from the airline. "I'm Mr. Schmitt," he said. The people who had come for him overheard him, and approached. Is that all the baggage you have? they asked. "That's all," said Jack Schmitt, an astronaut for the United States of America. He heaved his long suit bag over his right shoulder. "I have to get a new one, this one is falling apart," he said, and they headed down the corridor.

He walked swiftly. Not a head turned. He was wearing a dark, pin-striped suit and a bright white shirt, and no one stopped. "It's not like we're actors," Jack Schmitt said. "You have to understand that; it's not like we're actors." There was a limousine waiting, and he climbed into the back seat.

Somewhere it ended, the country's fascination with the men who went into space. It is hard to put a finger on exactly when it happened, but it happened. Somewhere between the Shepard-Glenn days of glory, when every American knew the faces and the names, and the Cernan-Evans-Schmitt mission, when no one paid much attention, it went away. He was here to address the Harvard Club of Chicago, and the limousine was speeding along the Kennedy Expressway.

"But you are wrong about that," Schmitt said. "The public interest hasn't diminished. The interest on the part of the press has diminished. The public's still just as interested. When I speak at elementary schools, the children ask me when we're going to Mars. The public still cares."

And yet the Apollo program is over; the days of throwing men into space on their way to the moon is dead, and there is no public mourning. It was an exciting time, a thrilling time, for a while. In the United States, however, there is a limitless capacity to become bored. And whether the astronauts can admit it to themselves or not, by the end of the last mission, the country was bored even with this, the greatest adventure in the history of mankind.

"I won't be able to go up again," Schmitt said. "That's a little disappointing. That's a little frustrating. To think that no one will go again, to evolve to the point that we have evolved to and then not do it any further. . . . Am I resigned to not going up again? I have to be resigned to it, don't I? It's either be resigned to it or go find a wall to beat your head against."

He is 37 years old and a bachelor, and everywhere he goes, he is asked about what it was like, what it was like to step on the moon. How can he answer it? He trained and trained and trained, and finally he became one of 12, 12 among all the people who have ever lived, and how is he supposed to answer the question?

"I suppose it's hard for you to understand the feeling we had when we landed," Schmitt said. "It's outside your normal experience. But don't you see, it was not outside our normal experience. It's what we had trained for. It was not that big a surprise. It was like a mountain climber reaching the top of a mountain. We knew what to expect. Gene Cernan and I felt something, we clapped each other on the shoulder after we touched down on the moon, sure. But we were prepared for it; we knew what to expect."

The limousine was in the Loop. Schmitt went into the offices of Bache & Company, the brokerage firm. Bache was sponsoring the speech before the Harvard Club, and Christopher Janus, an investment banker with the company, had made the arrangements for Schmitt's visit. Schmitt rode up to Janus' office in a crowded elevator, again unrecognized. He got off and walked down a carpeted hallway.

"Sure I look up at the moon sometimes," he said. "I don't know what the feeling is. I guess I think to myself, 'By George, I was up there.' Now let's find another one; let's find something else to do."

Janus led Schmitt down to the board room, where 50 or so people were watching the stock quotations flash by. Janus told some secretaries that the quiet man in the corner was an astronaut, that he had walked on the moon, and that he would say hello and sign his name for them if they wanted. Several of the secretaries approached Schmitt, and one of them asked him where he lived. He said he had a place in Houston, but that he was in Washington a lot. He had grown up in New Mexico, he said, and at the moment, because of the way his life has gone, he does not know where to call home.

"It's been a job primarily concerned with travel," he said.

It was time to go to the speech. The limousine took Schmitt to the University Club, where he would give his talk, and then stay for the night. The desk clerk handed him a telephone message. He read it.

"No way," Schmitt said. "I knew this was going to happen. No way."

The message was from a scientific group that would present Schmitt with an award in the evening. The awards dinner was a white-tie affair, and the message said that Schmitt should save some time in the afternoon to be fitted for his tuxedo.

"Now why is this white tie?" Schmitt said to the air. "This thing is taking hours. Literally hours! Everyone has black tie, and that's not so hard. But white tie? They want to come over here in two hours and measure me. White tie!"

He went into his bedroom. The man who went to the moon sat down on one of the twin beds.

"Mr. Janus," he said, "I was wondering . . . that secretary of yours? The tall blonde girl? I was wondering if she could get the rest of the afternoon off? To show me around Chicago?"

Janus said that would be all right.

"I haven't seen Chicago in a couple of years," Schmitt said.

Downstairs, outside the University Club, the limousine driver spotted someone who had ridden downtown from O'Hare with Schmitt. "You know that fellow we picked up at the airport?" the driver said. "We have to keep a record of who it is we pick up. I have to write it down on my trip ticket. Could you tell me, what was his name?"

Rock Star

ANDERSON, S.C.—There is no plausible reason for Rod Stewart, the world's current king of rock and roll, to be in this backwoods part of the Carolinas. But here he is, flat on his stomach in the grass, playing with two old black hound dogs.

"Bibbiboo, bibbiboo, bibbiboo," Stewart says to the dogs. The dogs roll their eyes and begin to look away. "Bibbiboo, bibbiboo, bibbiboo," Stewart says.

The dogs are losing interest. Stewart is at a country airfield. The other members of the Faces, the English band he sings with, are waiting in a nearby Lear Jet. They have just played a date at Clemson University and this is the closest landing strip that will handle a jet. There are no commercial flights at the field at the moment, just little planes. It is hot. The wind is bringing up the dust.

Stewart is a nervous flyer, and the first Lear Jet is already crowded. He decides to fly in a second Lear, the one that will carry the baggage for the Faces.

"Got your own plane now, do you, Rod?" calls bass guitarist Ronnie Lane from the first jet.

"Going to put your name on the side of the plane, Stewart?" yells pianist Ian McLagan.

"Bibbiboo, bibbiboo, bibbiboo," Stewart says to the retreating dogs.

This is a problem that Stewart and the rest of the Faces are learning to live with: it is Stewart, the lead singer, who is garnering huge personal publicity. He was chosen top male vocalist in *Playboy*'s reader poll this year, and *Rolling Stone* named him rock-and-roll star of the year. With the exception of Mick Jagger, he is probably the most instantly recognizable rock singer performing today. And the thing is growing.

Two hours earlier, the Faces had been eating another lunch in another restaurant of another Holiday Inn. Ron Wood, a guitarist, was fooling with a portable videotape unit he carries with him on tour.

Stewart took a felt-tipped pen from his pocket. He wrote in large letters, across the bottom of a white plate that had just held a mound of french fries: "HOTEL DE POOF."

Wood zoomed the camera in on the plate. Then he shifted to Stewart's face. "Hello," Stewart smiled. "When I find myself traveling, I always make it a point to stay at the Hotel de Poof. The people are very friendly here, and they send you away smiling."

It gets like that on the road, as day after day of airplane flights and anonymous hotel rooms and no sleep catch up. The first Lear Jet is ready to take off for Louisville. Drummer Kenny Jones is trying to sleep.

Stewart meanwhile is looking at one of the wings of the plane he will fly in. "Pilot," Stewart calls over. "Can you come look at this? I don't think the gas cap is on right. It's loose."

The pilot comes over and looks. "It's fine," he says. "Don't worry."

"Well, look at it," Stewart says. "It's loose."

The Faces' booking agent hoists himself up and sits on the wing. "Get off," Stewart says. "Don't sit there."

The agent continues to sit. "The wings are strong, Rod," he says.

"I'm not kidding," Stewart says. "I'm asking you. Get off. It causes metal fatigue."

It is time for the first jet to leave. The engines start with a howl, and the plane taxis to the end of the runway, next to an open field.

Stewart is alone on the tar-and-cement boarding area. He begins to walk. He goes out to a spot just a few yards from where the first jet will speed by on its takeoff.

He is a strange figure here in a quiet part of the South. He wears a multicolored plaid sport coat and a pair of white pants. Tonight he will be mesmerizing thousands and thousands of jumping kids who live for his music. He watches the plane start down the country runway. As it speeds past him, ready to climb, Stewart waves to the Faces. But the plane is moving too fast, and they cannot see. He is still waving as it disappears into the distance.

DiMaggio

. . . Sitting on a sofa
on a Sunday afternoon,
going to the candidates' debate,
laugh about it, shout about it
when you've got to choose,
Every way you look at it you lose,
Where have you gone, Joe DiMaggio?
A nation turns its lonely eyes to you. . . .

—From "Mrs. Robinson,"
a song by Simon and Garfunkel

"I had to get up at 4:30 this morning" Joe DiMaggio said. "Even then I almost didn't make it to the airport on time. It's impossible to get out of Houston today. Everyone is trying to get away from the Super Bowl. I am so tired."

DiMaggio did not look tired. As a matter of fact, he looked great. Now in his 60th year, DiMaggio was ruddy of face and trim of build, and he carried himself with the almost palpable feel of absolute confidence that most men will only strive for and never know. The DiMaggio grace was winning over even the arguably incongruous scene in which he found himself Monday, in the basement of McCormick Place, on the shore of Lake Michigan.

"Joe, come with me for a second," said Vincent G. Marotta. Marotta is the president of a company known as Mr. Coffee. He led DiMaggio to another man. "Joe," said Vincent Marotta, "this is Tom Dollnig, our national sales manager."

Thomas Dollnig reached out for DiMaggio's hand. "It is a real pleasure to meet you, sir," Dollnig said to DiMaggio. "Welcome aboard. Welcome to Mr. Coffee."

DiMaggio nodded hello. This was the first day of the National Housewares Exposition, and it was, in a sense, the first day on a new job for DiMaggio. The former Yankee Clipper was beginning his work as the national symbol for the Mr. Coffee quick-brewing home coffee maker.

"We went through quite a few names when we were looking for a spokesman," said Vincent Marotta. "But when it came down to the decision-making, Joe DiMaggio was the one. He has a wonderful credibility image. He has the image of an honest man. People believe in him. He doesn't do this sort of thing very often, you know."

So within the next few months, DiMaggio will be appearing in a number of television advertisements praising the speed and quality of the Mr. Coffee home brewer. The advertisements, produced under the supervision of the Tatham, Laird, and Kudner advertising agency, will appear on such programs as "The Match Game," "Let's Make A Deal," "Hollywood Squares," and "The Price Is Right." On Monday, it was DiMaggio's job to meet the manufacturer's representatives who had come to the housewares show.

"There are so many teams in the Major Leagues now," DiMaggio said to a buyer who had just asked him about the strength of a particular club. "I just don't know anymore. I can't even keep track anymore. The only time I could really remember was when there were six, eight teams in a league. Just the National League and the American League. Not those divisions they have now, with 24 teams."

It went on that way for several hours. DiMaggio, wearing a World Series ring, stood in the vicinity of a functioning Mr. Coffee machine and signed autographs and let the buyers look at him. "I don't know if you remember me," one man said. "I'm related to Mel Allen? Who used to do the Yankee broadcasts?"

DiMaggio said, "Yes. I see Mel every now and then."

"If you see him," said the man, "tell him that you ran into Ted Meisal. Remember to tell him that."

But Vincent Marotta was already leading DiMaggio to another buyer. "Andy, come here, you old reprobate," Marotta laughed. "I've got a young fellow here I want you to meet. Say hello to Joe DiMaggio. He can still hit it out there where it says '435,' by the way. And you should see him hit a golf ball."

Late in the afternoon, someone asked him if he had ever heard the Simon and Garfunkel song which held him up, to a new generation, as a symbol of an American era of heroism and hope and exuberant triumph that may be gone forever.

"Yeah, I have heard it," DiMaggio said. "You mean that Mister Robinson song? I was really flattered. I was surprised that those young fellows would think of an old guy like me. It made me feel good. When I was coaching at Oakland, some of the young ballplayers would play that song all the time in the locker room, and that's when I heard it. I don't have a copy. I think my sister might. But it really made me feel good."

John Adominas, 52, a uniformed guard for the Kane Security Service, touched DiMaggio's arm.

"I saw you in Comiskey Park," Adominas said. "Back in 1941. When you had the hit streak going. The Sox almost broke the streak that day. Luke Appling had his glove on the ball, but it got away from him, and you kept the streak going."

DiMaggio smiled. "I got lucky a couple of those times," he said.

"Yeah, it was 1941," Adominas said. "That was a long time ago."

"I know it," said Joe DiMaggio. "Don't I know it."

Travels with Howard

"Young lady," shouts Howard Cosell, "do you know what it is . . . to be suddenly beset . . . by an open passion . . . a gnawing hunger . . . a desperate yearning . . . for a woman?" Cosell is looking up from his seat at a dinner table in the Marriott Inn of Cleveland, Ohio. The young lady has just approached him for an autograph, and Cosell is addressing her in tones only slightly less amplified and frenzied than those usually reserved for a 90-yard-pass play in the last moments of the fourth quarter of an especially tight Monday night football game. "Do you realize what it does to a man, young lady? If my wife were not here . . . at this very table . . ."

Cosell's staccato voice is ricocheting off every wall in the dining room, and it is achieving its intended effect; namely, there is not a person in the room who is not staring at the Cosell table. Some patrons from the next-door barroom, lured by the unmistakable sound of Cosell, are rushing in to get a look at him. The other diners at Cosell's table are attempting to deal with Howard's performance in as unobtrusive a way as possible. Emmy Cosell, Howard's wife, is smiling silently at her husband's bloodless romancing; it is one of his standard jokes, and she has seen it before. Frank Gifford, the former New York Giants' halfback and currently one of Howard's two announcing partners on ABC Monday night professional football broadcasts, is rolling his eyes toward the ceiling. And Joe Robbie, the millionaire owner of the Miami Dolphins, is leaning over to a reporter to answer a question.

"Hell, yes, I'll help his fund raising," Robbie says. "Who do you think suggested Howard run for the Senate in the first place? Me, that's who. I'll not only help his fund raising, I'll start it."

So it is true. Howard Cosell, one of America's most familiar television faces, due to his acerbic, high-energy performance on broadcasts of athletic events, is not merely thinking quite seriously about making a run for the United States Senate in 1976; he has, in fact, already begun to make firm, detailed campaign plans. In a quiet moment he will discuss them in specific terms. The race would be against James Buckley, in New York, with Cosell theoretically running as the Democratic party's candidate. Election day is three years from this week, but Cosell is already measuring support, consulting with politicans, calculating the odds.

Tonight is not a time for such heavy talk, however. Tonight it is a Sunday in Cleveland, the night before the telecast of the Browns versus the Dolphins, and Cosell is doing what he loves best: allowing himself to be adulated in public. He glances around the room, greeting the gapers with a smile here, a nod there, a raise of his cigar over there. The fame he has built through television is what he is counting on to create his political constituency, and he visibly loves the turning of eyes that come his way each time his famous voice erupts. Frank Gifford tries to tell a story.

"Any of you ever hear of a restaurant in New York called The Grenadier?" says Gifford.

"No, but there is a place called The Grenadier in London," says

Cosell. "I remember once, Chris Schenkel, you know how thin he is, he has a very bad stomach, we were in London. His stomach was upset again. I needed to get him some American food. So we headed out for The Grenadier . . ."

A waitress approaches the Cosell table. "That gentleman over there in the glasses," she says, "he's from the Stop and Shop here in town, and he'd like to buy your table a drink."

"Tell him no thanks," says Gifford.

"Fine," says Cosell, "bring us another round."

"Howard," says Gifford, "if we let him buy us a drink, he'll want to come over here and talk."

"And if we tell him no," says Cosell, "all the local papers tomorrow will have headlines that say, 'Cosell Shuns Cleveland.' Now where was I in that story about The Grenadier?"

"Howard," says Gifford, "it was *me* that was trying to tell a story."

A band in the dining room begins to play. "Oh, listen, Howard," says Emmy Cosell. "Do you remember this song? It was 1939. I was at my peak."

"You, dear," shouts Cosell, "were at your peak . . . several years later. The date . . . June 23, 1944. You were nervous. You were excited. You broke out in pimples. The reason: you were marrying me. The stage was set. You were wearing a power-blue dress—"

Gifford interrupts: "You were wearing number 32 . . . you were a free agent from New Orleans . . ."

The whole room is gazing at the Cosell table. Howard waves. He is beaming. These are his people. The campaign has started. The making of Senator Howard Cosell has begun.

The television set in Cosell's hotel suite is turned on. A professional football game is on the screen, but the sound is turned down. Cosell is talking about running for the Senate.

"I do not have that many years left in my life," he says. "And I do not want to spend the rest of my life in the dugout. For once in my life I would like to come to terms with things that really matter. I simply am not interested in how good a particular baseball player is in a hit-and-run situation anymore.

"I'm 53 years old now, and I'd like to feel that I had done something important before I die. Yes, I have a certain amount of influence right now, because of the power of television, the large numbers of people that I reach. But you have to ask yourself: what is the *nature* of that influence? What does it mean to convince people that Larry Brown has lost a step? Such influence means virtually nothing. There is nothing more transitory in life, nothing more unimportant, than a sports event. But if I could influence X number of senators that my position on an issue is the valid position . . . now *that* would be influence."

Cosell is a self-defined liberal, an admirer of the late Senator Robert Kennedy. Cosell's daughter, Hilary, in a letter to her father, once wrote, "And while I in all honesty cannot, despite the greatness you possess, attribute to you all the greatness of the Senator [Kennedy], I can compare you. There is much that is comparable. And coming from me, you know that is the highest praise I can give." Cosell carries the letter with him.

"I think I can prove to my own daughter that I'm capable of living up to that kind of faith," Cosell says. "Look, who's to say that I could ever become a Robert Kennedy? Who's to say that I could ever have the mind that he did? I like to think that I do. I'm not going to lie. I think that I'm a pretty smart guy. And I think I'll win.

"I have already received extremely positive reaction from several Democratic party leaders in New York. I think that in the aftermath of Watergate, my kind of truthfulness, my kind of candor, will be a key factor in my favor. I doubt that, right at this moment, the Senate is ready for Howard Cosell. But I think it will be by 1976. Three more years of the disaster of the Nixon administration, if you can call it an administration. I just think that man is a national and international disaster. Spiro Agnew was a philosophical Neanderthal. And Gerald Ford will hardly add to the luster. Did you see that, when those senators stood up and cheered when Nixon named Ford? That was the sickest thing I have ever seen.

"Did I ever used to think of myself as a senator? No. But then, I never used to think of myself as a best-selling author, and now I am one; my autobiography is on the *New York Times* best-seller list. I am basically a deeply sensitive guy. I am far more than a sports announcer. I am probably the most recognizable face on television.

And I have confidence. When Dean Martin goes on television and tells his audience that I am a super talent . . . when Frank Sinatra toasts me and says, 'Here's to the other king' . . . well, that has to give a man confidence."

Cosell can talk for hours about his wide-ranging interests, his global view, his disenchantment with sports, and sometimes, in that Cosell voice, his statement of his positions takes on the sound of a eulogy to Jackie Robinson: "I want a country . . . without racial anguish. I want a country . . . without slums. I want a country . . . not crippled by drug abuse. I want a country . . . that is constantly concerned with its aged and its underprivileged. I want a country . . . that is committed to peace . . . this is what I want for my country."

And yet, for all of his protestations about despising the jock mentality, Cosell sits in his hotel room and interrupts a thought about the Nixon administration to scream at the NFL game on the TV set: "Jeez, he's a hell of a runner!" He stops talking about his election chances to bang his hand on the table and shout, "Look at that! Hold on a minute, I just want to watch this kick. The Giants are going to win this game!"

While talking about the seniority system in the Senate, he breaks off in mid-sentence to run to the telephone, call the room of Monday night football producer Don Ohlmeyer, and caw: "Ohlmeyer? Are you watching? You still think Chuck Knox is no coach, huh? You still think John Hadl is no quarterback, huh?" Watching Cosell, it makes one wonder, despite all his fine phrases, whether he would ever be truly comfortable completely removed from the sports context.

This was the same feeling that came on the night that Spiro Agnew made his farewell address on television. It was a Monday night, just before an ABC football broadcast, and the network was giving a cocktail party in a private club. Cosell, Gifford, and Don Meredith, the third member of the ABC announcing team, were all there. So were the owners and officials of both football clubs, men wearing blazers with the crests of their teams, and so were 100 or more fawning admirers of the Cosell-Gifford-Meredith squad. The three were being surrounded. "Didn't you used to play with Kyle Rote?" someone asked Gifford. Gifford finally managed to break away, and he joined an acquaintance who was standing in a corner of the room. "What a freak show, huh?" Gifford said. "Look at these people. This is a trip, man."

When Agnew came on the screen of a television in the room, Gifford and Meredith, who have been derided as the two jocks of the announcing team, hurried over to sit on the floor and watch.

With the exception of one or two other guests, they were alone. Everyone else in the room fled from the television set as if it were about to explode. "I knew this would clear the room out," Gifford said.

So Gifford and Meredith sat by themselves, watching political history. Across the room was Howard Cosell, sitting at the bar with NFL Commissioner Pete Rozelle, holding court. On television the former vice-president of the United States was saying that he had left office for the good of the country. In the private club Howard Cosell was being asked by a fan whether he would be harsh on the home team during the broadcast.

"No way!" said Cosell. "I will tell it . . . like it is!"

A few days spent with Cosell is convincing evidence that he would be a strong campaigner. He is tireless. He is up at dawn to do his network radio program, and he runs until after midnight. He talks to anyone who stops him. He will grant anyone an interview. A reporter from the local paper. A young film crew doing a documentary on Jackie Robinson for use in fourth-, fifth-, and sixth-grade classrooms around Ohio. A reporter from the University of Akron student radio station. A young woman from the commuter newspaper of a Cleveland junior college, who has left a note at the hotel for Cosell requesting an interview. Cosell has his wife call her and tell her to come on up. After she has completed her questions and left, Cosell says, "If you're going to run for the Senate, there is no better way to recruit young campaign workers."

Cosell bitches from time to time that he has given up all his privacy, but he seems unwilling to accept the few private moments that are available to him. His days are dotted with episodes where he could have been left alone, but instead he invited an onslaught of attention:

Cosell is being driven through downtown Cleveland. He is sitting by the window in the front seat of the car, which is caught in a traffic jam. No one on the street has noticed that Cosell is there. He sees Nathan Wallack, a vice-president of the Cleveland Browns, in front of the Theatrical Restaurant. Cosell rolls down his window and screams, "Where is Nate Wallack? I must see Nate Wallack!" Immediately, he is the center of attention as pedestrians recognize the voice.

Cosell is walking into Cleveland Stadium for the broadcast of the game. If he wishes, he can hurriedly be escorted to a private area where he will not be swarmed. But he walks through the crowd and shouts: "Monday night football is a carnival, it's a ticker-tape parade . . . there *is* no other game!" And he is surrounded.

Cosell is leaving the lobby of The Hollenden House Hotel. Amazingly, he has managed to slip through it without being seen. He fixes that easily enough. He spots Leroy Kelly of the Cleveland Browns standing across the room. "Number 44!" Cosell calls. "I must talk to Mr. Kelly, number 44! Leroy, what is your current position on the advisability of Jewish ownership?" It is autograph time.

He has taken the phrase "I tell it like it is," which was a moldering cliche five years ago, and has somehow made it his personal property. He uses it three or four times every hour, especially when encountering young fans: "Let's lay it on the table, son! Let's tell it like it is!" He often ascribes his success to the fact that "I am the only one around who tells it like it is," and the thought never comes up that there may be other men in the country who attempt to tell the truth, but who do not have the benefit of an audience of 40 million people every Monday night.

He is awesomely sensitive to criticism, and he can quote lines from stories that slighted him years ago. He is convinced that much of the press is consciously out to harass him, and every time he is stopped on the street for an autograph, he turns to a companion and says, "See, now is that hatred, do these people hate me?" When he is asked why he thinks his fellow journalists are so set against him, he says, "Envy . . . bitterness . . . all of the human frailties."

He is an absolute whiz at what he does; he is a master of the broadcaster's art, and of the art of creating a public personality for himself, and in case anyone is too dense to notice this, Cosell points it out. Cosell, reflecting on the success of Monday night football: "What I have done, surrounded by two jocks! What I have done! A miracle! I *am* the Monday night football package." Cosell, after taping the halftime highlights of other NFL games: "Arrogant, vain, obnoxious, verbose, a show-off. That is what they call me. But you just saw me do my work. And I am telling it like it is: there is no other man in the country who could do what you just saw me do."

Now he is ready to move on. "I have had a limited periphery," he says. "I know of no other world so utterly limited, so utterly devoid of intellectual thought, than the world of sports."

A race for the Senate would mean that Cosell would have to go off the air, at least temporarily. He says that—win or lose—he would never go back on.

Cosell is at the bar of the Wigwam Club, a private dining room inside the walls of Cleveland Stadium. The Monday-night broadcast is over, and Gifford has left the stadium immediately, to return to New York; Meredith, too, has departed for the hotel. They have been stars since they were teenagers, and they do not need any postgame plaudits. For Howard Cosell, though, the big fame did not come until he was almost into his 50th year. He drinks a vodka on the rocks and happily accepts the congratulations and good wishes of the people in the Wigwam Club, most of whom have not seen the broadcast, but have watched the game live in the cold of the Cleveland night.

The bartender in the Wigwam Club keeps sneaking glances at Cosell. The man is trying to work up the nerve to speak. He has seen Cosell on television so often, and now he wants to get just one sentence in, one interchange of words, just to cement the fact that their two lives have, indeed, crossed. Finally he does it.

"Mr. Cosell," the bartender says, "I have to admit that when you started doing the football games, I thought you were a jerk. But I've changed my mind. Now I think you're out of sight."

Cosell, wearing his bright yellow ABC sports blazer, turns to a companion at the next barstool. "Now what does that tell you about hate and love?" Cosell says. "Think about that, and then relate it to the Senate campaign."

Cosell takes another sip from his drink. He looks at his companion again. "I can sum it up to you in one phrase," Cosell says.

He pauses. He smiles. He sets his drink down on the surface of the bar. "Howard Cosell," says Howard Cosell, "knows where it's at."

Prince of the Church

"No, I wouldn't say that I had a best friend," said John Cardinal Cody, archbishop of Chicago, spiritual leader of the 2.5 million Catholics in the largest archdiocese in the United States, prince of the church.

"I wouldn't say that I had any truly close friends," Cardinal Cody said. "Everybody is my friend. No close friends, though. I don't have the time. No best friends."

But, the cardinal was asked, even leaders of state such as the president have one or two people they can turn to when the press of official business gets too tight, when they want to go out and have a private meal; a Bebe Rebozo to call when they feel the urge to pick up the telephone in the middle of the night and just hear the voice of another human being.

"I only go out to eat privately perhaps once in a month," Cardinal Cody said. "And then it's not with any one person. It's always with someone different. As I told you, I simply don't have the time to have what you'd call a 'best friend' or a 'close friend' or however you choose to say it."

But doesn't it sometimes get lonely? What about relatives? Do you see them much of the time?

"My relatives are all in St. Louis," said John Cardinal Cody. "But in my position as a religious leader, there is no need for any best friends. Everyone is my friend."

The idea had been to call on Cardinal Cody and talk about whatever came to mind. Not a discussion of the detailed internal problems facing the church; not a theoretical discussion of the changing roles of religion in relation to the world. Just a talk with the man, based on the fact that although he is one of the most famous people in the city, among both Catholics and non-Catholics, not much is known about what he is like. He has been a bishop since 1947, a cardinal since 1967, and that creates a certain distance between a man and those who would try to know him. The distance is there whether the man would choose to have it there or not; when a man is referred to as "your eminence," the atmosphere is not conducive to a lot of small talk and rambing discussion.

So the idea was to do just that: to sit down with him and see what happened. It turned out that the cardinal almost never meets privately with reporters; he has a press secretary, a young priest, the Reverend James Roache, to serve as a screen between himself and the people who would impose on his time with questions.

Before one even can think about talking to Cardinal Cody, one goes into a quiet, dark study with Father Roache and explains just what one will bring up if, by chance, the cardinal should become available. When one shrugs and says he simply does not know what he and the cardinal would talk about, no one ever knows about such things until the situation actually comes up, Father Roache offers old video tapes: a tape of a conversation between Cardinal Cody and Fahey Flynn; a tape of a conversation between Cardinal Cody and Lee Phillip.

When one says he would prefer not to watch the tapes, but would rather just go in and meet the cardinal cold, without feeling he is encountering Dick Cavett or Flip Wilson, or anyone else he has been conditioned to react to on the screen, Father Roache seems disappointed. He says the cardinal is always very busy, and often these things just cannot be arranged.

A number of months go by. The archdiocesan office does not like to move fast. And then one day there is a telephone message, saying that Cardinal Cody will be available at a certain time on a certain morning. There is no explanation why, and none asked for. It just seems like a good idea to show up and see what it turns out to be.

The cardinal was 20 minutes late. His office in the American Dental Association building on East Chicago Avenue looked like the office of a chief copywriter at an old-line advertising agency except, of course, that he was wearing his robes and there were crucifixes around the room. His attitude was quick and business-like, though; the John Hancock Center was framed in the window to his side, and the feel of the room was more commercial than religious.

"I've been working on some things about the teachers in our schools," Cardinal Cody said. "We pay their pension; we give them free hospitalization; we pay Social Security. I have it all on paper somewhere. Let me see if I can't get you a copy."

He hit a button on his desk; a secretary was instantly in the doorway and immediately dispatched for the requested records. "We pay $3 million a year to run the inner-city schools. That should be broken down on that statement when she brings it."

His photographs often make him look very fat, but it is not so pronounced up close. More like a once-a-month golfer in the country club locker room who just doesn't have the time to get out on the course more. He is 65 years old, born on Christmas Eve, 1907, in St. Louis.

He is an easy talker, accustomed to being listened to, accustomed to his words being the center of attention in any group in which he should find himself. He has made it very big in his chosen field; to be a cardinal is to gain automatic respect and deference, and his manner, although pleasant and gentle, is laced with reminders that he is always the one who sets the terms, who determines the rules for his interpersonal dealings.

"Oh, occasionally I'll watch the TV when I go home," Cardinal Cody said. "No particular show. I'll just turn it on and see what's playing. But usually I'm working. I read books when I can, but almost all the time I'm working. Take yesterday. I left my house— now I don't want to sensationalize things—but I get along with four, perhaps five hours of sleep a night. So I work late, and I'm up early.

"So yesterday I had a typist come in at 7:00 A.M. I wanted 4,000 teachers each to get a personal letter from me. Then I saw a priest at eight o'clock. I left the house at 8:45, and I was due at the seminary to ordain 38 priests. You may have seen that in the paper this morning.

Well, that started at 10:00, and I didn't finish up until 1:00. Then I greeted the parents and relatives, and then I had to back to the house and sign some letters. I always have an urge to get rid of the mail, so I try to sign the letters just before dinner or just after dinner. I even do mail on Saturday and Sunday. I finished dinner about 7:30, and I went to bed around 11:00. I got up at 3:00 for a while, and then I went back to bed and was up again before 7:00.

"You know, if I have something to write, I can do it right from my bed. See this machine here?" He pointed to a metal object next to his desk. "That's a Code-A-Phone. I can just dial a number from my bed and dictate to it. Watch." He buzzed for his secretary, gave her the number that he thought would activate the recording machine, and sat back to watch. She went back to her own desk and dialed. Nothing happened.

Cardinal Cody frowned. He buzzed for the secretary again. "Maybe you didn't get an outside line," he said.

She disappeared. The sound of her dialing the telephone came from the next room, but the Code-A-Phone remained silent. She came back into the doorway. "Could you have given me the wrong number?" the secretary said.

"No," Cardinal Cody said. "That's the number I dial from my bed. It always works at night."

"Well, I don't know what's wrong, then," the secretary said. "A business keeps answering at the number you gave me."

"Well, see if you can get it straightened out," Cardinal Cody said. "We'll just keep on talking in the meantime."

But for the next five minutes, Cardinal Cody's glance kept fading back to the machine by his desk, waiting for it to click on. The sound of his secretary dialing repeatedly continued to come through the wall. "I really have no hobby except work," he said, glancing at the machine. "I like classical music, modern liturgical music. I don't get any exercise. My real hobby is work." He stared at the machine.

Finally it happened. The machine clicked and hummed. "THERE," Cardinal Cody said. "That's the sound!" Like a kid with a new electric train with transformer trouble that has just been solved, the cardinal beamed at the machine and listened to it vibrate.

Moral leadership used to be an easy term to deal with. Determine the righteous course, and then point the way. In the '60s, when Cardinal Cody built himself a strong reputation as a proponent of equal rights for blacks and whites, his vision of how to provide moral leadership was clear. But now, like everyone else, the cardinal is sometimes uncertain.

People don't seem to want their morals tampered with. Morality has become a completely private matter, and the liberalized attitude in the country that has made "clap" and "smack" easily recognizable terms even in elementary schools creates a difficult situation for men of the church who, in past days, could assume that their moral judgments were expected and wanted. Now the world has changed.

"I won't say it's really a sense of pessimism that I have," Cardinal Cody said. "There has been social upheaval before; it's true of almost any age in society. But this current state of morality—the violence, the drug addiction—I don't mind telling you, sometimes I find myself being shocked. The poverty—you see a housing project, you see that sight, and what do you do? What do you do?"

The conversation with the cardinal was taking place before the Supreme Court decision that opened the way for a crackdown on pornography, and the pornography situation was one of the things on his mind. "It's terrible that we should permit X-rated movies," he said. "Those movies have an appeal to youth. And they're becoming more and more attractive as the sense of morality becomes less and less. Whatever happened to parental control? When I was growing up, we would have *never* been allowed to go to a show without permission from our parents. Now anything goes.

"The breakdown in law enforcement plays a part in it, too. Those kind of movies weren't permitted to be shown in public in days gone by. The greed of the people who are producing these things is responsible. That's where the real responsibility can be found.

"No, I have to say that I can't deny that there is a rather negative sense of morality about so many things. People say that we can't do anything about it, and I just don't know sometimes. With all this pornography it's so hard to keep it from the young people. Youth has always been adventurous. But the obscene material has never been so *available* before. After World War I the pornography was *there,* but at least it wasn't *thrust* at you. The only way to combat this is with law enforcement, and the way the Supreme Court decisions on obscenity are reading, anything goes. We just have to come up with enough people who will stand up and say, 'No, we do not buy this attitude.' We have the Legion of Decency in the Catholic Church, but I just don't know. . . .

"It is a very difficult thing for a religious leader to get a sense of morality across. There are millions of basically good families who just let their children go. The children are on their own. And with all of these temptations, some people are going to take advantage of it. Have you been around Old Town lately? Old Town is as bad as Paris or any of those places were in the past. First it's drugs, then it's sex, then it's violence. You can get the message to them, all right, but they don't seem to want to respond to it. There's a general breakdown in respect for authority.

"There is a malaise of distrust even of one another. Racial problems. Political problems. It certainly doesn't say much that's good for the future of the country, does it? If we can't even trust each other anymore, if we can't believe in the brotherhood of man under the fatherhood of God, what is there but chaos? I have such great hope for young people, I find them so sincere, they want to know the whys and wherefores, which is good. But you have to place this against the backdrop of what's going on in the society.

"It will require almost a miracle today to stop this. If the voice of the people under the proper leadership can't do it. . . . The only leadership I can give is moral. I can only warn. I can only warn of the dangers that the society is permitting, and if people won't listen . . ."

It used to be a concern only for men of the church, this deep thinking about setting a moral tone, and saving society from the devil, and restoring goodness to the heart of man. But the dark events of the last decade have shown that all of that is certainly more than pulpit talk, and now John Cardinal Cody finds himself but one among millions of Americans who are waking up to the fact that just maybe there is no temporal answer at all. But while the rest of the world can shrug and say how depressing it all is, a cardinal cannot have that luxury.

So he works at it, and he keeps track of precisely how long and hard he works at it, as if by the sheer bulk of hours spent at the task, the world will turn around. But one somehow feels that the cardinal must be harboring a suspicion that perhaps, with the world the way it is now, all the hours in the day cannot be enough.

And even with the job of working at it comes other problems. The lifestyle of a cardinal, for example: with the limousine and the fine house, Cardinal Cody lives very well by worldly standards, and he knows that there are those who think that by his very lofty position, he cannot relate to the people in the bottom half of society.

"When I go out on any ceremony, I make it my business to meet each and every one of the people," he said. "I went out to Chicago Heights, and I greeted about half of the people in Italian. I just got a card from a kid in the sixth grade, and do you know what it said? It just said, 'Hi Cardinal.' With the kids, you don't have that terrible awe that you see in some adults.

"I think that the times are a challenge, and I'm happy to be alive right now. Even with the bad things, even with all of the problems . . .

"You ask me about my worst moment? My moment of almost sheer horror? It was the day that the Supreme Court of the United States ruled to allow abortion. That was the beginning of the downfall of this country in many ways. First you allow abortion. Then comes sterilization. Then comes euthanasia. I can't even express to you how horrified I was by that. Horrified as a religious leader, and as an American, and as a person. You can't just brush all respect for life away like that.

"But you have to keep working for what you think is right. Do you know that in one six-month period, I saw 177 priests, and I attended 118 different functions? That was in one January 1 to May 30 period. Here, I have it on paper somewhere, let me see if I can get it for you . . ."

John Cardinal Cody says that his work is his whole life, that it does not give him time for leisure activities, and certainly not for pleasure vacations.

"Because of the church, though, I have been to Rome 71 times since the end of the '50s," he said.

But what, he was asked, what if someone told him that he *had* to take two weeks off, he *had* to stop working, and pick any place in the world, and just go there and see the sights and relax and forget about his duties as a cardinal for a while? What if he *had* to do that?

"But that would never happen," Cardinal Cody said.

What if it did, though, he was asked. Just for argument's sake, what if it did?

"I would go to Rome," Cardinal Cody said.

But he had just said that he had been to Rome 71 times in the recent past, he was reminded.

"Then I would go a 72d time," Cardinal Cody said.

But why? he was asked.

"I like it in Rome," said John Cardinal Cody.

Always Joan

Of course Manny Greenhill was there. There are a million Manny Greenhills; they are everywhere the music is, giving their orders and checking their watches and complaining that everything is running late. The manager, bringing the world of money and contracts into the auditoriums and concert halls, bringing the daytime harshness of the city to the night. So tonight, Manny Greenhill, with his gray beard and his gray suit, was there of course, but tonight it seemed wrong.

"Look, it's almost 7:40, we're ten minutes late," Manny Greenhill was saying to the manager of the Auditorium Theater. Manny had just finished a gin and tonic, over which he had been complaining that all the arrangements had been screwed up. "We have two shows tonight, two shows, and we simply cannot afford to run late," Manny was saying, but then everyone looked away from him, and no one wanted to listen to him anymore, because all of a sudden Joan Baez was there.

"Which way to the audience?" Joan Baez said, laughing and slinging her guitar over her shoulder. She was understated and lovely, her hair pulled back, wearing blue slacks and a white shirt, quiet and soft and beautiful like she has been for all these years.

An electrician in a blue shirt pointed to the curtain, then walked over to it and pulled it back for her. "Would you like a spotlight in the center of the stage?" he asked her.

"No, I'll just walk out," Joan Baez said. "Let me sneak out, maybe they won't see me. If I know they're looking for me, I'll probably trip all over myself."

And she walked out in the darkness, to the single stool in the middle of the stage. Four thousand people, reaching clear up to the heights of the last balcony, roared their welcome, thanking her once again, as people have been thanking her for ten years, and she smiled and began to sing "Joe Hill" in that voice that only one lady will ever have.

She was going to sing twice tonight, and all the money would go to the American Friends Service Committee. The only thing she asked was that no one have to pay more than $2 for a ticket, because she thinks her music should not be out of anyone's reach.

"Most of the ushers tonight are draft resisters," Joan Baez said. "We're glad to have you around for a while. And if you have to go to jail . . . well, you'll do it. It's a drag, but you'll do it." And that smile.

She has been right for so long. From the early days of the civil rights movement, when wanting the same freedoms for everyone in the United States was a radical thought, she was there and the enemies of change vilified her and she was right. And through the '60s, and through all of the things that have torn at the country, she was there and always right, singing her gentle songs and standing strong, quietly denying violence, knowing that refusing to be violent will never mean refusing to be steadfast.

For a whole, massive part of the country, she has come during these years to be more than a singing lady; every time the cause is just, she is there, helping and showing that she still cares, still hopes. While so many of the people who are supposed to represent America have turned out to be deceitful and vain and tainted, Joan Baez has remained as always.

She has been an easy target for those who oppose her ideas, and during Vietnam, she and her husband David Harris have been maligned and hated. But now it is becoming clear that, as that dirty little war dries up, Joan Baez and David Harris are perhaps among the real heroes—for seeing it was wrong, knowing it was wrong and, in their dignified ways, saying no, we reject it, it is not right.

So once again she was on a stage, once again to let them hear that voice and remember to care about something. During her last song, an usher came backstage to see Manny Greenhill. The usher said a group of paraplegic youngsters was in the audience and would like to see Joan, if only for a moment. Manny Greenhill politely said no, she would be too tired.

But as Joan Baez came off stage, the applause ringing behind her, the usher approached her and told her about it. Manny Greenhill started to interrupt, but Joan nodded to the usher and said of course.

It took about ten minutes for the auditorium to empty out, and she didn't have much time until her next show. They were sitting in a section near the back. The word "paraplegic" is bad to hear, but it cannot convey the horror of these people, so young, who have had something terrible go wrong in their bodies and who must spend every public moment in a contorted, wrenching parody of their youth. Joan was walking toward them.

"Hi," she waved, and they reacted immediately, calling to her, asking her to come over. Their voices echoed in the empty auditorium as she kissed them and reached out to touch their hands and have a word with each of them, and they were smiling.

She was slow and patient, making sure that no one was forgotten, that no one who had a question would go home with it unanswered. And when she headed back toward the stage door, she looked across the hall. There, alone, were five kids in wheelchairs who had tried to get up close to see her, but in doing so had drifted from the group she had just left.

So she scooted sideways through the seats, until she got to them, all the way at the other side. And she stayed with them, too. A girl got very excited and started to come out of her wheelchair, and Joan hurried over and calmed her. And she did not forget the boy in the rear of the group, too shy to talk; she went to him and whispered for a few moments.

It was not an important thing, just one more little thing that Joan Baez has done right when it would have been easier to look the other way. Manny Greenhill was at the stage door, beckoning to her and pointing to his watch. So she waved good-by to all of them and walked swiftly over to him.

"You're not going to have any time at all before the second show," Manny Greenhill said. "How'd you get yourself in a hole like that?"

Joan Baez was already walking toward her dressing room. She looked over her shoulder at him. "That's no hole, Manny," she said.

Psychic

The famous psychic, Uri Geller, was in town over the weekend, and so I went to call on him at his hotel.

Geller, as you may have heard, is the young Israeli who can bend keys and spoons by telepathy, can duplicate drawings he has never seen, can start clocks that have been broken for years, can pluck thoughts out of people's minds, and perform various other feats.

Skeptics say that any good magician can do what Geller does; believers (including a number of respected scientists) say that there is no trickery involved and that Geller apparently does have strange powers. Geller himself, both in conversation and in his autobiography, claims that a mysterious force within him is responsible for his abilities.

Geller sat down at a table opposite me, and offered to bend any keys I might be carrying.

"What is the capital of Idaho?" I asked.

"Pardon me?" Geller said.

"You're 0 for 1," I said. "Question two: where does Kup toss his half-smoked stogies during the commercials?"

"What's that you're saying?" Geller said. "What is a 'Kup'?"

"0 for 2," I said. "Question three: who were the original members of the Jordanaires?"

"I don't know," Geller said. "I am not an American. I am an Israeli. Please, give me your keys." He took my key ring, stroked one of the keys, and it bent upward. He smiled.

"Very nice," I said. "However, you are still 0 for 3. Question four: where do you change for the Ravenswood?"

Geller raised his arms. "Who is a Raven Hood?" he said.

"Tell you later," I said. "0 for 4."

Geller interrupted, and began to explain how he has fixed hundreds, perhaps thousands, of broken watches and clocks merely by appearing on television and willing them to be fixed.

I lifted my foot. "Fix this hole in my shoe," I said.

"No," he said. "It doesn't work that way. I don't fix holes in shoes."

"0 for 5," I said.

"Please," Geller said. "Let me show you what I do." He had me draw a design of my choosing. He then proceeded to recreate a close approximation of my drawing. He had me do it again. Again, he drew a close facsimile.

"Great," I said. "Now back to business. Question six: is Mike Royko going to the *Washington Post?*"

Geller's lips became tight. "I . . . don't . . . know," he bit off.

"0 for 6," I said.

"Look," Geller said. "Let's try something else that I do. I am going to draw a design. You don't look at me."

I looked away. "OK, I've done it," Geller said. "Now you draw a design."

I looked down and drew a shape. When I looked back up again, Geller was holding a piece of paper with the same design I had made.

I whistled appreciatively. "Good," I said, "Now, back to the questions. Let's try to make you 1 for 7. Here you go: for whom is the shrimp salad at Eli's named?"

"I don't know," Geller muttered.

"0 for 7," I said. "In case you're interested, the salad is named for Eli's son, Marc."

"Wonderful," Geller breathed.

"Don't give up," I said. "You have three more tries. Question eight: who wrote the Phi Ep Dream Girl Song?"

"I . . . don't . . . know," Geller said. "Do people know this? Do you ask everyone these questions?"

"Walter Schwimmer wrote the Phi Ep Dream Girl Song," I said. "You're 0 for 8. Question nine: who played Jimmy Olsen?"

"Where?" Geller said.

"I shouldn't do this, but I'm going to give you a hint," I said. "On the Superman TV show."

"I don't know," Geller said. "I don't know who played Jimmy Olsen. I know who played Superman, though."

"Who?" I said.

"Clark Kent," Geller said.

"Wrong," I said. "I should count that as two wrong answers, but I'll just count the Olsen part. 0 for 9."

"You don't understand the nature of my powers," Geller said.

"Who is Jack Mabley" I asked.

Geller sighed. "I don't know," he said. "A baseball player?"

"0 for 10," I said. I got up to leave, and shook Geller's hand. "One more thing," I said. "Would you mind straightening out my key before I go?"

"You fix your own key," Geller said.

Jack Benny

The reporter had made an appointment to see Jack Benny. The reporter was new in the business; he had no experience at interviewing celebrities, and instead of calling Benny directly, he had gone through a public-relations woman. The reporter arrived at the Palmer House at the appointed hour and asked for Benny's room on the house phone. There was no answer.

The reporter, by now more than a little nervous, took an elevator to Benny's floor, and banged on the door for a minute or so. Finally there came the sound of the unforgettable voice: "Come in!"

The reporter entered the suite, and there, alone, in the center of the room, was Benny. He was 75 years old at the time, near the end of a remarkable career. He had pulled a chair up to a room-service dining table; he was wearing a blue bathrobe over a white T-shirt, black slippers covering black, knee-length socks. He peered inquisitively at the reporter, and the reporter stammered out his reason for coming to call.

"I don't know anything about any interview," Benny said. "No one told me."

Benny had opened a window, and the night sounds of the city came into the room as the winter air ruffled the curtains. By the window was a table with a fifth of Scotch on it and a number of bottles containing medication. He was midway through his solitary dinner.

"I have to go downstairs and be on stage in 15 minutes," Benny said. "I've got to finish eating, I've got to shave, I've got to put my makeup on . . ."

The reporter turned to leave. "Can you come back in the daytime some time?" Benny said. The reporter said no; he was doing the interview on his own time, trying to make an impression on some bosses, and during daylight working hours his time was not his own. He apologized to Benny for interrupting him so close to show time and started to leave again.

"Oh, come on then," Benny said. "Finish dinner with me, and then you can come down and watch the show, and we can come back up and talk some more afterwards if you like. Sit down."

And Benny began to talk. He had gone through literally thousands of interviews before in the course of his professional life, and on this night he looked tired and a bit haggard. But he understood the inexperience of his visitor, and he went out of his way to tell stories, to recall memories, to embellish on the events of his years as a master comedian—to help make the reporter's job easier.

He excused himself to go shave, and from the other room his voice carried over the buzz of the electric razor: "My Kind of Town, Chicago Is . . ." He came out of the bedroom wearing a dark-blue business suit and motioned for the reporter to follow him, took the reporter with him down to the Empire Room, said something to the maitre d', and the reporter was shown to a table with a clear view.

Benny's performance was marvelous; his timing and his gestures and his understanding of how to play an audience were, of course, classic, and the years disappeared as he heard the waves of laughter, he became a young man again as he felt the approval of the customers. He no longer looked tired, and as the show passed beyond its normal time limit, and the laughs intensified until they were almost screams, Benny became a kid again, saying, "We might as well stay here all night. I mean, where are you going to go?"

After the performance, the reporter returned to Benny's suite. Benny had been visited by some old friends from Chicago, and he introduced the reporter around and poured drinks. The Chicago friends began to leave, but Benny and the reporter kept talking. They talked long and late, Benny telling about the dreary parts of his fame as well as the high points—the weariness that came from still being on the road at 75, a vaudevillian 50 years later.

"I don't know," he said. "I think I'll cut down some next year. Maybe not quite as much time away from home. My wife hates to travel, and I miss her too much being out here by myself. But retire? I couldn't retire. I just couldn't. I'm too much of a ham."

Finally Benny began to drift off to sleep even as he sat in his chair, and the reporter excused himself and made ready to leave.

"I hope I've given you enough for a story," Benny said, and the reporter said yes, he certainly had. Jack Benny was 80 when he died last week, and there were many words spoken in praise of his professional talent. It seemed that it might be well to speak also of a random kindness offered once by Benny to a beginning reporter on a winter Chicago night.

Spillane

I wanted to talk to an expert about the national crime wave. Suddenly crime is the hottest topic in the country; *Time* magazine devotes a special cover story this week to Crime in America, and most public opinion polls show that citizens worry about crime more than anything else. Fear of crime is rampant in the nation.

Most of the people being quoted about crime, however, seemed to be Harvard professors or Princeton sociologists. The opinions of these scholars may be perfectly valid, but I thought it would be a disservice not to contact the most astute authority on violent crime that I know. I dialed a number in South Carolina.

"What is it?" Mickey Spillane said.

I identified myself, and said that I wanted to talk about crime. Spillane, 57, is the creator of the Mike Hammer private eye books, a series of blood-drenched, gore-soaked crime novels that have sold more than 130 million copies. Spillane himself is a crew-cut, politically conservative, fedora-wearing representation of what Mike Hammer might look like in real life. I asked Spillane if he, like so many other Americans, is afraid to walk the streets at night.

"Ha, ha," Spillane said. "Don't be stupid. If you screw me, kid, I'll jump on you like a ton of bricks. I'll tear your ears off." He sounded as if he had just consumed six or seven carloads of the beer he endorses on television.

I asked him again if he is afraid to walk the streets.

"That's ridiculous," Spillane said. "Ha. I never had any fears. I'm not afraid of anything. You're making a mistake, kid, if you think you got more power than I do. You have no power next to me. I'll slaughter you."

I began to realize that the interview might not go well. Nevertheless, I brought up the *Time* cover story, and asked Spillane if he had any solutions to the new flare-up in the crime problem.

"Who needs this garbage?" Spillane said. "I'm taping every

word you say. They're always trying to get me, but they won't be able to this time."

I asked him who was trying to get him.

"The Canadians," Spillane said. "They do things."

I asked him what the Canadians had done to him.

"They can't do nothing to me," Spillane said, and the line went dead.

I called him back. I asked him for his specific thinking about street crime.

"I don't feel fear at any time," Spillane said. "New York is falling apart. You don't have one chance against me, kid."

I asked him how citizens could protect themselves against criminals.

"We don't need to protect ourselves from crime," he said. "Can you fight? When was your last fight? Did you win? How big are you? Don't try to hustle me."

I brought up the subject of the decay of America's cities.

"Tell me what you ever did to protect your city," Spillane said. "Did you ever kill anyone? Were you ever in a war? No war? Well, isn't that wild. No war. I'm an old fighter pilot. I'm recording everything you say. You even try to hurt me, I'll knock the hell out of you. If you think I can't, you're crazy. You'd better be pretty big, because I'm a big one."

I asked if he had a way to solve the crime problem.

"Yeah, I've got a way," he said. "It's the only way. I'm going to send you some literature. In the mail. I'm a Jehovah's Witness. Read Revelations, read Timothy. That's the way to fight crime."

I asked Spillane if he was concerned about crime.

"Who cares?" he said. "I don't give a hoot. Crime? I'm not for it or against it. Who needs it?"

I asked him if he felt safer living in South Carolina than he did when he was living in New York.

"Why didn't you volunteer for the service?" Spillane said. "I volunteered for the Air Force. I'll tear you up. I'm going to end this conversation."

I asked him to answer one more question.

"What's that?" Spillane said.

I asked if Mike Hammer would have been scared by the current crime wave in America.

"Boy, what a stupid thing to say to me," Spillane said. "Was he ever afraid? No way. I'm ending this conversation. I'm 56 years old. I will tear you up. I love you. I got you on tape. I will kick your ass."

Fonda the Elder

Henry Fonda, 68, talked in the shadows. He was on a couch at the end of a long, dark living room. The only light came from a small window directly behind him.

"It isn't the applause," he said. "The applause isn't what does it for me.

"That's not what acting is all about," Fonda said. "It can be just as exciting for me to do a run-through rehearsal, the first time you do a play from beginning to end. My God, that can be an experience. That first time, with an empty house, when you put the blood and the breath and the guts into a play. The first run-through rehearsal of *Mister Roberts* is something that those of us who were there will carry with us to our graves. What a remarkable, moving feeling, to see a play like that come to life for the first time. There was no one in the audience, but for those of us who were on that stage that day—I can't even tell you the feeling, it made the hair on the backs of our necks stand up. An audience, that comes later. And the applause, that, too. But the audience and the applause aren't what's important."

Fonda is back on the boards. He is one of America's premier actors, a legendary name, and he could afford to retire and let his fame rest on his long list of theatrical and motion picture accomplishments. "No," he said, "I wouldn't do that. I go back to the theater out of pure selfishness. It's where I get my kicks. I do it for myself. The scripts come in, and out of hundreds I'll find one, and in that first moment it will just get me going right away; it'll goose me and jar me, and I'll know it's right, I'll know I have to do it."

Fonda is in Chicago appearing as Clarence Darrow at the Civic Theater, beginning a nationwide tour for the one-man play. On Monday afternoon he talked with a visitor in his hotel suite in the hours before he was to take his daily pre-performance nap. He was not interested that one of his films, *The Ox-Bow Incident,* was scheduled to be shown on television that night.

"I've only seen a few of my movies," Fonda said. "I've done maybe 85 or 86 movies, and most of them I've never looked at even once. Not even screenings. I just don't want to see them.

"Sometimes my wife will be watching TV, and she'll yell, 'Hey, you're on television!' and it will be one of my old movies. But I don't watch them. I made myself look at some of them—I've seen *Mister Roberts,* and *Grapes of Wrath,* and *Young Mr. Lincoln,* and *Ox-Bow Incident,* and *Twelve Angry Men.* But I don't like to watch. It's because I don't like the look of my face, and I don't like the sound of my voice. People tell me that my voice has a distinctive sound, but I really dislike it. I'm very self-conscious about my face, too. I wish I could look like Cary Grant. The first time I saw myself in a movie, I wanted to slide down into the floor. I've never gotten over it.

"That's why acting is a kind of therapy for me. I realize that I'm introverted. I guess I'm almost neurotically introverted. When I was young, I'd cross the street rather than say hello to anybody. Even now, if a drama league is giving me an award or something, I'll sit through the luncheon with my stomach all tied up. I won't be able to eat because I'm so afraid about the time when I have to stand up and accept the award, say some words. Acting, though, that's a mask for me. Acting is being somebody else. I can do that."

Fonda said the four-year run of *Mister Roberts,* one of the great American plays, still is special to him. "That was one of the high points of my life," he said. "There's nothing in the book that says something like that will happen to you. God doesn't say, 'You shall have a *Death of a Salesman,'* or 'You shall have a *Mister*

Roberts happen to you in your life.' To have a *Mister Roberts* come along is just something that you remain thankful for."

The visitor asked Fonda how he would like to be remembered when his career is over finally. Fonda paused and looked out the window.

"I don't know," he said. "I never thought about that before. You want to be remembered as . . . well, I don't know, I suppose you want to be remembered as pleasing. I don't care if they put asterisks or exclamation points by my name. It would be enough if they liked me."

Chicken King

Colonel Sanders was dripping a little lentil soup into his white goatee. He looked over at the person who was having lunch with him, and who was eating a cheeseburger. "I never eat hamburger," Colonel Sanders said.

Why's that, he was asked by the person with the cheeseburger.

"I've seen what they put into hamburger," said Colonel Sanders, and then he made a grimace that told of unspeakable horrors. The colonel dipped again into the soup. The person with the cheeseburger put it down on the plate.

"Limburger cheese," said the colonel. "I can't get it in Kentucky. I would run my legs off for a Limburger cheese on rye. I can just never find it."

Harland Sanders is 82 years old, and the quintessential American success story: a chicken maker who has become internationally famous and is now looked upon with wonder and awe as he walks the streets of the world.

"I don't know about being a celebrity. I just want to be a

chicken cook," the colonel said. Yeah. He owns eight all-white suits, so that no one will ever see him in public looking like anything but the TV image of himself. He will not wear a topcoat over the white suit when people are looking.

"Once it was ten below at the Cleveland Airport," he said. "And I strolled in in my white suit, and someone said, 'Who's that?' and someone else yelled, 'It's Colonel Sanders, the chicken man.' So I started wearing it all the time."

Bob Montgomery, 23, is the colonel's traveling aide. The colonel travels every week, promoting Kentucky Fried Chicken, and Montgomery is still stunned at the public response his boss draws.

"You should have seen it," Mongomery said. "We're at Buckingham Palace, for the changing of the guard. We just wanted to watch it. So it starts. And everyone's looking at the colonel! No one's looking at the palace!"

The colonel was still working at his soup. "Bunch of damned shysters, sons of bitches, biggest sharpies you've ever seen," said the colonel. He was referring to a group of businessmen who bought the chicken business from him in 1963. The "shysters" are no longer in control; since then, the company has been bought by Heublein Incorporated, but Colonel Sanders is not one to forget so easily. Not that he loves Heublein so much either. The colonel hates the gravy that is currently being used with Kentucky Fried Chicken so fiercely that he refers to it in terms such as "wallpaper paste," and worse. The colonel has a public relations man who sometimes travels with him, but when the colonel begins to talk about the gravy, all the PR man can do is look the other way and hope it will end soon. Because Harland Sanders, although he no longer owns the company, is still the most valued asset of Kentucky Fried Chicken. He is paid a salary of $75,000 a year for being Colonel Sanders in public. He says what he wants to say.

Which isn't always what you would call your basic effete, liberal party line. "The most pitiful daggone thing I ever saw was that Democratic convention in Miami," the colonel said. The colonel appeared at the convention, promoting chicken on national TV. "Do you realize something about that convention?" he said. "Do you know that 16 of the delegates from California were on government assistance? That's the class of people they had down there, and do you wonder what kind of government we'd have had under McGovern? I told 'em I didn't want to go down there with that class of people, but they pay me the $75,000, and it was prime time, the whole world was watchin' on the tube, so I went. But I'm sorry about it."

The colonel, who dropped out of school in the sixth grade, said that he likes the young people of America, except "that hippie bunch in California, with that free way of life, careless, going from city to city." And he doesn't much see any point to young people postponing getting a job so they can travel and see the world for a while. "Unless you can travel in decency, it doesn't mean much," he said.

The colonel's limousine was waiting downstairs. He glanced at the market listings in the *Wall Street Journal*. Then he walked to the elevator, and when he stepped out, on the first floor of the Sheraton-Chicago, he did not go outside right away. Instead he leaned against a baggage cart until three older women stopped to stare.

"I don't believe it," one of them said. "I do not believe it. Colonel Sanders."

The colonel straightened up and pulled his white suit coat down on his shoulders. He twirled his hand-tooled wooden cane into the air, Mick Jagger with his red cape. It is odd to be a superstar at 82, especially a chicken-cooking superstar, but most people never make it at all. "Good afternoon, ladies," said Colonel Sanders.

Brickhouse Agonistes

"What am I proudest of?" Jack Brickhouse said. "Oh . . . you know, one thing I've learned, is that a voice may come over the radio or the television and become very famous, but that the man behind that voice may not have any character. I've seen guys in this announcing business who were idolized, but what do they do when they walk away from the microphone? They run from their bills, they get little girls pregnant, they charge anything they want to.

"What am I proudest of? I think that I've tried to give announcing a little dignity. That I've proved that an announcer can pay his bills, and date girls as opposed to boys, and sleep with his wife, and build himself a home. That an announcer can be a man with a little self-esteem. I think I've proved that."

Brickhouse took a long pull at his Scotch and water. He finished off the glass, motioned for a refill. The barroom was emptying, but Brickhouse was not finished talking. "All right, look at me," he said. "Here is a guy who likes to drink, who sprinkles his language with an occasional swear word . . . if I went on the air and talked like we're talking now, I'd be yanked off within 24 hours.

"Announcing is a form of self-hypnosis, in that we hypnotize ourselves into *being* ourselves, and yet stay within the *do*s and *don't*s of broadcasting. Look, I know what some people say about me. I know what they think of me. A hometown rooter. The mail is so strange, they'll call me a nigger lover, or a nigger hater. Maybe they all think I'm a fairly shallow guy who simply has found a good, safe way to make a living and who plays it close to the vest, Mr. Smile, Mr. Nice Guy. A guy who does all this and probably feels a little hypocritical about it.

"I know what they say. But I don't think I'm a square. I think I'm progressive, I think I'm pretty liberal in my ways. I don't let my hair grow long. I'm not wearing long, uh, muttonchops. If I Rush Street it, I'd just as soon it doesn't appear in the columns, although I'd be a damned liar if I didn't say I like publicity, because I do. Look, I'm probably attempting to go a little too deep here, and maybe I don't have the credentials to be talking about these things."

Brickhouse was in a quiet, reflective mood this night, and the talk was not of athletes or athletics. Brickhouse, at 58, had suddenly found himself somewhat troubled. For decades his voice and face had been synonymous with broadcasts of Chicago athletic teams— his voice was the first to be heard on Channel 9's initial telecast in 1948—and he is as closely identified with the Cubs and the Bears as are Philip Wrigley and George Halas.

As vice-president and manager for sports for WGN Continental Broadcasting Company, Brickhouse has been the prototypical representative of that corporation's Midwest optimism and civic boosterism. For years the thought of Brickhouse becoming an object of controversy was absurd. He was a local play-by-play announcer; "Hey Hey, Holy Mackerel, Attaboy Ernie"; he was a Chicago institution.

But in the 1970s, in the Age of Cosell, that began to change. The new school of sports announcers, following Cosell's "tell it like it is" cliche, were approaching sportscasting with all the seriousness and objectivity of political reporting. Brickhouse never had been shy about admitting that he was a fan. Now he was finding that in many quarters he was scorned for this very parochialism, and criticized for his happy, upbeat, purely positive approach to broadcasting sports.

His position as a member of the board of directors of the Chicago Cubs was a particular target, and there were those in and out of broadcasting who pointed to that as the perfect proof that Brickhouse was a dinosaur, a modern Babbit running out of time.

In the midst of the criticism, it seemed like a good idea to seek Brickhouse out, to get him away from the athletes and the locker room hangers-on and the sportswriters, and let him have his say. To steer him away from the sports personalities he has been talking about for 30 years, and instead let him talk about Jack Brickhouse. So on this night Brickhouse was sitting in a back booth of a deserted bar, and his words had very little in common with the ones that have become so familiar on WGN.

"Hell, yes, I'm a fan," he said. "I'd be a pretty sorry case if I wasn't. This broadcasting is all I've ever done. It's all I've ever tried, really . . . I was a soda jerk once, and I washed dishes, and I filled bottles with gin at Hiram Walker's distillery [in Peoria], but what I do for a living is essentially all I've ever done. If I didn't enjoy going to the ball games, then I'd be a pretty uncomfortable fellow.

"These people who want to nail any announcer who doesn't 'tell it like it is' . . . I mean, are you really a journalist in that broadcasting booth? Is broadcasting a baseball game the same thing as covering a train wreck? A bank robbery? Am I there just to report the facts? I don't think so. First it's entertainment. Only second is it news. It is an escape. It is a diversion. It's the fun-and-games department, and I don't think it's all that damned much important.

"Yeah, I admit it, I don't criticize the players I'm covering. I can't play that game. I can't knock people's brains out. I can't go out and hammer innocent people. If you want to shoot from the hip and the heart instead of from the head—well, you'd better think it out first, buster. A microphone or a camera gives you an awesome responsibility.

"I'm not a Cronkite or a Brinkley or a Chancellor. By no means should men like those men be on the staff of a political candidate, like I'm on the board of the Cubs. But we're not doing the same thing. Hell, I'm glad to be on the board of the Cubs. I can give them a little perspective on that ball club. I live in the trenches with that ball club; I travel with them; I know them. I'm on the firing line with them. If I owned General Motors, you can bet me that on my board would be a couple of guys who make their living assembling automobiles."

What about the Brickhouse image? Is the upright, wholesome, decent, Chamber of Commerce persona that comes over the air the real Brickhouse, or is he a secret reader of *Penthouse,* a back-row boy at the topless-bottomless joints in America's Major League cities?

"I'm no bluenose, if that's what you mean," Brickhouse said. "I'm by no means a moralist. I've never considered sex a spectator sport, but if a naked girl were to walk by here right now, I'm not going to turn my head away. If I were a swinger, I'd be a goddamn fool to admit it to you, but if I were single, I guess I'd probably be that way.

"I told my wife years ago, 'If a beautiful girl walks by, and I *don't* look, then you'd better start worrying, because it means one of two things: either I'm losing it, and I can't do you any good, or I'm turning queer.' But a guy like Namath doesn't do much for me. That business of trying to prove what a great big stud he is. I know athletes who are better than him in *that* league than he ever was on the best weekend of his life."

What about his identification with sports, and ball games? Does his enthusiasm for these contests never wane? Aren't there mornings when he dreads going to the ball park and sitting through nine more innings?

"Hell yes, I get bored," he said. "I get so bored I can hardly stand it. But this is where being a pro comes in. When you can stay alert, and on top of an audience even on a bad day, during a bad game, that's when you're a professional.

"I make myself get away from it. My biggest kick in the world is theater. I couldn't tell you how many trips to London I've made, just to go to the theater. I don't particularly dig rock music, but I go totally ape over Al Hirt, Pete Fountain. Give me a Dixieland outfit, you've lost me for the night. I have an absolute need to get away from sports, and from people who want to talk to me about nothing but sports.

"I go to France. Over there, if I say 'baseball' to a French bartender, he doesn't know what the hell I'm talking about. I take books with me. Poe, Pope, Shakespeare, Ellery Queen. That's where I'm most comfortable, in the south of France. I've got some golf buddies in Nice and Cannes. I love to do that, just get the hell away. That's one of the things that gets to me here at home, people who come up and want to talk sports all the time.

"Now I love people, and a lot of the time I'm more than happy to talk about the players with them. But there are times I want to go to a bar, and I want the drinks, I want the atmosphere, but stay the hell away from me.

"I don't like wise guys. I don't mind people coming around, but I don't like it if I'm in a little group, and I'm telling a story, and I'm just getting to the punchline and some guy muscles in and kills my punchline. And I don't like guys who are always talking negatively about the ballplayers, and trying to get me to talk negatively. I believe in positives.

"The way I look at it, any ballplayer I see out there on the field is one of the 600 greatest players in a world of two billion people. Every one of those 600 who are playing in the Major Leagues is entitled to my respect."

And that attitude does not make him uncomfortable, in this era when we are learning more and more about the foibles of American heroes, athletic heroes included? How does that attitude deal with something like *Ball Four,* Jim Bouton's best seller about the real world of Major League baseball?

"I think that anybody who writes a book like that is the world's biggest phony," Brickhouse said. "Under the guise of trying to tell it like it is, they try to build a career for themselves, and line their own pockets. I believe in the sanctity and the secrecy of the clubhouse. I believe that reporters like myself should be barred from the clubhouse if the team wants it that way. Anyone who violates that secrecy is going to get no sympathy from Jack Brickhouse.

"There's such a thing as loyalty, you know. I remember when I was first breaking into this business, at WMBD radio in Peoria, the people at that station who befriended me. Edgar Bill. Gomer Bath. Florence Munro.

"Why, those wonderful people would put their arm around me when I made a mistake. When I was so new at broadcasting that I couldn't pronounce my name, when I would muff a $9 commercial on a day when that nine dollars was the difference between a profit and a loss for the station, I was so frightened and frustrated, and Florence Munro, that wonderful, wonderful woman, would put her arm around me and encourage me.

"I was so low after broadcasting my first football game, when I had really blown it, that I just said, 'I know sports broadcasting is not for me.' And those people in Peoria said, 'You'll learn by it,' and sent me back to give it another try. I was trying to imitate all the great sportscasters back then, and one day Edgar Bill said it to me, I was trying to be another Bob Elson, and I guess it showed, Edgar Bill said to me, 'Did you ever think you might like to be the best Jack Brickhouse there is?' "

What about politics? Does Brickhouse's middle-of-the-road public personality extend to his personal political preferences?

"I'm probably slightly to the right of center," he said. "In Chicago I'm about 60-40 Democrat. In the state of Illinois I'm about 70-30 Republican. On the national level I'm about 85-15 Republican. In Chicago so many of my goddamn friends are in the Democratic party. But I'll tell you one thing . . . I have covered quite a few political conventions in my day, and I have never seen anything to match the complete and total arrogance of the McGovern organization in Miami Beach in 1972. Arrogance. Just plain arrogance.

"I was a hell of a strong Nixon man. I began to wonder about him because of the way he presented himself in public. I looked on it as a broadcaster. He was too evasive. The choice of words, the language he used bothered me. I admired Agnew for having the guts to turn on the press. I turned away from him as soon as I found out that he wasn't kosher.

"There was an arrogance in the Nixon camp, too. It started with Ziegler. By 1972 there was no dealing with them. I tried to get through, at their '72 convention, but Ziegler wouldn't let me get near to Nixon. Those politicians always like to play the network game, anyway. On a normal day, they'd drive to your house to be interviewed by a station like WGN, but at the conventions they don't have the time for a local independent station.

"I had an exclusive interview with Nixon at the 1968 convention, you know. I'm pretty goddamn proud of that. The way we got it was through Clem Stone. He's a big contributor, and he's a friend of mine, and I asked him, can you help me get to Mr. Nixon? And Clem got to the Nixon people, and got the promise.

"Now, once we got down to Miami, Herb Klein tried to back out of it; he was playing the network game too. But I told him, dammit, a promise is a promise. He said, 'What if we let you see Mr. Nixon with a group of reporters?' And I said, hell no, what am I going to get out of that, a picture of the back of my head? No, we were promised an exclusive, and we got an exclusive. Nixon was in one room, and down the hall was the big room where he was going to announce that he had selected Agnew as his running mate. And we had a room in between, and he ducked in there on his way down the hall, and gave me six or eight minutes, exclusively.

"Pierre did a bum job, too. Salinger. I tried to get to JFK in 1960, and Pierre kept ignoring me, playing the network game. I waited all week. Finally, at the end of the convention, I said, 'Pierre, I'm leaving now. This is the first time I've seen you without your nose stuck to Sandy Vanocur's ass.'

"I'll tell you about politicians, though. In politics we've all got fellows we can call up and get a favor from. But I'm not sure if I'd want any of them as a pallbearer."

Is the road still the same for him? Does he still like flying into America's biggest cities, seeing the country as a traveling sportscaster?

"New York is where you see the change," he said. "That used to be one exciting town. We were excited to go in there. We'd walk up and down Broadway, stop at Toots Shor's . . . but New York just isn't the town it used to be. It is no longer an impressive town.

Now instead of staying there overnight after a game, I'll give the driver a couple of bucks so I don't miss the last plane. Chicago is the best big city in the world. There are big-city people and small-town people, and I guess I've become a big-city person. Chicago's the best, although I really dig London."

He has been at it for so long—does he ever think about getting out, sparing himself the road life and the endless seasons and the hotel food, and just living the rest of his days away from a press box and a microphone?

"Nah," he said. "Retiring per se isn't for me. They can't send this guy out to Sun City for the Friday night socials and square dances. I love this big, wonderful, nutty world, though, and I want to get the hell out and see all I can."

And leave behind nothing to be remembered, save a million recollections of an excited Midwestern voice describing a ball game over the airways?

"I'd be a damned liar if I said I didn't want something of me left in Chicago," Brickhouse said. "Sure I would. If they would name a school or a street after me . . . sure I would. I think that would be very flattering. I remember Bert Wilson used to say he'd like it if they buried him in the bullpen at Wrigley Field. If they would name a school after me . . . I would like that very much.

"I just wish people would take sports for what it is. It's not an important thing. It's not a serious thing. The future of civilization does not rest on who wins the World Series. There's so much sadness and unhappiness at the top of the news, on the front page . . . by God, if we don't back off and recharge the battery, then how in the hell can we keep going? How can we? Should sportscasters go and look for things to find wrong with sports? Should we see a bogey-man behind every tree? Should we always be looking for skinflint owners trying to cheat their players? Should we? I told you, it's only fun and games . . . why take ourselves so seriously? Do we have to?"

And all of this talk of the pure pleasure and escapism of sports, the relative unimportance of what it means—if he really believes that, how does he evaluate the sum of his own professional life? He has spent a lifetime in the various sporting stadiums of the world, announcing the hits and the errors and the touchdowns. Has he done something of importance? Has he contributed to his world?

Brickhouse hesitated only momentarily. "Not really," he said. "I don't think I really have. I'd like to think I had contributed, but I can't think what the hell it would be."

Woodward and Bernstein

Woodward is having television makeup swabbed onto his face. Bernstein is reading the *National Lampoon* 1964 high school yearbook parody.

"I need from both of you a sense of urgency," says Phil Donahue, the television host, whose syndicated program will go on the air in a few minutes. "We can't be introspective, or sit around sucking on our pipes. Make 'em mad, sad, or glad."

Woodward flashes a quick look over at Bernstein. Bernstein shrugs. It is all a part of the game. For Woodward and Bernstein, the two young *Washington Post* reporters who uncovered the Watergate crimes and changed the course of the nation's history, it is just beginning. They are on the road, doing six and seven television shows every day to promote their book, *All the President's Men*, and with each passing day the two police reporters are solidifying their position as America's newest favorite couple, the Tracy and Hepburn of the '70s.

The irony of two city room types being fawned over as international celebrities is not lost on them, of course. They are dealing with it as best they can. Which, at times, becomes difficult. The paperback rights to their book have been sold for $1 million, and Robert Redford has been signed to play the part of Bob Woodward in the movie version, which is being written by the same man who wrote *Butch Cassidy and the Sundance Kid*. The part of Carl Bernstein is as yet uncast. Lately Redford has been following

Woodward around to see how he lives and moves, to try to get the part down right.

"That's the first time I got a little embarrassed," Bernstein says. "The first time Redford came into the newsroom at the *Post.*" The Donahue show is over, and Woodward and Bernstein are riding in the back seat of a black Cadillac limousine, on their way to the next TV station. "When Redford came in, it was like we were suddenly on deadline," Bernstein says. "You know what I mean? The noise level built up. There was a lot of traffic in the room. A sense of tension. But it was only 11 o'clock in the morning. I wouldn't look up from my typewriter. I could hear the whispers, and I knew what it was, and I didn't want to see it."

"I don't know," Woodward says. "I don't look at it that way. I guess I separate my emotions from it, just like it's another part of the job. I suppose that's an emotionally personal problem with me. I won't go to my feelings. I thought about Redford just like I'd think about one of Nixon's men. What is he here for? What does he want to do? What's the mixture?"

"Yeah, but still," Bernstein says. "When Redford walked into that newsroom, I started to think about everything that's happened, and I started hoping that this whole thing wasn't turning into something that it's not. I'll just be glad when this is all . . . settled."

For the talk shows, Woodward and Bernstein have their routine down smoothly. They have set answers to every conceivable question, including a neat, polite evasion to the inevitable attempt at finding out the true identity of Deep Throat, the code name for the man who was their key secret source. When their answers begin to ramble, they have unobtrusive signals that they flick at one another to make sure that they keep it short, and do not tax the attention spans of their viewing audience. They are purposely and consistently reluctant to criticize the president, feeling that talk show partisanship would hurt their credibility as reporters.

But as good as they are becoming at selling their book and themselves, there is a vague discomfort about them when they are sitting before the cameras and the microphones, and it does not go away until they are away from the studios, removed from their new celebrity role, and instead talking loosely about the things reporters normally talk about. Even if reporters don't normally talk about them in limousines.

"My first day at work at a newspaper," Bernstein says, "I was 16 years old. It was the *Washington Star*. I got a job as a copyboy. Summer job. I knew that I wanted to be a reporter literally the first time that I saw the city room.

"So it's my first day, and I'm wearing this brand-new cream-colored suit, because I figure that this is the way that you impress people and get a job as a reporter. And I'm loving the job, loving being around the reporters. At 2:30 in the afternoon, one of the older copyboys comes around, and he says, 'It's 2:30, and the newest copyboy always has to wash the carbon paper.' I look at him, and he says it again.

"He starts to raise his voice, and he says, 'Unless you wash the carbon paper at 2:30, it's no good for the rest of the day, and we won't be able to get the late editions out.' So I go around the newsroom, and I pick up every piece of carbon paper off of every desk, and I take it into the men's room. And I pile the carbon paper into one of the sinks, and I turn the water on full blast and I start scrubbing the carbon paper with my hands.

"The water is spraying all over me, and my beautiful new suit is getting all wet and grimy, and I keep scrubbing away. While this is going on, the managing editor walks in. He sees me, and he says, 'What in the name of Christ are you doing?' And I say, 'Washing the carbon paper, Mr. Noyes, it's 2:30.' And he starts yelling, and saying that if the copyboys ever pull a prank like that again, they'll be fired, and he tells me to get the hell out of the men's room."

Woodward is checking his watch, to make sure that the two of them will be on time to go to Jorie Lueloff's noon news show at NBC, and to tell again the story of how they exposed the reality of the Nixon White House.

"My first memory of Nixon?" Woodward says. "Let me think. I guess it was in 1952. It was when Eisenhower was running for president. General Eisenhower came through Wheaton, where I grew up, and he was supposed to make a train stop at the station. I was nine years old. My parents took me down so that I could see him. I just remember how impressed I was that Eisenhower would stop in Wheaton. Nixon wasn't with him, but I remember that everyone was wearing these buttons that said 'Ike and Dick.' There were 'Ike and Dick' buttons everywhere."

Woodward and Bernstein are in a small office at NBC, waiting to enter the studio. Woodward is reading a newspaper, and he stops at a brief caption underneath a photograph of Carol Burnett. He wordlessly hands the paper to Bernstein.

The caption reads, "Comedienne Carol Burnett quipped Wednesday that she'd be delighted to play Martha Mitchell in a Watergate movie. 'Oh, I would love that,' she said. 'I've always wanted a phone in the can.' Actor Robert Redford is producing a movie based on the book *All the President's Men.*"

Bernstein scans the caption. He lets out a long breath. "Jesus," he says.

All day long there are more shows, more interviews, more of the same answers about the one breaking newspaper story that has occupied the last two years of their lives.

"You know what I'd really love to be doing right now?" Bernstein says, on his way from one show to another. "Be covering the Hearst case. Now that would be fun. What a great story. There are so many sides to it. The kidnaping, the family, the father . . ."

But there is no time for that. Late in the afternoon, Woodward and Bernstein sit at a bar, killing an hour before yet another television program. Woodward sips a brandy; Bernstein drinks a beer. The talk is of the astounding changes that have come into their lives.

"The movie," Bernstein says. "Who should I get to play me? How about Desi Arnaz, Jr. And Mel Brooks as Deep Throat."

"We'd better get going," says Woodward. "We're supposed to be at CBS in 15 minutes."

"By the time we get to the Catskills, we'll have this thing down pat," says Bernstein.

Fats

Mr. Fats Domino, wearing a tan bathrobe over a white T-shirt, was watching television in his room in the Executive House and waiting for the room-service waiter to show up. Fats calls room service a lot. For example, he has been playing the Flamingo Hotel in Las Vegas for the last 13 years, three months every year, and he has been in the Flamingo's restaurant exactly five times.

"I watch TV and say some prayers and call room service," Fats said. "I'm not happy during the day, anyway. I'm only happy when I'm on stage. Anything else is no fun."

Fats had just hung up the phone. He had been speaking to his wife, Rosemary. Rosemary, as usual, was at home in New Orleans. Fats is on the road ten months a year, and Rosemary never travels with him.

"I wrote a song for her once," Fats said. He began to sing: "If you see Rosemary, tell her I'm comin' home to stay; tell her I'm tired of travelin', can't go on this way." Fats laughed. "Except I'm not going home," he said. "I'm never going off the road. Love the road. Lot of fun."

Rosemary has seen Fats Domino play music before. To be precise, she has seen him play once. That was before they were married, 26 years ago. "She real nice," Fats said. "But she doesn't like to go to the shows, I guess."

Fats is in Chicago, in the midst of a two-week stand in the London House. There is little chance that *Newsweek* will put Fats on the cover with a bannerline saying "Fats Is Back," but if you have been hearing a lot of talk about rock-and-roll legends lately, you might stop in one night and see a real one. From the moment Fats sits down at the piano and leans into "I'm Walkin' " and then goes straight into "Ain't That a Shame?" his show is so fine, so much what rock and roll is supposed to be about, that it is hard to believe he is playing for a roomful of salesmen in town for the housewares show, instead of before 18,000 people in the Chicago Stadium.

Not that Fats minds. "Same show I've always had," he said. "Same songs. Same show I used to do at the Brooklyn Paramount for Alan Freed. I play the same for 60 people as I do for 60,000. I used to play in front of 60,000 people. No difference. Just play and sing."

A visitor asked Fats if he had ever heard the story about how Mick Jagger learned to sing by listening to old Fats Domino records. Fats, not showing much interest, said that he had not.

Well, the visitor said, it's like this. Jagger likes to tell about the days when the Rolling Stones were first recording, and people complained that they couldn't always make out what the lyrics were. And Jagger told them it's supposed to be that way, that he had learned to do that by playing Fats Domino singles—Fats buried his vocals under the instrumentals, and it gave the songs a special sound, and so Jagger would do it, too.

Fats looked at the television. He still did not seem overly excited. "He said that, did he?" Fats said.

He picked up the phone. Before dialing he said, "I don't know why that is. I try to make it so people understand me. I don't try to make it so people don't understand me. I want them to hear the words. Maybe the microphone is bad sometimes. Yeah, I'll bet that's what it is. I never heard that before."

He dialed and then said, "Hello, Royal? Yeah. It's me. Listen. Go over to the club early tonight. Yeah. About an hour early. Yeah. Make sure my microphone is working right. Yeah. You don't forget now. Yeah. My microphone. Make sure it's working. Yeah."

Fats hung up the phone. He is the recipient of 21 gold records, all of them from the days when rock and roll was new. "Now that was a lot of fun," he said. "I knew something was happening. We'd play these shows, and people would start lining up at eight o'clock in the morning. The lines would be seven or eight blocks long.

"You know who came to see me in Las Vegas? You know who I met? The drummer. What's his name? Ringo? The one from the Beatles? He came to see me play. I met him afterwards. He said the Beatles were going back together. No, maybe he didn't say that. Maybe he said he was going out on his own. I forget. He said one thing or the other."

Fats studied the room-service menu. "The reason I don't go out of the room much is that something could go wrong," he said.

"Little things that could get on my mind. I'm not comfortable unless I'm playing, anyway. I try to give 'em what they hear on the record and more. You can't do that after staying up all night and all day. People come out in the cold weather to see me—well, if they're happy, I'm happy. Ain't too many fellows who hang around 12 years without a hit record and people still come out in the cold weather to see 'em."

Fats is 45 years old, and he has been on the road for 23 years. Most of those 23 years have been spent traveling to one-nighters. Fats never has had a manager.

"I make good money, and I spends good money," he said. "I like nice things. I like champagne. My band flies in airplanes."

6
ROAD SONGS

I like the road. Oh, it tends to make me lonesome and a little crazy at times, but a change of scenery can be good if you're looking for columns that you'd never find working out of the city room every day.

These columns have nothing in common save the fact that they were all done during times when I decided that I had to get out of town and take a look around. I sometimes find it easier to meet people on the road; when it's just me and the Holiday Inn, it becomes less of a strain to approach total strangers and begin talking. Columns like "Night Visitor" and "Chop Talk" are examples of this; maybe they never would have got written in Chicago.

A final note: the first piece in this chapter, "Moment of the Heart," was written from the National Student Congress in St. Paul, Minnesota, in the summer of 1970. (It was filed as a news story; this was a year before I began the regular column.) The last piece in this chapter, "Geezer at the Crossroads," was written five summers later, from the 1975 National Student Congress in St. Louis, Missouri. What they have to say about the country or the columnist, I'm not sure. Maybe just that we've both changed. . . .

Moment of the Heart

ST. PAUL—They had been having so many laughs during the long days and noisy nights, these young ones, and someone thought that another funny thing was in order.

So when the time came to put into nomination the names of people who may become the officers of the National Student Association next year, a kid in the back of Macalester College auditorium stepped to a microphone and nominated the boy named Randy.

There was some giggling from the people who knew who Randy was, and then they sat back to wait for the real fun. Because after all the names had been put up for nomination, the people had to get up and make their little speeches and either decline or accept their call from this very important convention known as the National Student Congress.

This boy Randy, you see, has something terribly wrong with his body. He cannot talk right because of it, and he walks funny and he does not look or dress quite as nicely as the other people at the student convention, who are of course the leaders of the nation's campuses and very contemporary and sophisticated.

All week long Randy had been at the congress. He is not a student, but he volunteers for anti-war groups in the Minneapolis-St. Paul area.

It is not hard to imagine how the life of a person with an affliction like Randy's must be, and when he heard the students were coming to town, he decided that he would be with them, because they believe in the same things he does, and they are young like he is, and they might give him a chance.

And throughout the week most of them did. But every time he would go to a microphone to question a speaker, and the halting and broken words would make their agonizing way through the amplifiers, there were a few in the audience who would see how funny it was and really get a good laugh out of it.

So now one of the young campus leaders at the back of the

convention floor had put Randy's name into nomination, and even though he was not a student and even though he was not eligible to be elected, Randy would have to get up and talk in front of the whole congress. And that would be a good one, that scene would.

They started to go through the candidates in alphabetical order. Each of the people made their strong pronouncements about Vietnam and racism and poverty and other important things, and it was getting closer.

Some delegates who say they are Yippies, and think that Jerry Rubin is the name of a god rather than that of a clever man who knows he can sell books by acting crazy, began to throw water balloons. That kind of humor is very big at the congress.

There was only one other candidate to go before Randy. One more until he had to get up, not really knowing he was being made fun of, and address the delegates.

The name of the candidate before Randy was Mary Lou Oates. She works for the National Student Association, and she does not want to be an officer next year. She could have simply declined and sat down.

But she stood up, and her voice was a whisper. She was out on the floor in front of a microphone. She was standing very straight and next to her, holding her hand, was Randy.

"I hope I can get through this without crying," she began softly. "Next to me is a friend of mine, a very special friend of mine, whose name is Randy.

"Randy has been active in the peace movement in Minneapolis," she said. "He has been here at our convention all week. Tonight someone in a burst of hilarity thought it would be a very funny move to nominate Randy for office."

Randy stood next to her with a grinning expression on his face. It was not a grin of joy. It is with him 24 hours a day. He cannot get rid of it. It is impossible to know just how much Randy understands all the time, so it was impossible to know if he could tell exactly what was happening.

"Maybe, at times, I have been hard on people," Mary Lou Oates said. "But I never have tried to do something like this to a person in front of a crowd like this. I never have done that."

Then she looked at Randy and said that he had told her that he was too busy in Minneapolis to run for a national office, but that he appreciated the nomination anyway.

And she gazed as the faces of the delegates, who have polished perfectly the art of looking like college students who are concerned with people. She told them that for once maybe they will understand that there are more important things in this world than being able to talk into a bullhorn and say the political cliches fashionable this season.

And she said that she had told Randy how much they all appreciated the work he was doing, and she asked them to stand up and applaud him to show their thanks. She said that perhaps the next time they were in the streets protesting, they could remember that a friend is a very precious thing, indeed.

They all rose and applauded for Randy, and by now they were on his side. He was waiting for the applause to die down, taking in a very important moment in his life, but Mary Lou Oates had already walked away.

She had brought a piece of dignity and humanity to a convention where those things are often only words. Now she was crying because she was sick of the whole business, and she just wished that it would end and everyone would go home.

Solo Flight

MEMPHIS—There didn't seem to be any reason for the huge trailer truck to be slowing down, but here it was, pulling over to the side of the highway, screeching and puffing as it braked to a quick stop. And then the girl got out.

"Bye. Thanks for the ride," she said. She smiled. God, what a smile, really lovely. You had to like her right there. She waved up at the truck driver.

"Stupid little bitch," he said to her. He spat out his window and, without looking back, ground the truck onto the road.

"Yeah, well thanks anyway," she said, the smile still there, but the truck was gone.

She shrugged a green knapsack up across her shoulder, walked a few feet. She looked funny, bouncing up and down in a laughable kind of way as she walked. But beautiful, really, really pretty, long brown hair and faded jeans and a blue wool jacket and the knapsack. Maybe a young-looking 19.

She had gone 30 feet or so when she decided to stop and sit down. She tossed the knapsack onto the gravel. She used it as a seat, resting her elbows on her knees, and kept an eye on the highway, waiting for a friendly looking car.

The guy who had been watching all this happen walked up to her. When his shadow blocked her sun, she looked up at him, no expression on her face.

How come you're a stupid little bitch? the guy said.

"Oh, that," she said and laughed. Great laugh. "The truck driver was all mad. I'd been riding with him for half an hour, and then he decided that it was time. So he kind of cleared his throat, you know, he kept looking straight ahead, and he asked if I wanted to pull off the side of the road and climb in back of the seat with him. I think the term he used was 'have some fun.' "

Yeah, so what happened? the guy asked.

"I just smiled at him and told him no, I was just along for the ride," she said. "He got mad right away and wouldn't look at me or talk to me. He drove for about five minutes without saying anything, and then he drove off the road and let me off. He was really a pretty good guy until he got all mad. I really liked him, kind of."

She squinted down the highway, waiting. She did not stick her thumb out or give any indication she was looking for a ride. Just waited, looking for a good car.

"I was in North Carolina," she volunteered. "Now I'm trying to get to Oklahoma City. What are you doing?"

It's too complicated, the guy said, and it doesn't make much sense or matter anyway.

"No, I want to know," the girl said.

OK, here we go, the guy said. See, he was supposed to be in St. Louis to meet this senator. The guy was supposed to write a story for a newspaper about the senator. But it was raining in St. Louis, bad, and the pilot tried three landings without making it and finally gave up and came to Memphis instead. And now the guy had five hours before he could get another flight to St. Louis, so he had decided to walk around and look. Which is what he was doing when he ran into the girl and the truck driver who thought she was a stupid little bitch.

"A senator?" the girl said. "That's pretty weird."

True, the guy said, pretty weird. Now drop it.

So she did. She started to talk about her travels. It was the usual thing: she had been a sophomore in college, had become sick of it, and had started out on her own. Except somehow she was not a usual girl because there was little of the jargon in her voice (the comment about being pretty weird excepted), and she had that incredible smile.

OK, so you're on your own, the guy said, but what about things like the truck driver—what do you do when that happens, doesn't it ever get to you?

"I told you, he was a pretty good guy," she said.

I know, terrific, the guy said, but what about the ones who aren't such good guys, what do you do then?

"Usually you just smile and talk to them and laugh," she said. "It's very hard for a man to attack someone who's laughing and smiling at him and talking. They usually just give it up or let me out. Which is fine either way."

You mean every time? the guy asked. It never works out wrong?

"Once," the girl said. "Just one time."

The guy said that since they were such tight friends, he'd like to hear about it.

"It was in Florida," she said. "I'd been down around Lauderdale, and I was hitching back up North. It was hot that day, I remember. These two boys—well, not boys; men, I guess—stopped in a convertible. I got in the back seat, not really thinking about it, and we started driving.

"Usually people will start talking to me right away because a chick hitching alone still makes a lot of people curious. But these two didn't say anything. Nothing. I asked them how far they were going, and still they didn't answer. It got dark, and they drove into the woods, just like they had it planned all along."

And? the guy said.

"And they raped me," the girl said. Just like that.

The guy didn't say anything, just watched the cars for five minutes or so.

"But you know something," the girl said. "As bad as it was, the thought of it was much worse. You know what I mean? All the time I'd been hitching, I'd been thinking, 'Some day it might happen.' And whenever I thought about it, I got scared, chills and all. But as awful as it was, the fear of it was worse."

So what happened? the guy asked.

"The second man got done, and they ran to the car, like they were scared, and they drove away. And I started hitching again."

You didn't tell the cops or anything?

"No. This real nice lady picked me up, and I was crying, and I told her about it. She wanted to take me to the police, but I told her to forget it, I was all right. And I just tried to forget about it."

But now don't you think about it? the guy asked. When something like the truck driver thing happens, don't you think about it?

"Sure," she said quietly. "I think about it."

They talked for some time, and a very pleasant conversation it was. She kept flashing that smile, and the cars kept racing by.

Don't mean to get personal, the guy said, but don't you ever get scared or lonely or sick or lost? It can't be as good as the cliche would have it; you're not in the middle of some highway movie, this is real life, and there must be some bad times, too. Aren't there?

"Yeah," the girl said. "A lot of them."

It was getting to be dusk, and the guy's plane was going to be leaving for St. Louis, and he had to get back to the Memphis airport in time to catch it.

"Look," the girl said. She stopped.

Yes, what? the guy said.

"Look," she said, "If you want to, you can come with me. I mean, I'm going to Oklahoma, I told you, but that's pretty far away, and if you want to, I wouldn't mind it. I mean, only if you want to."

Yes, the guy said, he wanted to, but that didn't matter, really, he said, because he had to meet that senator who probably was already gone from St. Louis, so he had to get on that plane and go to St. Louis and somehow track the man down. But yes, he wanted to, and no, he couldn't.

"OK," the girl said. The smile again. She lifted herself up and walked forward ten yards until she was right beside the highway again.

The headlights came streaking by, and the guy sat back and watched it all. After about five minutes a new Pontiac pulled over. The driver opened the door on the passenger side. The light inside the car showed that he was about 40, with graying, slicked-back hair.

"Need a ride?" the driver said.

The girl nodded her head and threw her knapsack in. Then she turned to the guy sitting by the side of the road again and smiled a last time before getting in. The guy sitting by the road just looked at her.

The driver saw the guy sitting on the side of the road, too. The driver looked at the guy and gave him a greasy little wink. The guy wished very hard that the driver would drop dead.

Then the car joined the line of other cars on the highway. The guy watched it until the red taillights disappeared, and then began to walk. Had to get to St. Louis.

No Regrets

VALPARAISO, Ind.—He is, in an ironic and somehow poignant way, the ultimate victim of Watergate. Less than a year ago he was a national oddity, an outrageous headline figure in the news. That was when he was a member of Congress, the last congressman in the United States to stand behind the presidency of Richard Nixon. Today he sits in a local restaurant, sipping coffee before going to work at his trucking firm. His name is Earl Landgrebe; he is no longer a congressman, and he is still puzzled about how it could have worked out this way.

"Maybe I am a country boy who went to the big city, got stars in his eyes from being around the president and his wife," Landgrebe says. "But they were and are great people. I am ashamed of nothing. I have no regrets. I am extremely proud."

To read about Landgrebe in the papers last year was to experience a combination of rage and astonishment at a congressman who could behave the way he was behaving. With all of the evidence piling up against Nixon, Landgrebe said, "Don't confuse me with facts; I've got a closed mind." He said, "I will stick with my president even if he and I have to be taken out of this building and shot." As congressional support for Nixon dropped away to no one but Landgrebe, he stopped angering people and instead became a joke. When the Republican national committeeman from Indiana was asked about fellow Republican Landgrebe by a reporter from the *Wall Street Journal,* the committeeman would say only, "I didn't know the *Journal* had a comic page."

After Nixon left office, Landgrebe continued to defend him, and last fall the voters in his highly conservative district replaced him with a Democrat. Landgrebe had come to be an embarrassment. So he is home again, working at the Landgrebe Motor Transport Company, and still trying to figure out how his own life became enmeshed so inextricably with that of a President of the United States.

"I guess if the president can be throwed out, then sure enough this little truck driver can be throwed out, too," Landgrebe says. He is 59 years old; to sit and talk with him for most of a morning is to find a pleasant, open man who is not very sophisticated, not very worldly, not much of a questioner or a thinker—and who is so fearsomely trusting of what he had grown up believing about the White House that he could be fooled by Richard Nixon even after virtually all of his fellow countrymen had regretfully accepted the truth.

"I didn't mean that quote about the president and me being taken out and shot to be a rhetorical flourish," Landgrebe says. "I meant it as an actual happening. Thousands of men died with live bullets for their country."

He still believes that Nixon was guiltless of wrongdoing. In a patient, bloodless way Landgrebe says he does not even think that the man uttering the profanities on the White House tapes was really Nixon. "I never even heard him say 'darn it,' or tell an off-color story," Landgrebe says. He smiles, almost apologetically. "My warped brain shows through here," he says, before explaining his theory of the tapes:

Landgrebe says that he had seen, on television, a mimic—he thinks it may have been comedian David Frye—"who looked and sounded just like President Nixon." It is Landgrebe's thought that someone, perhaps this same comedian, might have impersonated Nixon's voice, "and made tapes and put them in the stack."

It is not difficult to draw quotes like that one from Landgrebe; he has not learned from the Nixon experience, and, indeed, is even more adamant about Nixon's innocence now. But to talk quietly with him is to come away feeling for him. "I loved being in the Congress," he says. "It was the joy of my life. I miss it very much." One does not necessarily have to wish that Landgrebe were still in Congress to understand that there should be no glee felt over the bittersweet story of a rural Indiana small businessman who got in over his head, and who was done in while defending the deeds of men far cagier and more calculating than himself.

"My God," Landgrebe says, "it was the presidency. My wife and I are flag-waving Americans. We were taught to appreciate the system." And when one suggests to Landgrebe that perhaps the departure of Richard Nixon from office represented the working of the American system at its very finest, Landgrebe can only hesitate, and then reply, "Ha, ha, ha."

The talk in Landgrebe's district is that, because of his handling of the Nixon situation, he is washed up. "I'm not a has-been," Landgrebe says. But then he says, "You know, there was a little meeting at the church last night, and Helen and I went to it and were home by 10:00. I brushed my teeth and fell into bed. Why, many nights when I was in Washington, I was too tired to brush my teeth at all. I'd have to wait until morning."

When he looks back on the events that led to his own political downfall, Landgrebe is a little confused. "The hell of it is that there weren't enough Landgrebes to come out and defend Nixon," he says. "Just one little weak voice. I guess my little weak voice got lost."

Richard Nixon never thanked Landgrebe for his continuing support. But Landgrebe does not seem to mind this, either.

"There are ways of telling your sweetheart that you love her

other than embracing her and licking her in the face and telling her
that you love her," Landgrebe says. "There's a look in the eye or a
handshake. I didn't stand by Nixon for glory or for honor. I stood by
him because I was totally convinced. I don't need pats on the back.

"I wish you had some kind of scope so you could see inside my
heart," Landgrebe says. "I don't feel sorrow or shame for what I did.
This man was elected president. He was a president I had the
privilege of knowing. I think he is a really nice man." And with that
Earl Landgrebe excuses himself and goes off to work.

Flower of Fatherhood

NEW YORK—The long wait was over, and now she had the
purple orchid. The orchid, and her memories; she was taking them
both home with her, on this Saturday afternoon in May.

Her name was Linda King, and she was on her way back to
Browns Mills, New Jersey, where her husband would be worrying.
He had wanted to come with her on this trip, but she had told him
no; had said that he must understand, she had been waiting 27 years
for this, and it was something she must do by herself.

She looked out the window of the American Airlines flight,
and she gingerly touched the orchid. It was real; it was proof. She
smiled easily to herself.

When Linda was six months old, her parents had been
divorced. She had never seen her father. Many times he had tried to
come and visit her, but her stepfather had forbidden it, had said it
would only do the girl harm. And so she had never known the look
of her father's face, never heard the sound of his voice.

Soon the father had stopped trying. He was not heard from.
Linda had grown up. She had worked as a cocktail waitress, and as a
go-go girl, dancing over the bars at highway truckstops like the

Stage Door, and the Seven Gables in Elizabeth, New Jersey. This year she had gotten married, and had quit the bar dancing. She had a better job now, working for a major airline.

Still, though, there was not a week when she did not think about the father—if he was alive, what he was doing, if he remembered her. Sometimes it would be when another person would say, "I haven't seen my dad in a long time"; sometimes it would be when she was watching television, and a show would feature a good, loving father. Usually it was at night.

This spring, she did it. Her vacation was coming up, and she knew she would have the time. So she searched out her birth certificate, and she found out her real name. She started making telephone calls. In Salt Lake City she found her father's mother. Yes, the old woman said over the telephone, he is alive. He lives here in town. He is not married. He has no other children.

Linda did not know what to say when she called the man. She hesitated. But the grandmother had given her the telephone number, and Linda dialed, and when the man answered, she said, "This is Linda, do you want to see me?"

"I have always wanted to see you," the father said.

So on the Wednesday before, she had flown, alone, to Utah. Her father had not been waiting at the airport. But the grandmother was there; the old woman told Linda that the father was nervous, he was afraid to come. He was waiting back at the old woman's house.

They drove. When they arrived, there were two men in the kitchen. The grandmother pointed at one of the men, and said, "This is your Uncle Don." She pointed to the second man, and said, "And this is your father."

Linda looked at the man, and she thought, This is my father; this is my blood.

They did not speak for a moment. Finally Linda talked. "Can I call you dad?" she said.

"You better," the father said. They looked at one another. "You better," he said again, and he touched her face.

In the next few days Linda spent all of her time with him. She found out about him; that he had no job, that his life had been mostly troubles. She found out, from the grandmother, that the father had been afraid that the daughter would see him and not be proud of him, be disappointed after all this time.

"You're my father," she said to him one afternoon. "I love you."

Since she had been a child, she had not been able to sleep well. In Utah she slept all night, every night. The father had no money, and neither did the grandmother, so on the second night, Linda had said, "Let me take you to dinner." But the grandmother said, "If we couldn't feed you, we wouldn't have asked you to come here," and they ate at home.

Sometimes Linda thought how old her father looked. She knew that he was no more than 50 or so, but he appeared to be 70. She wondered what he had looked like as a young man.

On Friday night, at the dinner table, the father handed Linda two small photographs. They were of an infant girl.

"That's you," he said. "When your mother and I separated, I took these from her wallet. I've carried them all these years."

There was a box on the table, and the father pushed it toward Linda. "I bought this for you," he said.

It was the purple orchid. Linda knew that the father did not have the money to buy the flower, but she did not say anything about that. She said, "It's beautiful; thank you," and she pinned it to her blouse.

In the morning she had boarded her flight, still wearing the flower. "I'm not going to say good-by, because I'm coming back soon," she said. "You will meet my husband then." The father had nodded.

In Chicago she had changed planes, and now she was coming into New York, from where she would drive home. A stewardess on the flight saw Linda's orchid, and stopped in the aisle. "What a beautiful flower," the stewardess said. "Did you just get married?"

"No," Linda said. "It was a gift from my father."

Modern Wedding

SHORT HILLS, N.J.—It has been several years since I reported on the style of modern wedding ceremonies. The last time I checked, the fashion was for both principals to wear garlands of flowers in their hair, say their marriage vows in an open field and recite self-composed poetry to each other while a Simon and Garfunkel song featuring the words "organdy" and "crinoline" played in the background.

So when a wedding invitation arrived in the mail recently, I welcomed the chance to take another look. My initial thought was that the flowers-and-meadows style of wedding might have passed on by this time. And when a closer examination of the invitation revealed that the prospective groom was none other than Mr. Lee Ottenberg, I was sure of it. Mr. Ottenberg, regular readers of this space may recall, is the horrid facsimile of a photographer who has accompanied me on a number of stories. Although Mr. Ottenberg has yet to produce an in-focus photograph, he has gained entrance to events ranging from Alice Cooper tours to the Watergate hearings, always in the guise of a member of the working photographic press corps. The thought of Mr. Ottenberg getting married with daisies in his hair and a pristine toga on his body is beyond comprehension, so it seems that the Ottenberg wedding will be as good a place as any to examine the new, 1973 wedding style. It only makes good journalistic sense to get on a plane for New Jersey.

1:05 P.M.—Arrive at Newark Airport. Think about finding a cab. Discover this will not be necessary, for standing in the concourse, by the metal detection shed, are Mr. Ottenberg himself and old college chum Max Levin. Max Levin's airport garb consists of Hawaiian swimming trunks, Super Fly shoes, and no shirt. Mr. Ottenberg, in the hours before this sobering and momentous event in his life, does not seem to be especially nervous. Mr. Ottenberg is leaning against the metal detection shed, practicing with his newly acquired Duncan Imperial Championship YoYo. Uniformed security guard requests that Mr. Ottenberg move somewhere else just as Mr. Ottenberg is perfecting "walk the doggie" technique.

1:12 P.M.—En route to motor inn. I ask Mr. Ottenberg if he is having any poignant, last-minute thoughts before his wedding. Mr. Ottenberg turns up volume on car radio so he can clearly hear "We're an American Band" by Grand Funk. "You know who I saw at the Hamburger Haven outside Washington the other day?" Mr. Ottenberg says. "H. R. Haldeman. He was sitting in a booth for two by himself. He was eating a bleu-cheeseburger with bacon and reading the *Washington Post.*"

3:10 P.M.—Mr. Ottenberg is watching "Boxing from Madison Square Garden" on a motel room television set. He is asked directions to the building where the wedding will take place. "I don't know, it's a small town, I'm sure we'll find it," Mr. Ottenberg says. He is asked where he and his bride will be spending the night. "I don't know, I didn't make any reservations," Mr. Ottenberg says. "Have you ever known me not to find a place to sleep? Look, I think that guy in the dark trunks is about ready to take a dive."

5:05 P.M.—Wedding time is fast approaching. Mr. Ottenberg is watching ABC's "Wide World of Sports" and simultaneously performing "rock the cradle" with his Duncan Imperial. Also in the room are Max Levin, second college chum Steve Kolker, and this correspondent. "Don't you think we ought to buy you a nice bachelor dinner?" Kolker says to Mr. Ottenberg. "Yeah," Mr. Ottenberg says, his eyes on the TV screen. He picks up the phone. "Room service?" Mr. Ottenberg says. "Send me 12 orders of fried clams and some tartar sauce and three six-packs of beer and a side order of vodka."

6:15 P.M.—Mr. Ottenberg is dressing for the wedding. He is putting his tuxedo shirt on over the Led Zeppelin T-shirt he has been wearing for three days. This is the traditional time for the friends of the groom to help him on with his bow tie and suspenders. But Max Levin and Steve Kolker are too busy. They have not seen each other in two years, and each does not want the other to think he is falling behind in the world of business. Each is 25 years old.

"I would like to put up a high-rise condominium in Cincinnati," Max Levin says, "and I would like you to help me finance it."

Steve Koiker nods. "I will be glad to," Kolker says, "but I must be quite frank with you. I cannot even consider it unless you have a million dollars in capital."

Max Levin gestures expansively.

"No problem," he says.

Both Steve Kolker and Max Levin had hidden in the bathroom when it was time to give the room service waiter a tip. Mr. Ottenberg slips on his tuxedo jacket and leaves the motel to go to his wedding.

7:10 P.M.—The three friends of the groom arrive at the site of the wedding. It is a building constructed so that a large number of weddings can be run off simultaneously; its owners are prospering. When we find the room designated for Mr. Ottenberg's wedding, the guests are eating from a 60-foot buffet table and dancing to a full symphony orchestra playing "On the Street Where You Live." We make the only logical assumption: we have missed the wedding, and this is the reception and dinner.

7:12 P.M.—"You have not missed the wedding," Mr. Ottenberg says. "This is merely the warm-up." Mr. Ottenberg is not even married yet, and he is being surrounded by well-wishers. The older gentlemen at the wedding keep asking Mr. Ottenberg what he thinks of the Watergate situation. It is very hard for Mr. Ottenberg to discuss this since his interest in politics never got past the stage of "Dump the Hump." Approximately 650 pounds of food have already been consumed by the guests, and the wedding ceremony still shows no sign of starting.

8:05 P.M.—The wedding is starting. Mr. Ottenberg and his bride come walking down a runway long enough to accommodate a 747. Similar ceremonies are taking place all over this wedding factory. Mr. Ottenberg looks distinctly uncomfortable about being a guest at a public function to which he is legitimately invited. All the excitement is gone for him.

8:12 P.M.—The man performing the ceremony says, "As you are joined as man and wife, before the eyes of God in this consecrated hall of Short Hills Caterers, Short Hills, New Jersey. . . ." Mr. Ottenberg turns around to make sure the visiting correspondent is taking notes. Mr. Ottenberg need not have worried.

8:32 P.M.—The wedding is over. There is more food in another room. But Mr. Ottenberg and his bride are not in the reception line to greet the guests. Before there is time to wonder about this, the lights in the room go out.

8:33 P.M.—The guests are all standing in the darkness. Suddenly a spotlight hits the door. There is a drum roll. "Ladies and gentlemen," comes the amplified voice of a professional announcer, "will you give a big welcome to . . . MR. AND MRS. LEE OTTENBERG!!!" The symphony bursts into song. In walk Mr. Ottenberg and his bride. Mr. Ottenberg is trying to imitate the swagger Mick Jagger used in the movie *Gimme Shelter* when the Rolling Stones came on stage for "Jumpin' Jack Flash." He gives up as the symphony launches into the strains of "Summer of '42."

9:10 P.M.—The ninth course of the sit-down dinner is in the process of being served. The orchestra is playing "These Are a Few of My Favorite Things." There will be no Simon and Garfunkel. 1969 is over. There will be no self-composed poetry or flowers in the hair.

9:47 P.M.—Max Levin, who has been missing for 15 minutes, hurries into the dinner room. "Quick," he says, "come with me. I've been checking out the other weddings in the building. And I went to the reception down the hallway, and I walked in, and the bride and groom were dancing their first dance . . . and I swear to you, the bride was trying to make eye contact with me. I would not lie about something like this." Mr. Ottenberg overhears this, and asks if he can come along to the other wedding. He is given a polite but firm no. The orchestra is playing "Lara's Theme." Mr. Ottenberg returns to his table. The fourteenth course is being served.

Night Visitor

LOUISVILLE—It didn't look like his kind of place. The saloon was too noisy, too new, too full of young laughter. But he didn't hesitate. He walked past the tables filled with people out for the evening, and pulled up a chair at the bar.

"I would like," the man said, then paused as if pondering a question of major importance—"I would like one Schlitz."

He reached forward to take the glass. The hands were those of an old farmer—rough and scarred and hard. He wore a red shirt and an old gray coat. His hair was white, cut close to the scalp and high around the ears.

He tried to start a conversation with the man on his left, a salesman in town on business. "The name's Judd," he said, offering his hand. "Cecil Judd, from Greensburg, about 80 miles south of here." But the salesman, made uncomfortable by having the greetings of the old farmer thrust upon him here, made a quick excuse and walked out of the room.

"Wonder what his hurry was," Cecil Judd said. "Say," he called to someone sitting nearby. "How old would you say I was?

"I'll give you a hint," Judd said. "I've been married 40 years. I won't keep you waiting, I'll tell you. I'm 70."

He said that he decided a long time ago that he would not let his life rot away before his eyes in rural Kentucky. "A man could go crazy down there," he said. "Me and Maggie, that's my wife, we decided a lot of years ago—if she goes her way and I go mine, we'll be all the happier. And we're still living in Greensburg, and we're still married. I don't know where the hell she is tonight. Probably at some women's club or something. But I'll see her by the time it's time to go to sleep. If she's having a good time tonight—more power to her, I say.

"Me, I get up here to Louisville whenever I can. I like this place especially. This is where the fun is. Have me some drinks and raise a little hell." He was still holding the first glass of beer, and he had hardly sipped any of it.

"You ever meet anybody famous?" Cecil Judd asked. He did not wait for an answer. "Well I did. It was in Macomb, Illinois. I went into a tavern, and there was this man at the bar. I didn't know who he was, and we started to talk. I thought he was just a fellow like anybody else. Then these people come in and start asking for his autograph. And he signs them, just like he's used to it. So I say to him, doesn't that bother you, all those people asking for your autograph? and he says, 'When they stop asking, that's when I'll be bothered.' And you know who it was?

"Harry James! The famous bandleader! Talking to me just like we were old buddies. I says to him, 'Hey, how's Betty Grable?' and he says, 'Now why's everyone always asking me, how's Betty Grable?'

So I right away change the subject, and everything is fine after that."

He said that tonight he was waiting for a man to meet him, but the man was late. The saloon was in a big hotel, and the friend was attending a meeting in the hotel. "He's a surgeon," Cecil Judd said. "He takes me a lot of places with him. If he doesn't know to look for me in the barroom, then I give up."

He kept talking, about old times and horse races and Kentucky life, and after a while it seemed that maybe there was no surgeon friend, and maybe he was alone. And he kept holding the one beer, hardly touching it. "Don't know where that pal of mine might be," he said, but not very convincingly. He didn't even bother to look over at the door.

He started to bring up Harry James again, then thought better of it. "I come to this bar too often and spend too much money," Cecil Judd said. "It's about time to get home to Maggie, anyway. She's a hell of a good girl, and I'll fight you from here to now on if you tell me she's not. Bartender," he said, pushing his single beer away, "I think I'll stop here." He paid for it with a dollar bill.

"Lots of luck to you," he said as he got up to leave. "Whatever you try to do, I hope you do it." And he left the place.

The bartender came over. "Did that old fellow say he comes in here a lot?" the bartender said. "That's what I thought I heard him say. I wonder why he said that. I've never seen him before in my life."

Stealing Time

TREMONT, Ind.—Thoughts on getting out of town:

Maybe it's the sense of winter ending, or maybe it comes from a more personal changing of the seasons. Whatever, you find yourself doing it again: getting on a train and riding it out of Chicago and renting a room for the night in some town where you don't know anyone, and they don't know you, and that's the plan.

You can still do it, although it seems that before too long the railroads will all be gone, even the few escape routes that are left, and then the road will be made up only of freeway exits, and part of the random feel of picking a stop by instinct will be dead. But it is still worthy of a try, and for some reason you are willing to try it more and more often.

To watch the city disappear mile by mile is a luxury whose appeal is made stronger by its unexpected nature; it shouldn't feel so good. But it does, and the feeling is heightened by the thought that no one knows where you will end up, not even yourself, and so there will be no telephones to ring you awake, no voices to hail you on the street.

The others on the train are all going somewhere, but you are only going away, and that can be the truest vacation of all. The time factor does not count; you can leave in the afternoon and be back by the next noon, and no one will know that you were even gone. If it is important enough to you, hours and minutes have nothing to do with it.

If you tell yourself that you are looking for the country, you will be disappointed, because that is hard to find anymore. There are too many fast-food restaurants, and too many motels with national names you have seen advertised on your television, and if you are searching for a place that has not been touched by the urbanization of America, your search may take longer than the time that you have stolen for yourself. But if you accept that, and tell yourself that all you want is a smaller place in which to keep company with yourself, then it can be all right.

Because if you look, you can still find that there are places that help. You can still find a real town square to walk around, with the police station and the town hall and the dinner restaurant all within sight of one another. You can still find a community movie theater that has one show each night, and devotes the first ten minutes on the screen to slides advertising for local merchants who know that it is a sure way to reach their people. You can walk in a neighborhood where you will see four cars in the course of an hour.

And if you don't want to, you won't hear the sound of your own voice. You can walk all evening, or just sit and watch this part of the world, and never be compelled to make a conversation or look to see who else is around. You may surprise yourself when ten o'clock comes and you don't even have the urge to turn on the news, and you don't care what you may have missed.

It can be so good that you find yourself not wanting to go to sleep, even though there is nothing better to do. You go back to your room and sit by the window with your legs draped over a chair, one light burning over on the table, and you look out at the night and lose track of time. The hours go by without a sound, and you let them.

In the morning you go outside early and watch the highway before breakfast. You eat by yourself and don't hurry, and you don't look at your watch to see if you're making anyone else check their watches in some office in the Chicago Loop.

And when you leave, it should be with the understanding that you won't be back, not to the place you have been this time. Because if you're out to grab a moment for yourself, you can't do it in a place you've ever seen, or on a road you've ever walked. You've got to be selfish enough not to let your memories intrude.

When you take the train back to Chicago, there is no reason to let anyone know where you have been, or what you have done, or why. There should be a part of your life that is allowed to remain your own. You shouldn't share it, or it will lose whatever there was in it for you. You should never put it in a newspaper. . . .

Chop Talk

SACRAMENTO, Calif.—In the morning he was drinking whisky. The bottom of his glass made wet little circles on the Formica tabletop, and he called for another. There were only a few people in the airport bar, and the rest of them were drinking bloody marys.

Outside the big picture window, one 747 after another approached the runway, almost touched down, then pulled up and away. Someone said the airport was being used for pilot training, but no one knew for sure. They just watched the giant planes come down and then lift up again.

All around the airport they were looking, but he was not. He just took the top off his latest glass of whisky and glanced at his watch. For Robert Locasto, it was time to leave another city.

He was at the table by himself. On the carpet, next to his feet, was the old leather case that is the story of his life. The top of the case was unbuckled, and you could see what it was carrying.

It was one of those machines that chop up fruits and vegetables and ice. You've seen them on television thousands of times. Locasto noticed that someone was looking at the case, and he kicked it under the table and out of sight. Then he apparently thought better of it, and began to talk.

"Use it as a mixer, a dicer, a chopper, a slicer," he said in a rapid, nasal voice. "Make the kiddies snow cones. Chops potatoes, even tomatoes, with no mess at all. Just run it under your kitchen faucet to clean it quickly and completely."

He said it without a smile and then returned to his drink. He looked up, and the person who had been watching him was still there. "Don't say it," he said. "I know. *Death of a Salesman*, right?"

He asked the other person if he wanted to sit down. "I've got about an hour until my flight anyway," Locasto said. "I seem to spend more time in airports and bus stations than I do at home."

He sells the things. It is what he has been doing all his life, in one form or another. Sometimes it has been knife sharpeners, and sometimes can openers, and now it is these choppers. But Locasto is 50 years old, and he is in trouble.

"It's the one thing I've ever been able to do," he said. "I can talk to a crowd and make them want to listen. I used to be able to say that I could sell anything. but the damned TV, it's killing me.

"I go into a store and set up my display, and people don't even look at me. They see these things advertised on television every day, and they watch a guy doing it in a store and they figure you're seedy or something. You know, like it's OK on TV, but it depresses them to see a man making his living by pushing this stuff."

Locasto says he sets up the chopping machine and goes into his talk, and then at the end he takes orders and money. But it isn't working anymore.

"You know how many orders I got in this town?" he said. "Four. And that's in a day-and-a-half of working. And I can guarantee you, just by looking at the people, that at least one of those checks is going to bounce. And my commission comes out of that.

"I remember the state fairs, we used to have to get the cops to make the people stand in line. It was a gold mine. We were all like stars at the fairs, people would talk about which of us put on the best show. Now, it's like there's something distasteful about a man who's trying to sell people something face-to-face. I don't know why it is, why people feel that way. Sometimes I get done at the end of the day, and I feel like I've been committing a crime or something. I think people get scared at the personal touch anymore, they feel more comfortable with no human contact at all."

The announcement of his flight came over the public-address system, and Locasto buckled up his case. "I'm a jetsetter these days," he said. "I used to like the train stations better."

David's Chance

SAN FRANCISCO—Another hip crowd in another muggy auditorium on another California night. Everyone in the dressing room was so involved in discussing where they could score some cocaine and other matters of importance that they did not pay any attention when the young man came through the door. When they turned, he was just there. Some of them laughed when they saw him.

He introduced himself. "My name is David Sewall," he said,

and it came out in nervous, embarrassed, soft gasps. The backstage people got a kick out of that one; they are the ones who move on the periphery of the rock and drug scenes, who hang around the important people, and they do it without benefit of talent or worth. They do it on the basis of loudness and persistence and pure arrogant self-confidence, a knowledge that they can barge their way into the glamour world solely on the basis of pushing until they are there. And to see a young man like this David Sewall, who was so nervous just to be backstage—well, this was one to smirk about and to exchange glances over.

Besides, look at the kid. He had a short haircut. He was wearing a black tuxedo, and he had a top hat. By now all the blue-jeaned backstage people were looking at him and waiting for him to do something else. He started to say something, then shook his head and walked to a corner. The smiles were spreading around the room. The people had come for a rock-and-roll show tonight, but this David Sewall was giving them an extra comedy act.

He reached into a case he was carrying, and he pulled out a very old violin. Without saying a word, he began to play. It was beautiful, lilting music. It was hard to hear, because the sound of the opening rock act was blasting through the walls from the nearby stage. But there was no mistaking it; this kid in the tuxedo could play the violin.

He stopped in the middle of a quiet passage. "I was just kind of wondering," he said. "I mean, if it's not all right, I understand. But I mean, I just sort of hoped . . . I didn't know who to ask, but I thought I should try." He looked around the room, and was met with silence.

"I want to play in front of people," he said. More silence.

He began to explain that he had always wanted the chance to make his violin music in front of an audience, but that the only place young people go for entertainment anymore is to rock-and-roll shows. He said he was wondering if he could play in this auditorium tonight, just for a few minutes between sets, just so a real audience could hear how he performed.

But the people in the dressing room were losing interest, because the members of the featured rock-and-roll band were beginning to drift into the room to swig some whisky before it was their time to go onstage. So David Sewall went back to the corner and played his violin a little more. By this time no one was listening.

The sound of the opening act stopped. It was time for the equipment men to go onto the stage and shift the gear around in preparation for the featured band. David Sewall walked out to the wings.

And then he did it. With a dozen equipment men moving drums and wires and amplifiers all around him, he walked onto the stage. He took a breath, lifted his violin, and began to play.

Without the aid of the massive sound system used in the auditorium, it was very hard to hear him. Most of the people were filing out to the lobby for a smoke and did not see David Sewall. The ones who stayed in their seats during the intermission did not know what to make of it. A kid in a tux playing the violin while people pushed past him with crates and guitar cases.

The people in the audience did not stop their talking or their moving around, but David Sewall did not seem to mind. He was smiling broadly as he played away. From close range it sounded sweet and wonderful. The sweat had come to his forehead, and he looked very happy.

It lasted only a few minutes. The rock band's equipment was ready, and the people were starting to come back to their seats. He sensed it was time to get off. "Thank you all very much," David Sewall said, and a couple of people near the front applauded for a second or two.

Within a minute the featured rock band was on the stage, and the crowd was on its feet and whooping. David Sewall was wandering around the deserted backstage area, looking for someone to talk to about his big moment. But the only person he could find was a uniformed security guard, sitting in a folding chair by the stage door.

"Did I do all right?" David Sewall asked.

"Didn't see you," the security guard said.

Geezer at the Crossroads

ST. LOUIS—The old geezer was at the end of his rope. Ever since he had packed his bag in Chicago and headed down to the 1974 National Student Congress, his petulance had been building. Now in the middle of a convention session, his patience was gone. He limped over to one of the student delegations.

"Name's Greene," the geezer wheezed. "Northwestern. Class of '69. Political power comes at the barrel of a gun."

The students looked at him with bemusement in their eyes. Some fought to repress giggles.

The geezer coughed. Dust billowed from the front of his shirt. "If you're not part of the solution, you're part of the problem," he croaked. "What's wrong with you whelps? You call yourselves students? Stop the war in Vietnam, bring the boys home!"

There was muffled laughter from the student delegation. "Here, old timer," said a representative from Northern Illinois University. "Let me fix you a drink. What would you like? Gin? Vodka? Tequila? Imported champagne? We have it all here on the floor of the convention."

The geezer shakily waved his fist in the air. He drew a rheumy breath, and began to sing in a decrepit, off-key wail: "All we are saying, is give peace a chance . . ."

A crowd began to gather. Up at the podium a speaker was advising the assembled students on how best to invest their money in tax-free municipal bonds. But in the audience the attention was being drawn to the geezer.

"Why, you ought to be ashamed of yourselves!" the old fellow rasped. "When I was your age, we were stopping an unjust war, we were! We shut down a thousand campuses in a single week! And you! What have you done? What have you got to tell your grandchildren?"

A woman student said, "Try to relax, sir. You're only exciting yourself. Remember your heart. We're not bad people. We're just interested in going to college and having a good time without hassling anybody."

The old man was wracked by a sudden coughing jag. A student tried to pound him on the back to bring him out of it, but the geezer jerked away. He wagged a quavering finger at the students. "I don't need your help!" he wheezed. "Get your hands off me!" The coughing continued, and the old fellow struggled to talk between asthmatic bursts. "Ho, Ho, Ho Chi Minh, NLF is gonna win," he managed to murmur, before weakening again.

A concerned student laid down his copy of the *Wall Street Journal* to focus full attention on the geezer. "Sir, perhaps you'd better go up to your hotel room and rest for a while," the student said. "You could come back down here to our convention after you feel a little stronger."

"Stronger?" the old man hissed. "You're telling me about strength? We are the people our parents warned us against! Death to the fascist state!"

"Yes, yes," said a sympathetic co-ed. "You'll feel much better soon, I'm certain." Up at the podium, a student leader was praising the President of the United States.

The old man pounded his hands unsteadily on the table, attempting to set a rhythm for a song he was determined to try: "Tin soldiers and Nixon coming, we're finally on our own: this summer I hear the drumming, four dead in Ohio. . . ."

As the old fellow gasped the words to the song, the students looked at one another warily. One suggested calling the police.

"I heard that!" the geezer snapped. "Off the pig!"

"Sir, we're not trying to be rude," a delegate said. "It's just that we can't relate to you. We don't mean to be making fun. It's just that . . . well, we don't know exactly how to deal with you."

This latest rebuff seemed to throw the geezer into a geriatric frenzy. His wheezing intensified, and he appeared to become delirious. He raved at the students and rocked unsteadily in his chair. "Free Bobby!" he said. "Jerry Rubin, be like him, dare to struggle, dare to win! And it's one, two, three, what are we fighting for; don't ask me, I don't give a damn, next stop is Vietnam! Revolution's the only solution! Free all political prisoners! Paul's dead! Power to the people!"

The students were clearly becoming bored. They began to drift away, to listen to a convention speaker discuss career opportunities in Today's Army. Within a few minutes the old fellow was ranting to himself. He saw that he was alone, and he got up to look for a pay telephone.

When he had found one, he placed a long-distance call to a familiar number in Chicago.

The call was answered after two rings. "City desk," said a voice on the other end.

The geezer cleared his chest. "You don't need a weatherman to know which way the wind blows," he croaked.

"Oh, it's you," said the voice. "We've been wondering when you'd call. We think it's about time you came home."

The geezer hung up the phone. He saw a woman student passing by, and flashed her the peace sign. She slapped him across the face, knocking him to the floor. "Fresh," she said.

7

"THIS IS NOT JOURNALISM"

The column goes out on the *Sun-Times* wire service to 110 or so other newspapers, and after I had been writing for three or four months, I received a letter from the managing editor of a client newspaper in North Carolina. Attached was a clipping of one of my stories, and this was the letter in its entirety:

> Dear Mr. Greene:
> This is not journalism.

I think I know what he had in mind. Some of the things that I have tried to do with the column have not exactly fit into the traditional mold of the professional journalistic societies. For example, when Elvis Presley released an album offering snippets of his clothing enclosed inside each record jacket, I ran a column saying that any readers who would like a piece of my blue jeans could send in a stamped, self-addressed envelope and get the patches back in the return mail. It was supposed to be a joke, but almost a thousand readers wrote in, and so I had to cut up the blue jeans and send them out.

On another occasion, when an attorney general of the United

States named Richard Kleindienst was making all kinds of demands for reporters' notes, I suggested in print that every reporter in the country clean off the old press releases, coffee cups, discarded leads, magazines, undecipherable scrawlings, and worn-out mittens from on top, beneath, and around their desks (if you've ever seen what a city room looks like, you know what I mean), put the garbage in bags, and send the bags along to Kleindienst. The *Bulletin of the American Society of Newspaper Editors* liked the idea so much that they reprinted the column; if Kleindienst wanted reporters' notes, then he was going to get notes. I never did get a thank-you letter from the attorney general, but then he left office in kind of a hurry.

The point of all this, of course, is that if you're lucky enough to have a daily column at your disposal, you might as well have a little fun with it. Other reporters in the profession seem to have more trouble dealing with these kinds of columns than does the general public, and I would say that the first piece in this chapter, "The Ballad of Bobby Greene," set some sort of record for hostility within the newsroom. But within a week of the ballad stunt, the following events occurred:

1) Between 500,000 and one million persons attempted to get through to the song on the automatic telephone answering machines.

2) Three of Chicago's highest-rated radio stations began to play the song in prime time.

3) A "greatest hits" record company acquired rights to the ballad and included it on an album that was advertised and marketed nationally.

So . . . as for the ballad column, and the others in this chapter, I suppose that "this is not journalism." But it's sure not a bad way to break the boredom.

The Ballad of
Bobby Greene

If you pick up your telephone and dial 555-7600, you will hear this column's new theme song: "The Ballad of Bobby Greene."

A little background is in order:

As you may recall, several weeks ago we printed a column concerning "chemistry" in the news business and how important it has become. I stressed that television news shows have demonstrated that reporting, accuracy, and integrity have nothing to do with journalistic success these days. Rather, "chemistry"—the transmission of a favorable image to the public—is the only factor that counts.

Well, the more I thought about it, the more I realized that a theme song was essential. After all, Bill Kurtis and Walter Jacobson began to make it on Channel 2 only after their highly sincere "It Takes Two to Track 'Em Down" song was played enough on the air to become a part of the public consciousness. That fellow Mister Geraldo Rivera has his own song, and it's got him a network variety show. Larry Lujack and all the big Top 40 disk jockeys have their own jingles that they play 22 times an hour.

So I figured it was time to make my move. I went to Happy Day Productions, a hot young Chicago-based jingle company that has produced singing ads for such products as Seven-Up, Bisquick, Archway cookies and Betty Crocker brownies mix. I told them what I wanted.

The three men who own the company—Bruce Bendinger, Roger Pauly, and Vince Ippolito—asked what exactly I had in mind.

"Oh, anything at all," I said. "As long as it sounds like 'High Noon' with Frankie Laine backed by the Allman Brothers Band."

"You are really twisted," they said.

"I will put your names in the paper," I said.

"We'll do it," they said.

And so, with the aid of Bendinger's eight-year-old daughter Jessica, they sat down and wrote a cowboy-rock song called "The Ballad of Bobby Greene." Here are the lyrics:

He rode out of Ohio with a pencil
in his hand,
Now he's ridin' through Chicago,
tellin' folks across the land,
He's chasin' down the truth cause he's
got nothin' left to lose,
Bobby Greene's out ridin', ridin' for
the news.

Bobby Greene! Bobby Greene!
With his sidekick Johnny Deadline by
his side,
When there's a story that needs writin',
Bobby Greene is out there fightin',
Ride, Bobby Greene, Bobby ride.

Some folks ride together, only
Bobby rides alone,
Cause Bobby does his writin' and
his thinkin' on his own,
When you're brave it doesn't matter if
you've never paid your dues,
So keep on ridin', Bobby, keep on
ridin' for the news.
Yeah, keep on ridin', Bobby, keep on
ridin' for the news!

I listened to them go through it. "Very tasty," I said. "Honest, yet humble and understated."

"Do your editors know about this?" they asked.

"Oh, they're very busy men," I said. "I don't think we should go bothering them with a little thing like this. Let's just go on to the next step."

So we booked time at Streeterville Studios, 161 E. Grand, a major Chicago recording facility in the advertising and music field.

The Happy Day boys, aided by session guitarists Bob Thomas and Mitch Hennis, got the final version of the ballad on 16-track tape within four and one-half hours. A Streeterville engineer played it back for us over the studio's massive speaker system.

"This is the most wonderful song I have ever heard," I said. "I have not been so moved since the first time I heard the Davy Crockett song. I think I am going to cry."

"Yeah?" said the Happy Day boys. "Seeing that you aren't a TV station, and you aren't a radio station, but merely a newspaperman, how are you going to get people to hear our song?"

"Oh, relax," I said. "If you knew me better, you would not doubt me. Just give me the tape."

I went to call on Earl Kuntz, president of the General Telephone Answering Service, one of Chicago's largest business and personal telephone answering companies. I explained about the ballad.

He began to shake his head and moan.

"I know what you are thinking," I said. "That you have enough problems and crises on your mind, and why did I have to pick you?"

Kuntz nodded.

"So will you do it?" I said.

"Sure, why not?" Kuntz said. "If I say no to you, you'll just hang around here all day and talk me into it anyway. I might as well save myself the time and not argue."

Thus, "The Ballad of Bobby Greene" is now hooked up to a multiline automatic answering machine. If you dial the number I gave you in the first paragraph of this story, you will hear the song. Just like calling the weather.

And to those readers who feel that this is the most appalling piece of self-aggrandizing gimmickry in the long and checkered history of this column, and that it makes all previous such self-promotional stunts seem positively tasteful in comparison, I have one suggestion:

If you get a busy signal, wait a few minutes and dial again.

Missing Miss America

This is a bit late to be running a story about the Miss America Pageant, but I had some checking up to do. And now I am ready. It turns out that Laurel Lea Schaefer, the new Miss America, did indeed go to high school with me. It was a very small high school, 800 students. And I am here to tell you that I thought I knew every girl that went to Bexley High School when I was there, and I never heard of Laurel Lea Schaefer.

What's more, I just checked with my old high school friends, who were among the youngest dirty old men ever to be raised in the state of Ohio, and none of them ever heard of Laurel Lea Schaefer either. Which goes to prove that everyone who used to say that we were running with a bad crowd just may have had a point.

I was amazed to learn from the newspapers that Miss Schaefer and myself were old schoolmates. So I decided to conduct a thorough survey, tracking down all my old friends and getting their comments on her. If you want to verify just how thorough this survey was, call the *Sun-Times'* auditor in about a month, for by that time he will be quite familiar with my September phone bill.

First I called Jack Roth, who was the sports editor of the high school paper and was going out with the homecoming queen behind her boy friend's back. Jack is now a schoolteacher in the day and a graduate student at night, and he was amazed at the whole thing.

"I know, I know," Jack Roth said. "I can't figure it out either. When I found out she went to school with us, I closed my eyes and began repeating her name over and over. 'Laurel Lea Schaefer, Laurel Lea Schaefer, Laurel Lea Schaefer,' I said. After about an hour, I began to hear flutes. Do you think she could have been in the marching band?"

Jack suggested that perhaps we had been too busy hanging around the Whitehall Recreation Center on weekend nights, looking for girls with beehive hairdos and stretch pants, and we were too preoccupied to notice a girl with the qualities that represent the best in American youth.

Next I called David Frasch, the quarterback on our football team and an early exponent of the theory that even minor celebrities should have groupies. He too was puzzled.

"I've done some investigating of my own," Frasch said "And believe it or not, she did go to school with us because someone looked it up in the yearbook. But I can't seem to picture her. I believe I went to church one Sunday when I was a junior, and I may have seen her there. But I can't swear to it."

Frasch, now a law student at the University of Michigan, was another one to espouse the theory that maybe a girl with all-American teenage qualities is not the type that appeals immediately to average American teenagers.

My next call was to Tim Greiner, the captain of our high school baseball team and a keeper of odd training rules. On nights before games he would consume quite a few bottles of Stroh's beer, which he claimed sharpened his eyes. He still lives in Bexley, and he was not anxious to discuss it. "I don't want to hear that name again," Greiner said. "This whole town is going nuts over Laurel Lea Schaefer, and I'm through with it. Here I was a high school big shot, and Miss America was in our midst and she never even had the good grace to let us know she was around. I have no use for her, whoever she is."

My last call was to Chuck Shenk. Even as a high school kid, Shenk could have been the character Philip Roth was thinking of when he wrote *Portnoy's Complaint.* Shenk was finding it hard to accept the fact that he was in school with Miss America and never even noticed she was there.

"Give me a hint," Shenk said. "Look up some stuff in your paper's clippings file and read it to me; maybe that will bring it back."

So I read him a UPI story that ended with the line "on the subject of premarital sex, Miss Schaefer said that she was 'stunned' when Miss Universe declared herself in favor of it."

Shenk paused for a moment. "No," he said, "I'm sure now, I never knew her."

So it's still a mystery. Laurel Lea Schaefer, where were you when we needed you? If you could have shrugged off your admirable, good, clean, all-American qualities for just a little while, I'm sure we would have found you. You might not have ever made it to the point where you are Miss America, but on the other hand we would have shown you some pretty interesting times, I bet.

Shoot Smokers

I went to court Wednesday. My reason for going had nothing to do with the pursuit of justice. I went because I wanted to see blood. I wanted to see people get beaten. I wanted to watch people be hurt.

I went off in search of Branch 95 of the Circuit Court, at 321 N. LaSalle. I walked into the crowded lobby of the building and told the first court official I could find, "I want to see these defendants stretched out on a torture rack. I am not kidding. Punish the scum."

He asked me what court I was looking for.

"The new one," I said. "Smoking Court."

"Room 136," he said.

I went to the appointed room. I was full of adrenaline. What an opportunity: the chance to see all of these despicable swine in one room. Due process and presumption of innocence are fine in innocuous theory, but there comes a time when protecting society comes first. I wanted to sneak up on some of these defendants and break their knees with a baseball bat.

Perhaps we should back up for a moment. Branch 95 is a new court announced by the city. The idea is right on the mark.

Branch 95 is a court dedicated to putting on trial persons arrested by Chicago police for smoking where prohibited in stores, elevators, public transportation, and other public places. In the past, these people were tried in courtrooms all around the city; now they are being brought together in one place.

Great. Move 'em in, convict them, and sentence them to death. Do it as quickly as possible.

The slime. No one is more offensive or worthy of public loathing than the man or woman who smokes cigarets, cigars, or pipes around other citizens. Forget the laws about where you can smoke and where you can't smoke; they are much too lenient. It should be against the law for any person to smoke in any public place, including—especially including—the out-of-doors.

As a matter of fact, giving the smokers a special courtroom is far too good for them. Any police officer should be empowered to shoot on sight any person observed smoking in public. People who smoke are so stupid. Do they think the cigaret companies put those little death messages on the sides of the packages because they need to fill up space? Smokers are killing the rest of us. Also, they smell.

Well, back to the story. I walked into the courtroom. I was immediately disappointed. First, there were no gallows, stocks, pillories, or other pain-inflicting devices. Second, the people on trial before the presiding judge seemed to be arguing not about cigarets, but about domestic spats.

I approached the court's clerk. She told me that Smoking Court was supposed to have opened Wednesday, but because of a delay in transferring cases onto its docket, it would probably be next week before the first smoking and other public-safety cases were called. I broke my pencil.

I sought out Associate Circuit Court Judge Francis X. Poynton, one of the men who came up with the idea of Smoking Court.

"Let's get this thing moving," I said. "I hate these people."

"Me too," Judge Poynton said.

"I want these people off the streets," I said. "I want them put away for so long that by the time they get out their families will have forgotten them."

"Nah, we can't do that," Judge Poynton said. "All we can do is fine them."

"That's all?" I said.

"Yeah. They'll probably spit tobacco juice in our faces," Judge Poynton said.

Well, there are other methods. When this Smoking Court

begins to operate next week, we just may be covering the thing like it was Al Capone on trial. If the city editor won't assign other reporters to it, I'll do it myself. You talk about abuse of press freedom; I'm going to go crazy. You want to smoke in public? If you end up in Smoking Court, don't be surprised if you find the following items in the next morning's paper: Your name. Your address. Your telephone number. Your photograph. Your place of business. The names of your spouse and children.

Is that an invasion of your privacy? Really? Any more so than expecting the rest of us to feel like we're the odd ones because we don't like to walk around in a haze of other people's poisonous smoke?

Gee, I feel much better about this already. One final note: if today's column should somehow fail to appear in the paper or show up in garbled form, don't blame it on me. I am now looking up toward the front of the city room, where I see Frank McHugh, the night managing editor, and Tom Moffett, the night copy chief. They are waiting for this column to be brought to their desks. At least I think it is them; both men I am looking at have cigarets dangling from their lips, and both of their heads are encased in clouds of noxious smoke.

I'm calling the cops. They can tell it to the judge.

Public Enemy

The accused Public Enemy sauntered into the courtroom.

He didn't look exactly like Capone or Dillinger. Missing were the pearl-gray fedora, the diamond stickpin and the snow-white spats.

This one was wearing black Converse All-Star basketball sneakers, a black sweater and a pearl earring in his left ear.

His name was Phillip Westmoreland, 23, of 2111 E. 67th Street. He glanced into the press section and spotted the lone reporter on the scene.

"Oh, no!" Westmoreland said. "Not that dude! I don't need this! Man, get me out of here!"

"All you criminals will be brought to justice," the reporter announced to him. "And the gallant free press will carry the news to the people."

"I read that thing you wrote," Westmoreland said. "You want me to get the death penalty."

"Tell it to the judge," the reporter said.

As if on cue, Associate Circuit Court Judge Edwin Kretske entered the courtroom and took the bench. Court Clerk Nancy DeFranco, her voice wavering only slightly under the stress of the historic moment, announced the case.

And it was under way: the first trial in the county's wonderful new Smoking Court.

Regular readers of this space may recall the column several weeks ago where the formation of this court—dedicated to trying cases involving the mad dogs who stalk our streets smoking cigarets in places where they're not supposed to—was announced.

The column proposed a series of rather severe penalties for the villains who insist on fouling the air with their smoke, and lamented the fact that the Smoking Court would not begin to try its cases as early as expected, because of a paperwork backup. But by Tuesday things were running on schedule, and Westmoreland was the first accused lawbreaker to face the music in the courtroom—officially known as Branch 95 of the Cook County Circuit Court, and located in room 136 at 321 N. LaSalle.

"I'm going to beat this rap," Westmoreland hissed cockily at the reporter.

Judge Kretske called the participants to come forward.

Sergeant Eurel Jackson, the courageous police officer who made the arrest, testified that he had boarded an eastbound CTA bus on 63d Street near Racine Avenue on July 1.

"What did you observe when you entered the bus?" said Assistant Corporation Counsel Richard Friedman, the valiant prosecutor.

"I observed four young men smoking cigarets in the rear of the bus," Sergeant Jackson said.

The prosecutor asked Sergeant Jackson what happened next.

"I asked the young men to put out the cigarets," Sergeant Jackson said. "I told them that smoking was not permitted on CTA buses."

"And then what happened?" prosecutor Friedman asked.

"Three of the four men put the cigarets out," Sergeant Jackson said. "The fourth man—Mr. Westmoreland—did not."

"What did Mr. Westmoreland do?" the prosecutor asked.

"He turned to me," Sergeant Jackson testified, "and then he said . . ." Sergeant Jackson repeated an obscenity.

"Aw, man!" Westmoreland said.

Judge Kretske then asked Westmoreland to tell his side of the story.

"Me and these other fellows were talking about something that was happening in the sports pages or something," Westmoreland said. "We were smoking some cigarets. This man here comes up and says to put the cigarets out. I say, 'Do you have a badge, officer?' And he said he was arresting me. I said, 'Hey, why me?' and he said that I was a smart aleck. And then he lets the other guys go, and he takes me to the station house at 61st and Racine."

"Did you put your cigarets out when he asked you to?" Judge Kretske asked.

"Yeah," Westmoreland said.

"Didn't you see the 'No Smoking' signs when you got on the bus?" Judge Kretske asked.

"Yeah," Westmoreland said.

Judge Kretske paused for a moment, and then delivered his verdict.

"Guilty," he said.

"Aw, man," Westmoreland said.

"Fifty dollars in fines and $5 in court costs," Judge Kretske said.

"Aw, man," said Westmoreland.

The dramatic trial was over. Justice had been done. Westmoreland and the reporter walked out of the courtroom together.

"You are only the first to feel the swift sword of society's vengeance," the reporter said.

"You know, you're crazy, man," Westmoreland said.

Coke Tale

There is something terrible going on in our country. Some days a fellow wants to thank his lucky stars that he is a crack investigative reporter, and is able to get to the bottom of a matter like this.

I called the headquarters of the Coca-Cola Bottling Company of Chicago.

"Good afternoon," I said. "This is an investigative reporter speaking. Why can't I find a normal-sized bottle of Coke anymore?"

"Pardon me?" the voice on the other end of the line said.

"Don't be coy," I said. "I want answers, not evasions."

"I'll try to connect you with someone, sir," the voice said.

I was switched to a functionary in the marketing department.

"Why can't I find a normal-sized bottle of Coke?" I said.

"You mean the old 6½-ounce bottle?" the woman said. "That's obsolete."

"And just why is it obsolete?" I said.

"Perhaps you had better talk to Mr. Gerber," the woman said. "He's out of town right now, but . . ."

"Never mind," I said. "Where are your international headquarters?"

"Coke's main offices?" the woman said. "They're in Atlanta."

"The telephone number, please," I said.

The woman gave me a number. "But Mr. Gerber will be back . . ." she began.

"This is a little too big for your 'Mr. Gerber,' I'm afraid," I said.

I dialed the number in Atlanta, and as I waited for the connection to be made, I mulled over the problem.

I am addicted to Coca-Cola. When I am without it, I become physically ill. Since the time I was six years old, I have consumed, on the average, three bottles of Coca-Cola a day. I sat down and figured this out. In my lifetime—and this is a conservative estimate—I have swallowed 4,893 quarts of Coke. This is the equivalent of 9,786 pounds.

Certain do-gooders are opposed to Coca-Cola. One consumer group, known as the Center for Science in the Public Interest, has composed a list of the "Terrible Ten" foods—foods that are supposed to epitomize what is wrong with the American food supply—and have included Coke on the list, charging that it "provides only empty calories for more money than it takes to buy milk."

I have no idea what milk tastes like, but it can't be better than Coke, or I would have had an urge to try it somewhere along the line. I know instinctively that Coke is good for you. I make this point because it pains me to take the actions that I am taking against Coke. Now I know how heartsick the *Trib* must have felt when they went after Nixon.

The trouble is this: I grew up, and you grew up, drinking Coca-Cola out of the standard Coke bottle. It was a classic. It held 6½ ounces of Coke. You removed the cap with a bottle opener, and you drank the Coke, and you were finished. You never thought about the bottle; like the sky, it was just always there.

Well, it is no longer always there. In recent months I have had great difficulty finding stores that carry the normal-sized bottles. Now the smallest size that you can find are 16-ounce "resealable" bottles, or 12-ounce cans. Each of them presents a serious dilemma: they don't taste like Coke. The bottles go flat after one usage, and the cans taste like metal. You can't even reach your hand around the bottle. This may seem like a small matter to you. To me? Allow me to put it this way. I am well aware of the problems of air pollution, and yet I have never uttered a peep of protest about that. I am well aware of the consequences of industry fouling our water supply, and yet I have never said a word about that. But every man has his breaking point. Which is why I was on the phone to Atlanta.

The Coke switchboard operator put me through to an executive named John White. I presented my case.

"Let me assure you, the 6½-ounce bottle is alive and well," White said. He sounded like Ron Ziegler.

"Then how come I can't find it?" I said.

"Well," White said, "there are some areas of the country where they don't use as many of the smaller bottles. We have more that 800 locally owned and operated bottlers, and in some areas the consumer preference is for the larger-sized bottles. You may be living in one of those areas."

"Why?" I said.

"Consumer preference," White said. "I already told you."

I could tell I wasn't going to get anywhere with him. I hung up and called the Chicago offices again. I was connected with Coke's Chicago controller, Bill Fullerton.

Fullerton confirmed that, in the Chicago area, stores are ordering fewer and fewer of the old one-drink bottles, and that because of this the classic Coke bottle is making up a smaller and smaller percentage of the company's business. He said that there are still some stores where you can find the one-drink bottle, but that the trend is undeniable. He said that one reason for this is the economy: there is more drink for the money in the bigger bottles.

"The old Coke bottle has been chewed up," Fullerton said. "It has been cannibalized."

So now it is time for me to make a decision. One alternative is to move out of town, of course, to an area served by a different Coke bottler. It may have to come to that. But there is another possibility. I have been greatly attracted to those hillbilly "Me and My RC" commercials for Royal Crown Cola on TV. They seem authentic and enticing and real. True, the only RC franchise owner I ever knew was one Harold Schottenstein, and if he was a hillbilly then I'm a feminist, but still. . . .

Marijuana Affair

"Stop!" the reporter commanded. The order was being directed at Fred, the bartender at Riccardo's, who was, at that very moment, attempting to dump another shot of vodka into the reporter's glass.

"What's wrong?" Fred inquired.

"I have had enough," the reporter said.

"But you've only been here three hours," Fred said.

"And now it is time to go to work," the reporter said.

"What kind of story you working on?" Fred inquired.

"A marijuana party," the reporter said. He pulled an invitation out of his back pocket and flattened it out on the damp surface of the bar. The invitation was professionally printed: "The Board of Directors of the National Organization for the Reform of Marijuana Laws (Illinois) Invites You to Celebrate the Approval of Proposed Legislation by the Board of Governors of the Illinois State Bar Association." The address was a town house on Crilly.

"A marijuana party, huh?" Fred said. "You smoke that stuff?"

"I'm no beatnik," the reporter said.

"No, really," Fred said. "You smoke that stuff?"

"Wouldn't touch it," the reporter said. "But an assignment is an assignment."

"You sure you're . . . uh . . . in shape to be going out on the street?" Fred said.

"Are you kidding?" the reporter said. "I'm just trying to get myself ready to deal with those putty-brained dopeheads at the party. I wasn't born yesterday. You go in there straight, they'll eat you alive."

The reporter wandered out of the bar, hailed a cab, and gave the address of the party. When he arrived and walked to the door, though, he realized that he had come to the wrong place. The guests inside the town house were clearly assembling for a combined prayer meeting of the Illinois Young Republicans and the Fellowship of Christian Athletes. Suits, ties, cocktail dresses, and neat haircuts were the order of the evening.

"Sorry," the reporter said. "Wrong party. I'm looking for the marijuana people."

"You're at the right place," the man at the door said. "Come in."

The reporter entered. The living room was brightly lit. Fine books lined the walls. Men and women sat drinking wine, engaged in quiet conversation. A baby held her mother's hand. It may have been an illusion, but Billy Graham seemed to be in the next room.

The reporter was confused, but only momentarily. He decided to challenge the host. "Got any dope?" the reporter asked.

The host, Paul Kuhn, smiled. "Look at your invitation," he said. Kuhn pointed to a line on the invitation, which said: "Wine and cheese." Kuhn said, "Come pour yourself a glass of wine and have some cheese."

The reporter struggled for a witty rejoinder. Several seconds passed. "Got any dope?" the reporter said.

"The purpose of this is not to get people together to smoke," Kuhn said. "The purpose of this is to get people in our movement to meet together."

Kuhn began to lead the reporter around. Kuhn explained that he, in private life, was an investment counselor. He said that the pro-marijuana group was referred to as NORML and he introduced the reporter to the other members of NORML's board of directors. One was an attorney. One worked for Governor Walker. One was the owner of a fancy restaurant. They were among the most dignified, polite, successful, solid, prosperous citizens the reporter had ever met. The reporter sought to make small talk.

"Got any dope?" the reporter said.

There was uncomfortable laughter. Kuhn explained that the reason for the gathering was that the board of governors of the Illinois State Bar Association had drafted legislation that, if approved by the state Legislature, would legalize marijuana use in Illinois.

Many of the guests at the party were wearing tiny gold marijuana leaf pins on their lapels, to demonstrate their support.

The reporter asked Kuhn what would happen if anyone at the party began to smoke marijuana.

"That person might be asked to leave," Kuhn said.

"But I thought . . ." the reporter began.

"First of all, you do not have to be a smoker to be in Illinois NORML," Kuhn said.

"But . . ." the reporter said.

"And second of all, this is my apartment, and it's illegal," Kuhn said.

The reporter looked around the room. Kuhn anticipated the next question before it could be asked.

"Look, none of us are hippie-dippies," Kuhn said. "I'm very much aware that we appear to be fairly conservative. That's good. That's one of our strengths. It gives us some credibility."

David Samber, another member of NORML's board of directors, started to explain some of NORML's goals for marijuana decriminalization to the reporter. Samber was very low-key and persuasive. Other guests at the party began to gather and to discuss their programs. "Can I get you something to eat or drink?" Samber said.

"I would like a fistful of Quaaludes and a glass of warm milk," the reporter said.

"We have wine and cheese," Samber said.

After a while the reporter said he would have to leave. The people at the party bid him good-by, much in the manner of a group of very established and very conscientious suburban parents sending their child off to camp.

The reporter took a cab back to Riccardo's, and returned to his seat at the bar.

"Vodka," the reporter said.

"How was it?" Fred said.

"Freaks," the reporter said.

The Ms. Greene's World Pageant

Now, there are some people who are going to be highly offended at the very idea of conducting a beauty contest through a newspaper column. All of us here at contest headquarters realize this. You will simply have to go to the trouble of reading all the way through the column to understand that this is *not* really a beauty contest.

We must begin at the beginning. As you may be aware, at this time every year this column conducts a giveaway or a contest. In the past these have centered on such items as pieces of blue jeans and keys to motel rooms. Fellow newsmen from respected newsgathering organizations around the world have almost unanimously taken note of this practice. They lumped it under the general heading of the Death of Journalism.

For the last few weeks, those of us at contest headquarters—namely, the proprietor of this column and deskmate Roberto Suro (a reporter who, when informed that he was now a column item, insisted on being referred to as the Wizard of Wabash)—have been pondering over what nature this year's contest should take.

"It is time for you to be serious," Mr. Suro said. "It is time to take a stand. This is, after all, International Women's Year."

He had a point. It seemed only right to honor women during this special year. And yet how to do so without the risk of offending sensibilities made tender by the increasing politicization of women?

As if delivered by fate, the answer came to us in the mail. A woman reader wrote: "I see by the commercials on television that it is time for the beauty contests to start up again. Will this never stop? After all these years of lobbying for equality, am I to believe that American mass culture still centers on a bathing suit parade on a runway? Are there no other ways to judge a woman's worth?"

A very good point. The Wizard and I perused the letter and found ourselves nodding in unison.

"Damn right," Mr. Suro said.

There was a momentary silence.

"It is time to drag out the Miss Greene's World pageant again," Mr. Suro said.

A shudder could be felt running through professional journalistic societies the world over. Miss Greene's World, it should be pointed out to those who are too young to remember, was a contest featured on a now-dead radio show known as "Greene's World." Some communications experts will testify that the Miss Greene's World contest was the immediate cause of the death of "Greene's World" and the departure of a station manager.

"Wash your mouth, Suro," the proprietor of the column scolded. "We have all, it is to be hoped, matured and grown since those juvenile days. We are not simpering children anymore. The day is long past when the public will accept something as pandering and piggish as a Miss Greene's World contest."

"OK," Mr. Suro replied. "How about Ms. Greene's World?"

"You got it," the proprietor responded.

"A new kind of contest," Mr. Suro said. "A contest that will judge women not merely by traditional ideas of 'beauty,' but by the qualities that a truly modern woman should have in order to get by in this world—independence, heightened consciousness, humanity, social awareness, sense of self."

"Yeah, exactly," the proprietor responded.

So here are the rules. Read carefully:

Entrants in the Ms. Greene's World contest should send a photograph of themselves to the contest headquarters, in care of this column, The *Sun-Times,* 401 N. Wabash, Chicago, Illinois 60611. The photographs will be judged on the basis of independence, heightened consciousness, humanity, social awareness, and sense of self. The judges will be Mr. Greene, Mr. Suro, and Nat Lehrman, editor of *Oui* magazine.

For the purpose of a tie-breaker, contestants are free to include an essay outlining why they wish to become Ms. Greene's World. The winning pictures and essays will be published in a future column. There will also be a lavish prize—so far, we are thinking in terms of a copy of "Chevy Van" by Sammy Johns, currently the favorite song here at pageant headquarters.

"You realize," the proprietor of the column said, "that some critics are going to say that we still don't have this thing right."

"Let them complain," Mr. Suro said. "A journey of a thousand miles begins with a single step."

Both black-and-white and color photographs, snapshots and professional prints, are eligible for entry in the contest. Polaroids are fully acceptable. Essays, if included, must be written in English.

The Winner

Mary Lipman, a 36-year-old mother of two from Winnetka, has been chosen Ms. Greene's World for 1975, the pageant committee announced Tuesday.

Mrs. Lipman was selected as the winner from a field of more than 122,000 women who submitted photographs and essays to the contest. "It was a tough decision," said *Sun-Times* reporter Roberto Suro, speaking for the judges. "But in the end we went with Mrs. Lipman because she was so obviously willing to hold herself up to scorn and ridicule among her peer group just for the cheap thrill of seeing her picture in the paper. We felt that this was most in keeping with the spirit of the man for whom the contest was named."

Simultaneously with the declaration of Mrs. Lipman as the winner, the American Newspaper Publishers Association announced that every newspaper in the country will slow its Goss printing presses to half-speed Wednesday in protest of "the great institution of the Fourth Estate being dragged through the mud by a gimmick as sleazy and transparently salacious as this so-called 'Ms. Greene's World Pageant.' This is not journalism."

Mrs. Lipman, when informed that she was the winner, said, "It's a major damn tingle, is what it is."

She rejected the proposed first prize of a copy of "Chevy Van" (currently the favorite musical composition of the proprietor of the column), saying, "My six-year-old plays it at home 50 times a week already, think of another prize."

Mrs. Lipman then was presented with a lavish 30-minute cocktail hour at the Executive House and Riccardo's. She seemed too choked up by emotion to express her thanks, but upon entering Riccardo's she did muster up enough composure to state, "Is that Roger Ebert?"

The pageant was judged by a three-man panel consisting of Reporter Suro, Nat Lehrman, editor of *Oui* magazine, and the proprietor of the column, who lost a commentary job on WLS radio two years ago after using the public airways for a similar contest. After it was determined by Dan Feldman, attorney, that the Federal Communications Commission could exert no sanctions over such a contest run in a newspaper, the pageant was revived.

Rules of the contest were that any woman could submit a photograph of herself and, if she wished, an essay stating why she desired the title of Ms. Greene's World. The purpose of the contest was to honor the New Woman in America: photographs were to be judged on the basis of independence, heightened consciousness, humanity, social awareness, and sense of self.

Mrs. Lipman submitted two photographs of herself (neither was fit for publication here). She stated that she possessed a high degree of independence: "I decided all by myself to have Touch-Tone phones installed in my house, without consulting anyone."

Mrs. Lipman also demonstrated a heightened consciousness by testifying that she has taken up the hobbies of backpacking and outdoor camping, but that she still maintains enough fear of the dark that she pops a Valium by the campfire before going into her tent for the night.

The coming year will be a busy and exciting one for the new Ms. Greene's World. She will represent this column at various events, including sock hops, drive-in openings, and breaking news stories that seem to offer a danger of physical violence or bodily harm.

Next year at this time Mrs. Lipman will turn over her crown to her successor. For those women who did not win, the committee suggests a try again in the 1976 pageant. A helpful hint to many of this year's losing contestants: there is such a thing as being too forward. This is a serious business, and the baseness to which many women will sink in pursuit of fame proved a shock to some of the judges not accustomed to big-city ways. Remember, ladies, there must be losers in any contest, and you have to live with yourselves after the pageant is over.

The committee already is working on plans for next year's pageant, including several proposed reforms designed to help the contestants, One such reform would provide for the addition of a modest entrance fee.

Transportation to and from the Ms. Greene's World Pageant is provided by the Chicago Transit Authority. While in Chicago, Ms. Greene's World stays at the *Sun-Times* cafeteria.

8
LISTENING

There has been debate over what quality is most important to a reporter: aggressiveness, tirelessness, skepticism, perseverance, curiosity. I would say that right up there near the top is the ability and desire to listen. Each column in this chapter required that above all else. They say, in an athlete, the legs go first; in a funny way I would guess that with a reporter, it's the ears. When you get tired of hearing people tell you their stories, then maybe that's the day you know you're tired of being a reporter.

The Letters

The letters started to come two summers ago. When you have a job like this one, it is not unusual to receive letters from strangers; I made myself a promise a while ago to try to answer every piece of mail, but it is easy to get careless, and I responded to her first three letters by sending stock replies, without realizing that the letters were from the same girl. Her fourth letter set me straight; she returned my first three form letters, all of which said: "Thanks a lot for writing, glad you enjoy the columns," and she asked me to pay closer attention.

For two years she wrote every week. At first it was a little unsettling; she was a teenager, a high-school girl from the suburbs, and I didn't know if I wanted to be let in on the secrets she was telling. Any one of the letters, taken alone, could have been misclassified as "nut mail"; the letters ran to 10 and 12 pages, and they were full of the kinds of details that a person tells to a best friend. I did not know how to reply; I decided not to try.

It didn't matter to her. "I'm not looking for anything," she wrote at the beginning. "Sometimes it's easier to talk to someone you don't really know. Do you understand?" She didn't need an answer, apparently; the letters kept arriving.

At first I showed the letters to some other people; it was so curious that this girl would choose to reveal her life in such detail to a person she had never met, and I wanted to know if my friends found it as puzzling as I did. Soon enough I stopped showing the letters; to make them public seemed to be a betrayal of sorts.

Some of the letters were unbearably sad. The girl's life was no more full of problems and worries and doubts than the life of any other young woman growing to adulthood in the '70s, but most people keep their demons and torments to themselves, hide them away. Reading the letters often seemed to be an intrusion; more than once, the girl would write: "I hate to burden you with this . . . ," and then she would relate a small agony that she said she had entrusted to no one else.

She made it clear, almost every time, that she expected no answers. "It's enough to know that someone is listening," she wrote once. "I just hope you aren't throwing these away as soon as you see who they're from." She seemed to know that the rule was that she would never meet the person to whom she was writing; the distance and the mystery were giving her the courage to put her life down on paper.

"Sometimes I feel like I'm five years old," she wrote once. "Sometimes I feel like an old woman." The letters told of her family, her friends, her solitary thoughts; she was a good, spare writer, and it wasn't long before I felt as if I was reading a strangely moving, free-form autobiography, in serial form. "I don't mean to bother you," she would write, but it was no bother; I found myself looking for the letters in the mailbox, wondering what was happening in her life. "No one knows I'm doing this," she wrote once.

She fancied herself an artist, and sometimes there would be drawings along with the letters. More than once I found myself wondering if something truly crazy was going to show up in one of the letters, if the slim strangeness of what she was doing was going to turn ugly and frightening. But it never did; she was just a girl who was sharing her life with someone she had never met, for reasons of her own.

"I'm going to make myself stop writing these soon," she wrote last summer. "Have to do it sometime, I guess." I had a feeling that she would, and she did; just two years after the letters had begun, they stopped coming. That was three or four months ago. There was nothing in the last one to indicate it was anything special.

Then, last week, a new one was in the mailbox. I recognized the writing right away. Inside was a piece of white paper with just a few words. "I'm OK now," it said. "Thanks." Down at the bottom of the page, she had drawn a small butterfly, in colored pencil, and next to the butterfly she had written something else. "The End," it said. . . . .

Killer

"I don't know how many times I killed," Marvin Scheffler said. "I can remember a few, but I can't remember all of them. You don't feel much at the time. You just get so caught up in the excitement of it all. You perform automatically. You just do your damndest to kill. You get really twisted."

Scheffler is 26 now, and he lives on the North Side. From April of 1968 until June of 1969, he fought with the Marines in Vietnam. He did not actively oppose the war when he was in the Marines, but now, back in Chicago, he has decided to testify in court on behalf of a man who is accused of destroying Selective Service files during the war.

"I feel that it's the least I can do," Scheffler said the other day. "Now I can see that the people who tried to stop the war at home were showing real courage—a different kind of courage, but courage just the same. And now I'm willing to do whatever I can to help the ones who still face going to prison for what they did.

"I think someone should say that those of us in Vietnam didn't hate the anti-war people back home. I know that the government always tried to give the impression that the men in Vietnam resented the war protesters, that we felt the protesters were putting us in danger. But that's not true. I was an average Marine; I had no qualms about killing people in the war. But I was sympathetic to the anti-war movement; I think most of us were.

"Even while we were fighting, we knew that we had no constitutional right to be in there. We thought the war was a bad joke, just a chance to try out our war toys. We knew we weren't fighting for the preservation or safety of our country. But I was like a lot of guys; I thought that it was the manly thing to go and fight just because we were told to.

"But even then, a lot of us knew that even though our own personal lives and philosophies were probably different from the anti-war people's, they were doing a good thing. We figured that they were doing their best to get us out of there, and if they were successful, they might save some of our lives. There was no hate for the protesters."

Scheffler talks matter-of-factly about his own actions in Vietnam. "I remember once, I was firing mortar shells at a couple of North Vietnamese regulars," he said. "I had them in range. I could have killed them right away, at will. But I didn't. I played cat and mouse with them, made them run around, to make it last longer, before I did it. I was really warped.

"That's how you get after a while. You got to the point where you didn't really care. After you've killed somebody, you figure, 'Well, I've done it; I'm already damned, so let the show go on.' And you go with the flow.

"I would say that most of us were unable to justify in our minds what we were doing. We weren't looking to be heroes. In fact, we looked at the few guys who tried to be heroes with disdain. But still, when it came time to get out there and fire a rifle, we did it without complaining. I was no different from anybody else. If I would have started to think seriously about it, I might have cracked."

Scheffler wants to help the war protesters who are still facing prosecution as a gesture of reconciliation, a sign that he understands what they were trying to say.

"They were justified in what they did," he said. "They were working in a positive way to bring what was going on over there to the attention of the public, knowing that they might eventually have to pay for their acts by going to prison and being harassed. It took a lot of guts to go against a machine as powerful as our government. And I just know, inside myself, that time has shown that the people who were protesting at home had a better concept of what was going on, and what was right, than I did at the time."

Scheffler is not a member of Vietnam Veterans Against the War and has never been a part of any organized pacifist group. His decision to try to help people under prosecution for anti-war activities was a private one.

"When I came back from the war, I joined the American Legion, but I quit after a year," he said. "I'd go down to the Legion hall, and there'd be all these guys from Korea and World War II sitting around in their T-shirts, drinking beer. They had no idea of what Vietnam had been about. So I just quit going there. I couldn't relate at all."

Lincoln Bolton

It started with a phone call. "I have a story for you," the man said. He would not say what it was.

He called every afternoon for the next few days. "I have a story for you," he said. He would not talk about it; would not even say what it was about. One day he showed up at the newspaper building.

He seemed awkward and afraid and without anything to tell once he was face to face with the person he had been calling. He wanted to talk about other things: his life, his family, his sorrows. Finally he was told that time was short, and that he would have to reveal the story he had come to give. Either that, or he would have to leave.

He paused, and then he began. "Look, I have been a thief," he said. "I admit it. But I don't want to do this. I don't want this on my conscience."

His name was Lincoln Bolton. He was a black man, 47 years old, in a baggy blue blazer, a too-tight thin white shirt, a red tie, a gray pair of pants, and a black trench coat. He said he came out of Detroit.

His story was a strange one, and it did not take too many minutes of listening to know it could not be true. In his story, crime syndicate men forced him to sell drugs to high school students and threatened to beat him until he could no longer walk if he refused. He was clearly improvising as he went along; the details became fuzzy, and he became eager to say anything that he felt his listener might want to hear. He did not want to be made to leave.

So he attempted to continue with his story, and even as he was talking the real reason for his calls and his visits made itself evident. He was a lonely man with no one to speak to and no one to share his thoughts with. He had been like that for years; it had done something to his mind, for he seemed to half-believe the tales of criminal intrigue he was telling. He rambled and he swayed, and finally he was persuaded to stop the fable about the drugs and to tell the truth about himself.

He became embarrassed; he said that his days were spent in an alley near Harrison and Clark, behind a printing factory, and that his hours were passed sitting behind parked cars and drinking whisky from the bottle. "When I finish talking to you, I know I'll go back to the alley and drink until it's dark," he said. "I can't help it." He said his only companion was a transistor radio, and he pulled it out of his pocket to show it.

He left. After he had gone, the person he had come to see did some checking. It turned out that the clothes Bolton had been wearing were given to him by the people who run the Pacific Garden Mission, where homeless men can find a bed and a meal. The police said they knew of Bolton; he had a long record of small wrongs, things like loitering and being drunk and disorderly. He was one of those men who lose their fight with life's harshest elements early, and live every day with that knowledge displayed to the world.

In the months after his first visit, he would call often. He was back to the story about the drugs, using it in the hope that it would make someone want to spend time with him. Sometimes he would bring notes by, and leave them for the person he had visited; some of the notes were on the stationery of a YMCA, and the desk clerks at the Y, when asked, said that, yes, Bolton would come in and buy a room whenever he had the money.

The calls and the messages became more disjointed. The drug tale faded away, and in its place came a plaint about his mother and father in Detroit, and how he missed them. He began to sound like a child. Once, when it was mentioned in the newspaper that the person whom Bolton had visited would be at a certain public place at a certain time, Bolton was there too, waiting, wanting to talk.

It has been more than two years. The calls and messages still arrive. They have become worse. There will be no climax to Bolton's story, no neat summing-up. There are thousands like him in the city, and when they go, the world takes no more notice of their deaths than it did of their lives. Bolton's passing will be announced by the cessation of his pleading calls and messages. No one ever writes an obituary for the Lincoln Boltons among us.

Love of Country

I hate to bore you with a Vietnam story today; I know that they don't get read anymore, now that 19 out of 20 Americans are blubbering that they always knew we didn't belong over there right from the start. But there are young men who were saying it before it became so easy, and who are in prison cells this morning, and once in a while it seems proper to mention something about them.

This Friday, Pete Bezich, a 54-year-old carpenter who lives at 8114 S. Keating and who was awarded the Silver Star for his service in the Pacific during World War II, will drive the 800 miles to visit his son again. If Bezich can get someone to go with him, he will share the driving, do it in 14 straight hours overnight. If he does it alone, he will sleep for a few hours in Lebanon, Missouri, as he always does. Bezich's son, Steven, 25, is in a federal prison in El Reno, Oklahoma, because he decided that he should not fight during the American experiment in Southeast Asia.

Steven Bezich was not a college anti-war marcher. He was a young construction worker who had a brother who had fought in Vietnam, and who decided that it would be wrong for him to go and kill. He said that he would rather go to Vietnam and help build hospitals for eight years than to be forced to fire a gun even once. He volunteered to do just that, as alternative service.

U.S. District Court Judge Julius J. Hoffman did not agree. He sentenced Steven Bezich to three years in prison.

Since then, once a month, Pete Bezich has been driving to prison to see Steven, to visit and talk with him. At first it was only eight hours one-way, to the prison in Sandstone, Minnesota. But then, without explanation, prison officials transferred Steven to the Oklahoma prison—and his father continued to travel to see him.

"He's still the same way," Pete Bezich said Monday. "He is not bitter at anyone. He's very passive. His attitude is, 'Here I am, if you want to beat me, fine.' He would not lift a fist to anyone."

The father said that Steven has refused to co-operate with the prison work routine. "He says that he won't work for the prison system. He says that they can have his body, but they can't have his mind, and that he's in the prison because that's what society wants, but that's as far as he goes. He says if they want labor, they can hire it. He won't even put in for parole—he said he'd rather serve his three years and come out a free man than be paroled and have to come out under government supervision."

For this attitude, Steven Bezich has been put in solitary confinement at both prisons. "When I went to visit him two Saturdays ago, his right eye was all black and blue, and he had cuts on his mouth, and he said that the guards had got their pound of flesh, dragging him from his cell to the hole," his father said. "I called Senator Percy's and Senator Stevenson's offices, and now he's out of solitary—that has helped before. Steven says that he just won't compromise, that they can keep him in their prison, but that's all they can do to him."

There are 16 months left in Steven's sentence; his father said that he will continue visiting until the end. "First they moved him from Minnesota to Oklahoma," he said. "Maybe it'll be California next, or Puerto Rico, if they can find a federal prison there. But I'll still go to see Steven.

"Steven was against the war and killing, and as far as I'm concerned, he did the right thing. The Beziches have given 30 years and more to their country's military, if you count my brothers, but this last war was a different question.

"I love my country. I've done my bit for it. I've traveled this country, and I've traveled all over the world, and there's no better place in the world than the United States of America. I'm very proud of my country.

"But I'm proud of my son, too. Steven loves his country; all he was trying to do was offer it some constructive criticism. I've watched him as he's done it, every step of the way. And I'll tell you, I couldn't be prouder of him."

Love Story

A passion play:

The two of them were never seen apart. That was when it was new, when they were beginning. On the campus of a Midwestern college, it was easy. "He's my best friend," she would say. He would smile and shake his head.

They had met after both of them had been at the school for two years. She had been living with a boy who had always been able to make her laugh when she was down, but lately the boy had begun to seem unfunny and too young. She was just beginning to think about how to move out of the boy's apartment when she met him.

He had seen her around, but had never really thought about her one way or the other. The first day he talked to her, though, and he found out that she was living with someone else, he became immediately attracted. He asked her to come home with him, and she did. She stayed that night and never moved out.

"We're both free to see anyone else we want to," he said. She said: "But the nice thing is, we don't want to." The year 1967 was one for such thoughts.

He had a roommate, but when it became clear that she was there for good, the roommate moved out. She began to help pay the rent. His friends began to say that they never saw him anymore. He said that he knew, he knew—but that he felt bad when he left her alone, all by herself at the apartment with nothing to do.

They both said the idea of marriage had nothing to do with it. "Why ruin a good thing by adding something artificial like that?" she said. He said, "We're fine this way. And this way if either of us wants out, it's no problem."

His friends would get on him about never seeing any other girls, and he would say he'd thought about it, but it would mess her up too badly, and he didn't think that was worth it. Then one night, while he was at the apartment studying, he noticed that it was 3:00 A.M. and that she had not come home from the library.

She did not show up until the next afternoon, and when he asked, she said she had run into the boy she had lived with before and that they had stayed up and talked all night. When he became angry and asked her why she had not at least called, she said, "Look, it's not like we're married. You can't have it both ways."

Their wedding was the month after they were graduated from college. "We're doing it for our parents' sake," she said. He said, "It's good that we lived together for so long, because now we know exactly what we're getting into."

She wanted to live in Boston, but his grades had been indifferent, and he did not want to work yet, so he said he was going to the only graduate school he could get into, in Arizona. She said it was unfair, that she, too, should be able to go where she wanted. He said that after he got his master's degree, she could. In the meantime they moved to Arizona and she got a job in a drugstore to pay the rent while he went to graduate classes.

"Sometimes it's hard, because we're our own people," he would say when his old friends would call long distance. "It's not like our parents' marriages, where you have a man and a woman pretending they're happy all the time, when you know very well that no one is happy all the time."

She would say to her old friends, "I'm starting to like the idea of working. It's nice to get out of the house for eight hours a day. Any person can get on your nerves if you never are away from them. Even someone you love."

They talked about open marriages, and they both said they were lucky that they were living in a day when married persons could have other close friends of the opposite sex.

One night a girl called the apartment while she was there and asked for him. He stayed on the phone for two hours, and when he hung up, she would not sleep in the same room with him. Later he found out that she occasionally had been going home with one of the pharmacists from the drugstore after work. He confronted her with it, and when she shrugged and did not deny it, he slapped her so hard that it left a bruise, and she had to wear heavy makeup for a week.

"If I felt I had something real to hold onto, it would be better," she said. "If I had a baby to take care of, then I wouldn't feel so tense all the time." He said, "How can you talk about taking care of a baby when you can't even keep the apartment clean half the time?"

When he moved out, he said it was only for a few days. He stayed with friends from the graduate school. He went back home in a week to find that she had asked the pharmacist to move in. She said that she felt it was her apartment as much as it was his, and besides, the pharmacist gave her any kind of pills she wanted, and she was finding that she did in fact want pills.

She stayed in Arizona. He left and has just returned to his old college town, where he is wondering if he is too old to be with the freshman girls. "I still think the two of us can be friends," he said. "We were always friends, right from the first day." It has been six months since he has seen her, three months since he has heard her voice on the telephone. . . .

Ghosts of a Barn Dance

> Kentucky,
>   You are the dearest land outside of
>   Heaven to me.
> Kentucky,
>   Your laurel and your redbud trees. . . .
> I know that
> My mother, dad and sweetheart are
>   awaiting for me.
> Kentucky,
>   I will be comin' soon.

—From "Kentucky," by Karl Davis
Copyright, 1942 by Advanced Music Corporation

Karl Davis was a star. His voice was heard all over the country in the '30s, '40s, and '50s, back in the days before WLS radio went to a rock-and-roll format. Every Saturday at 8:00 P.M., the WLS National Barn Dance would be broadcast live over the station's clear channel, and the fine young voice of Karl Davis, singing along with his sweet mandolin, would race across the night to cities and towns all over the United States.

The other morning Davis, now 67 years old, went to work as he always does, put on a set of earphones, and did what he now does every day. He took the latest rock-and-roll records by 19-year-old millionaires, and he placed them on a turntable, and he put a needle on them. Then an engineer pushed a button so that the songs could be transferred onto tape cartridges and could be played over WLS all day every day.

Karl Davis' job classification is "record turner," and this is how he has been earning his living the last 13 years.

"Oh, I guess we just came along a little too early, that's all," Davis said in the voice that still has rural Kentucky laced into it. "I guess we were before our time. This rock-and-roll music—I've come to like it, though. I hear it at the station every day, and I have heard some wonderful songs."

He comes out of Mount Vernon, Kentucky. In 1930 there were 700 people in Mount Vernon, and two of them were Karl Davis and Hartford Taylor. They came to Chicago to join the Barn Dance cast, and they made it. They called themselves "Karl and Harty," and they were a hit.

"We were trying to make a name for ourselves," Davis said. "We were trying to do our best so we could stay."

They stayed. Davis wrote the songs, and he and Harty expanded their duet into the Cumberland Ridgerunners. They were very famous, and then, in the '50s, rock and roll was born, and the live Barn Dance died. Davis had no place to play his mandolin anymore, and he was not wealthy.

"It's not like these singers have it today, with big money," he said. "We'd make a personal appearance in a place like Ishpeming, Michigan, and we would get $25. So when there was no more Barn Dance, I was very grateful to be given this job as a record turner at WLS. It allowed me to keep my wife and family in Chicago."

He has not performed in public in 20 years. "I guess I'd feel funny playing without Harty," he said. "We played together since the time we were ten years old. When the Barn Dance died, Harty didn't get a job as a record turner. He worked on the tollway, in one of the booths as a toll taker. One day I was driving, and I saw Harty down a couple booths away, but I didn't get a chance to talk to him. And then he died a couple of years ago."

But Karl Davis still plays, and he still sings. He goes home after work, and he takes out a guitar or a mandolin, and he sings to himself. He sings the old songs, and he sings some new ones that he writes from time to time. He has four mandolins and two guitars. His favorite is a Martin Dreadnaught guitar.

"You can hardly get those," he said. "They're made by hand, by old men in Nazareth, Pennsylvania. Oh, it makes beautiful music. My children heard me talking about that guitar, and one Father's Day they chipped in and bought me one."

There are country music shows in this area, including a festival presented at the University of Chicago every year, and Davis would like to go on a stage again, but he hasn't. "No one ever asked me," he said. "I'm kind of bashful about it, and no one ever asks me to play anymore, so I just play for myself. Just this morning, I got up half an hour early. So I took out one of those guitars, and I sat in the breakfast room, and I played and sang until it was time to come to work."

He talked some more, but the afternoon was getting late, and he had more work to do in his job as a record turner. WLS was putting together a program of rock-and-roll oldies, and Davis lifted "Dead Man's Curve" by Jan and Dan onto a turntable.

"I do have one kind of secret dream," he said. "I've thought about it a great deal. I would like it so much if I could have a half-hour show on television, maybe every Saturday night. There wouldn't be any whoopla, no cowbells, no applause. Just singing and playing.

"I've even got a name for it. I would call it 'The Old Cabin Home.' It would just be me and my family, singing together. We'd have a big picture of the Cumberland Ridgerunners on the mantel, and we'd show the people that and maybe some antiques and old instruments. I've even thought of how I'd begin the show every week."

Davis looked around him in the WLS recording room. He cleared his throat. Then he began to sing, in a country voice so clear and beautiful that it almost hurt to hear it:

> Down in the old cabin home
> The welcome mat is always at the door:
> We'll sing a song or two
> And we'll play a tune for you
> Down in the old cabin home. . . .

He stopped suddenly, as if he didn't want to think about it anymore, and went over to place the needle on the Jan and Dean record.

"I know that show will probably never happen for me," Karl Davis said. "It's just a dream of mine."

Civilization

A story for a Sunday in June:

David Mack is a uniformed security guard at Roosevelt University. He is 52 years old. He works the night shift, 3:00 P.M. to midnight. He grew up black and poor on the West Side of Chicago; his father made him drop out of Marshall High School in 1936, at the age of 14, to help earn money for the family.

For most of his life, Mack did menial labor. He performed the lowliest, harshest jobs in steel mills, on road-tarring crews, in factories. After a while, he assumed that he would be doing that until he died.

On Monday night, he will not be going to work. He made arrangements to work an extra night some other time so he could get the night off. He will show up at Roosevelt anyway Monday. But instead of changing from his street clothes to his guard uniform, he will change into a cap and gown, and he will walk across a stage and receive his master's degree in public administration.

Last week he waited for the day that will mark the culmination of a lifetime of silent prayers, and he talked about what has happened to him.

"In 1954 I got the job that helped give me the determination to do what I have done," he said. "I was hired as a caretaker for the Second Presbyterian Church of Evanston. Working up there in that environment was a new experience for me. I was immersed in quietness, in a place where I could meditate and do some reading. It was the first time in my life I ever was away from raucousness and noise. It was a fine feeling.

"I heard about a program that the University of Chicago was running downtown. It wasn't a part of the regular undergraduate school, so I didn't have to fill out an application and be accepted in order to attend. I enrolled in a Great Books course. It was a new world.

"Sometimes I would call up the university office in Hyde Park and ask them if my name was on their list of special students, and they always told me that it was. I just wanted to hear them say it, to make sure that I was associated with a university.

"After a year or so, I shifted over and became a regular part-time student. They let me do it because I had been in the Great Books program. I took a number of courses, and sometimes I said to myself, 'Gee, Dave, Lord, look where you are. Oh, my God.'

"Some of the professors were very kind to me. I went to my first dinner gathering in Hyde Park, at the home of an academic man. The quiet air of things. . . . We had a buffet, and candlelight, and there was a low hum of conversation. To use an expression of the youth, it knocked me out. I thought it was so wonderful . . . a different life, where one could deal in ideas.

"The little money I was making at the church, I used to pay my tuition. Then, in 1969, I took a part-time job on the weekends as a guard at Roosevelt. And I found out that they had a program where their employees could take academic courses free of charge. It offered a chance to poor men. I accepted a full-time job, and I began to take courses every quarter. I never missed a quarter. I would go to class, and then I would go to my job."

Two years ago, Mack had accumulated enough credits to qualify for a bachelor's degree. On graduation night, the university gave him an hour and a half off from his guard job. After the graduation ceremony he returned to his post.

He was supposed to turn in the cap and gown immediately, but he kept delaying; for three months he stored them in back of an old shelf of drawers by his guard desk, so that he could look at them from time to time and remind himself that it was true. He continued to work—and to take more classes.

"America is a youth-oriented society," he said. "When one goes before an organization to apply for a job, it is understood that they would rather hire a youth than an oldster. The people who hire wonder how much output they can get from a 50-year-old. If they hire a 25-year-old, they can expect 30 years or more of good work from that young man.

"But there is a way around it. If one has an expertise in a specific area, one achieves equality with youth, So I determined that I must earn my master's degree and be qualified."

Now that he has reached his goal, Mack is planning to decide what kind of work he would like to pursue. He is in no hurry; he has no family, and he lives by himself at the Lawson YMCA. He plans to continue his security-guard job for a while, until he is sure of what he should do next.

"It's a great feeling," he said the other day. "A wonderful feeling. To tell you the truth, I feel a little tearful. I don't drink, so I won't go out and celebrate in that manner. I may have a nice dinner, though.

"I know it's a cliche, but I think of Harry Golden's *Only in America*. It's that kind of happiness. There's a singing in my mind. I believe that the presence of an educated man enhances civilization. That's what the singing is about."

On the Train for a Year

We are riding on a train. The commuter is reading his evening newspaper, taking his time with each page, pausing even for the one-paragraph shorts. He is going home, toward the western suburbs.

He is surprised when someone interrupts his reading to ask some questions about the most distant stops on the line. The commuter does not seem used to being spoken to on his way home. But he is helpful; he pulls a schedule from his briefcase, and explains that Geneva, Illinois, is the last point on the line, and that to go beyond, one must hitch or find a ride. The commuter says that he, himself, has never been as far as Geneva on this train.

He goes back to his newspaper, and when the other passenger continues to talk to him, he hesitates for a moment, as if he does not wish further conversation. But then he puts his paper down and says, "I didn't mean to be rude. It's just that most people don't talk much on this ride."

The other asks the commuter if he has been riding this train for a long time.

"Twenty-two years," the commuter says.

Does he never talk to anyone? the other asks.

"No one really does," the commuter says. "There are some people who travel in twos and threes, and they take the same seats every night, and they talk to each other. Sometimes we will say hello to each other, because a lot of the faces become familiar. But that's about it."

The two talk for a time. The train stops in Oak Park, in Maywood, in Bellwood. The commuter says he no longer looks out the window until he hears the conductor call his stop.

"In the morning, riding into the city, I used to get excited," the commuter says. "As soon as I could see the buildings downtown, I would feel like I was doing something important. That was a long time ago. Now I usually read the morning paper until we're stopped in the North Western station. Everyone always gets up and pushes to be the first out of the car. I read my paper until everyone's done pushing. You don't save any time by fighting in the train."

The other asks the commuter if he ever thinks about saving himself the ride, about moving into the city.

"I grew up in the city," the commuter says. "I wouldn't move back. I feel better out where I live. My wife and I have three children, and I think it's good for them to be able to live in the suburbs. At least when I go home at night now, I feel as if I'm going somewhere. If I lived in the city, I don't think I'd ever feel like I was leaving work."

The other asks the commuter what he thinks about while he is riding every day.

"Nothing," the commuter says. "I used to look at the other people's faces and think how tired and empty they looked at the end of the day. But then I thought that someone was probably looking at me and thinking the same thing, so I don't do too much looking around.

"I remember my first train ride. When I was a kid, my father took me down to Springfield with him one time, in a parlor car, and we ate on the train. Big adventure. The other day I added it up in my head. Do you know how much time I've spent riding this train to work and back? Almost a year. One year out of my life.

"That's the kind of thing, if you think about it, it could drive you crazy."

Has there ever been a time when the commuter just didn't get on the train at the end of the day? the other asks.

The commuter nods his head. "One time, before a holiday, some of us from the office went out for a drink, because we got off work at noon. We drank all afternoon, and then we had dinner and drank some more. There were some women. I called home and said that I had to work late and would just stay downtown. My wife never questioned me about it. The next morning, I took the train home at the same time I'd usually take it downtown. It felt pretty good. That was the only time.

"Sometimes I think about leaving the office in the afternoon, and instead of going to the train station, I'll just go out to O'Hare and get on a plane to Las Vegas or somewhere and stay for about a week without telling anybody where I am." The train is pulling into the Glen Ellyn station, and the commuter picks up his briefcase and prepares to leave. "But I know I'll never do it," he says. "I'd probably feel guilty before I even got to the airport."

A Secret Soul

Lenny was the loneliest of dreamers. No one knew; we wouldn't have, either, except for the fact that the afternoons got long, and the only way to make it through was to talk. After a time we even talked to Lenny.

He worked in the shipping room of a bottling plant. They manufactured soda pop. Lenny was a thin, slight man in his middle 40s, with a stammer and a sad face. We worked at long tables. Lenny was the only full-timer at our table; the rest of us were in school, and we came in whatever afternoons we could spare and picked up pocket money for the weekends. For us, the job was a dreary way to kill time. For Lenny it was his sustenance.

The other full-timers in the room liked to kid Lenny. Most of them were in their 20s, and they passed the day with talk of women and late-night intrigue. Lenny had no wife or family, and he never spoke of a woman. So when the full-timers became bored with their own talk, they would call over to our table and rag Lenny some. They would ask him about his romances, and when he would become embarrassed and turn away and try not to answer, they would not let up until they became bored with that, too. They didn't mean anything by it.

He never said much, and for a while we didn't offer. We would come in after classes, nod hello to him, and start loading boxes. Lenny had spent most of his life being invisible; we sensed that without really thinking about it. He just seemed happy that we didn't rag him like the others did.

One afternoon, though, he started to talk. He didn't slow up what he was doing, but as he worked he began to ask us about the classes we took in school, the courses we were studying. He asked if any of us were studying English as a major; he wanted to know if any of us were studying the great poets.

None of us thought much about the questions at first; I know I didn't. But after that, a couple of times every week, he would ask the same things. It was always about the poets. On the way back home in the evenings, we would talk about it, and wonder what he meant. One night we determined that we would find out.

So the next day at break time, we asked Lenny to sit down for coffee with us. This never happened before; usually Lenny would disappear on his break. One of us asked him about the poets.

"I just wondered," Lenny said. But we pressed.

He avoided it, and so we dropped it and finished our cups. Just before we were due back at our table, Lenny said, "Sometimes I write poems."

We went back to work and tried to make him tell us more. It was so unlikely, the idea of Lenny, who seldom had the nerve to speak, and had trouble when he did, spending time committing his thoughts to paper. When we attempted to question him further, he became uncomfortable and flushed.

"Don't talk so loud," he pleaded. "The others will hear."

We asked him that day if he would let us see his poems, and he said no. We kept it up, though; we wanted to see. Finally he said that he would like to let us see them, but that he was afraid that if he brought them in, the others would find out and make fun of him.

We told him we would go with him to see them. He said he would think about it, and we did not let him forget. One day he said that we could come home with him if we wished.

After work we rode the L. He lived in one room. There were not enough places for us to sit. He brought out a large scrapbook. The poems were inside.

They were written all in longhand, with a fountain pen. Even before we started to read them, they looked elegant. Lenny's hand moved with strokes full of flourish and style, confident and strong where Lenny was timid and quiet. And when we did begin to read, the poems were beautiful. The verses were long, and rich with imagery and detail. They told of love, and of spiritual triumphs, and of life in faraway places. They were music. We must have sat and read for an hour, saying nothing. When we finished and looked up, there was Lenny, in his rented room, staring away from us.

"Please never say anything to the others," he said.

We tried to tell him how good the poems were, how he should be proud of what he had done, and not ashamed to let anyone know, but he cut us off.

"Please," he said. "I have to work there."

We went home, and the next day Lenny let us know, without a word, that we were not to talk about the poems again. For a few months we continued to work, and Lenny continued to take the joking from the other full-timers. Then school ended for the summer, and we left the job, and Lenny. We never went back.

The reason I am thinking about this is that I saw him the other day. There was no mistake; it was him. It was on a crowded street, and there was Lenny. I motioned to him, and called his name, and started walking toward him. He saw me; I know he did. He turned around very quickly and walked away, and I knew that I was not supposed to follow. . . .

9

WASHINGTON AND BEYOND

When I began the column, I had no ambition to be a political reporter. But when the presidential campaign year of 1972 started up, I found myself following the candidates, not out of any great interest for strategy or policy positions, but rather to observe the campaign as a massive American road show.

What started for me as a lark, of course, turned into the greatest political drama in the nation's history. A relatively boring presidential race grew into a scandal that changed America, and ended with, for the first time, a President of the United States having to leave office in disgrace.

This chapter provides, in rough chronological order, some snapshots from that continuing drama. "The Outsider" and "View from the Back Seat" were drawn from the political conventions of 1972 in Miami Beach.

The five following pieces, "Then . . . the Unthinkable," "Journal of a Political Sightseer," "On the Campaign Jet, Tears," "Barricades of Freedom" and "Wake for a Campaign" were written during the summer and fall campaign between Richard Nixon and George McGovern.

Then the scene jumps ahead to the following spring and summer of 1973, when "Watergate" became an American catch-phrase, and the nation's mind could not be torn away from the Senate Caucus Room in Washington. "The America of One Sad Man," "Irresistible Force," "President Ervin," "'Kind of Hard for Me to Watch,'" and "No Escape" are reporting from that remarkable year.

In the summer of 1974 impeachment hearings were held, and Richard Nixon's world dissolved. Four pieces—"Spirit of America," "History Lesson," "Over and Done," and "Serene"—are taken from that period.

By 1975 things were supposed to be back to normal. But we all had changed, all of us who had lived through it, and "normal" had to be considered in a new context. The final two columns in the chapter consider this. "Rodino, One Year On" is a look at how the events of Watergate altered the life of one man. "The Lesson Learned"— written on the eve of a visit to Chicago by the new president, Gerald Ford—is a look at how those events altered all the rest of us.

The Outsider

MIAMI BEACH—It all went away from him so quickly. For a few precious months he had it all, the idealism of a nation's young, the fear of its political bosses. And then, gone. So on this sultry afternoon at the Fontainebleau Hotel, most of the people filing past him did not even notice the man in the gray suit, standing with his back to a blue wall, watching them with a bemused smile on his face. In 1972, Eugene McCarthy is an outsider at the Democratic Convention.

"Where are you going to be?" he asked a friend. She had just offered to him, as tactfully as possible, an invitation to watch the convention sessions on television with her and some others. There will be no convention hall trailers and floor operatives for McCarthy this time. He is looking at TV with the rest of the country. "Where exactly will you be watching?" he asked.

Four years ago he came to the Chicago convention and his thousands were cheering at the airport, still drunk with the thrill of knocking off Lyndon Johnson, floating on the hope of winning the nomination. But that was a lifetime ago.

This time there was no chartered jet, and there was no crowd. McCarthy was scheduled to fly into Miami on a night commercial flight from Roanoke, Virginia. But the Piedmont flight was canceled at the last minute, and there were no more that night. So the man who became a part of history in 1968 spent the night by himself, and came quietly into Miami the next morning.

And at this moment he was at the headquarters hotel, watching the people go by. He has no Secret Service agents assigned to him, no one to clear his path through the lobbies. He does not need them. There is no crush.

"Where are we going next?" he said to a young man who had come to the hotel with him. The young man gave the name of a hotel.

"How far is that?" McCarthy asked.

"It's about four blocks," the young man said.

"That's not too bad," McCarthy said. "I'll walk it."

The young man said nothing. It was awkward; the presidential candidates are not allowed to walk anywhere; their security guards hustle them into limousines and surround them as they walk from car to hotel. Even if McCarthy had no security men, at least he could go through the act, the young man was figuring.

"Uh, maybe we should drive," the young man said. "It's too hot to walk, don't you think?"

"Oh, I don't know," McCarthy said. "It seems to be cooling off a little bit. We can walk it."

A few friends from other years recognized him, and came to say hello. McCarthy looked handsome and at ease, and he smiled a lot, the bit of gold between his front teeth showing. The trousers were a little wrinkled, but he still had the aura of quiet dignity that the others can only hope for. He talked easily with his friends, and once again he sounded more like a human being than a politician. The others can only try for that.

"Think we should do it now?" he said to the young man who stayed by his side. McCarthy had decided to hold a press conference. But he had arrived ten minutes early, and the La Ronde Room was only one-quarter full. To make matters worse, many of the people were ladies in bathing suits, and little kids with cheap cameras, and the lobby dwellers who have haunted the hotel all week. Since he has no Secret Service, no one was checking them as they came into the room. All week they have been kept out of the political press conferences, and now they were going to get to see one.

So McCarthy waited until the room had almost filled, and then he went forward. When he looked out over his audience he saw what he had—saw that the national press was by and large ignoring him, that the correspondents who had trailed him in 1968 had found other, more important stories to cover this afternoon.

He did it anyway, talking loosely and smiling to himself as he made private jokes. Did he prefer himself for a vice-presidential nomination? "No, I don't prefer myself for vice-president; I prefer all the others for vice-president." How should the convention vote? The smile, and, "Oh, I don't know, I'll talk to my four delegates about that."

It looked like it was going to end like that, but then something very bad happened. A young boy, one of the youth press representatives who had been admitted to the convention by the Democratic National Committee, raised his hand. "Senator McCarthy," he said, "If George McGovern is nominated, will you support him?"

McCarthy looked at the boy with undisguised scorn, "Oh, listen," he said, "we'll have that question from some senior members a little later on."

The room went silent. No one knew what to say. The kid looked like he was about to cry. The press conference ended soon after.

As McCarthy was leaving the room, a girl shouted, "What have you got against youth?"

A young photographer who had known McCarthy in '68 hurried up and said, "Senator, you know, a lot of these youth media are the people who worked for you in 1968."

McCarthy stopped. "I answered three questions for him," he said. "He just works for a high school paper in Milwaukee or something."

Maybe the high school kid was feeling awful, but McCarthy had to be feeling worse. To be ignored after having what he has had is a terrible thing. The people in the room were muttering that he had forgotten so soon, but that is not true at all. Eugene McCarthy has not forgotten a thing. He walked to the revolving doors. It was not cooling off at all, it was still steamy outside, and he had a four-block walk ahead of him.

View from the Back Seat

MIAMI BEACH—Nothing makes sense anymore. The cabdriver is 22 years old, and we are stalled in traffic. It should be a $1 ride, but the meter is already up to $3.90, and we aren't even close to where we are going. The problem is that cops and protesters have filled Collins Avenue in front of the Fontainebleau, and nothing is moving. The meter keeps clicking, a dime at a time.

"So people ask me if it doesn't bother me about my girl, and I tell them yeah, it bothers me, I cry all the way to the bank," the cabdriver says. He is referring to the fact that he sells his girlfriend to the riders of his taxi. Going rate during the convention is $100 a throw. His girl friend is an 18-year-old blonde and she had been known to bring in $700 in an evening.

"She doesn't have to do it if she doesn't want to," he says. "But look, when this convention's over we're going down to the Bahamas, all expenses paid by her. She's been doing it for about a year. The first week it was bad; she got real upset. But now the tricks aren't even people to her. Just a job, man, you know? She never got beat up or anything. She's real little and cute; you'd have to be crazy to beat on her."

Flaming youth, 1972. The cabdriver looks as though he could

fit right in at Flamingo Park, but he says he would not mind it if a few of the demonstrators got filled with bullets. He says they are hurting his business, and thus that of his girl friend, who he is living with but does not yet know if he will marry.

In front of the Fontainebleau, a bleeding carcass is on the sidewalk. A kid with a red bandanna around his forehead is leaping on the hood of a Cadillac limousine. The police are moving in, clubs held chest-high. Republicans in evening dress are trying to make their way inside the hotel, but eggs are being tossed at them by the young idealists, and they have to keep looking over their shoulders to avoid getting hit. There is a lot of sweat and noise and heat. Ten feet behind the surging line of policemen, Rocky Pomerance looks as if he is at a garden party.

"Oh, what a delight. Of course I remember you," Pomerance says to a writer from *Life* magazine. Pomerance, the Miami Beach police chief, is wearing a perfect dark blue summer-weight blazer and a pair of white duck bell-bottoms. He is puffing on a pipe, watching the scuffling in front of him as if it were a Miami Dolphins game on his television. He has become a national media celebrity by virtue of playing the role of the cool cop, and by God he's going to stay cool no matter what happens. He is in the middle of Collins Avenue, and he has to raise his voice to be heard over the chants of the Cream of American Youth and the marching steps of the policemen.

"Was it done nicely?" Pomerance asks. He is talking to Barbara Walters, the TV lady, who is in a black evening dress and is also in the middle of the busiest street in Florida, watching the bullfights. "Oh, you just got here, you missed the first part of it, didn't you, Barbara?" Pomerance says.

"You know," he philosophizes into the muggy Sunday night air, "they say that you become half of all you meet. At this point I feel like I'm half hippie."

Gardnar Mulloy, the tennis player who, with Billy Talbert, used to be part of the finest doubles team in the world, is leaning against a car, racket in hand, wearing his whites. Ever since 1968, street fighting has become just another wonderful, wacky part of Life in These United States. Just something else to watch and shake your head at. No one thinks it is in the least unusual for Mulloy to be out here in his tennis duds, or for Pomerance to be making idle conversation with his media pals, or for Miamians to be pulling their cars into the middle of the tumult, then locking the doors and turning the air conditioning up full blast and leaning back in the front seat to watch. All of this within a couple of yards of the pushing and shoving.

A kid has climbed to the top of a 15-foot-high column in front of the Fontainebleau. He is not a part of the demonstration, but he looks as if he might be. He is very scared. There are three men in suits at the bottom of the column, trying to get him down so they can tear him apart. All he wanted to do is watch the policemen and the Brave Young Americans, and now he doesn't know how to get away.

"Get down here, you little scumbag," the men yell. "They never look so brave when they're alone, do they? Come on down here, we've got something to show you!"

The cops make a tentative move toward the Leaders of Tomorrow, and the spectators in front of the Fontainebleau burst into heartfelt, lusty cheers. The cavalry has arrived. Without John Wayne, though. He's inside at the $500-a-plate dinner. Rocky Pomerance sucks on his pipe and smiles at something Barbara Walters is saying. Gardnar Mulloy taps his racket on the street. An egg flies through the air and splatters by the bleeding carcass. The kid on the column looks for a way to get down and run away. The people in the driveway applaud. The cops move forward. The 22-year-old cabdriver looks for someone to go to bed with his girl friend. Nothing makes sense anymore.

Then...the Unthinkable

CUSTER, S.D.—Please, just for a second, let us forget the presidential campaign.

The rain was coming hard in Custer. Lou Thebo, 72, was in his barber shop, cutting hair. He had a rancher in the chair. They were talking about the rain, of course, and about the price of beef, and about the fact that George McGovern, a man who is running for president, was up the road, over by Sylvan Lake, taking a vacation.

The gas heater in Thebo's shop, which is on 6th Street just off Rushmore Road, was turned off, because it is hot here this week. A pile of yellowing comic books, some of them dating back to 1968, went unlooked at on top of a shelf. There were four empty card table chairs around the room. Lou was the only barber. A Stephan's Dandruff Treatment poster and a Ralph H. Gates Insurance calendar decorated the wall. Lou's sink was stained from years of hot water rushing out of the faucet.

"I've got no use for McGovern," Lou Thebo said. "My daughter Mary's got a son over there in Vietnam. My grandson Stevie. He's over there fighting. When that McGovern joined up with the peace marchers in Washington, that was enough for me. I want no part of him."

Lou went back to the price of beef, and slowly cut the rancher's hair. And then, as if in a horrifying snatch from a dreadful, perverted afternoon soap opera, Mary Trant appeared in the doorway. Mary is Lou Thebo's daughter. She was crying, almost choking as she called out.

"Dad, dad," she sobbed. "A man from the Army just came. Stevie's dead. They just killed him in Vietnam."

So Lou Thebo locked the door of his shop and walked his daughter Mary up to his home, at 632 Montgomery Street. Mary's husband left her a couple of years ago, and she lives on the other side of Custer, in a trailer home. Lou did not want her to go back there alone and think about Stevie being dead.

They sat in the living room, on two green couches with faded cloth covering. An endless succession of quiz shows came across the

television screen, but the sound was off and no one was watching.
And as had to happen, as would happen in the worst melodrama
conceived by the most pitiful Hollywood script hack, the mailman
came, and he was carrying a letter from Steve Trant.

"Dear Mom and All," the letter said. "Well, I finally got here.
A lot of my old friends are still here, so it's not like going to a new
place. Most of my friends think I'm crazy to come back over here.
They can't believe that I'm here again.

"I'm glad I got back in the same area. At least I know what to
expect here. So it's not bad. Did Vicki apply for a job at the state
hospital? If she's still in Custer, tell her I've been writing her at her
address in Hot Springs. Well, everyone, that's about it for now.
There's not much more to say, so I'll sign off for now. God bless all of
you. I miss everyone. Kiss Mickey for me and write soon. Your son
and brother, Steve."

Over in a corner, Vicki Broyles was reading the letter and biting
her lip and trying not to let it all come out of her. She was wearing a
pair of red shorts cut almost up to her hips and a black-and-white
tie-dyed T-shirt that she did herself. Vicki is 18 years old, and until
the man from the Army came to Custer she thought that she was
going to marry Steve Trant.

"I met him over in Hot Springs, where I used to live, when he
was home on leave last month," she said. "We only knew each other
a couple of weeks, but we were going to get married. You know that
'Mickey' in the letter? That's Steve's brother Michael. Michael's
retarded. He lived at home until Steve went into the Army, but
when Steve went in, there was no one to take care of him. Mickey's
19 years old and Steve is . . . was . . . 20. That's why I was going
to work at the hospital. They keep Mickey there, and I could kind
of watch out for him for Steve and make sure no one did anything wrong to him."

Mary Trant kept bringing the wad of Kleenex up to her face,
but the tears wouldn't stop. Her boy was dead, and there was
nothing to do but look at the soundless TV and let it all wash over
her. "He didn't like the war," she said. "He enlisted in July of 1969.
He was in Germany, and then he was in Vietnam for a while. He
reupped when it was time to decide, because there was nothing for
him here."

And indeed there was not. Steve Trant graduated from Custer

High School and saw no other way to get out of town but to join the Army. There was no reason to stay around town. He met Vicki Broyles on his last leave before going back to Vietnam early this month. He told her that he wished he had met her before, that he would have quit the Army if he could have known that there was a girl like her in South Dakota. She moved away from her home in Hot Springs right before he went back to Vietnam. He asked Vicki to wait for him, and she said she would try.

Now they were all in Lou Thebo's living room. Steve Trant's 14-year-old sister Becky was face down on one of the couches, her head buried in a foam rubber pillow. Tom, Steve's 18-year-old brother, was beside her. His hair was moderately long, and he had just started to grow sideburns.

"I'm not going over there, ever," Tom said. "They can't force me. It's stupid."

Vicki Broyles had left the house. She was walking slowly around the neighborhood. Finally, she sat down on the grass and looked down the hill toward the main street, where the tourists were parading up and down.

"I just don't know," she said. "I don't know what I'll do. I can't go home to my folks in Hot Springs. There's nothing for me to do there. But there's nothing for me do here, now, either. I don't even know if he would have married me, really. Maybe he was just feeling lonely, you know?"

So George McGovern was up in the hills, planning a presidential campaign based on a pledge to end a war that has become so much a part of us that we are deadened to it. After all, look at the numbers. There are only a handful of American kids dying over there every week. It's winding down.

Mary Trant, her son dead, said that she had better start thinking about dinner. "If you ask me it was senseless for us to be over there in the first place," she said.

Lou Thebo, her father, leaned toward her. "Someone's got to do the fighting," he said. "Someone's got to stand up for what we believe in."

In the morning, the man from the Army would come back and talk about how the body would be shipped home, to a little hill town in South Dakota where the population had just been decreased by one. Mary Trant brought the Kleenex to her face again, and Becky pulled up into a ball on the couch, and Vicki Broyles sat on the neighbor's lawn and tried to figure out what she would do from now on, now that her boy friend was dead, another one sacrificed to a long and famous war.

Journal of a Political Sightseer

HARTFORD, Conn.—One of the many glamorous and exciting side benefits of traveling with the McGovern campaign is the leisurely, sophisticated manner in which one can meander through the United States and savor the civic and cultural highlights.

It would be selfish to keep the rewards of this languid, studied examination of the country's notable spots to oneself. So the following is offered as a journal of one recent day's relaxed sightseeing.

5:45 A.M.—Alarm rings in your room of Leamington Hotel, Minneapolis. Soon after, telephone rings. It is front desk calling to inform you that of the six shirts you sent to the laundry yesterday, five have been washed and returned.

7:30 A.M.—Baggage call, Minneapolis Room, Leamington Hotel. Secret Service, in their never-ending quest for security, go through your suitcase and leave the five clean shirts wrinkled and bent and ready to be sent to the laundry.

8:12 A.M.—Eggs are placed in front of you in Leamington Hotel coffee shop. You are about to bite into eggs, when McGovern staff girl calls that McGovern is coming, and everyone must board buses. You wave good-by to eggs and board bus.

8:45 A.M.—You look out window of parked bus, waiting for

McGovern to come out of Leamington Hotel. You daydream of eggs and toast.

9:04 A.M.—Arrive Twin Cities Airport; board charter jet. Stewardess offers bloody mary. You say no. She walks on. You look at day's schedule. You call stewardess back and accept bloody mary.

10:37 A.M.—Plane arrives Chicago Midway Airport. Mayor Daley is waiting at Sherman House for 11:00 A.M. meeting with McGovern. "We'll never make it," McGovern aide says.

10:44 A.M.—There are no cars on Stevenson Expressway. City trucks block entrance ramps. Police cars lead way. "We'll make it," McGovern aide says.

10:59 A.M.—Arrive to meet Daley, one minute early.

12:22 P.M.—Raining very hard in Loop. "I say it is unfair for the rich businessman to write off his $20 martini lunch as a business expense when the workingman can't write off his bologna sandwich," McGovern says. Rally applauds. Your feet are getting wet. You make a note to buy new shoes without holes in bottom, if there is a day when you have time.

1:38 P.M.—Arrive Midway Airport. Look for restaurant. McGovern is ready to go, staff girl says. You stop looking for restaurant.

1:55 P.M.—You sit on airplane. Airplane is on ground. You look out window of plane for McGovern, daydream of cheeseburger and french fries.

2:05 P.M.—Airplane is in sky. Stewardess offers bloody mary. You say no. She walks on. You look at wallet calendar and see there are eight weeks to election day. You call stewardess back and accept bloody mary.

3:10 P.M.—Arrive Metro Airport, Detroit. You ride bus to Sheraton-Cadillac Hotel. McGovern goes to suite for private meeting. You go to lobby for nap on couch. Desk clerk warns you not to put feet on couch.

4:50 P.M.—You ask girl on street where Kennedy Square, site of rally, is. She laughs. "What's wrong with you, aren't you from around here?" she sneers. She do s not give directions.

5:05 P.M.—You are late for rally. You eat luxurious expense account dinner at filthy downtown Detroit diner with Doug

Kneeland of *New York Times.* You eat chocolate pie and red pop; Kneeland eats Coney Island hot dog and orange pop. Both will be filets by the time *Sun-Times* and *New York Times* auditors see them.

5:20 P.M.—Misty and windy and cold in downtown Detroit. "I say it is unfair for the rich businessman to write off his $20 martini lunch as a business expense when the workingman can't write off his bologna sandwich," McGovern says. Rally applauds. Your feet are getting cold. You begin to sniffle. You make a note to buy a bottle of aspirin, if there is a day when you have time.

7:02 P.M.—Board airplane at Detroit Metro Airport. Stewardess offers bloody mary. You say no. You look in airplane window and see your reflection. You call stewardess back and accept bloody mary.

9:10 P.M.—Arrive Hopkins Airport, Cleveland. Board bus. Bus driver must think he is on a regular downtown run, for he stops at every corner on way to Cleveland Arena.

9:32 P.M.—Muggy and fetid in Cleveland Arena. "I say it is unfair for the rich businessman to write off his $20 martini lunch as a business expense when the workingman can't write off his bologna sandwich," McGovern says. Rally applauds. Your feet are numb. You sniffle. Your throat is sore. You make a note to check into a hospital, if there is a day when you have time.

9:47 P.M.—Pretty Cleveland blonde girl comes up to you at rally, is nice to you, welcomes you to Cleveland, and asks where you are staying tonight. You look at schedule and tell her Pittsburgh Hilton. You begin to cry.

11:05 P.M.—Board airplane, Cleveland Hopkins Airport. Stewardess takes one look at you, does not have to ask. She knows. She places bloody mary on tray table.

12:30 A.M.—Plane arrives Allegheny County Airport, Pittsburgh. It is wet and gusty. Two hundred people are waiting for McGovern, even though there is no rally scheduled. McGovern decides it would be nice to shake each of their hands. Your feet are gone. You cannot breathe. Your throat is on fire. You see angels. You make a note to draw up a will, if there is a day when you have time.

1:20 A.M.—Arrive Pittsburgh Hilton. You are informed that

you are being billed $2 as a "gratuity" for having bags carried to your room but, because it is so late, you will have to carry bags yourself. Assistant manager says you have your problems, he has his.

2:30 A.M.—You lie in bed, stare at ceiling in darkness. You know that you have forgotten something. You remember. You have forgotten to write story for newspaper. You remind yourself what a wonderful experience this is. You get dressed and head for pressroom.

On the Campaign Jet, Tears

ST. PAUL—It should have been a private moment, but there are no private moments when you are a presidential candidate. So when the tears came to George McGovern's eyes, he had to turn his head away, because three or four people were watching him, and he did not want them to see him cry.

He was in the cramped back compartment of his campaign jet, the Dakota Queen II, on his way from Boston to Minnesota. The silver Prisoner of War bracelet he wears on his right wrist was showing under his cuff. He sat on a table, suit jacket off, tie loosened, his stockinged feet lifted up off the turquoise airline carpeting. He looked out the window for a brief moment. Then he pulled a handkerchief from his pants pocket and dabbed at his eyes to stop the tears.

The tape recorder had just been clicked off. It was a Sony stereo model, with the two speakers taped to the wall of the plane, above some campaign photographs and a hand-drawn "Would you buy a used car?" poster of Richard Nixon. For the last six minutes McGovern had been listening to a tape, and now there was only silence.

"They came into the villages after they dropped the napalm,

and human beings were fused together," the voice had said. "Fused together like metal, sometimes you couldn't tell if they were people or animals."

The voice had been soft and full of breath and struggling to hold back a frantic kind of sobbing.

"You go into a village," the voice had said, "and—not even the bugs, you can't even find bugs. That's how fantastic and devastating it is. When you're there you accept it, you rationalize it, you condone it because they're the enemy. . . . You didn't have the courage to open your mouth against killing people, animals. You have no idea if it's a human being or an animal. You come home and live with that because you didn't have the guts to say it was wrong. . . ."

All these months McGovern has been trying to say why the war slices him up inside, and he just hasn't been able to get it across. His manner is too shy, his voice too soft, to convey the seething that he feels. And then Thursday morning, a man in Boston handed him a reel of tape, and all of a sudden there was a voice saying everything that McGovern has been feeling, everything that everyone who hates the war so much that it makes them sick has been feeling.

The voice is that of a young man who, on Labor Day, made a telephone call to the Jerry Williams radio talk show in Boston. The young man told Williams that he was a Vietnam veteran, and he went on to talk for six minutes of the things he had done and the things he had seen. Several times the young man lost control of himself when he spoke of the bombed-out villages.

McGovern was a guest on the Williams show Thursday, and Williams told him about the young man, and the tape. He told McGovern that it would be worth listening to. But McGovern was behind schedule, and did not have the time. He said he would take a copy of the tape with him if Williams had an extra one. Williams did.

So midway into the flight to Minnesota, McGovern came walking down the aisle. That is not unusual; his office is in the front of the plane, and the staff working area is in the back, and he comes back and forth all the time. A few of the reporters looked up and said hello, but most of them continued to eat their lunch or play cards or talk or sleep.

It wasn't until a few minutes later that the people on the plane began to notice that McGovern had not returned right away. He was listening to the tape, of course. He was staring at the recorder as if it were a television set, his mouth tight. When you came into the little work area, the first impulse was to ask what was happening, or to make a joke with McGovern about the stockinged feet. But right away the voice from the tape cut into you. No one was saying anything, just listening.

The soldier's words may not be that powerful on paper; all of these years of millions of words about Vietnam have not been powerful enough to stop the war. My Lai was not powerful enough. The words of Eugene J. McCarthy and Robert F. Kennedy and McGovern himself have not been powerful enough.

But somehow the anguished voice of the young man who helped do the killing brings it home. We hear all this talk about withdrawal plans and Kissinger trips and winding down, and we forget that those, too, are not only words. The war is not words. It is this:

"We have jets that drop rockets, and in the shells they have penny nails and those nails—one nail per square inch for about the size of a football field—you can't believe what they do to a human being. I was there a year and I never had the courage to say that was wrong. I condoned that. I watched it go on. Now I'm home. Sometimes I—my heart—it bothers me inside because I remember all that and I didn't have the courage then to say it was wrong. . . . You go into a village that has had a thousand-pound bomb. It's called the daisy cutter. . . . You don't worry about taking prisoners because there are no prisoners. You don't know if you killed Viet Cong because you can't put the people together. . . ."

The young man never gave his name. But no one who heard the tape thought to question its validity, because the sickest thing of all is that what he was saying is not especially controversial; it is not something that we disbelieve. We drop bombs on people in Asia, and they die horrible deaths. There are 30 days in September. Cats have four legs. Just another fact of life.

When we arrived in the Twin Cities, we drove to the University of Minnesota for an outdoor rally. McGovern spoke, and received the usual warm, polite, grateful reception. The students liked him very much.

And then, after the speech was over, McGovern asked the students to wait for a few minutes, because he had something he thought they should hear. The tape of the young veteran's voice came over the loudspeakers. For six minutes there were 15,000 people standing outside in the chill, numb, unwilling to move, hearing the same voice that had brought McGovern to tears on the airplane.

When the tape had ended, McGovern told the crowd that there was not much else to say, and they began to drift away. A guitar player started to play "This Land Is Your Land," the traditional song that ends McGovern rallies. But this time the people were not singing along. This time, no one was making a sound.

Barricades of Freedom

PHILADELPHIA—The place is called Independence Park. The Liberty Bell is here. So is Independence Hall where, on July 4, 1776, the Declaration of Independence was signed. The park is a national shrine, big and grassy and dotted with trees. People come here every day to wander around and look at the country's history.

But not the other morning. On this particular morning there were policemen standing shoulder-to-shoulder around the entire periphery of Independence Park. On the streets surrounding the park, other policemen rode patrol on big horses. The side streets were barricaded. If a person wanted to come to see Independence Hall, he had to go through an elaborate series of checkpoints. And if he did not have a special invitation, he would not make it past the first checkpoint, he would not get within a block of the park.

Electronic metal detectors like the ones now common at airports had been set up at the one point in the park where a person with an invitation could enter. Sawhorses had been arranged so that the invited people could be funneled into a single file, then led through the metal detectors one at a time before they were taken to a roped-in area where they were allowed to stand.

From the air it must have looked ludicrous. Here was this calm, gracious park on a chilly autumn afternoon, and it had been completely cleared except for a small group of people jammed into a tiny area closest to the hall. The rest of the park was empty, save the security agents with walkie-talkies who patrolled it as if it were some Vietnamese jungle.

But then, no one was going to see it from the air. The only thing in the air was a helicopter. Inside the helicopter were the people who were the reason the park was being closed down for the day. Their names were Bob Haldeman, John Ehrlichman, Ronald Ziegler, Walter Tkach, and Richard Nixon. They were coming from the South Lawn of the White House to Independence Hall for something called a "nonpolitical visit."

Mr. Nixon, at the invitation of an ex-policeman named Frank Rizzo who is mayor of Philadelphia, was coming to sign the revenue sharing bill. Mr. Nixon would sign the bill in the shadows of Independence Hall, and the ceremony would be filmed for use on television. Both Democrats and Republicans were among the people who had invitations that would let them in, which was one of the reasons the visit was called "nonpolitical."

A man who had never been to Independence Park before went up to a policeman who was on duty on the lawn, and said "Could you tell me where the Liberty Bell is?"

The policeman turned around and said, "Where's your invitation?" The man convinced the policeman that he was cleared to be inside the barricades, and repeated his question.

"Look," the policeman said, "no one sees the Liberty Bell when the president is here."

The program's master of ceremonies, Spiro T. Agnew, was saying, "Too much power has been flowing away from the people." A block from the park, a small delegation of labor people, older men with signs asking for a revision in the wage-freeze guidelines, were being surrounded by the mounted policemen. They wanted Mr. Nixon and Mr. Agnew to see their signs. The mounted cops' assignment was to make sure this did not happen.

Thomas Dunn, the mayor of Elizabeth, New Jersey, was not carrying a sign. Neither was Eldon Hout, the commissioner of Washington County, Oregon. Nor was H. F. Jacobberger, a councilman from Omaha, Nebraska. These were the people who had been invited, and who had been allowed inside Independence Park—people from local, state and national government, people whose deportment could be depended on. Mr. Nixon gave them each an autographed pen when the ceremony was over, and the chant of "Four More Years" went up at the nonpolitical event.

The oddest thing to think about is the question of why, with the public opinion polls as overwhelmingly in favor of the president as they are, there should be an attempt to limit the citizens who are allowed to set eyes on him.

Surely, with that huge park available, and so many police present to prevent trouble, and the millions of Americans who are supposed to favor Mr. Nixon, it would make sense to let them in.

What better setting than a National Historical Park for the president to look out over the people and say, "The Constitution of the United States begins with the words 'We the people,' and the bill I shall sign is a demonstration of a principle that we have faith in people, we believe in people, and we believe that government closest to the people should have the greatest support."

Instead he said the words in the desolation of a top-security encampment, and it was a little sad. Because it is not a pleasant thing to see naked fear, and the Republicans are very afraid of something, or else they would not be running their campaign the way they are.

Is it anti-war demonstrators they are afraid of? They shouldn't be. It is not 1968 any more, and most of the people in the country apparently approve of the way the president is handling the war. If the Republicans were to let Mr. Nixon make a speech and allow anyone in who wanted to listen, there would almost certainly be a staggering majority of plain citizens who would simply like to see a president, and that in itself would be an answer to whatever demonstrators did come.

But the fear is there, so only the invited get in.

When the ceremony at Independence Hall ended, Mr. Nixon walked out to his car. Across the street were rows and rows of people who had not been allowed into the park. Among the crowd was a small group of young anti-war people. Their chants were almost lost in the cheering from the rest of the sidewalk crowd. But the chants were still audible, so a plan was put into effect.

From large loudspeakers that had been hung above the people, painfully loud military music began to boom. It was so loud, so piercing, that it completely drowned out both the cheers and the boos from the people who had come to see Mr. Nixon. Many of the people put their hands to their ears to try to shut the awful clamor out.

The president approached his car. He looked across the street at the people he could not hear, smiled, and waved to them. The smothering blanket of music remained until he was gone, the nonpolitical visit to Philadelphia and Independence Park over.

Wake for a Campaign

SIOUX FALLS, S.D.—You can sit around and watch it die, or you can do the proper thing, which is to head for the closest bar and make them turn the jukebox up full blast and try to forget that it is happening.

That's not much of a choice. So, in a chilly South Dakota town, you watch the local ladies cruise in and out of the bar and tell yourself that it had to happen, it was going to happen all along, and if you were a little more grown up and a little smarter you would have known it months ago. Even as the Hollies are singing "Long Cool Woman in a Black Dress" on the jukebox, even as the barroom ladies are twitching their bottoms in the brown leather chairs, George McGovern is losing it all.

It's not like it ought to be. The place ought to be packed with election-night people, at least people getting drunk to block out what is going on. But it's not; it's half empty. There's not a familiar face in the joint, except the guy across the table from you, Hunter S. Thompson, who has been following the campaign all year for *Rolling Stone* and is trying one more time to find something good in what is going down in Sioux Falls.

"Maybe something's up," Thompson says. "They ought to be here; the staff people ought to be out in one of these places. We haven't seen any of them. Maybe something's up; we ought to find them."

So you leave the bar for a minute, and you go to look for the McGovern people to see if they know something startling, but they don't. They are in their hotel rooms, and it is still early in the evening, and they already know it is all over, dead, stomped to hell. If it looked good, they could celebrate, and if it looked doubtful, they could drink to pass the time until the important states came in. But it is neither of those things; it is simply hopeless, and they are by themselves.

Dick Dougherty is keeping the game up. He is McGovern's press secretary, and if he has been a bit reluctant to act like a typical fawning PR man, that is probably because he is a better writer than 90 per cent of the newsmen on the press plane, which is an oddity for press secretaries. But he did it for George McGovern, and on this night, even though it is all gone, he will go through his act one more time.

He goes into the hotel press room and tells the national correspondents what McGovern's suite looks like, and who is in it, and what he had for dinner. With all the hopes fading away, someone shouts out, "What kind of dressing did he have on that salad?" and Dougherty closes his eyes for just a moment, and then say, "Roquefort."

In a second, though, he is over talking to the girls who are his assistants, telling them that the airplanes back to Washington will leave early Wednesday. In 24 hours all this will have disappeared from South Dakota, and there will be no sign that there was any campaign at all.

The last time for smiles was in the afternoon, at the Minnehaha Country Club, when McGovern and the reporters who have followed him got together for one last party. It was supposed to be relaxed and loose, but there were only two hours left until the polls would close, and anyone who was acting like he was at a typical cocktail thing was not doing a very good job of pretending. There have been some bad times between McGovern and the campaign reporters, especially during the Eagleton thing, but the fact is they like him. He is, quite simply, a nice man. They like him, and it was hard for everyone to pretend that they did not see what was going to happen.

By the time the party ended, dusk had come to Sioux Falls. McGovern went to his room, and that was when you began the wait, the wait that would not last very long.

The official statements and the tears will come later. Now it is just the three television sets, lined up next to each other on a tall table covered with white tablecloths. All three networks are bringing the same news.

Rob Gunnison and his wife, Jan, are sitting together, across the room, next to the tub of cold beer. They have traveled the whole campaign, arranging baggage and plane logistics for the McGovern tour party, getting up early and going to bed late. It is odd to see Rob doing anything other than lugging suitcases, and Jan doing anything but checking over the charter jet passenger list. But tonight there is none of that to do. Jan looks over and slowly shakes her head. She pauses, then shakes it again.

There is not much to say. George McGovern's campaign was a nice dream, but like all dreams it was only a matter of time before reality wiped it out. And your choice comes down to whether to watch the death scene or to walk away from it. The night in Sioux Falls is getting colder.

Four more years. Time to go home.

The America of
One Sad Man

WASHINGTON—It starts in the White House, with a president spending four and a half years issuing dire warnings about national security and threats from within and demons walking among us, and in the end, on the bottom line, this is where it ends. With a nervous, puzzled, perspiring middle-aged man drumming his hands on a witness table Thursday and explaining in a quavering voice why he now finds himself living in a jail cell: "I get confused about these things. . . . It was a matter of national security. . . . It was my duty to help my country."

Bernard L. Barker, another of the convicted Watergate burglars, came to the Senate Caucus Room wearing a seersucker jacket and thick glasses. He had none of the cockiness of the previous witnesses; none of the understated, self-assured professionalism of James McCord, or the educated, law school glibness of Gerald Alch.

Barker came to the brown-clothed witness table with his hands shaking, and he began to talk in a thin, jumpy voice. His language was imprecise, and he had to struggle to articulate his thoughts. He did not try to hide the fact that he does not pride himself on the workings of his mind: "If I was a wise man, I probably wouldn't be sitting right here. . . . I was not there to think. . . . I was there to follow orders, not to think."

Barker is a sad, confused, anonymous little man with a sad, confused idea of what patriotism is, and he would be a humorous figure had he not come to this end. For he is a product of the White House talk of national security; when the sophisticated man in the White House used the nation's security as fodder for clever political statements, this not-so-sophisticated man named Barker took the words at face value. He believed all of it; he believed it so well that he thought burglarizing the offices of the Democratic Party constituted an act of service to the United States.

So confused. Barker thought he was dealing with an enemy of America when he broke into the Democratic headquarters, and Thursday he tried to explain what he was thinking when the District of Columbia police caught him: "When you're captured by the enemy, you do not talk." And later, becoming desperate at the sound of gasps and laughter in the hearing room as he revealed his poignant state of mind, he tried again to explain, tried to explain to make everyone understand how he felt during the burglary. It was an impersonal, patriotic act, he said, much like "when I was a bombardier in Germany and bombed a town."

He breathed heavily as he struggled to make the people in the hearing room see that he was not a ludicrous man. He knew that after he was arrested he would be taken care of by attorneys. He said: "The philosophy was that if you were caught by the enemy, every effort would be made to rescue you."

Barker was perfect for the Watergate assignment—and for the break-in of Daniel Ellsberg's psychiatrist's office which he carried out—because he is such a trusting, dull man that he did not even think to question what he would be told to do. Better still, he didn't even want to know who was giving him his orders, other than E. Howard Hunt, his immediate boss. To Barker, Hunt, the man from the White House, represented everything decent: "the liberation of Cuba, and anti-Communism, and the government of the United States in current form."

When Joseph Montoya, the Democratic senator from New Mexico on the Ervin Committee, stared at Barker and said, "As a matter of fact, Mr. Barker, you were in there for the purpose of political espionage, and not for internal security," Barker looked hurt that anyone would accuse him of that. And when Howard Baker, the Republican senator from Tennessee, kept asking Barker why he did it—"Why? Why? Why?"—Barker could only keep repeating what he must truly, in his limited way, believe: "It was a matter of national security. It was my duty to my country, sir."

Even as Barker struggled through his testimony at the witness table, Richard Nixon was on the other side of town telling an auditorium full of returned prisoners of war that "it is time that this country stops making national heroes out of those who steal national secrets and publish them in the newspapers."

The president got his expected standing ovation for that, as if the current troubles in this country have anything at all to do with what he casually calls "national security" when the mood strikes him. But using the term so cheaply will create more Bernard Barkers, who really, deeply believe that a president saying that something is vital to the nation's good automatically makes it so, who believe it to the extent that they will commit felonies against other Americans in their obedience to it. Just as the same president loosely talking about "bums burnin' up the campuses" helped create a national climate that ultimately led to four dead bodies in Kent, Ohio, so his calculated, selfish use of the idea of the security of the nation will bring us more Bernard Barkers, more people who look upon Watergate as an act of patriotism.

When Barker had finished his testimony about the domestic enemy, and duty to country, and what he called a "paramilitary operation" in the capital of the country, he was near tears. He tried to explain that he feels a close kinship with the other burglars: "In a certain way the things I said do not represent me as a person. . . . I am part of a team which I am very proud of . . . devoted anti-Communist fighters . . . family men who believe very deeply in a cause. . . . We are not criminal elements."

One of the senators, leaning too close to his open microphone, could be heard to murmur, "That is the most frightening thing I have ever heard." But by that time Bernard Barker, a burglar who believes that his way of thinking is what America is all about in 1973, was on his way to the door. For a brief moment, the hearing room was strangely quiet.

Irresistible Force

WASHINGTON—Herman Talmadge, the senator from Georgia, was finally getting his chance, and in his perfect rural red-clay voice he was talking to John Ehrlichman about principles of law rooted in ancient England. "I believe that students learn early in law school," Talmadge said slowly, "about the principle that no matter how humble a man's cottage, even the king of England can't enter without permission."

Ehrlichman, behind the witness desk at the Watergate hearings for the second straight day, smiled thinly at Talmadge and began to lecture, as if he were speaking to a particularly backward worm. "I'm afraid that's become considerably eroded over the years, hasn't it, senator?" Ehrlichman said.

Talmadge raised his voice, squinted and leaned toward Ehrlichman. "Down in my country, we still think it's a pretty legitimate principle of law," Talmadge said.

The crowd in the Senate Caucus Room burst into applause, and Ehrlichman sat back to wait until they stopped. He did not bother to answer Talmadge. Just another enemy, an enemy like everyone else in the room, an enemy who, not so long ago, could have been dealt with. John Ehrlichman is no longer in the position to deal with anyone, though, so he pushed his lips together and waited for the next question, waited for the next insult to the lofty, rarefied position that he had held only last spring.

He was one of the three most powerful men in the government of the United States, and so what if no one ever elected him, so what if his sole source of power derived from the fact that Richard Nixon liked to have him close at hand? At this time last year, a telephone call from John Ehrlichman carried all the thunder and trauma of a call from the president himself, and even now, even after Ehrlichman has left the White House in disgrace, he cannot get rid of the manner he developed there. Even though he has no power base anymore—even though he is unemployed, for that matter—he cannot stop acting like the government still belongs to him, and he cannot hide the fact that he feels that the indignity of appearing under oath before this select Senate committee is somehow beneath him.

The hostility in the hearings room is almost palpable, and it flows both ways. If Ehrlichman is scornful of the senators, they are just as scornful of his attitude, and the attitude he always held toward Congress when he had the ability to make things difficult. The tinge of hatred is never buried very far beneath the surface, and it is likely to poke out at any given moment.

Ehrlichman is a lawyer, and so are all of the seven senators on the Watergate committee. "Mr. Ehrlichman," asked Senator Daniel Inouye of Hawaii during Wednesday's afternoon session, "as the president's most trusted attorney, I assume that you are familiar with the code of ethics?"

Ehrlichman stared coolly back at Inouye. "Of the legal profession?" Ehrlichman said.

Inouye returned the stare, ice on ice. "We have certain ethical codes," Inouye said as if he were tasting sawdust, and for a brief moment the two men locked eyes and would not look away.

It is far more than a game. The senators want to make Ehrlichman look as bad as possible before the nation, and Ehrlichman wants to do the same for the senators. So when Ehrlichman testified that White House operatives had been assigned to carry out an undercover assignment that the Federal Bureau of Investigation would not, Herman Talmadge paused for a second, and then said, "You don't mean to imply in any way, shape, fashion, or form that J. Edgar Hoover was soft on communism or on national security, do you?" leaving the impression that in Talmadge's mind Ehrlichman was implying just such a thing.

And even if Ehrlichman were to decide that he would like to put on a false, pleasant facade for the committee, it would be impossible. For the way that he thinks cannot be hidden, and it keeps coming out in the middle of his testimony.

At one point he said that he would never even consider shredding documents, that such a practice would never cross his mind, and for a moment it seemed that perhaps some moral force would prevent him from doing such a thing. But in the next second, he was explaining why: "We have a great disposal system at the White House—if you want to get rid of a document, you just put it into a burn bag, and it's never seen again; it's completely destroyed." His voice rang with genuine pride that, when he was running the White House, the burn-bag method had been found to be even more effective a means of obliterating government records than so unsophisticated a device as a mere paper shredder.

And when Inouye asked him about the canon in the code of ethics that prohibits an attorney from committing acts that would demean the propriety of the judiciary in the eyes of the public, Ehrlichman shrugged and said, "I'm afraid that's a great catchall."

It intensified by the minute. The senators kept trying to make Ehrlichman answer their questions, and Ehrlichman kept letting them know that he would say exactly what he felt like saying. And what he usually felt like saying was filled with the catchphrases that made the Nixon-Haldeman-Ehrlichman White House what it was. "Hunt and Liddy simply went off my screen, so to speak." "By September of that year, the bureau was clicking on all eight cylinders." "From July on I knew what the marching orders were." "That's a story that had an out-of-town tryout, like many of Mr. Dean's episodes."

Talmadge was asking Ehrlichman about the break-in at Daniel Ellsberg's psychiatrist's office by White House burglars, and Ehrlichman said that perhaps there were ways other than break-ins to get the desired medical records. And again there was a flickering thought that possibly Ehrlichman had some higher, more ethical means in mind. But he was asked what methods he was talking about, and he said, "Oh, one way it could be done is through false pretenses," and he looked surprised when he heard the gasps and laughter from the gallery.

There will be a third day of the senators versus Ehrlichman on Thursday, and the scenario will begin anew. John Wilson, Ehrlichman's attorney, was talking to Sam Ervin during Wednesday's testimony. "I believe you know what happens when an irresistible force meets an immovable object," Wilson said.

President Ervin

WASHINGTON—The pretenses all disappeared on Thursday. The facade of surface friendliness was knocked to hell. The day before had set the tone when Senator Daniel Inouye had muttered "What a liar," after questioning John Ehrlichman, and when it was announced early Thursday that President Nixon was refusing to give his tapes or his papers to the Watergate committee, the final lines were drawn.

This is how it was. Ehrlichman, the president's former assistant, was at the witness table for the third straight day. He sat expressionless as Sam Ervin, chairman of the committee, read the letter from the president aloud. Ehrlichman is the personification of the Nixon White House, and the sight of his placid face, accompanied by the reading of the president's words of refusal, combined to provide a stark, memorable tableau in the Senate Caucus Room.

During the day's testimony, the committee members were buzzed to a roll-call vote on the floor of the Senate. Ehrlichman stayed in the room, though. In front of him was a pile of telegrams. The one on top congratulated him for being "tough," and for "not crumbling under." Next to the telegrams was a copy of the legal profession's Canons of Ethics.

Ehrlichman waited for the senators to return, and then a Washington newspaper columnist, who has been particularly vituperative about the Nixon administration, came walking by the witness table.

"Well," Ehrlichman said, "what have you been writing about?"

"You," the columnist said.

"See," Ehrlichman said. "That shows I don't read you."

"It's just as well," the columnist said.

"I learned that three years ago," Ehrlichman said.

A voice came from behind Ehrlichman. "Are you writing a book, Mr. Ehrlichman?" the voice asked.

Ehrlichman heard the voice, but looked directly at the

newspaper columnist. "No," Ehrlichman said, "but I might write a column."

"Not in our paper, you won't," the columnist said.

"Haven't you talked to your editors lately?" Ehrlichman said. "I understand they have a space opening up."

"Where you're going, you won't be able to get your copy out," the columnist said.

The thin layer of civility that until now has been maintained at the hearings began to be chipped away. Ervin, his glasses balanced precariously on his nose at a sharp angle, read the letter he had received from Richard Nixon, and he could not manage to disguise the scorn and anger in his voice. When Ervin got to the line where the president had written, "In my July 6 letter I described these acts of co-operation with the select committee as genuine, extensive, and in the history of such matters, extraordinary; that co-operation has continued and it will continue"—when Ervin read those words, he looked as if he had bitten down on some terribly foul and evil-tasting substance.

Ervin finished reading the letter, and his voice was shaking. He was incensed; not only had the president refused to supply any tape recordings to the committee, but he had also refused to turn over any documents, because he wanted the committee to specify exactly which documents were wanted before deciding whether to allow them to be seen.

"Now how the president expects this committee to specify each document which he says falls within the ambit of one of these subpoenas is a very surprising thing," Ervin said, his voice rising anew. "We are not clairvoyants. . . . It is a manifest impossibility. . . . You can't identify a document you've never seen. . . . The chair finds it a little difficult to see what co-operation comes from the president on this matter. . . . He can't furnish it to us because we might misconstrue 'em. . . . If the president would provide us with the papers, the Constitution wouldn't collapse and the heavens wouldn't fall, but the committee might be aided in finding the truth of the matter."

And a few minutes later, when John Wilson, Ehrlichman's attorney, attempted to restrict the way in which Senator Lowell Weicker was asking his questions, Ervin cut in: "I'm not going to undertake to tell any senator of the United States how he should conduct himself."

It was another day in which Ervin became cemented in the consciousness of the country. There may be some out there who hate him for the vigor with which he is prosecuting Richard Nixon's White House, but for another segment of America—perhaps even a majority of the country—something very dramatic has happened since the Watergate hearings began.

It is this: Sam Ervin, in a real way, has become the moral leader of the nation. He is corny and he is partisan, yes, but he is corny in a way that brings to mind characteristics that America had seemed too jaded to think about anymore: love of country, and devotion to making things right, and respect for honesty. With his Biblical passages and backhome stories, he has grandstanded, but he is being forgiven for that, because in a baseball player the legs may go first, but in a public person the ego goes last, and the country is willing to give Sam Ervin this attention at such a late stage in his life.

He is too old to lust after the presidency, too old to have any ambitions other than carrying this one duty out right. And because of it, millions of people all over the country have come to hold Ervin in a kind of gleeful awe since the Watergate telecasts began. The reaction he gets on the street and in the halls of the Senate can only be described as idolatry. Quite simply, he is being treated like a president. Certainly more so than the man who currently holds that position. For many, many Americans who have rejected the ways of Richard Nixon, it can be said that Sam Ervin has become the President of the United States.

Perhaps even John Ehrlichman senses that. Ehrlichman has faced Sam Ervin for three days now, and he has heard the reaction of the spectators in the room to himself, and the reaction to Ervin. And especially on Thursday, Ehrlichman just may have begun to realize that there is, indeed, a remarkably big world outside the walls of the White House. At one point, replying to a question from Ervin, Ehrlichman said, "I assure you, Mr. President . . . uh, excuse me, I assure you, Mr. Chairman."

If Sam Ervin was flattered, he did not show it. He simply launched into a Biblical parable. In the parable, Ervin likened the White House and the Committee for the Re-election of the President to a pair of would-be Good Samaritans on the road to Jericho, who see a man who has been beaten by thieves, and pretend not to notice the man. Strong stuff, but it was that kind of a day.

"Kind of Hard for Me to Watch"

WASHINGTON—It was a private dining room in the Senate wing of the Capitol, and the lunchtime patrons were not entirely anonymous. At one table, Mrs. Richard Nixon talked quietly to Mrs. Mamie Eisenhower. Five feet away, Sam Ervin and his wife looked over the menu. Howard Baker ate with three colleagues over by the far wall. Lowell Weicker came in the door and glanced around for his meal companions. And over in the corner, drinking a cup of coffee and waiting for his omelette to arrive, was another man who knows a thing or two about the nature of fame and political happenstance.

"No, I really haven't watched the Watergate hearings too much," said George McGovern. "Oh, once in a while when I go into the Senate cloakroom the TV set in there is turned on, and I watch it for a few minutes. But I don't watch the reruns at night. It's kind of hard for me to watch the hearings anyway; I guess I feel a little more personally involved in what they're about than most people do."

McGovern looks fine. The jowly, weary face that he had earned by the end of his presidential campaign against Richard Nixon is thinner and tanner now, and the smile and the casual conversation come to him easily. But he is no longer the star of the Senate; the seven Watergate committee members have taken over that role, and George McGovern is simply a senator from South Dakota who must compete in a potentially difficult re-election battle next year. He has his memories, though. He has plenty of those.

"What did you think?" McGovern asked a luncheon guest who had traveled on much of the 1972 campaign. "When you were riding the planes and looking at the crowds every day, did you think we'd lost it? Did you think we never had a chance from the convention on? Because it was the crowds that convinced me that the polls were wrong. I simply couldn't conceive that the crowds could be so big and enthusiastic, and that the polls could be so drastically negative at the same time. That's the one thing that still puzzles me a little."

McGovern had just come out of a meeting of a Senate Agriculture subcommittee. It was tedious work, and he would have to be at it all afternoon, too. He must pay attention to such things, though; he is no longer a national candidate, and the voters of South Dakota might not take kindly to the thought that their senator is skipping committee sessions that deal with the problems of farmers. So he sits in meetings all day, talking about how to solve the problems of America's farms, while another, more glamorous Senate committee does its work before live television cameras that carry the testimony into every town in the United States.

"I've been thinking about asking to appear before the Ervin committee, as a witness," McGovern said. "I'm not sure if I'll do it or not. But I really would like to help clear up the public's idea of what a campaign can be. The real damage of Watergate may be that it's deepening the political cynicism in this country, which was deep enough to begin with. I just don't like these allegations that Watergate isn't so bad, that all political campaigns are like this, and these guys merely happened to get caught. That simply isn't true. What happened in 1972 was unprecedented, and it's not fair to tell people that things like that are no different from what always goes on. I think I'd like to go before the committee and just say in straight-out English how we conducted our campaign."

McGovern turned to John Holum, an aide who was also at the table. The night before, McGovern had attended a party at which President Nixon had also been a guest. McGovern had gone through the receiving line, and when he had reached President Nixon, the cameras had clicked. So on this morning, on Page One of many of the nation's newspapers, a picture had appeared showing

Richard Nixon and George McGovern smiling broad, if fragile and uneasy, smiles, and shaking each other's hands.

"Have we had much telephone response on that picture?" McGovern asked Holum.

"Sure have," Holum said.

"How much?" McGovern said.

"Oh, I'd say maybe 50 calls by noon," Holum said.

"Positive, or negative, or what?" McGovern said.

"All of it negative," Holum said.

"That's what I figured," McGovern said. "As soon as I was invited to that party, I knew the situation was going to come up. That's the first time I've seen Nixon since the election. I was determined not to smile when the photographers took their pictures, but I ended up doing it anyway. I didn't think that was the picture they'd take. There was another time when Nixon and Kissinger and I were all going to be standing together, and I figured that was the picture they'd take. I don't know, though. What did people expect me to do when I got to Nixon, do this?" McGovern scowled and began to wave his finger scoldingly in the air. "Couldn't very well do that."

McGovern has been spending a great deal of time in South Dakota lately, laying groundwork for next year's election. When he travels, he often must change planes at O'Hare Airport in Chicago. There are no Secret Service men anymore, and no legions of national media, and people are often surprised to see McGovern standing around the airport alone.

"People come up," McGovern said. "Some of the time someone will come up and say, 'I voted for Nixon,' but then they'll follow it up with 'but I regret it now.' No one comes up and says that they voted for Nixon just to be saying it. Oh, I guess one man did. But usually you don't encounter any face-to-face hostility."

The hostility to McGovern came in the voting booths of America. But even though the landslide against him was of historic size, there were 28 million people in the country who turned to McGovern for leadership even before the full truth about Watergate began to come out. Because of that, McGovern's mail is still heavy; he is still the politician millions of Americans believe in and trust. And it is of small consolation to him that he talked about corruption in the Nixon administration back before it became public knowledge. Because not too many people seemed to be listening.

"When we talked about the Nixon administration being the most corrupt in history, we knew we were right; we knew it was a big issue," McGovern said. "But we didn't know the exact details; we didn't know the exact names and dates and places. But it sure is even more flagrant than we imagined.

"At first I tried not to talk publicly about Watergate. But when I go back to South Dakota, there's no avoiding it. I'll be giving a speech, and I'll make a brief reference to Watergate in my opening remarks, and then—always—in the first six questions from the audience, there'll be two or three about Watergate. And you'd be surprised about the number of people who are interested in knowing about Cambodia, about the bombing. They really are. They mention it to us just about every time."

The thing that still weighs most heavily on McGovern, of course, is that the majority of the country apparently saw him as some kind of villain, a political pariah to be avoided even at the cost of re-electing Richard Nixon. Not surprisingly, McGovern still thinks about that. A lot.

"Those twisted television commercials, those were the worst," McGovern said. "The weathervane things. Over the years I've been as consistent in what I stand for as anyone on the national scene. Even if what I was saying was unpopular. And then they took those two issues, the vice-presidential thing and the welfare proposal, and they helped create an image of me not as a person of constancy and consistency, but of a vacillator who didn't know where he stood.

"But even with everything, I didn't feel that we'd lost until the last two days. Up until then, I still believed we could do it. Monday before Election Day I felt very down, and then Tuesday, Election Day itself, I became very, very discouraged. But it wasn't until then."

That was yesterday, though. Today the problem is staying in the Senate. "I think we'll win next year," McGovern said. "But I think we'll have to work at it. If we were to take it for granted, we might not win."

He is writing a book about his presidential campaign, and he is thinking about calling it *A Case of Mistaken Identity*. He is also reading all other books that are beginning to come out about his losing effort against Richard Nixon, and with each new book that he receives, each new analysis of why he was defeated so badly, he realizes once again that the life he led in 1972 is, indeed, now history.

"It's very painful for me to read some of that," said George McGovern. "Yeah, it's not particularly enjoyable."

No Escape

WASHINGTON—Wednesday morning, inside the White House. Four television sets are tuned to NBC's live coverage of the Senate Watergate hearings. One set is color; three are black and white. The volume on all four is turned up. This is in the press briefing and workroom area, directly off Ron Ziegler's office, perhaps 30 paces from the Oval Office of Richard Nixon.

The voice of Lowell Weicker, one of the Watergate senators, comes out of all four television sets and fills the suite of rooms. It is loud, loud enough, perhaps, to carry to the Oval Office. Richard Nixon, the White House has reported, does not watch the Watergate hearings.

Weicker is asking questions about dirty campaign tactics carried out in behalf of Richard Nixon. He is talking to the witness, H. R. Haldeman, who used to be the president's closest assistant. During the days when H. R. Haldeman ran the White House, the reporters who cover the president almost never got to see him and virtually never got to talk to him. So these same reporters are staring at the screens of the four televisions with great personal interest.

The color television set is placed against a window on the north wall of the room. Through the window you can see people coming from the main entrance of the White House. Tourists. Citizens who have come to take a quick tour of the historic building. On the TV, Senator Joseph Montoya is asking about lists of White House enemies.

Haldeman is replying. "Well, certainly," his electronic image says, "certainly they had the right to their own views. But they did not have the right to be extended the president's hospitality to express those views."

Haldeman's voice is drowned out by another voice. This second voice is coming from a loudspeaker in the ceiling. "We'll have a photo opportunity on the south grounds," the voice says, "so you can get moving."

The men in the briefing area abandon the television sets. They head for a side door. A cameraman from ABC retrieves his motion picture camera atop the color TV set, directly above the talking head of H. R. Haldeman.

The people move through a series of hallways and out into the White House Rose Garden. The grass is wet, and the air is heavy and damp, and there are tiny, flying insects everywhere. The announcement of the "photo opportunity" means that Richard Nixon will be making an appearance soon.

"Step back, please," says a Secret Service agent in gray. "We're going to make this one over there. Make some room, please."

Straight ahead, in that office with the double doors, Richard Nixon is meeting with Kakuei Tanaka, the prime minister of Japan. With his entire political life crumbling around him, the president has decided to carry through a string of these state visits to show that he is still an international power, still a world statesman. But he has yet to answer questions about the crimes of Watergate that were carried out in his name, and that is what the nation wants to hear from him. It is on his mind. The night before, at a state dinner in honor of Prime Minister Tanaka, the president had offered a toast, in which he said:

"We are total friends and co-operators in working for peace. So let others spend their time dealing with small, murky, vicious little things. We will spend our time building a peaceful world. . . . We should build a better world and not be dissipated in things that don't matter."

Inside the near-empty briefing room, a few correspondents linger to watch the hearings. Outside, on the South Lawn, next to a curving cement driveway lined with limousines, an all-service honor guard begins to chant in cadence.

Richard Nixon walks out of his office. He is wearing a dark blue business suit, with his American flag lapel pin on the left side. The national press corps of two countries, the United States and Japan, push against a wet row of hedges to try to hear what the two men are saying.

Richard Nixon, his face pink and unreadable, grabs Tanaka by the arm. The president points majestically toward a small tree. "That," says Richard Nixon to the prime minister of Japan, "is a crab apple tree."

The president leads the prime minister across the lawn to the limousines. The prime minister climbs into the back seat of the lead car, and the president remains to watch him drive away. The reporters are within five feet. The reporters have spent so many of their working hours over the last year writing about Richard Nixon and Watergate, and hoping the president will answer questions about it. And Richard Nixon has spent so much of his time avoiding opportunities to do so. Here they are, then, on a muggy August day, within breathing distance of each other, and there is stark, unbroken silence.

Such are the rules. The president has said that he will not answer questions about Watergate, and any random query at this moment would draw no answer. It would only cause trouble for the White House correspondent who might call it out, and covering Richard Nixon's White House is full of enough troubles as it is.

So the silence sticks. The reporters stare at Richard Nixon, who avoids looking back at them. The president bends toward the limousine, and he salutes, quickly and crisply. Then he turns and, by himself, begins to walk swiftly back toward his office.

"Did you have a good talk, Mr. President?" someone calls to him. But Richard Nixon will not answer. Instead, he hastens his pace even more, and by the time he reaches his doorway, he is leaning forward with the effort of the rapid walk. He enters the office alone. In days past, H. R. Haldeman would have been at his side.

But on this day, H. R. Haldeman is answering questions before the country. Haldeman's face is still on the television sets in the briefing room. As the reporters come back inside, Haldeman and Weicker are again arguing. "Do you mean to tell me," Weicker is shouting, "that as the man closest to the President of the United States, you would sign a memorandum linking the Democratic candidate to Communist money because you THINK it is the case. . . . That is a disgrace!" The face of H. R. Haldeman looks coolly back at Weicker.

In this White House, where the occupants would pretend the Watergate hearings do not exist, the secretaries emerge from an inner office, carrying official announcements on long sheets of white paper.

The announcements are of normal things, pleasant things, things the men who run the building wish that people would think about again. "The president today announced his intention to nominate Theodore L. Eliot, Jr., to be ambassador to Afghanistan." "The president today announced the appointment of Patrick E. O'Donnell of Washington, D.C., as Special Assistant to the President for Legislative Affairs." "Prime Minister Tanaka and President Nixon met in Washington July 31 and August 1 for comprehensive and fruitful explorations on a wide variety of subjects of mutual interest."

But as the secretaries circulate through the room, handing out these messages of presidential workings, the television sets remain on. Even here, even inside the White House, there is no avoiding it. The voice of Sam Ervin booms out, and laughter fills the Senate Caucus Room and comes out of the four television sets, and even here, inside the fortress of no laughter, 30 paces from the office where Richard Nixon sits by himself, there is no escaping Watergate.

Spirit of America

MALTA, Ill.—At first the urge had been to get on an airplane for Washington, to watch it all up close. But somehow that seemed unsatisfactory; somehow, being in the room full of arguments seemed the wrong place this time. It might be better to simply head out for the country, and sample the days of a nation in trauma from there.

If ever the damage were confined to Washington, that time is long over. With Congress moving ever closer to the eviction of a president from his office, Washington seemed, in an odd kind of way, precisely the city not to seek. The ripples have spread too far by now.

So just go, if you will. Take a train to the west, and then hitch a ride even farther, and buy yourself a room for a night or three. Outside your window there are wide green and yellow fields, and lightning bugs flickering in the dusk. Switch on your television and you are there, even in the middle of the corn and the empty skylines. "Mr. Chairman, we are talking about the very gravest of offenses," a man you have never seen before says into his microphone. "We are all aware of our historic role." From the road, there comes the distant sound of motorcycles cruising in the country, on their way to something.

In the morning, you take a walk along Route 38, staying in the dirt off to the side of the road when there is no pathway. The sun feels hot and good; you are by yourself, and you kick at a stone and watch it hop across the furrows a tractor has left behind. There is a massive cross-country trailer truck pulled up on the shoulder; its driver sleeps in the shade of the cab.

You can do this for hours; there is no one to disturb you, nothing to remind you that there is anything else going on in the land, nothing any more important than walking along this strip of cement and trying to decide where to stop. You choose a clearing in the middle of a patch of tall brush, and you lean back and watch the traffic. You do this for some time, thinking about nothing at all.

When you start back, a lady sees you by the side of the highway, and she asks if she can give you a ride. She is on her way to pick up her young son somewhere; you get in, and her radio is playing. "I have the greatest regard for any man who holds the office of the presidency," the voice from the radio is saying, "but I have an even greater regard for the Constitution." The lady says that she has been watching the hearings all afternoon, but that now it is time to do her errands. She drops you where you are staying.

You have dinner, and go back outside for a while. When you return to your room, the President of the United States is on the television screen. He is smiling broadly; he appears to be ready to make a formal speech, in front of a large gathering of handsomely dressed businessmen. The president begins his speech, and you hear him say, "We are on the right road toward our goal of full prosperity." His audience applauds, and he smiles once more; you have been seeing that smile all of your life. You hit the switch on the television set, and the president becomes a tiny dot; when you turn it back on half an hour later, the hearings into his impeachment have replaced him on the screen.

It is so puzzling to comprehend this. In future centuries, the events taking place right in front of you will comprise entire chapters in history books, books of their own, even. The United States will be described as having been on the verge of moral and emotional collapse. The people will be said to have touched a low point in the national spirit. And yet when you abandon the televised hearings, and head out to the road again, it is an easy matter to leave it all behind you, at least for the moment. Perhaps it is made easier because out here you are by yourself, without a thousand voices on the telephone and in the office and on the street telling you what their owners think about the breaddown of a presidency.

There is a motel with a bar attached on the outskirts of De Kalb, and you stop in for a beer. Thankfully, there is no television, no radio. Even the jukebox is unplugged. Tonight there is live enter-tainment. The singer's name is Gary Hiland; he has no other musicians to accompany him, but instead sits alone on a stool, a man with a guitar, and sings his songs. He is fine; the other patrons of the bar are more concerned with playing an electronic darts game on the other side of the room, but it doesn't bother Hiland; he knows how good his stuff is, and he is playing more for himself than for them anyway. Above the noise he sings in a deep, sure voice:

"Get your fingers like this," the official said, swinging the racket behind his head and looking at an imaginary tee. "Lock them like I am." Ashe copied the golf grip on another racket.

Gonzales moved silently to the end of a bench and started to change to his tennis clothes. "You play golf today?" he asked Ashe.

"Yeah," Ashe said. "I'm still doing something wrong, though. I shot 103."

Gonzales tossed his dark blue sport shirt into a locker. "My God, Arthur, that's pitiful," he said. "The first time I ever played in my life I shot 108, and that was off the back tees at the Masters course in Georgia."

"I know," Ashe said. "I think I'm coming into the tee wrong."

Gonzales picked up a racket. "Here," he said. "The best way to practice for that is to pretend that you're hitting a backhand volley in tennis. It's the same kind of wrist action."

In less than an hour, they would be playing each other for important money, but it was nothing to be tense about. They could talk about golf and kill the time until the match. There have been too many nights on too many courts for Gonzales to try to work up an artificial grudge against an opponent.

He looked at Ashe, who was snipping the top and bottom strings on one of his rackets with a nail clipper. "What are you doing?" Gonzales asked.

"These strings are shot," Ashe said. "I'm cutting some of them so I can take the pressure off the frame until I can get it restrung."

Gonzales walked over and took the racket from Ashe. "Well you're not doing any good that way," he said. "You're not taking any pressure off at all." He took the clippers and quickly ripped at all the strings, making a big cross in the middle of the face of the racket. "You've got to cut all of them up to do any good."

Ashe leaned back against a metal locker and picked up a copy of *Playboy*. He was reading an article about Dick Butkus. "This is one guy I'd hate to run into in a dark alley," Ashe said. "Or a light one, for that matter."

Gonzales was studying some scrawls on a green chalk board, apparently some of Northwestern University's football plays. "Who's that?" he asked.

"Dick Butkus," Ashe said.

"Who?" Gonzales said.

"You know," Ashe said. "No. 51 for the Chicago Bears, Butkus."

"Oh, yeah, him," said Pancho Gonzales.

The promoter came in and said the doubles match was almost over. Gonzales bent over and pulled on two pairs of white wool socks. He folded the top sock down on each ankle.

He examined each of his rackets as Ashe went out the door. This cannot go on for too many more years. Gonzales has the body of a teenager, but 43 is old even for the most remarkable of athletes. Upstairs, the place was filled, at $10 top for the best seats. It was a well-turned-out crowd, full of country club ladies with end-of-summer tans, looking good in their September woolens. All of them were there to see him play, so that when the time comes that it finally ends for good, they will be able to say, yes, I saw the great Gonzales once.

He climbed the stairs and walked onto the court and accepted their cheers. And he played another match of tennis for money. Ashe, the young man, was too much for him. Ashe won the first set 6-2. At 5-2 in the second set, with Ashe in the lead, many of the people in the fieldhouse started for their cars, walking out on Pancho Gonzales. He lost the set. He picked up his check, $1,000 for an hour's work, the wages of a professional player of games, and headed back for the little locker room so he could get dressed and put on his jacket and get started toward the next place.

Game Day

A quiet Wednesday afternoon in suburban Palatine. The skies are threatening. Most of the men in the expensive neighborhood have been off to work for hours. Inside the big house at the center of the block, though, the owner is pacing all around the living room, waiting for the daylight to end. His work will begin after the sun has set.

"I've got to baby-sit today, anyway," Bob Love says. "I'm very nervous. There's not much for me to do except sit around here and try to keep my mind relaxed. That, and watch the TV."

The curtains in the house are drawn; Love has shut out the rest of the world. Within six hours he will be in the Chicago Stadium, in the uniform of the Chicago Bulls, competing against the Golden State Warriors in the National Basketball Association playoff series. He is a certified star, and that is how the world knows him: in his uniform, on the glistening floor, surrounded by screaming strangers.

This afternoon he is wearing jeans and a sport shirt; his four-year-old daughter, Basha, plays on the carpet. The furnishings are lavish. Love lives on a block populated by executives and professionals.

"We didn't have anything when I was growing up," he says. "It was in a little town in Louisiana, called Bastrop. There wasn't any money. But we always had enough there to eat. We'd grow it and catch it ourselves. No steaks, nothing like that. But that garden—we had greens, tomatoes, beans, okra. And we could fish all year 'round. Perch, catfish—there was plenty of that."

Love is paid $147,000 a year to play basketball. That appears to be a large sum, on the surface, but it keeps Love unhappy. At 31, he is not a young man, by professional athletic standards. He knows that other major stars are paid much more—Nate Archibald of the Kansas City-Omaha Kings draws a reported $400,000 annually; Nate Thurmond, currently on the bench for the Bulls, earns $300,000—and Love knows that his ability to draw a big salary will not last forever. Love is not as well-known as many other athletes of his caliber—he never is interviewed on television or radio, because his speech is flawed by a stammer that can become severe—and the situation has him in a quandary.

"It's always on my mind," he says. "I'm good enough to play every minute of the game; they count on me to score and to rebound; they figure I'm good enough for all of this—but I guess they don't figure I'm good enough to be paid what I deserve. I'm trying not to think about it during the playoffs, but I can't. Mental attitude means a lot to anybody. I've stuck it out. I want us to get into the championship round. That's my purpose. But after the season's over, I don't know what I'm going to do. I don't see how they can expect me to come back next year and play under the same terms."

This afternoon, however, Love is just trying to keep the jitters away. His wife, Betty, is out shopping. "Late in the afternoon, when it's getting close to game time, I always put on some music. Bobby Blue Bland, Tyrone Davis, Gladys Knight—something I can move to, so I can stop pacing and try to relax. I won't be able to eat, though. I can never get that relaxed."

Love is a man who is capable of making gracious gestures. Much of his time is spent working with inner-city children on his own initiative, and this is seldom publicized. Recently, when the story of a paralyzed young man named Tony Williams appeared in this column, there was a flurry of publicity about how Tony had been taken to a Bulls game and had been presented with an autographed basketball. The next day—after the pictures had appeared in the paper, and the Tony Williams story was "over"— Love showed up at Tony's meager apartment on the West Side, just to spend the morning with the boy.

Love is slightly embarrassed to talk about such things. "Oh, I don't know," he says. "It's just something I like to do. A lot of guys get in the pros, all they want to do is spend this, spend that, live on top of the world. They don't realize that it's all going to go away. So why change the way you are?"

The Cubs baseball game is on the television set, and Love is pretending to pay attention to it. "I can't really keep anything in my mind but playing basketball tonight," he says. "I can't watch the Cubs. I've got to go to work. That's what it really is. I leave here with my lunchbox—only with me, my lunchbox is my gym bag with my game shoes and my jock."

Love and his wife have four children. When the night's game is over, he will come home to them, and to his first real meal of the day.

"This is the only place I'm really comfortable," he says. "Sitting around the house, I'm just daddy. If you've had a bad game, something like that, if the fans are mad at you, the coach is on you, you can come home and your kids hug you and stuff, and you talk to your wife—it can really keep you going. It can take your mind off a lot of things. It can be your backbone. It can carry half the load.

"On the court, I have a different life. This so-called superstar thing is strange. Even my wife, when she's at the game, she looks at me like I'm a different person. I see her hollering for me to score, and I know that she's looking at me as Bob Love the basketball player, not as her husband. You get used to it, I guess."

The sound of Jack Brickhouse announcing the Cubs game fills the room. Love stares absently at the set. "It happens as soon as I walk into the stadium," he says. "I can almost feel myself change. That's when I become the basketball player. Everything else goes away. The only thing that matters is being the basketball player, and winning the basketball game." The afternoon is turning dark, and the work day is about to begin. . . .

Ali Alone

His hands were moving faster than you could see, and his feet kept bouncing on the rough, unvarnished plank floor. He was pounding a light punching bag, hitting it and hitting it and hitting it until his fists and the bag became a blur, and the sound was a constant, single thwack.

No one was looking at him, though, because he was not a fighter with a name. He was just a young man who could hit hard and who thought that maybe, somehow, if he did this often enough and well enough, he could end up in an arena someday, making real money and being on theater television and having people turn around when they hear his name.

Not today, though. Because this afternoon at the Johnny Coulon Physical Training Club, under the L tracks on 63d, one of the very few boxing gyms left in the country, there was another attraction.

Muhammad Ali, in a blue pullover shirt and blue bell-bottomed pants, training for his July 26 fight with Jimmy Ellis, had just jogged up the three flights of darkened stairs, and the eyes were on him, not on the young man who kept flailing at the light bag.

So the young man toiled in solitude as Ali nodded to the people who were hanging around the gym. Ali walked quickly to a little dressing area and closed the door behind him. In the nailed-together cubicle, he looked tired. Coulon's gym is not air-conditioned, and it was steamy and uncomfortable as he talked softly about little things, nothing things.

Here at Coulon's, somehow, the glamour that has come to surround Ali was stripped off. That is for the Cavett and Carson shows; it is for the college lecture tours, where there are always a few students around to tell him how much they admire him for the stand he took in his draft case. But here, in a boxing gym in a dismal neighborhood where many of the fashionable do not choose to venture, it was different.

Jack Dempsey and Ray Robinson and Carmen Basilio are on the walls, and the posters are there for all the young men who come to Coulon's and who need a dream to look at. The young men see the posters and they keep hitting, and maybe it would be wrong to ask them why. The only boxing matches you hear about are the ones once or twice a year involving the famous heavyweights; there don't seem to be many other cards, so where can these young men go when they want to step beyond Coulon's, and what good things are going to happen for the man pounding the light bag while the handful of people wait for Ali?

Earlier Ali had been training at Navy Pier, so that the downtown people could see him and gape. But that was mostly for show, and by this time, with the fight moving closer, he was down to the real work. He banged the bags while someone timed him, letting him go three minutes at a burst. And between the three-minute sessions, he wandered the gym by himself, sweat coming to his face, thinking.

The lights reflected dully off the tile ceiling, at one time white but now grimy beyond cleaning. So much has happened here. But the days when Jack Dempsey would come in on a Saturday afternoon just to get some exercise are over. Something has gone very wrong with boxing. There are so few names left that stir the imagination, and the sight of Muhammad Ali, who has so much, hitting on one bag, directly next to the other young man, who hopes for so little, hitting on another, tells much of the story.

Finally the young man moved, perhaps uncomfortable to be so close to Ali and yet many worlds apart. The young man walked to a distant, dim corner of the gym and began to jump rope. He was alone, and as the perspiration flew off him, it made little dots on the floor.

He would sneak a glance at Ali every few minutes, and he continued skipping the rope as if by the sheer effort of skipping so fast and so well there would be a match for him somewhere, a ring where people would pay to see him fight.

Ali, who has earned millions of dollars for a single fight, was alone, too. He had moved to a heavy bag. He is known everywhere in the world, and people gravitate to him, try to get near to him, want to do things for him, to be a part of his universe. But in the end there is no one else who can do this particular job for him, can do the job of toughening himself up until he is ready to put himself against another man in a major fight. And at Coulon's gym in the shabbiness of 63d Street in Chicago, he grunted as he leaned into the unyielding bag, again and again and again.

Benny's World

"Just a minute," says Benny Bentley as the phone rings. "Let me take this call, then I got something to show you. Just hold on." He picks up the phone. "Hello. Yeah, this is Bentley. I got no tickets at all, not a one. But wait a minute, for you I think I can scare up a couple. That's all right, don't thank me; the tickets'll be in your name at the box office." Bentley hangs up. "My tax accountant," he says. "How can I say no to him? He screws up one figure and I end up in jail."

Bentley is in the headquarters of the Chicago Bulls. He has been the Bulls' Publicity and Public Relations Director for the past six years, and of course he is good at it. Benny Bentley can hustle anything; he has done it for most of his 50 years, and a successful NBA club is no trick at all for him. But somehow, swiveling in his chair in the Bulls' offices at the Sheraton-Chicago, Bentley does not look right. After all these years, he is still a boxing man, and he does not fit in here.

"Yeah, but how can you fight it anymore?" Bentley says. "Who do you have trying to run boxing? A bunch of guys who talk about images and ask you to write them out proposals. *Proposals!* A real fight man never wrote out a proposal in his life. Think about Al Weill. This man was not the best-liked human being ever to walk the earth, but he had a shrewdness in him you couldn't get at Yale or Harvard. You can't show me a Yale man who could take a crude kid like Marciano and make him the heavyweight champion of the whole world. A man like Weill, he could tear your heart out for two and a half per cent. That's what you need in boxing, that kind of mind, not some guy in a button-down suit who's going to ask you for a *proposal,* for chrissake."

The phone buzzes again. Bentley picks it up, listens for a moment, then rolls his eyes toward the ceiling. There are a lot of ways to describe the man, but maybe Mike Royko of the *Chicago Daily News* put it best:

"Most people, when they think of a fight promoter, envision a burly man, wearing sunglasses, a diamond ring, houndstooth slacks, a wine-colored shirt, a white tie, a blue blazer and a cigar between his teeth. In the stereotype, the promoter talks like he was born near Humboldt Park and can snap your spine like a wishbone. As a matter of fact, that's the way Benny Bentley looks. I'm told he looked that way when he was nine years old."

Bentley lets the person on the other end of the line talk for a few seconds, then cuts in. "No," he says firmly. "Just no. I'm going to call Milwaukee and tell them to forget it. I told them I'd get tickets for those guys only if we had a check in the mail by today. The check's not here. They can forget it. They didn't pay, they get no tickets." He hangs up.

"I'm getting sick of this phone," he says. "Let's hit the street. Oh, wait a minute, I wanted to show you that thing." He reaches into a pile of papers on his desk. "Here," he says, "take a look at that."

It is a letter from Evel Knievel, the daredevil motorcyclist. Knievel had been in town the week before, and he had hired Bentley to promote his visit. The letter is a handwritten thank you.

"How do you like that?" Bentley says. "He writes it himself. I tell you, he never got treatment like this in his life. Usually, some guy sends out a press release. Not that I'm putting it down, but who needs press releases? I hit the street. I use my ankles. A press release they can throw away. When I walk into the office, they have to say hello. Knievel never got better press in his life."

Bentley slips on a belted trench coat and a Rex Harrison hat. He sticks the cigar into his mouth. "The street," he says.

There are not many left like Benny Bentley. Now there are Public Relations Counsels, and Publicity Advisors, and Directors of Sports Information. But Bentley calls himself a press agent, just like he did back in the boxing days, and he knows that his real key product is himself.

He grew up on the West Side of Chicago, and as soon as he was old enough he got a job as a traveling nightclub MC. In 1949 he was hired as press agent for a Chicago fight club called the Marigold Gardens. When the International Boxing Club came into prominence, in the early 1950s, he was hired to handle publicity for the fights at the Chicago Stadium. Eventually he became publicity man for the entire IBC operation, then ring announcer for the major fights.

Then Izzy Kline, a matchmaker, left the IBC, and Bentley was named matchmaker for the Wednesday night television fights. He also made matches at the Chicago Stadium. He handled publicity at training camps for Rocky Marciano, Ray Robinson, Bobo Olson, Carmen Basilio, and other big ones. But then the IBC ran into trouble, folded, and the decline of boxing followed soon after. Bentley tried to promote on his own, but had uneven luck. He began to do publicity for other sporting ventures, and finally found his present, lucrative position with the Bulls. Which he enjoys. Except that the Bulls are, after all, a basketball team, not a fighter.

Every day he drives downtown from his home in Rogers Park, on the far north edge of the city. There he lives with his wife and two teenaged daughters, one middle-aged businessman among many in that residential area.

His neighbors could never fully know the life Bentley has led. They know he is big with the Bulls, and that he does other public relations work, too. He has handled the Roller Derby, and a benefit football game or two, and he has some steady accounts among Chicago restaurants.

But the boxing thing, that is a part of the indiscernible past for his neighbors. Yet, if they paid attention, they could see it in him. He still has the look of the training camps. The eyes are always moving. The cigar is in and out of his mouth 15 times every minute. He is not a big man, but he charges through life with absolute confidence, and absolute knowledge that there is some way to get everything he wants. It is not possible to imagine Benny Bentley shrinking into the background of any scene. The action travels with him.

The ring announcer's voice has never left. Bentley can order dessert in a restaurant and make it sound like he is introducing the world's middleweight champion. Understatement is not a part of his style. A person is either one of the earth's greatest human beings, or a no-good sonuvabitch.

Benny Bentley feels that the rest of the world is his supporting cast. He will walk along a busy street at noontime, shouting his opinions and gesturing wildly. He is not at all self-conscious about the attention he draws. He accepts it as his due.

Occasionally, on a rare down moment, he will acknowledge that there are not many of his kind left. He will talk about the other boxing press agents, and only be able to come up with one or two names that are current. He speaks fondly of Muhammad Ali; it is clear that he believes that Ben Bentley and Ali are the only genuine articles left in a now-shoddy sport.

He still has his stories, though. All day long he can deal with rebound statistics and glossy pictures of Chet Walker and tickets that must be left for out-of-town basketball writers. But once in a while he gets away from it. Once in a while his memory stirs and brings back the boxing world.

Bentley's walking along Michigan Avenue now, talking loud to be heard above the cold wind. "The late, great, much-maligned James D. Norris," Bentley says. "That's what I call him. He was very maligned. Everybody had a bad word to say about him. But the IBC was a success, and when it died, boxing went. People realized how great James D. Norris was after his International Boxing Club was gone. When Norris was around, the check was always there, out front, before the fight. It gave the game stability. Forget the hoodlums. There have always been hoodlums in boxing. Norris inherited the hoodlums like Nixon inherited Vietnam. You think he wanted them? Let me tell you something: Norris offered J. Edgar Hoover a million dollars over a period of ten years to become the czar of boxing. This is a fact. Norris had Walter Winchell approach Hoover with the offer. This is how serious Mr. Norris was about cleaning up boxing. But Hoover turned it down, said he didn't feel like leaving the FBI.

"I'm telling you, the feeling in those training camps was like nothing else on this earth. The rustic living! The camaraderie! The poker games! I remember at one training camp, every afternoon at three, Carmen Basilio would come up to the press room and we'd play poker until dinner time. Basilio's wife, she'd never let him have any money. But he'd put it in his socks, right next to the ankle. He never said much, just looked at the cards. But every once in a while he'd bend over and he'd peel some money out of the stocking and toss it onto the table.

"That's when the boxing writers were really boxing writers. I was always in awe of those newspaper guys back then. Some guys have John Wayne; I have Jimmy Cannon. I could listen to his stories for hours. These genuine boxing writers were the greatest. Now that boxing's not a regular beat anymore, you have a writer come out to cover a fight, and he's probably covered a tennis match two nights ago. He don't even know anything about boxing. He's probably never even been in a training camp."

Bentley goes on with his staccato delivery: "I remember once, we're up in Holland, Michigan, with Rocky Marciano. I know this barber back in the city, and I know the barber's a big fan of Marciano. So I figure it's a good gimmick, I bring the barber up to camp. I have him come in and cut the champ's hair. A good publicity thing, right?

"Well, he gets done with Rocky. Then the trainer decides he wants a haircut, so the barber cuts his hair. Then the manager. By this time everyone in camp is getting wind of the free haircuts. What a great thrill for this barber. I'm thinking, getting to cut the champ's hair, and then getting to work on all these big-time writers to boot.

"So the guy cuts hair all afternoon. Finally, everyone's going into dinner, and the barber says, 'Who's the guy who pays me?' This man wants to get *paid* for cutting the hair, do you believe me? He's in *Rocky Marciano's* training camp, and he wants to get paid.

"Now I feel like telling him off, but I don't want to make a scene. So I reason with him. I pay him a deuce a haircut, plus I let him come in and eat a steak dinner with us. What the hell can you do with a guy like that?"

We approach the squat, steel-and-glass *Sun-Times-Daily News* building on Wabash Avenue, where he will drop off the latest Bulls' statistics, and fish for better coverage with the sports editors.

Bentley passes through the *Sun-Times* newsroom, flips his handouts onto the sports copy desk and makes a few jokes with the writers. "Oh, Motta just called," he says on the way out the door. "Love's OK. He'll make the trip."

The cigar moves back and forth in his mouth. "This walking is getting to me," he remarks. "Now where was I? Oh, the camps. A thousand stories in the camps, these guys'd come up and interview the trainers, the cooks, etcetera, etcetera. Once a columnist, a very big man, was so drunk he was falling off the barstool. He came to me in a panic. 'Benny,' he says, 'I'm on a deadline, and I've been drinking all day, and I don't have a story. You got to help me.' So I give him this stuff about the champ's childhood, and the next day all over his home paper's first sports page is 'Smell of Shoe Leather Made Rocky a Fighter.' Great sob story. The guy's editor calls him to congratulate him on this human interest angle. Says the guy must really be working double-time to get that deep stuff."

Now Bentley makes a quick pass through the *Daily News* sports department. He makes his hellos, and automatically picks up the early editions of the afternoon papers to see what kind of play the Bulls were getting. Then down a back elevator and toward the *Tribune* Tower.

"Now Ray Robinson, there is an intimidating man," Bentley says. "He's in Chicago training for a fight with Jake LaMotta, I would say this is 1950 or so. This is the first time I'm assigned to handle Robinson. I am filled with awe. I am scared, if you can imagine that.

"There's this 6:00 P.M. TV show that Bob Elson has on WBBM here in Chicago at the time. I'm trying to get Robinson on the show. So I go to where he's working out.

" 'Mr. Robinson,' I say, real soft, just like I'm talking now. And he looks up and I tell him about the TV show. I tell him that Elson'll give him a free radio for appearing. Robinson says, 'My man, be in front of my hotel at 5:30.'

"So I'm at the hotel, and he's waiting on the street for me. We do the show, and afterwards Elson gives Sugar the radio. Sugar hands me the radio and says, 'Here, kid, this is for you.' Me. Kid. But I don't say anything. I take the radio. And from then on, we get along fine.

"All right now, the scene changes. Ray Robinson is no longer middleweight champion. I'm Bobo Olson's boy now, I'm handling his camp. Olson's fighting Robinson for the title. And I keep running into Robinson, and he's behaving very cold toward me. I begin to feel uncomfortable.

"Well it turns out that Robinson is mad because I'm handling the press for Bobo. I go to Robinson. I say, 'Look, I work for the IBC. I do not make my assignments. I take what I get. They say I handle Bobo, I handle Bobo. I have no choice.' But Robinson chooses not to understand this.

"So it's fight night. I'm the ring announcer. Bobo gets knocked out. I raise Sugar's hand in victory. And Sugar looks down at me and says, 'Bentley, aren't you raising the wrong guy's hand?' "

By this time Bentley is crossing back over Michigan Avenue. He will stop at the *Tribune* sports desk, then go on to *Chicago Today*.

"Let me tell you a few things about that Bobo Olson," Bentley said. "This man was without a doubt one of the greatest Lotharios outside the ring I have ever seen. The women used to flock to him. Picture this. We're in Asbury Park, New Jersey, and Bobo is training for a fight with Archie Moore. Me, I should be on my honeymoon, I'm just married, but I'm assigned to take care of him.

"The camp is crawling with newspaper guys. And Bobo gets word to me that he's got a broad coming in. A *broad*! He wants me to sneak her into the camp. This shoud be a case for Olson's manager. But Olson happens to be managed by a fellow named Sid Flaherty. Flaherty owns a ranch or some damn thing, and he gets word that there is a cow sick in Montana. A cow. I am telling you the truth about this. So Flaherty goes to Montana to look after the cow. He's got a championship fight to worry about, and he leaves camp for a cow.

"I do some thinking. I figure, the best thing I can do is sneak this girl in to Bobo without any of the newspaper guys catching on. So I meet her at the airport. This is one outlandish broad. Very flamboyant. Hawaiian girl. Muumuu dress, gloves up to her elbows, all this.

"I get her in camp and up to Bobo's room by some miracle, and no ones sees. Now my room is directly underneath Bobo's. I'm in there with a bunch of guys from the papers. A wire comes in for one of the AP men. It's a query. It says: 'Please check rumor that a woman traveling in Olson entourage.'

"All the reporters turn on me. 'Did you see a girl in camp?' they say to me. I look back and say, 'Did you? You've been up here for three days.'

"But I tell Bobo, we got to get this broad out of there. He says OK, but he wants to take her to a movie. A movie. What can I do. I say I'll take them to a movie the next day.

"I go out and I get Bobo a blond Liberace wig and he puts on dark glasses. Me and him and the broad drive to Philadelphia. Here's Bobo walking down the street thinking he looks like Liberace. And some little kid comes up to him and says, 'Bobo, can I have your autograph?'

"I say, 'Bobo, does this convince you? We have *got* to get rid of this broad.' So even he agrees. He insists on coming into the airport terminal. And what does he do? He stands there at the gate and kisses her for five minutes. I'm going through the floor. That damn Bobo."

He walks into the *Tribune* sports department. Everyone is busy, but Bentley hardly seems to notice. He is so caught up in his boxing stories, and he keeps pulling them out.

"I think maybe it can come back. I don't know, if the time seems right, I'm willing to try. I figure maybe the ethnic angle can help boxing. Mexicans. It's very big in California now. Maybe it can spread. I remember when a leading boxer would walk down the street and people would stop him and run off at the mouth. Now who gets that kind of action? Ali, that's all. Maybe the tide's going to turn again, you know?"

Bentley's final stop of the morning is at *Chicago Today*. He walks into the sports department in a fake rage. He was moderately angry with Rick Talley, the *Today* sports columnist, for a slightly negative piece about the Bulls. Bentley figured the best way to handle it was to overact.

"Where the hell's Talley?" he yells. "I'm gonna take a punch at him."

Harry Sheer, a *Today* sports writer, motions Bentley over. "He's not here, Ben," Sheer says. "Sit down."

The two men talk quietly about things in general for a few minutes. Then Bentley says, "Hey, how'd that poll come out?" Sheer had conducted a reader survey to find out which spectator sports are now the most popular.

"Pretty good," Sheer says. "1,826 votes came in."

Bentley chews on his cigar. "Not bad," he says. "How many votes for boxing?"

"None, Ben," Sheer says.

Bentley is quiet for a moment and then looks at Sheer. "Really, Harry, how many?"

"Zero, Ben," Sheer replies. "Boxing didn't get a vote. I was kind of surprised, myself."

Bentley gets up to leave. "Well, I don't believe that."

"Check it yourself, Ben," Sheer says. "The ballots are all in that file over there. Take a look."

"I don't have to look," says Bentley. "I know when the fix is on."

Nesterenko

Sometimes, late in the night, during those hours when you know there is no reason to stay out and yet something keeps you from heading for home and sleep, you will see him at the end of the bar. Always he will be alone, with his thoughts and his memories.

For 16 years he was a star in this town. Now the name is starting to be forgotten, but the man is still here. Eric Nesterenko is 41 years old; his days of skating for the Chicago Black Hawks are over; his winters of traveling the world as a National Hockey League regular are all past. The sounds of the thousands calling his name from the distant reaches of the stadium are just a private echo.

Some nights you join him. He is good company. Nesterenko was always different, a reader of books in a professional world where most of his companions chose to pass the days in front of a television set. His athletic colleagues used to refer to him as an "intellectual," and even though they were speaking the word and not writing it, you could hear the quotation marks. His need to examine his life, to question the meaning of the fame and glory that had been his since he was a boy, made him a loner among the others, and he was made to know it every day and night of his working life.

Now the nights are different, and Nesterenko is still thinking about it, still wondering how it all came to pass. Sometimes he will look down at the bar and talk about it.

"The adulation you receive as a professional athlete is such an odd thing," Nesterenko will say. "To be made to feel that you are that important . . . when in reality you are just a kid, just a boy. I know that I was just a boy. I was 18 years old the first year I skated for the Toronto Maple Leafs. I had grown up in a tiny town called Flin Flon, in Manitoba, and I was truly an innocent young boy. And there I was every night in Maple Leaf Gardens, with 20,000 people screaming and shouting down at me, counting on me. The adulation . . . I was a virgin. I had never slept with a woman."

As Nesterenko talks, you sense that here is a man who has come to terms with his own weaknesses, his own limitations. He is not one to dwell on the peaks of his athletic career, the statistics and the numbers that now exist only on paper. Rather, he will be quick to turn to the other side of it—to the moments when a boy's doubts became a man's truths.

"The hardest thing in the world for any professional athlete to recognize is that he is not the best in the world," Nesterenko will say. "There are so few who make it to the major leagues of any sport. All of us were the very best in our schools, the very best in our neighborhoods. Until you become a pro, you just don't comprehend that this will change. It took me two or three years in the National Hockey League. Then one day, I just knew it was true: 'There are men here who are better than me. I can play my very best, I can play at the absolute top of my ability, and still there are men who are younger and much better. There's nothing I can do about it. It's a fact.' And that's when you start realizing what it means to get old playing a sport.

"Even now I see it. I work with teenagers, coaching them in hockey, and on several occasions a kid of 17 or so will skate into me and square off. He wants to fight. He wants to prove that he is man enough to fight with me. And I think to myself, someday he, too, is going to have to face it. You can't fool yourself forever. There are men younger and tougher and better than you are. That's what life is about."

Nesterenko will try to turn the conversation away from this. His interests are strongest when he is talking about a world not his own; he would much rather hear about a way of life he has never tried than discuss the years of his past. If you press him, though, he will tell you about it.

"I was never really with the rest of the players," he will say. "We got along well enough, but I always seemed to be on my own. For me the real fun of skating, the true joy of it, disappeared as soon as I started to get paid for it. There was never a moment in the National Hockey League that compared with the sheer joy I had as a boy skating outside in Flin Flon. That's something you can never recapture—doing it because you want to be doing it. Now, that is sport."

The hour will near closing time, and Nesterenko will know that it is time to head back to Evanston, where he lives with his wife and three children. But he will be reluctant to leave; there is something about going out into the night that keeps him inside the bar a bit longer.

"It's kind of funny," he will say. "I played in this town for 16 years, and I don't have one friend left here. I had two men who I could really call my friends, but they're both gone now. Do you know what I do for fun? I ski. I'm not very good at it; really not too good at all. But I'll go out there by myself to a place where there's snow, and I'll start down that course, and it will make me feel wonderful. Maybe not being good at it has something to do with it. I can't even tell you how fine it makes me feel. It's just me, trying to do something because I want to. It's like I'm back in Flin Flon again, learning to skate for the first time. It makes me feel like a boy."

A Professional Named Tiny

A snowy day in Kansas City. The two people in the front seat of the new Grand Prix were both young, both black. The young woman turned to the young man at the wheel, who looked to be about 16 years old. "The milkman told me it's early in the year to be getting so much snow," she said.

The driver said nothing. He was wearing a black leather hat pulled down hard on his head, and he was nodding in time to a slow rock song playing on the car's tape deck. The road was coated with ice, and the snow was blowing directly at the windshield, but it did not seem to be bothering the driver. He leaned forward, both arms resting on top of the steering wheel.

"I'd rather be in San Diego," the woman said. "I'd rather be driving in the rain than in this. Look, it's starting to hail."

Still nothing from the driver.

"Don't forget to stop at the bank," the woman said. "We've got to get that check cashed before we go downtown." The driver took a left, and pulled into the parking lot of a suburban bank and plowed his way through the slush, up to a side door of the bank. The woman walked inside. The driver got out of the car, pulled a snow brush from the trunk and began to knock the ice from the back window. Short and frail, wearing a pair of brand-new, stiff-legged Levi flares, he looked like a kid who might be doing this for tips on somebody else's pretty Grand Prix.

His name is Nate (Tiny) Archibald, and looking at him slipping and sliding in the deserted parking lot, it was hard to imagine that he was an athlete, even a high school athlete. The thought that he might be a professional athlete seemed simply ludicrous. A professional basketball player? In the NBA? Too silly to even consider. This little kid?

Tiny Archibald's wife Shirley was still in the bank. She was cashing a check that had been lying around the house, a check for $700. While Tiny (who at this moment was somehow, incredibly, leading the National Basketball Association in scoring *and* assists, who was becoming one of the most important names in professional sports) was living a fantasy known to every kid who was ever too short and too scrawny to let anyone else know of his basketball dreams.

The Kansas City Municipal Auditorium is a hopelessly dreary arena; it is much too dark and much too high, perfect for a rock band but not for basketball. Which is unfortunate for a first-year franchise such as the Kansas City-Omaha Kings. The team had to move out of Cincinnati; no one was coming to see the Royals play anymore, and they figured that if they divided the team's home town between *two* Midwestern cities, they might make it. They installed 40 bare light bulbs encased in steel reflecting covers, and hung them from the ceiling of the KC arena with long, skinny black wires, and that brought the candlepower just over the minimum level acceptable for television, meaning the minimum level acceptable for a professional sports franchise to live.

So the lights helped, but the thing that is really giving the Kings' franchise a chance to make it is the fact that Tiny Archibald shows up to play every game-night. Like tonight, with the Atlanta Hawks in town. It was camera night, with free film for everyone, courtesy of the Kansas City Area Photo-Mate Stores. At first the camera-carriers were all gathered around Pete Maravich. And then Tiny trotted out to warm up.

What an amazing sight. It's not just the size, although that is certainly part of it. The program lists him at six-foot-one, 155 pounds, and those figures are a pair of lies. But everyone knows that, everyone has heard it a million times, and you are prepared for Archibald to be physically small.

But it is the face that is the truly amazing thing. Here are all these professional athletes on the floor, and the miles of basketball travel are chopped into their faces. The faces are tired and hard and set. And then there is Tiny. He has not shaved this day, but the beginnings of a beard only serve as a contrast with his face. It is a kid's face, open and young and almost puzzled. He is different. Even before the game starts, he is different from the rest of the players on the court. Tiny is 24 years old, and going into this game he was averaging 34.3 points and 11.9 assists every time he stepped onto the floor. But all of that is not what drew the people with the cameras to him. Instead it was the unmistakable impression that for some reason, a young man from the playgrounds was being allowed to try his stuff against the money players tonight. The illusion is transparent enough, but it's also about half-true.

When the teams came out for the opening jump, Archibald could not stand still; he looked as if he did *not* think of this as a job he has to perform every night, that maybe he had forgotten about the realities of professional athletics for a moment. His mouth hung open, and he almost twitched, so eager was he for the shooting to start. The Kings have their names printed on the back of their shirts, but Tiny's back is so narrow that when he turns away from you, it looks as if his name is "RCHIBAL."

And when it started, he was incredible to watch. He missed an easy layup right away, but then he drove on Maravich and scored, and from that point on he did not stop. You could not look at him without a dumb, helpless grin coming onto your face; he is the kind of athlete who makes you smile whether you want to or not. There is just no other proper expression to be wearing while you are seeing him work:

Archibald waving teammate Dick Gibbs out of the way so he can take his own shot. Archibald passing behind his back while he looks in the opposite direction. Archibald being shoved aside, then shooting and making it anyway. Archibald driving on six-foot-eleven-inch Walt Bellamy, and scoring. Archibald faking Maravich off balance. Archibald sneaking under the basket, among all the huge Hawks and Kings, to take a feed from Tom Van Arsdale and score again.

And shooting, shooting, shooting. Archibald loves to shoot, and the inevitable playground comparison comes back every time he does it. He looks almost apologetic, like a school kid who knows that he's better than the older players and knows it's not cool to shoot so much, but also knows that the only way to prove just how good he is is to put the ball up there, time and again. Every time Archibald came down-court with the ball, you could see it in his eyes: he was thinking about scoring, thinking hard about it. Every time.

During each time-out, while the rest of the players would sit on the bench and hock the phlegm out and gasp for air, Tiny would stay on his feet, pacing, looking back to the court. The game was never close, the Kings had it won from the start, but after every referee's whistle, Tiny would shoot anyway—and when it would go in, he would turn wide-eyed to the ref, hoping that somehow he'd be allowed two more points.

Four minutes left, the game won by a mile, and still he yelled "He stepped out! He stepped out right there!" whenever a Hawks player came near the side stripes. "*Archibald!*" the PA announcer would scream every time he scored, and the organ would sound. He was taken out with 3:49 to go, and he looked like his world was ending. He had scored 41 points.

He went to the end of the bench, but he could not sit still. He shouted and changed seats a dozen times, and kept stepping toward the court. The game was sealed up, and he had enjoyed a sensational night. But there was a game still being played, not ten feet away from him, and he wanted to be in it, shooting a basketball. He looked very nervous and unhappy, pacing back and forth until the final buzzer went off.

The coach was in the practice gym early. He was shooting one-handed push shots from behind the key. A very large number of his shots were going clean through the net, without touching the backboard or the rim. The coach is not a young man anymore, and the gray is coming to his hair, the weight to his legs. He is still a stone cold poet on a basketball court, though. The coach's name is Bob Cousy, and as the Kings came into the gym in their street clothes, he kept putting those push shots right into the center of the net.

"I'd like to take credit for Tiny. I'd like to say that there's a lot of me in him, but I can't," Cousy said. "He's all Nate Archibald. That's all there is to it. He's all his own."

The comparison is natural. There is so much in Archibald that is reminiscent of the young Cousy, starting, of course, with the idea of the very little man in a world of very big men. During a game Cousy and Archibald do an instinctive eye contact thing, Tiny on the court looking over at Cousy on the bench all the time. During the time-outs, Cousy is always reaching out to lay a hand on Tiny, even when Tiny is wandering around.

"He has so much ability," Cousy said. "So much speed, so much quickness. I've talked to him at great length about taking charge, becoming a leader. When we're running I want him to be the one out there who's on top of things. When we've gone up and down the court three or four times without scoring, I want Tiny to be the one to put the brakes on. He absorbs pretty well, he's just got to convince himself that he really is the leader out there.

"He's got a tendency to go schoolyard on you, though. He doesn't really discipline himself as much as he should. I was always fairly disciplined when I was playing—but then, I had nowhere near the ability to go to the basket that he does. He's so good at that, it tempts him to be a little bit loose."

Cousy started flipping hook shots toward the basket. Some people who had wandered into the gym stopped to stare. His movements were absolutely hypnotic.

"Sure I feel good that Tiny is the kind of player he is," Cousy said. "He's a playmaker, and I like to see that. When he makes a great pass, I feel better than if it had been a great shot.

"I think I appreciate a good play more than the average guy," said Bob Cousy.

"We almost didn't make it back for the game last night," Tiny Archibald said. "We were in Baltimore the night before, and yesterday morning we went to the airport for a ten o'clock flight back to Kansas City. But it was foggy, and we had to get out of there some way, so we got in a bus and then they finally got us to some airport somewhere, and we made it just in time for the game."

We were riding in Tiny's car, on the way to his home. At the moment it was hot as a jungle inside the Grand Prix, because Tiny had just flipped the heater switch to full blast. He had already done this three or four times in the past 15 minutes. After the car steamed up, he would switch the heater back to "off," and it would become frigid inside the car. Then he would switch it back to full blast again. Apparently, the idea that there is a method of doing things halfway has not occurred to him.

Tiny is not much of a talker. Not that he is unfriendly; he is, in fact, gracious and polite and eager to make strangers feel comfortable. But talking is not what he's about; he is not very good at it, and he is almost pathologically shy, and he would simply rather not fill the air with words when there is no reason to.

This is not surprising; he came out of the boys' clubs and schoolyards of the South Bronx, New York, out of a broken home with no money, and it was not fancy talk that brought him to where he is right now. Tiny Archibald never bluffed or wheedled his way to anything. He was always the littlest person on the court, and he always kept his mouth shut and played better than anyone else. That is what he is interested in: playing basketball.

Newsweek did a big story on him. I asked him what he had thought of it, and he evaded the question a little, and finally he admitted that he had not read it. "What did that story say?" Tiny asked. "I looked at the picture and said 'Yeah, that's me,' and then I put the magazine down. I never even read the sports pages after our games. You can get your head all swelled up if you start reading about yourself."

We pulled up to Tiny's home, a townhouse near Kansas City International Airport. Inside, a reporter and photographer from an Omaha paper were interviewing Shirley about what it is like to be married to the leading scorer in the NBA. Tiny came in, flopped into a double-width chair, and began flipping through a stack of records.

The Archibalds have four children, and they came in and started climbing all over him, pulling themselves up onto his lap, grabbing at the bottoms of his jeans. Tiny was wearing a T-shirt that said "Central Intelligence Agency" on the front, and the kids began to yank the shirt out of shape. Tiny didn't stop them. He selected a record called *The World Is A Ghetto,* by a group called War, and put it on the stereo. The Omaha photographer snapped away, and tried to make conversation. Tiny said "Yeah" a couple of times, and concentrated on the record. "Your wife's so talkative, and you're so quiet," the Omaha reporter said. "Yeah, that's what people say," Tiny said.

Later, when the Omaha people had left, Shirley Archibald brought in tuna fish sandwiches for Tiny and me. Tiny said that if I wanted to do a formal question and answer thing, it was okay with him. He got up and turned the stereo down, and then came back to the plate of sandwiches.

It was strange. He was really trying, really making an effort to do the right thing. He wanted to be helpful. But all the ease and grace and relaxed confidence that he shows on the basketball court were gone. Now he was nervous and ill at ease, and there was no question about it: he would rather be anywhere but right here, being made to talk about himself. This just isn't what he *does;* it had nothing to do with him.

So we went through the motions as best we could. And Tiny responded to questions about his life.

On the idea of a poor black kid from the Bronx winding up as a wealthy superstar in the Midwest: "I don't mind being out here. I kind of like it. It's better for the kids, anyway, than the city. They can go outside and play, and we don't have to worry about one of them getting hit in the head."

On the current glamour being attached to ghetto street life in movies and songs: "I saw that *Super Fly.* I don't understand how any kid can believe in that stuff. I mean, they see the way it really is, right on their own block. You take 100 young black kids who are impressed by that movie. Maybe two of them are going to end up a big man on the corner, nice clothes, good cars, selling dope. The others are going to end up like Freddy, the junkie in the movie. And Freddy's dead, remember that. He ends up dead."

On his own experiences with dope: "I never did it. My friends were all gettin' high, but I just didn't indulge. It was kind of a struggle, going to school and making money for my family. I was 14 years old when I became the man of the family. A lot of people doing drugs come down on you when you won't do it, but I was playing basketball and I just didn't do it. One of my younger brothers got messed up with it, and he's just getting over it now. I don't even drink beer. They have those little bottles of . . . what you call them, those little bottles on the airplane? I don't even take them."

On his recognition of his own ability: "I didn't even realize I was any good until last year, in the NBA. In elementary school I was just one of the crowd, trying to play. I had a lot of problems even making the team in high school. They didn't even let me play a complete season until I was a senior. And then in college, at the University of Texas at El Paso, we weren't a high-scoring team, so I didn't really know. Last year, when I started scoring big against everyone, it hit me that I was really making it."

On going back to the Bronx: "Some guys I used to play ball with are still standing on the same street corner they were on when I left. A lot of them are taking a lot of dope. Just standing around. After a while, I stop talking to them so much. There's nothing you can tell them. A lot of them ask me for money, and you know what they're going to use it for. I can't tell them about dope, they know all about it, they know what they're doing. I can't tell them."

When we were done, Tiny had to go run an errand.

"Tiny, you'd better wear a coat," Shirley called to him.

"I've been wearing a coat," Archibald said.

"I mean a heavy coat," she said. "You know how you get when it's cold out."

So Archibald went back to the closet and picked out a heavier coat. Then he walked to the front door of the townhouse, and on his way he did something that any 12-year-old who has ever fantasized about being a professional basketball player would recognize instantly. Tiny Archibald, the leading scorer in the National Basketball Association, took a little jump into the air, and tapped his hand against the top of the door frame.

The Paterson Housing Project, on Morris Avenue in the South Bronx, is part of a world that knows a lot more about junkies and prostitutes and strong-arm criminals than it does about inspirational success stories. Tiny Archibald grew up in the Paterson project. His mother, Mrs. Julia Archibald, still lives there.

"The basketball headlines haven't changed my Tiny," Mrs. Archibald told Sam Goldaper of the *New York Times* recently. "He doesn't forget his family. He comes back here all the time, visiting family and friends and playing basketball in the same playgrounds and centers where he grew up. He loves the game almost like life itself. He makes me proud. He has never forgotten who he is and where he comes from."

That sounds like standard proud-mother-giving-predictable-quotes stuff. But in the South Bronx, it means more. For every boy on the street who carries a basketball under his arm and hangs around the playground, Tiny Archibald represents the only hope, the only sign that there *is* a way out. They talk about him in the hallways of DeWitt Clinton High School, and they feel that they are a part of him, that they can somehow identify with the good things that have happened to him. It's not going to happen to many of them; maybe it will not even happen to one of them. But the fact that Tiny came up the same way they are coming up, and that he is making it as big as an athlete can make it in America, gives them a little something to reach out for, and that counts for something in the South Bronx.

They all know Tiny's official biographical data: one of seven children; DeWitt Clinton High School, Arizona Wesleyan Junior College, UTEP; second draft choice of the Cincinnati Royals; starter in rookie year; passed over for the NBA All-Star game last year, after which he went on a scoring binge that stunned the league; brightest star in the NBA this year.

But that isn't why Tiny is so big in his old neighborhood. The reason they love him is because he has not turned his back on them. When he was a young boy, a man named Floyd Layne convinced him that basketball could get him out of there, could give him a better life than the street. Archibald knows that if Layne hadn't been there, urging him to play, he might be on the corner with so many of the other South Bronx 24-year-olds. So he goes back. He coaches. He advises. He sits and talks. He makes a point of just *being there,* an example of what can happen if things fall right.

One day last summer, Tiny and Shirley drove nine hours straight to get to New York from the Midwest. Tiny went directly to the Wagner Center in East Harlem, where a team he helps was practicing. He worked them for four hours straight, and got to his mother's home at 2:30 A.M. The next morning he got up early and drove to Newark, New Jersey, where he gave a clinic for young boys, and talked with them afterward. Then he drove to Temple University to appear in an exhibition game. He scored 52 points.

There are all kinds of stories around the South Bronx about fine young playground basketball players who end up in jail, or nodding out in some doorway every day, or dead. Some of the players have collapsed right on the schoolyard courts, the heroin getting to their systems even as they are doing the one thing that might get them away from it. So if Mrs. Julia Archibald sounds corny when she says, "It's a big day around here when my son comes home," forgive her. In a place where there aren't a whole lot of big days, she knows what she's talking about.

John Green is 39 years old. He has been playing basketball as a professional for 14 years, which is a long time to pick up the paper in the morning and see yourself referred to as "Jumpin' Johnny." He was a college star when Tiny Archibald was seven years old, and now the two are teammates, and Tiny is the star. On this day Green was sitting in the fieldhouse of Rockhurst College in Kansas City, waiting to get his official team portrait taken. The Kansas City Municipal Auditorium was being used today, so after the picture-taking the Kings would practice here.

"It'll be about five minutes, sorry," one of the jeans-and-flannel-and-hair photography crew called to Green. He went and sat down on a bench. We struck up a conversation, and I told him I was in town to do a story on Tiny.

"Boy, he sure got hot all of a sudden," Green said. "He's a real superstar, man. But he's so quiet. That's good. Some guys who get all the attention all of a sudden let it mess them up. Tiny's so shy, he'll be okay. He's really going to be big."

Just then Archibald came into the gym from the parking lot. No matter how many times you have seen him, the impression is always the same each time he rejoins his teammates: this can't be the leading scorer in the NBA; this must be the team's equipment kid. He was wearing that leather hat, and a pair of blue-and-red platform shoes, but the added height did nothing but make him look like a teenager trying to appear taller by wearing a hat and stacked shoes.

Everyone was shouting and making jokes during the picture-taking. Everyone except Tiny. He paced the perimeter of the gym, his blue shorts ballooning over his skinny legs, waiting for all this to be over, so he could play basketball. Finally he took a ball and went off to shoot by himself, at the far end of the court. When they called him back for his individual picture, he sat uncomfortably in the chair, turning his head when they told him to turn, smiling politely at the photographers' gags, offering nothing of his own. As soon as they were done, he ran to a ball, dribbled downcourt and was shooting again.

When practice started, Tiny and Cousy teamed up to bring the ball downcourt. It was something to see. They were, of course, the littlest men on the court, and Cousy by all rights should not even have been competing with these present-day athletes. But here they were, Cousy looking far into the distance as he dribbled, Tiny cutting under the basket, lost among the giants except for his hand sticking up, yelling "Whoooo!" as he broke into the clear for a moment, grabbing a hard underhand pass, putting it in.

The Kings would rotate, some of them taking the court while the other ones watched from the bench. But Tiny never went to the bench. When he was told to stay out of the scrimmage, he would stand just behind the halfcourt line and watch. He would bend over, his hands on his knees, and follow the play with his eyes. He would talk under his breath, and sometimes he would giggle a little when someone made a silly mistake. He would move, too; he would mimic the play, even though he was not in it. He would move as if he were the guard with the ball. Sometimes he would go in the same direction as the man who really was in control of the ball; but often he would look another direction, see another man open under the basket, and even though it was only practice, a pained look would come to his face. He had seen his opening, and he couldn't take advantage of it.

Late in the practice three men came into the gym. Two of them were wearing jerseys that said "WHB." They were local disk jockeys. The third man was in a suit. He was the disk jockeys' promotion man.

Their radio station basketball team would be playing an exhibition game during the halftime of a Kings' game the next week. The disk jockeys' names were Johnny Dolan and Phil Jay, and they had come to practice to have some promotional photographs taken with the Kings, and to cut some tapes for their shows.

The WHB promotion man went into a coach's office and placed a telephone call to the station. He had an engineer get a tape ready. Then, one by one, he led the Kings' stars into the office, handed them a script, and told them to repeat their lines twice.

It went smoothly enough at first. The disk jockeys were turned on to be in the presence of the professional athletes, and were full of hip, happy patter.

It was a good enough way to get away from the practice grind for a few minutes, and the Kings were more than willing to hang around the coach's office and talk with the disk jockeys. When it seemed to be all done, the WHB promotion man said, "Wait a minute. We're missing somebody."

Tiny Archibald was out on the court. He was still shooting. He had not come into the office to do the radio spots. When he saw the disk jockeys and the promotion man coming after him, he began to dribble quickly away from them. But they called to him: "Come on, Tiny, we just need you for a minute."

He took the ball inside the office with him. Johnny Dolan and Phil Jay were talking at him, and the promotion man was shoving the script into his hand. Archibald seemed almost scared. His eyes were darting from one man to the other, and he tucked the ball tightly under his arm.

"Nate, if you'll just read it twice, that's all we need," the promotion man said.

Tiny looked at the script. "Over and over again?" he said. He was almost whispering.

"That's right," the promotion man said, "Easy as that." He handed the phone to Archibald.

The line that Tiny was supposed to say was: "This is Nate Archibald of the Kansas City Kings, and even if Johnny Dolan was smaller, I don't see how he could be any big advantage for the WHB Basketbawlers."

Archibald looked at it for another moment. "Any time you're ready," the promotion man said.

Tiny started to talk. It was awful. His voice was still a whisper, and he hurried through it, in a nervous little monotone. The disk jockeys and the promotion man looked at each other.

"Let's give it another try," the promotion man said.

Archibald held the basketball even tighter. He read the line again. It was just as bad as the first time. He was out of place. It was not right for him to be here, doing this.

"I've got an idea," said Johnny Dolan. "Why don't you just say, 'This is Nate Archibald of the Kings, and Johnny Dolan . . . forget it.' "

Tiny looked at the telephone receiver. "This is Nate Archibald of the Kings, and Johnny Dolan . . . forget it," he said. The line was so short that Archibald's uncomfortable giddiness sounded like tough-guy cockiness, which was fine for the WHB spot.

"Beautiful!" the promotion man said. "That was better than the first bit anyway. . . ."

But Tiny was already running out of the office, toward the sound of basketballs pounding on the court. When he got there, though, the Kings were gone. Practice had ended, and a physical education class from the college had come into the gym and taken over the court.

So Archibald went into the locker room. The rest of the Kings were naked, heading for the showers or talking to the trainer. Archibald went to his locker, turned the combination, opened it. He sat on the bench, and he started to unlace his shoe. Then he stopped.

He laced the shoe back up again, and walked down the hallway of the locker room. He headed back out toward the court. The boys in the gym class were running a layup drill.

Tiny picked up a ball. He dribbled a little bit, standing out of bounds. Then he began to shoot.

At first, the gym class players didn't pay any attention to him. They knew that the Kings used the fieldhouse to practice; but practice was over, and this new kid on the court was smaller than most of them, anyway.

Then the shots started to go in. One. Two. Three. Four. Five. Six. Little by little, everyone in the phys ed class stopped shooting, and turned to look at Tiny Archibald.

Some of the Kings, in street clothes, were already walking out toward their cars. All action on the court had halted, except for Archibald. He drove toward the basket, he twisted in the air, he flipped shots from behind his shoulder. He picked up the ball, dribbled back toward the halfcourt line, wheeled, jumped high, arched a shot off toward the distant hoop. It went right in. "WHOOOOO!" yelled Tiny Archibald. He looked around him. All the phys ed players were gaping in amazement. Tiny grabbed the ball and drove for the net again, a huge grin on his face. He looked very happy. He looked like a man who was doing exactly what he was meant to be doing.

The Wimp at Work

The U.S. Open Pocket Billiards championships were about to begin, and the location was not a neighborhood pool hall, but a fancy downtown hotel. Many of the contestants were young, and they were dressed in colorful clothing like pro golfers. "No, I don't know where the Wimp is," the man from the tournament committee said. "I guess he's kind of a loner after all these years, and I hear he didn't even show up at the players' meeting last night. Usually he just stays to himself."

They weren't really thinking about the Wimp, who is known by that name in poolroom circles and whose real name is Luther Lassiter. The players were busy warming up in the Crystal Room of the Sheraton-Chicago. The room was bright, and it was just a few feet away from the Grand Ballroom, where the tournament matches were being played. The word was out that ABC television's "Wide World of Sports" program was coming later in the week, and the new breed pool players were anxious at the thought of appearing on national television.

So many of them are new to this, are the kind of men who hold jobs as salesmen and teachers during the week and play pocket billiards as a sideline. And while they were scurrying around the hotel, Luther Lassiter, age 52, pool player from Elizabeth City, North Carolina, was climbing out of bed in his room.

"I couldn't sleep last night," Lassiter said. "I'm getting a damn cold and it's going to take two or three days to break itself down. So I walked around the city. This town certainly has done some changing."

The only world he knows is pool. He has given up three-quarters of his stomach to an ulcer patch job and he has a bad gallbladder and his eyes are losing much of their ability to perceive depth. He has very little in common with the kind of situation where pool tables are in basements and suburban bowling alleys, and championships are played in hotels for television audiences. But the tournament was offering $5,000 to the men's champion. So the Wimp was in Chicago.

In the main ballroom, the women were playing. Lassiter had no interest in a woman's pool tournament, especially one in which a 12-year-old girl was one of the strongest contenders. The ballroom had four pool tables set up, with risers on all sides for the paying fans. Scores were flashed up on screens behind each table.

It was not until the first round of men's competition had begun that Lassiter went downstairs. He took a look into the main room. A young guy named Pete Margo was winning his match. Margo was wearing two-toned shoes with raised heels, a dark blue shirt with a white tie, and a wide-lapeled windowpane-pattern jacket. Lassiter took one look and went over to the warm-up room.

He removed his cue from its ancient alligator-skin case and

started to shoot. He looked wonderful. He wore a dark gray suit with pants that drooped over his shiny black tie-shoes. His white shirt was pulled out near the waist. A skinny blue brocade tie was yanked down enough for him to open his white shirt at the top. He chewed on an antacid tablet.

A man with a Polaroid asked to take a picture of the Wimp, and asked him to smile. He went on shooting pool. "Smile and laugh and giggle and you'll have a heart attack," he muttered as he circled the table. "Everyone knows that."

You did not have to know a thing in the world about pocket billiards to watch Lassiter work and realize what you were seeing. Old, yes. But the way he moved with the cue, effortlessly flicking the balls into the pockets, was poetry. His short-cropped white hair dully reflected the fluorescent lights. There may have been young men in the tournament who are better technicians at the game of pocket billiards than the Wimp. But one look at Lassiter and you never had to look for a pool player again.

"Most of the players I guess have jobs," Lassiter said as he knocked a ball into the side pocket. "Or they own pool halls. There are some of us who don't, though. I'm broke. I've won more tournaments by luck, and I'm still broke."

His people were beginning to gather. Milwaukee Lou and Cue Ball Kelley and the little men with cigars and gray skin who look like they have never seen the sun. Men who feel a little uncomfortable playing pool in a room where people have danced to orchestras on other nights.

He kept working, then went into the big room and sat to await his match. He was to play another old one, Richard Riggie, called "Socks" because he wears droopy white anklets in snappy shoes.

"He's a hard one for me to beat," said the Wimp. "He's a sly one, and he's even older that I am, but he looks 15 years younger."

The tournament was a double elimination affair, meaning that a man has to lose twice before being knocked out for good. But no one wants to lose in the first round because that means to reach the finals you cannot afford to make a single mistake from that point on.

The young players watched Lassiter respectfully as he waited. "I caught this damn cold on the plane," he said. "I wish I didn't have to ride those things. I hate to fly, the only time I want to fly is when I'm going toward heaven."

Lassiter went out and once again played a game of pool on a 4½-by-9-foot table featuring a slate bed covered with a very fine-grade felt cloth. It took three hours, and he was behind much of the time; he finished it with a run of 16 to win 150 to 110.

He removed his rimless bifocals. "I guess I need new ones again," he said. "I'm not getting any depth perception at all. I just got a new pair six months ago."

The natural question was: If he couldn't really see the length of the table, what did he use to spot the balls?

"Forty years," he said. "I use 40 years of doing this."

Bulls

A potential tragedy is brewing in Chicago. Ever since the Chicago Bulls were eliminated from the National Basketball Association playoffs, there has been talk of a mass housecleaning by the Bulls management, with the present players being traded away and a new breed brought in.

In any other city this might make sense. But in Chicago it must not be allowed to happen. Never in the history of sports has a team been so representative of the flavor of a town as the present-day Bulls are of Chicago. The Bulls epitomize the personality of this city so well that they have built a huge following even among persons who are not sports fans, this one included. The Bulls transcend athletics.

Let other towns build sports franchises with bright-faced, young, superbly talented, homogenized stars fresh out of college.

Let the members of other teams profess their love for one another, and brag that—blacks and whites together—they are striving for a common goal. Let other teams use slogans like, "you gotta believe," and bring the old school spirit into the pros. Let other teams pose as happy, satisfied, enthusiastic warriors.

None of that for the Bulls. If Chicago stands for anything, it stands for a rejection of fantasy notions of a nice, perfect, friendly, utopian world. Chicago is real-life, and the Bulls are Chicago.

The Bulls are old and foul-tempered.

The Bulls do not like each other.

The Bulls hate their coach.

The Bulls hate their owners.

There is strong evidence of festering racial animosity among the Bulls players.

The Bulls do not like to play basketball very much; they readily admit that they are only in it for the money.

The Bulls cheat and play dirty even when they don't have to.

In other words, the Bulls are a priceless treasure. We need them here. What would this town do with a bunch of Rhodes scholars and yoga enthusiasts? If a Bill Bradley came to Chicago and started espousing his high-IQ theories about the transcendental significance of basketball, he would be greeted with laughs in his face. If Bill Walton showed up with his birdseed lunches, he just might get his legs broken.

Let the Bulls stay here just as they are. Who cares if they win? How many winners have you ever met in this town, besides the mayor?

The Bulls are terrific roving ambassadors for Chicago. In other towns around the league, there has been evidence of hostile fans attacking players on the visiting teams. But only the Chicago Bulls have charged into the grandstands in an effort to attack the fans.

The Bulls are terrible losers, blaming one another, their coach, and the referees when the score goes against them. In fairness, it must also be said that the Bulls are terrible winners, often denigrating opponents and hogging individual credit when they are victorious.

Lots of teams have players who work with children and set

shining examples of respect for authority and good citizenship. Only the Bulls have a guy who once charged headlong into a small-town police station and started a full-scale rumble.

Lots of teams have eager young players who want to get into the game so badly that they will beg their coach to use them. Only the Bulls have a player who, after being kept on the court for the whole game, will call his coach stupid for not taking him out, and say, "I am not a mule."

Lots of teams will not make it to the championship in a given season, and bravely vow, "We'll get 'em next year." Only the Bulls, even before the season is over, will say that their teammates are making too much money, and demand, "Trade me."

Lots of teams have fuzzy, wishy-washy, undefined images around the country. Not the Bulls. Two of their players, Norm Van Lier and Jerry Sloan, are known around the NBA as borderline sociopaths, and the Bulls are despised by players, coaches, fans, referees and religious leaders of various faiths from coast to coast.

Coaches of other teams know what kind of hearts their players have, and after a playoff loss will console their men and tell them that they have a right to be proud. The coach of the Chicago Bulls knows what kind of hearts his players have, and after a playoff loss told his men that they ought to swindle two of their teammates out of playoff money so they could keep more for themselves.

We must not allow this team to be dissolved. They are the stuff of which legends are made.

In South Bend, the story is told of Knute Rockne informing his Notre Dame football players that George Gipp, a star of the team, was in the hospital, seriously ill. "Let's go out there and win one for the Gipper," Rockne said—and the team does just that, scoring a thrilling victory.

With the Bulls, they would have broken into the Gipper's locker, found his wallet, and cleaned him out.

12

THE END OF OUTRAGE

The title piece in this chapter originally appeared as an essay in *Newsweek* magazine, and its theme sums up what I was trying to say in all of the other pieces in the chapter. Whether reporting on the anatomy of the Alice Cooper phenomenon (the story here is from *Harper's* in 1972, and grew into the idea for the book *Billion Dollar Baby*) or examining the machinery of the Billy Graham Crusade, the stories say something about America in the '70s that is not awfully pleasant to think about. The last piece, "Where Have All the Young Men Gone?" was written in 1975, and appears to be done in a much lighter vein, but I'm not so sure how abundant the laughter should be.

The End of Outrage

The first time I thought about it, I guess, was last year, backstage in a big auditorium in Sacramento, California. I was working on a story, traveling with Alice Cooper, the male rock-and-roll singer. Alice was onstage, 15 feet away, chopping a baby doll to pieces, hacking at it with an ax, throwing the arms and legs to the little girls in the audience. There was a cop standing next to me. He was chuckling softly, shaking his head a little. I asked him if what Alice was doing in front of the teenagers of Sacramento was making him angry. "Angry?" he said with a puzzled smile, as if he thought he might have misunderstood the question. "What for?"

And he was right. There was no reason for him to be angry, or shocked, or outraged. Those are outmoded words, and those of us who grew up in the last ten years can probably take a lot of the responsibility for that. Nothing is forbidden. We cannot be shocked in the United States anymore.

That doesn't sound like much of a loss when you put it next to all the other things that we have lost in this country in the years since 1963. But still, it means something. We are so cool and so hard and so hip anymore, we are so wisely cynical to every one of life's darkest possibilities, that there has grown a large dead spot inside us all. Somewhere along the road to becoming smartly self-protective at all times, our last remaining bits of innocence got stomped to death.

I stood behind an amplifier in Sacramento and watched a hall full of 14-year-old faces almost calmly taking in the sight of Alice performing mock murder on the baby doll, accepting it as just another weird, funny part of the show. Outrage is supposed to be a part of the package now; it is advertised and promised and sold and expected, but of course when you have to try that hard for it, it is never really there. And as I watched the kids blissfully take in the chopping of the doll, and then the ritual hanging of Alice from a gallows, I recalled an evening early in 1956.

All over the country, all of us nine-year-old kids were sitting in front of our families' cabinet-model, black-and-white television sets when this duck-tailed *hood* sauntered out and said, "Ladies and gentlemen, I'd like to do a song now that tells a little story, that really makes a lot of sense—Awopbopalooboopalopbamboom! Tutti-frutti! All rootie! Tutti-frutti! All rootie!" And then Elvis started to sneer that sneer and grind his hips, and he had us. Our parents wanted to rip the plug out of the wall. They were furious. We were delirious. It was forbidden. The lines had been drawn.

Now the lines have all been erased. Nothing is forbidden in 1973. The parents are Elvis Presley fans. The ABC television network put Alice Cooper's sex-and-violence show on one Friday night, and the next day no one was even talking about it. ABC put Chuck Berry on, too, and he had a whole audience singing "I Want You to Play With My Ding-a-Ling" with him, and no one thought anything about that, either.

We quit caring about things like that after we saw a president get shot in the head, after we saw a war built on calculated lies, after we saw people of our own age getting beaten by police because they knew about those lies. During those years one *real* shock came after another, until finally we could not feel them anymore. We really couldn't feel anything, and we called for an end to the little hypocrisies, for an end to one generation's telling another what it could and could not do. Surprisingly, the older ones were instinctively willing to go along with us, because they were feeling just as empty as we were by what the '60s had done. And before we knew it, we really were in an age of Anything Goes. "Nothing is wrong or immoral if no one gets hurt," we said, and we believed it. If It Feels Good, That's Cool.

But things did not get better. Heroin addiction and gonorrhea became so common that both were soon acceptable dinner-table conversation. More and more public figures were shot down after John Kennedy, and the newspapers always reported our reaction as "shock and disbelief," but we weren't shocked, and we believed it, and our only question was: who's next? All the sexual barriers came down, and we saw the manifestations everywhere from Woodstock to the live shows in the downtown section of every city, but the psychiatrists reported that they were finding *more* people with serious sexual problems in this open society, not fewer. We called each other "brother" and "sister," but we weren't crazy enough to walk the streets alone at night. And the biggest change of all, of course, was our inability to even work up any feeling about what was going on. Everything's OK, nothing's forbidden, so why do things feel so vaguely wrong all the time?

At least when we were growing up, before these last ten years, we could always blame our disappointments on someone else. When things were forbidden us, we could assume that they were good and pleasurable, that no one would try to keep them from us if they were not worth having.

Now there's not even that, and I feel sorry for a kid growing up in 1973. A movie called *Deep Throat,* which is about a woman who has the physical ability to take a man all the way down to her tonsils, was recently featured in *Newsweek* and *Time* the same week—and on a recent Sunday, the *New York Times* ran *two* feature stories about it. It is currently the accepted motion picture for young dating couples to attend.

But what kind of kick can it be for a teenager to sneak in to see a movie that is fast becoming a chic, respected part of our contemporary national culture? I remember when I was 15, in Columbus, Ohio, my friends and I would go down to the Parsons Art Theater on a Friday night. Jack Roth, who was the tallest of us, would go to the ticket counter while the rest of us waited on the corner. He would lower his voice about five octaves, and say, "Four tickets, please."

If we got lucky, and the box-office guy sold Jack the tickets, we could go inside and see a grainy print of a movie in which a woman would take her blouse off and let us look at her breasts for about three and a half seconds. And I guarantee you, we got more turned on by that than any kid today does who goes to *Deep Throat* because he read about it in his mother's copy of *Women's Wear Daily.* But the Parsons Theater was in 1962, and that was an era ago.

Torture

"He's so cruel. It's not bad enough that he killed my little girl. But now he has to call up and say that my baby was a ten-year-old whore. Every time the phone rings I think it's him, and I'm so shaken up at this point that I don't know whether I want him to keep calling or not. I just don't know."

Mrs. Ann Moore did not think it could get any worse for her than it was the night of March 8. That was the night her daughter, Denise, was killed by the driver of a red semitrailer truck at the intersection of 63d and Kedzie. The driver kept on going, leaving Mrs. Moore and her husband, Freeman, with a daughter to bury.

But that has not been the end of it. Soon after Denise's death, there was a phone call to the Moore home in the middle of the night. "Mommy," a man's voice said, "I'm here. Come and get me."

And then, last month, the real torture began.

Because the hit-and-run killer had not been found, Mrs. Moore began running a series of classified ads in several newspapers. The advertisements asked for any witnesses to the accident to call and give her any information that might help the police catch the driver.

Immediately a man called. He told Mrs. Moore that he had seen the accident. She asked him to give the information to her attorney or to the police. He refused.

A week later the same man called again. "I have a confession to make," the man said. "I'm not just a witness. I killed your little girl."

The man said that Denise could not be brought back to life, and that Mrs. Moore should stop running the advertisements. "He says that I'm harassing him and ruining his life and his family's," Mrs. Moore said. "I begged him to turn himself in. But he just told me that I'd better not keep trying to find him. He started to taunt me. He said, 'Ain't got any clues, do you? The police haven't come to get me, so I know you don't have any idea who I am.' All I can do is try to get him to stay on the line and plead with him to turn himself in."

When the newspaper ads continued, the caller became more twisted. "Once he called after midnight," Mrs. Moore said. "He told me that my little girl was alive. He said, 'She's not dead, she's right here with me, do you want to talk to her? I have Denise right here with me.' And then he started to say these horrible things about Denise. I hate to even tell you what he said about my baby. It makes me so upset when he says those things. And then he said what he says every time. He said, 'You can't get Denise back,' and then he said that I should stop running the ads and stop looking for him."

Mrs. Moore said she is convinced the caller really is the killer, and not just some sick stranger. "He is too concerned that I stop running the ads," she said. "It's more than him just wanting to hurt me. He's scared that he will be caught, and he's trying to frighten me so badly that I'll stop looking for him. But I won't stop."

The caller sometimes telephones Mrs. Moore dozens of times every day. Sometimes he will say, "Denise, let me talk to Denise." He has told Mrs. Moore that he is 35 years old. One day a little boy's voice sounded in the background, and the caller said, "Georgie, Georgie. That's my son, Georgie." Mrs. Moore asked the caller, "How do you look at your own kids when you have killed mine?"

Recently, after Mrs. Moore's plight had received some publicity, the man began to threaten her. "He called and he said, 'I know where you live and I'm going to come get you,'" she said. "I jump every time I hear a foot hit the stairs. And he has said he's going to set our house on fire in the middle of the night."

Mrs. Moore suffered a mild heart attack on the morning of her daughter's funeral, and the calls are tearing her apart. But at least part of her does not want them to end, because she feels they are the only chance she has to find Denise's killer. On Monday afternoon, Mrs. Moore said the man had not called in three days, but that she has not felt any relief because of it. She feels that he will call again, and she is trying to think of more ways to convince him to turn himself in.

Mr. and Mrs. Moore have closed down their place of business, the High Star Grill at 3233 W. 63d Street, to be at their home on West 71st Street, in case anyone should come forward with information about the killer. Mrs. Moore said she does not think she will reopen the grill until the man is caught.

"I will never give up," Mrs. Moore said. "The man told me that he's been drinking for two weeks. He'll kill again, if he's driving around drunk. And I loved Denise too much to stop looking. If it takes everything I've got to find her killer, then that's what it will take.

"I rot when he calls. I fall apart. But I make myself talk to him. I tell him that God will help him if only he will turn himself in. I'm going to pay for some more newspaper advertisements. He thinks that he can hurt me so badly that I'll stop trying to find him. But Denise's loss was so great that I don't think I can be hurt any more than I am. She was my daughter, and I won't be scared out of finding the man who killed her."

Early Alice

On a warm night in San Francisco, Alice Cooper was running his fingers through his hair and watching a Danny Kaye movie on television. Alice is a male rock-and-roll singer, enjoying for the moment the rewards of a sudden and gigantic success. He was drinking a Coors Beer from the bottle as he stared at the tube in the living room of a suite in the Fairmont Hotel. Shep Gordon, manager of the Alice Cooper band, came out of one of the bedrooms carrying a briefcase. He opened the case and pulled out a newspaper clipping. "Alice," he said, "I have something you're going to love."

The clipping was from the front page of the *Charlotte* (North Carolina) *News*. Alice put his beer bottle down and began to read. The Danny Kaye movie blared on. The newspaper story caused Alice to laugh.

ROCK SHOW
"SICKENED" GIRL
By Brooks McGirt
News Staff Writer

A 16-year-old Charlotte high school girl said she was sickened and disgusted by a rock show in town this weekend.

The student, who asked not to be identified, said she had to leave in the middle of the show after the rock group Alice Cooper performed alleged sadistic acts, which included the chopping up of a doll.

A girl in front of her fainted, she said.

The student said the leader of the group first brought out a big snake which she believed to be a boa constrictor, and "let it crawl all over him—his face and everywhere" during a number.

Then, she said, he brought a plastic baby doll on stage, "felt it" and then undressed it. He tore off one of its arms, she said, took an axe and chopped at it.

The doll was filled with red liquid which ran out as the doll was hacked, she said, and members of the group screamed during the chopping.

He then held the doll up to the audience, she said.

"I left then," the student told the *News*.

"I'm not one to get sick at things," she said. "But I just couldn't take that. It was too realistic for comfort."

The student's mother said her daughter called her from Park Center, where the performance was held, and said the show had "absolutely made her sick."

"Well," said Shep Gordon, "how do you like it?"

"It's really nice," Alice said. "Did you get that part about 'alleged sadistic acts'? Where do they get that 'alleged' from? I feel like Sirhan Sirhan."

Gordon retrieved the clipping and put it back in his briefcase. "I called that newspaper," he said. "I told them I couldn't thank them enough. I told them I couldn't have written a better story myself."

But by this time Alice Cooper was being drawn back to the televised movie. "We'll be leaving for the show in about 45 minutes," Gordon said. Alice nodded, his eyes locked on the screen, taking another pull from his beer.

In the dressing room of the Berkeley Community Theater, the Alice Cooper band waited to go on stage. Assorted groupies and hangers-on cluttered up the room as the band prepared to begin what would be an extended tour of the United States and Canada.

They would be playing to capacity houses every night—the word had begun to spread about this band. The story in the Charlotte newspaper had been accurate, if incomplete.

At a time when rock and roll has gained respectability and stature, the Alice Cooper band sets out to be disgusting. It operates on the theory that if the show is hateful and revolting to parents, then the kids will go to any length to see it. The increasing profits (more receipts on each successive night) appear to prove the correctness of the theory.

In an age when advertising executives look far freakier than the Beatles did on their first arrival in the United States, the problem was one of standing out among the hundreds of rock-and-roll bands. To begin with, there was the name. When people first found out that Alice was a man, they assumed that the members were homosexuals or transvestites. The band did not discourage this thinking. They dressed in half-drag and affected a swishy stage manner.

In the dressing room, Alice had painted evil-looking black spider shapes around his eyes, and he had drawn sharp fangs from the corners of his mouth. He wore thigh-high black leather boots and a ripped black leotard. Across his chest, the name "Alice" was written in sequins.

The other members of the band—guitarists Mike Bruce, Dennis Dunaway, and Glen Buxton, and drummer Neal Smith— were dressed in bright one-piece uniforms made of simulated foil. Their fingernails were extremely long and covered with dark polish.

Their hair was tremendously long, even by rock-and-roll standards.

Out front the kids were clamoring. "And now," the announcer screamed, "the most exciting group in the world—the legendary *Alice Cooper!*"

They ran on stage and went through the same routine they perform virtually every working night. The music is solid rock and roll. But with the music alone, this would be just another band trying to make it. It is the show that is making the Alice Cooper band rich.

As soon as the crowd sees Alice, they rush toward the stage. By the time he is into the opening song, "Be My Lover," they are just inches from him. As he sings, he unsheathes a long sword and swings it over their heads. They do not flinch as the sharp blade flashes past them; they stare, fascinated. Alice brings a glob of spit from deep in his throat and it sails out into the audience. They are repelled and thrilled at the same time; the band apparently holds to no conventions at all.

Alice goes behind an amplifier and brings out a long, mean-looking boa constrictor. He holds it near the first row of fans. The snake's tongue whips in and out of its mouth. Alice winds it around his neck. He kisses the snake. He lets it stick its head in his mouth. He sticks it between his legs. He dangles it over the audience. They are breathing hard, not knowing what to expect from this man.

The band begins to play a loud, hard song called "Dead Babies." Alice comes to the front of the stage with a cute baby doll. The song is about a baby who ate a bottle of aspirin and died. As he sings the words, he fondles the doll, rubbing it across his body. He slowly undresses it, playing with it as he does so. Then the music quickens, and he tears at the doll's dress, ripping it. He begins to tear the doll apart. He slams it to the floor, turns around, and raises a hatchet above his head. The sounds of a crying baby are heard from a tape recorder somewhere backstage. Again and again and again he chops at the doll; fake blood turns the stage floor red. All the while he is singing. And the little girls in the audience are singing too; their eyes shine as they watch Alice kill the baby doll, and they sing along with him, "Good-by, little Betty . . . so long, little baby."

After chopping up the doll Alice places its head on top of a microphone stand. It rests there, obscene and taunting, as he flails a whip out over the audience. Some reach for him; he kicks out at them and spits some more. Then the lights go off.

Smoke fills the stage as the lights come back on. The rest of the band dons hangmen's masks. The music continues. They drag Alice, crying and kicking, to the side of the stage. There is a genuine gallows, massive and ugly. They hit at Alice as they carry him up the stairs to the platform and fasten the noose around his neck. He begs them to stop. They do not. They pull a lever; the floor under Alice opens, and he plunges downward. The noise is overwhelming as the young fans scream and shout with excitement. The lights go down again.

Within minutes Alice and the band are back, singing, "We've Still Got a Long Way To Go." Alice begins tossing rolled up posters into the swarming crowd. He throws one, then another, then another and another and another. The kids begin to fight for the posters. They hit at each other and swing and scratch at the people next to them. Girls faint, but there is no room for them to fall. Everyone in the auditorium is coming toward the stage. The unlucky ones, passed out on their feet, are pummeled from every side. Alice, laughing, continues to throw posters.

When it seems that it can get no worse, Alice brings out his last trick. He brandishes the sword again, but this time there are dollar bills strung on it, from handle to tip.

"Do you like money?" he screams. They roar and push forward once again. "How much do you like money?" he screams, and thrusts the sword at them. They leap at it, the last barriers down. They do not know why they are up there, fighting for the stage. They just know they cannot stop.

Which is how this night at the Berkeley Community Theater ended, as Alice and the band ran offstage and into the dressing room. They wanted to hurry and be gone; the limousines would take them to a local pizza parlor, where Warner Brothers Records was giving a party, complete with a stripper and free drinks.

"Everyone is trying to convince people that kids are interested in ecology, that kids are interested in politics," Alice Cooper said. "That's bullshit. Kids are interested in the same things that have always excited them; sex and violence. That's what they want, that's what they'll pay to see."

Alice was in another motel room in another town, drinking another beer and looking at another television screen. "You know, when I was a kid, I used to go to the movies every Saturday afternoon," he said. "If it was a funny movie or a love story, I'd go home with the vague feeling that I'd been cheated out of my money. But if the movie scared the hell out of me—man, I'd love that.

"So I think it's good if the kids are disgusted or frightened by our show. Because inside, it turns them on, they love it, they have to see it. They won't go home and shrug their shoulders; they'll talk to their friends about it, they'll try to figure it out, they'll wonder if we all go back and go to sleep in coffins after the show. They'll be fascinated."

Offstage, Alice is a quiet young man. He and his band have put the show together with a deliberate purpose, and the purpose is being achieved. But the thinking was all done long ago, the dead-babies idea and everything else. Now it is only the people in the anonymous towns who have the spontaneity for outrage. For the Cooper people it is a matter of logistics and mundane worries. How much time do we have to make it to the airport? Did anyone remember to buy mice to feed to the snake? Has the gallows been torn down and prepared for shipment? Has someone filled tonight's baby doll with fake blood? Are there enough posters to inflame the audience with? These are the problems that are important at this stage: the more complex questions have been forgotten by the band long ago. All they know is that the kids are coming to see them, and the money is piling up. (They can begin to afford luxuries; in San Francisco, for two days at the Fairmont, the hotel bill for the band amounted to $1,700.)

"All these rock groups are talking about getting into politics." Alice said. "That's so stupid. Politics is boring, I hate it. Rock and roll is political by its very nature—it's anti-parent, and that's a political statement in itself. You don't have to go beyond that."

Alice says he is repelled by random, offstage violence; he hates the thought of getting into a fistfight. The notion that young Americans eagerly pay to see brutality occurred to him by accident.

"We were doing an outdoor show a long time ago," he said. "This chicken wandered onto the stage. I picked it up: I figured it could fly, so I tossed it into the air. But chickens, you know, they can't fly, it turns out. It came down and it broke its neck. I didn't know what to do. So I kind of tossed it into the audience. You know what those kids did? They tore it apart, just ripped it to shreds! The kids were just like a pack of piranhas. It was amazing to see. It taught me a lot.

"Then all these rumors started to spread, like that we killed chickens onstage every night, and drank the blood. Never happened. It just happened that one time with the chicken, and we didn't drink any blood. But we couldn't convince people, and we began to figure that's the kind of thing they wanted to see. When we got to Atlanta a couple of weeks ago, there was a court injunction waiting for us.

"The injunction said that we supposedly made a practice of smashing kittens with sledgehammers every night and ordered that we not do it in Atlanta. Really."

For a moment only the sound of the television game show filled the room.

"I wish I'd thought of it first," Alice said. "Kittens . . . Jesus."

On a plane heading for Hollywood, a long-haired girl was sitting near the Alice Cooper band. She had the best body anyone in the band had seen in years. Conversation revealed that she was on her way to her father's funeral. She was to be picked up at the airport and driven directly to the cemetery.

"Ask her to bring her father's body to the Palladium tonight," Alice said to Shep Gordon. "We could bury him on stage."

On the way out of the plane, Mike Bruce, the guitarist, handed the girl a piece of paper. She looked at it and smiled, then waved at him and walked into the terminal.

Cadillacs were waiting to take the band to the headquarters of Warner Brothers Records, where gold albums were to be presented to the group for their LP, *Killer*. But when the band arrived, Warner's president Mo Ostin and executive vice-president Joe Smith were both out to lunch. The band walked into Ostin's private office anyway.

"Look at this," said Dennis Dunaway. "He's got one of those happy face notepads."

"Give it to me," said Neal Smith. "Let's burn it."

An autographed picture of Frank Sinatra hung on the wall. Alice sat directly beneath it. A secretary came in and asked the band to move to Joe Smith's office, which they did. Road manager Dave Libert brought in a boxful of drive-in tacos, and the band spread the food over the carpet as they reclined to eat. Which is what was happening when Smith and Ostin came in.

"They're all over the place," said Joe Smith. He said it out loud, but he was talking to himself. "They're all over my office, and they have tacos all over the place."

Ostin and Smith behaved as you might expect them to behave. They are middle-aged men who make their livings off the appeal of singers half their age; they live very comfortably because of it, but there is still something wrong. So they were full of overly friendly good cheer as they greeted the band and made loud jokes. When the band lined up for promotional photographs, holding framed gold albums, Joe Smith and Mo Ostin pushed into the picture. "Let's all put our arms around each other," Smith said. "What are you trying to do, make us look like homosexuals?" said Alice Cooper.

After the picture-taking, the limousines took the band to the Continental Hyatt House on Sunset Strip. The girl from the plane was in the lobby. She had come straight from the funeral, and she was waiting for Mike Bruce. They walked into the elevator together.

An hour later, a middle-aged couple bustled through the hotel's revolving doors. They looked like any other middle-aged couple on vacation in California; maybe a little straighter than most. The woman looked at the wall behind the registration desk, where a clerk had pinned up a photograph of Alice Cooper in full makeup and costume. "Oh, look at that," the woman said. "They've got Vince's picture up."

Alice Cooper's parents. They called his room on a house phone, then walked to a couch to wait until he came downstairs. His mother was carrying an envelope that was inscribed, "Happy Birthday Vince."

"We still call him that," she said. "I don't know, I just can't call him Alice. Mothers are funny, I guess."

They were from Phoenix, Arizona. The father is a minister. Their last name is not Cooper, and many of their neighbors do not know that their son is a rock star.

"I understand why they do the things they do," the mother said. "There are so many groups today, you have to attract attention the best way you can. I keep hoping that when they feel they've really made it, they'll go back to more normal types of entertainment.

"I love to watch the show. Vince has explained it all to me. The whole dead-babies routine is a warning to parents that they should not abuse their children. That's why they hang Vince after he does it; to show that he should be punished. I'm just sorry it's my son who has to take the blame.

"Of course, sometimes it gets pretty frightening. The audience, especially. But we're proud. Mothers are like that. Sometimes I get scared for him, though. You don't realize how many crazy, weird people are running around these days."

Alice came off the elevator and hurried to his mother and father. "Twenty-four, Vince," his mother said. "You're twenty-four years old today."

Alice smiled "I know, Mom" he said, "I'm getting up there."

His father moved close to him. "What's that we read about kittens down south?" the father asked.

"Oh, that Atlanta thing," Alice said. "Nothing happened. It was just a rumor."

"We thought so, Vince," his mother said. "We know not to believe what we read about you."

Later that evening, after a performance more frenzied than most, the band was toweling off in the dressing room when the door opened and Alice's parents entered with another middle-aged couple.

Alice called to them: "Mom! Dad! Uncle Lefty! Aunt Sue!" Things got quiet for a moment. No one seemed to know what to say. Finally, speaking of the evening performance, Alice's mother said: "It was a goodie, Vince."

Alice's father shook his son's hand. Aunt Sue stayed in a corner, looking uncomfortable and unhappy.

Uncle Lefty just gazed at his nephew for a few moments. The makeup was still on, and the "Alice" sequins shone brightly on the chest of the leotard.

"I try, Vince," Uncle Lefty said. "I try to understand, Vince, I really do."

The jet was on its way to Sacramento. On board, the band was playing blackjack, killing time until their contract called for them to take the stage again and titillate more thousands of California children.

Of course, everyone on the plane was staring at them. That always happens. But one little girl was staring especially intently, like a bird watching a snake. She was about 15, blonde and scrubbed and even innocent looking. She knew who these people were; she had listened to the albums and heard the rumors about the shows, although she had never seen an Alice Cooper performance. But she had never thought she would see them this close, and she was fascinated. All the horrid things she had heard, and here she was on the plane with them, and they seemed fairly subdued and almost human.

The stewardess handed the little girl a can of soft drink. She began to drink from it, at the same time not letting her eyes move from Alice Cooper and Mike Bruce.

She brought the can to her mouth again, and just as she was swallowing the soda, Mike Bruce leaned over to her.

"I just read in the paper where that stuff causes cancer in rats," he said calmly.

The girl choked on the drink as Bruce turned around and Alice Cooper dealt him another card.

Advancing Billy

"Why, right at this moment we have anywhere from 20,000 to 40,000 women praying in front of their radios, all around Chicago," Charles Riggs said. "They're praying in clusters of six or eight each. This is the week. . . let me think. . .this is the week that we've got them praying for the choir."

Charles Riggs was figuring all this out while he doodled on a pad of paper in front of him. He was in a little conference room at McCormick Place talking to an official of the huge exhibition hall.

Charles Riggs is director of the national Billy Graham Crusade. What Graham is to the spiritual side of his crusades, Riggs is to the side that makes the whole thing work. This was two weeks before Graham's Chicago crusade began June 3.

"Look, it's simply a problem of organization," he said. "For this June crusade, we started in October. We go from nothing, and on the week before the crusade we have 50,000 or 60,000 people praying. It's a set routine; it doesn't vary much from crusade to crusade."

Riggs, who looks a little like a bulldog in a light blue blazer, came off the Texas oil fields in 1952 to join the Graham crusade. He became crusade director in 1964, and now spends his years traveling from site to site making sure that by the time a crusade begins, nothing has been left to chance.

"Think of it like this," Riggs said. He drew a little box on his pad of paper. "The box is a church, all right? Now here's a minister's committee." He drew a line into the box. "Here's a men's committee." Another line. "Here's a women's committee." Another line. "And here's a youth committee."

"Now that's four teasers into each church, and that's a lot," Riggs said. "You have that many teasers, and you find people are asking each other, 'Do we have a block of seats for the Graham crusade?' Or, 'Do we have buses lined up to take us to McCormick Place?' "

Riggs snapped his fingers. "You don't miss often when your organizing is done right," he said.

"In my day," Billy Graham explained to 32,000 people, "when the young people wanted to rebel, they would get up on a pole and sit for 30 days."

This was youth night at the Graham crusade, and the Reverend Dr. Graham already had quoted from Simon and Garfunkel and the Beatles. A black cord was trailing from his sport coat. It was attached to a microphone pinned to his shirt, and it enabled him to walk around the stage while he talked. From the side, it looked as if Billy Graham had a tail.

"When you come forward tonight, you are not coming to me," Graham said. "You are coming to Jesus Christ." Graham has a beautiful voice, and when he says the word "Jesus," it sounds as if it has seven syllables.

Graham stared at one of the television cameras that were on a raised platform in front of him. The cameramen did not look like regular cameramen; they were dressed as neatly as Graham and everyone else in the spotless audience.

Graham smiled at the camera and invited anyone in the viewing audience who would like to receive the same literature as the people who had come forward for Christ to write Billy Graham, Minneapolis, Minnesota, and they would be sent the material.

A girl who had come forward to offer her commitment to Jesus was sobbing uncontrollably, shaking and crying and gasping for air. It was hard to understand. This was not a mysterious, holy roller experience; Graham had explained in detail exactly what was going to happen when the people came forward, and none of it was traumatic. It was mostly just a matter of filling out forms and receiving pamphlets, much less disturbing than a visit to the dentist's office. But the girl was out of control anyway.

The cameras were drawing back to show the people coming forward toward Graham and Christ. Soon the video tape of the Chicago crusade would be shown all around the country, and millions more would hear Graham's message.

Over in a corner with his arms crossed was Charles Riggs, crusade director; counting the house, as it were.

But that was during crusade week itself, and you have heard and read as much as you need or want to about that. The real work of the crusade was done in the months before.

"Trouble?" Charles Riggs asked weeks before the crusade. "What kind of trouble? Oh, there are some things that could conceivably go wrong. But that's what we're here for, to make sure that they don't. For instance the sound could be bad. But we try to make sure that it doesn't happen, and we go over and over and over and over it. There are very, very few times that there's a foul-up, and that's usually in a foreign country."

Riggs is much like the political advance man whose job it is to precede a candidate to a city and make sure that his campaign stop there is a success. Only with Riggs it is religion, and he is working for the most successful evangelist in history.

"Billy Graham has no part in setting this thing up whatsoever," Riggs said. "He shows up the night before, and if we've done our job right, he can drive up to McCormick Place, walk out, and deliver his sermon. He shouldn't have to worry about a thing."

The man from McCormick Place was looking over a parking chart. He was saying that getting people up to the main exhibition hall would be no problem because all the escalators would be switched so they were running only from the ground level to the hall. But he was worried that parking would be a major problem because the exhibition hall would be able to accommodate only 16,000 cars, and there was seating for 38,000 people.

"We'll take care of it," Riggs said, making a note to himself. "A lot of the churches will be sitting in blocks, and we'll encourage them to rent buses. Also, we'll encourage people who don't come in buses to drive to their churches, park there, and come to the crusade six to a car."

Basically the ground work for the Graham crusade works like this:

All the land around Chicago is divided into 12 areas. Each area has a chairman, responsible to the main crusade office. The areas are divided into districts. Each district has a lieutenant, who is responsible to his area chairman. The districts are further broken down into neighborhood subdivisions, each with a crusade representative directly responsible to his district lieutenant.

All of these volunteer workers devote their time to making sure people come to the crusade. Churches are organized as Riggs described. Four weeks before the crusade, five-day-a-week Graham radio programs are aired, and neighborhood residents are urged to listen together and pray. Two Sundays before the crusade opens, volunteers go into 20,000 homes to spread the word.

The purpose is to fill as many of the 38,000 seats at McCormick Place as possible each night of the crusade. The machinery for making this work has proven itself over the years. But it is up to Graham's staff to keep it moving.

Jack Cousins, office manager for the Graham Chicago Crusade headquarters at 180 W. Washington, was hunched over a huge layout sheet of McCormick Place's main hall. He was trying to explain what happens when the people Come Forward for Christ.

"All right," he said, "it works something like this. When the people first answer Billy's call, they all walk up to the front of the hall. They're met there by people we call counselors. Many of the counselors are the same people who sing in the choir.

"Before the crusade we have a four-week session (in the city) to train the counselors. We tell them what to do, and after they've gone through the four weeks of training, they apply to be accepted as counselors. We have ministers there to make sure that we don't accept any duds." He picked up a little booklet. "This is the training book we use to show the counselors. . . . Oh, wait a minute, this is the wrong one." He lifted the phone and dialed another number in the office. "Winnie," he said, "can you get me some of the red and green brochures from the counseling classes? I have the Texas one here, but I don't seem to have any for Chicago.

"Anyway," he said, "when the people come forward, they first talk with the counselors. The counselors determine if the people really want to make that commitment.

"Then they go to the advisers to fill out a card. The advisers are mostly church people. If you want to talk about numbers, on a given night we have a couple of thousand counselors and four or five hundred advisers. The advisers help the people complete their cards.

"The adviser shoots the completed cards into what we call the co-labor corps. The co-labor corps is responsible for notifying churches in the people's neighborhoods that they have made a commitment to Christ. That's used for follow-up, which comes later. But while the people are still at the crusade, the counselors help them fill out a test booklet.

"When they've finished the booklet, they mail it in to our headquarters. Then we send them another booklet for them to study and fill out. When they've completed and mailed all four tests, then we send them a book from Billy.

"Meanwhile, we ask the counselors to call, write, or visit each person who has come forward within 48 hours after the crusade ends. If the counselor doesn't do this, or for some reason we don't hear from the person who has come forward, we ask a minister to follow up.

"If we don't hear from the person and we get no response from the minister, then we transfer the person's card to another church and try to get in touch with him that way. Billy's very concerned about this lack of following up. The local committee in Chicago has been after Billy for nine years to come back to Chicago; our crusade here is operating on a budget of a half million dollars, and that doesn't include television, so you can see that we are upset if people don't follow up on their commitments through their neighborhood churches.

"Then we have another program," Jack Cousins said, "designed to draw people to the crusade who are not associated with a church. It's called Operation Andrew. But that's a different story."

When a person goes forward for Christ, he is handed a little red booklet titled "Knowing Christ."

Inside is a card on which he must check one of three separate ways that he has come forward: "Acceptance of Christ as Savior and Lord," "Assurance of Salvation" or "Rededication."

That means, roughly, that a person is coming forward for the first time, that he is following up to confirm his present beliefs, or that he is reaffirming something he has done a number of times.

The card is printed on the kind of paper that automatically makes a carbon. The original copy is kept by the counselor; the carbon goes to the co-labor corps for follow-up work.

A Decision for Christ card with a space for the counselor to write his name, address, and phone number also is stapled in. The person coming forward is supposed to carry this with him.

Also stapled in are four Bible passages and a little green envelope to carry them in. The envelope instructs, "Carry these cards with you . . . review the verses daily . . . say the references before and after . . . memorize the books of the Bible on the memory cards." The envelope is titled "Promises from God."

Finally, a larger envelope is stapled in. It is pre-addressed to the Billy Graham Evangelistic Association Follow-up Department, Minneapolis. It instructs the person coming forward to "Return Lesson 1 in this envelope."

Edward J. Lee, general manager of McCormick Place, looked up from his desk. "There is only one word to use when you're describing these people from the crusade," he said. "That word is pro.

"They're complete professionals. We just co-operate with their staff. You might think that because it's the Graham crusade, people would give them a price break on a lot of services. But they insist on paying their way, first class all the way. And they're smart. Because if people are giving you something and you become dissatisfied, you just have to take what you get anyway. But when you're paying for excellent service, then you demand that everything be perfect. And if it's not, you yell. Which they do."

Charles Riggs was asking when the risers would be constructed, if the choir would be able to use them for rehearsal.

"It's not essential that we rehearse on the risers, but it'll help," he told the man from McCormick Place. "That's a sight to see. We bring 3,000 people in, and they've never sung together. And in two and a half hours, Barrows has them sounding great."

On the night before the Billy Graham Chicago Crusade was to begin, the men and women who would make up the crusade choir were filing into the gaping exhibition hall. A huge blue-and-white sign read, "Jesus said, 'I am the way, the truth, and the life.'" Union laborers smoked cigarets in front of it, hauling banks of lights into place.

You just do not see crowds this neat and formal anymore. Ties and dresses. All in orderly lines to get manila packets full of sheet music, but no one pushing or impatient, just waiting their turn.

The risers weren't ready, and the people would have to sing from seats in the audience. Charles Riggs surveyed the scene. "We want 3,000 tonight," he said to someone. "We'll tell them that we want all of them to show up every night of the crusade, and that way if we're lucky we'll get 2,000 a night in the choir."

With all the men on machines putting the stage together, it looked like a combination of an industrial shop and a church convention. A voice came through the amplifiers: "Good evening, choir, I'm glad to see you. This hall is so big, you may not be able to see me or where this voice is coming from, but you will soon enough, I'm sure."

The voice was that of Cliff Barrows, director of the Billy Graham Crusade Choir. In front of him the people were divided into areas marked "bass," "alto," "soprano," and "tenor." As Barrows called out each section, they cheered for themselves, just like at summer camp.

As the workmen sweated through their shirts, with the city visible through one set of windows of the steel-and-glass barn, Barrows called for quiet and prayed for mastery of the songs.

It looked like most of the men in the choir had just gone out that afternoon to get haircuts so they could look nice as they became part of this faceless group. "How many of you have had a hard day?" Barrows asked. Many hands shot up.

"Put 'em down, you've come to the right place!" Barrows said. "It's great to lift your voice in song!"

They went through the crusade songs, and one by one, the people clipped their red choir identification buttons to their lapels and pockets, a sign that they were part of the Billy Graham team.

Barrows pumped his arms and pointed to the different sections. "Take the fourth verse, please. It's a great tune!" he called.

At the end, Charles Riggs stood next to Barrows. "We need a good offering tonight to help the crusade," Riggs said. Only a few of the people looked startled that, after coming here and volunteering their time, they were being asked for money. "We've given you the music, $5 worth of music at least, and we've got buckets on the side of the aisles," Riggs said. "Before we bow our heads, let me tell you that you can make out a personal check to the Billy Graham Crusade. Make sure we get those buckets around. All right, now, let us bow our heads." And he offered a short prayer, concluding with "in Jesus' wonderful name we pray."

Forrest Layman, assistant crusade director, was wearing bell-bottoms and a cowboy belt, which seemed strange. He was in the Washington Street Graham headquarters, three days before the crusade was to begin.

"We have psychiatrists and psychologists on hand if there's a real problem," he said. "We've had suicidal cases. But we try to get them separated and taken care of so there's no real disturbance.

"Security? We have our own, mostly volunteers. Of course, Dr. Graham has had FBI agents assigned to him for personal protection for a while. Why? It was right after the death of Martin Luther King that it started. I guess it was President Johnson who started it. It just seemed to be the wise thing to do."

There were more than 30,000 people in the exhibition hall when one of the local crusade organizers stepped to the microphone.

"This is One Dollar More Night," the man said. "If you were going to offer $50, offer $51. If you were going to offer a hundred, offer a hundred and one."

The man then referred the audience to the programs. He noted that there was a blank check inside each program plus a simulated charge card that would be honored by a major credit card company if the people didn't happen to have the cash on hand.

"We are certain that each and every one of you will allow the Lord to use you in your giving," the man said.

Charles Riggs, standing by a television platform, looked bored. His job was over. Now it was Graham's show.

"You have come tonight to Jesus Christ," Billy Graham said. "I want to tell you that He forgives you, for that is why He died."

Censor

Clarkstown, New York, recently established a nine-member "obscenity committee" to pass judgment on whether pornographic films, books, and stage shows should be allowed. Chairman of the committee is Marty Snyder, age 60. Snyder has been totally blind for the past four years.

"I don't see why that should be such a big factor," Snyder told me by telephone Wednesday. "I feel I can do the job and make an intelligent judgment. Take the case of X-rated movies. There is a lot in a movie that is voice. My hearing is excellent. Haven't you ever been in a motel room and heard voices and sounds coming from the next room? Now don't tell me you don't know what's going on in that motel room next door. You can't see through the wall, but you know exactly what they're doing in there."

The Clarkstown obscenity committee was set up as a result of the recent Supreme Court decision that allows local communities to establish their own standards regarding pornography. Snyder said that in his opinion sexual frankness has been getting too blatant.

"When I was a kid growing up in Baltimore, we used to go down to the burlesque house," he said. "We knew what sex was—if we didn't, the country wouldn't have populated like it did. I remember those shows. There was always a bedroom scene. This gal would come out, and she would be wearing something flimsy. She would

get into the bed. Then Miles Murphy, the comedian, would come
out in red flannel long johns. He'd get in the bed, too. Then the gal
and him would cuddle up a little bit, and then the lights would go out
and the curtain would go down. Today, as I understand it, you
would be seeing complete nudity and sexual intercourse."

Snyder said that his committee also has been empowered to
determine which magazines are fit for the people of Clarkstown to
see. "We may make a decision on this new magazine, *Playgirl*," he
said. "I understand that's a pretty bad one, and people around here
might not want their kids to see it."

He is not swayed by the suggestion that perhaps a person
without the benefit of eyesight is not ideally suited to be passing
judgment on what movies, books, and magazines are fit for the
townspeople to view.

"Why shouldn't I have the job?" Snyder said. "Just because I
can't see? Let's suppose we're examining an X-rated movie. Someone could sit next to me and fill me in on what's going on. There's all
kinds of dialogue and movement sounds in an X-rated movie, and I
can draw conclusions on that basis."

Snyder has been active in Republican politics. During
Richard Nixon's 1972 campaign against George McGovern, Sny-
der would telephone local radio talk shows and, using the name
"Mr. Truth," defend the president against charges made by pro-
McGovern callers. In his current position as the obscenity commit-
tee chairman, he is a bit upset about one of the committee members.

"It's a woman who has just admitted that she is a member of the
American Civil Liberties Union, and that she opposes any form of
censorship," Snyder said. "I think that she is a plant; I think the
ACLU got her on the committee on purpose. Now how can she be an
effective committee member? She's already said that she's against
shutting down X-rated films. She has a closed mind on the subject.
How can our committee be aided by a member with a closed mind?"

A Paralyzer
in Every Pocket

Additional social notes from the age of love:

In every guest room of every Holiday Inn in the United States this month, there is a copy of the *Holiday Inn Magazine*. And in every copy of the magazine is an advertisement for a currently popular product that carries the brand name, "The Paralyzer."

The advertisement is aimed at potential distributors for the product. "Get rich quick," the ad urges. "The product is The Paralyzer. The demand is phenomenal. The market is gigantic. The profits are unbelievable."

"It is the hottest item in America today," the ad continues. "The Paralyzer is a pre-sold item, because of assaults, robberies, rapes, and riots. In fact, three of the very best salesmen you can find are continuously working for you: TV, radio, and newspapers. Not a day goes by that you don't see, hear or read about the tremendous increase in crime. *Everyone* in this country is a potential victim, and people live in fear of criminal attack, not only on the streets, but in their own homes as well."

The advertisement goes on to say that The Paralyzer is a pocket-size cartridge of CS tear gas, which can easily be carried around and sprayed at people. "It will instantly stop even a 300-pound man," the advertisement says. "You can start immediately to profit from it. Every adult is an easy sale."

On Wednesday I called John Boal, the vice-president of Defense Products Incorporated, the St. Louis-based firm that manufactures The Paralyzer. I asked him exactly what it is that The Paralyzer does.

"Oh, it's super-painful, all right," he said, in a warm, pleasant voice reminiscent of a kindly general store owner offering the latest in farm implements. "It will blind a person instantly. The eyelids will close involuntarily. Tears will pour profusely from the eyes. The skin will feel like hot acid is being poured on the face. It will feel as if someone is trying to remove the skin from the face with a dull razor."

Boal said that he has had the opportunity to use The Paralzyer himself on several occasions. "If you aim it at a person's face, and he inhales, he will get the feeling that he's being strangulated," Boal said. "He may even throw up. He may collapse to his knees."

Boal said he has such complete faith in his product that he carries a pocket Paralyzer with him "24 hours a day," and also keeps a larger model stored between the bucket seats of his automobile. He said Paralyzers are sold over the counter in stores, and that except in Massachusetts and New Jersey, buyers are not required to register or to meet a minimum age requirement. (In Illinois, any person can buy one; if he gets caught carrying it, it's a misdemeanor).

"We know that we have a couple of million of these being carried by citizens right now," he said. "The market looks unlimited. Our orders are increasing every month. We sell them to the better classes, as well as to people with lesser incomes. You don't need a Paralyzer just on the Southern Side of Chicago. Crime is everywhere. We sell Paralyzers in towns of 20,000, just as we do in cities of a million or two."

When I asked Boal if he were not concerned about the prospect of millions of people roaming the streets with Paralyzers in years to come, ready to zap one another with the painful gas at a moment's provocation, he seemed more that prepared to deal with the question.

"First of all, The Paralyzer is completely safe," he said. "All of those symptoms I told you about wear off after 15 minutes or so. But, just hypothetically, let's assume that somewhere, some day, there is a case of misuse of The Paralyzer. Isn't that one case of misuse a small price to pay for the hundreds of thousands of lives that The Paralyzer saves?"

Boal said each of the pocket-sized Paralyzers contains enough of the company's product to shoot at 53 separate persons, with each person feeling the full brunt of the blindness, the choking, the facial-skin-being-peeled-off effect, etc. "It is a very personal type of product," he said. "We like to think that everyone should have one."

The National Binge

The thunderstorm had come up with dark, sudden fury. It was late afternoon on the road, and I hurried toward the green neon of a Holiday Inn sign. When I arrived in the lobby of the motel, he was there: a young boy, stretched out on the carpeting, his eyes wide open, a blanket over his body. The desk clerk said that the boy had been out in the storm, and that he had been trying to run for shelter when a bolt of lightning cracked out of the sky and struck him down. He had been carried into the inn; he was alive, but ashen and trembling, and as he waited in the lobby for an ambulance to arrive, a crowd was beginning to gather. The people circled around the boy, and even though he was fully conscious, they began to speak as though he could not hear.

I stood and listened to them talk. Within minutes I felt as if I had walked into a horror movie. With only one or two exceptions, the people in the lobby voiced no concern for the boy in front of them, no sorrow at what had happened to him. Instead, the sentiment I heard expressed over and over, in almost the same language each time, was this: "I never saw anyone get hit by lightning before. I wish I would have been here to see it when it happened."

The guests of the motel were clearly miffed; a thrill had been denied them, an opportunity to jack up the titillation one more notch. It is that kind of time: an amphetamine age, an era of giddy excess, when we have all become so dulled to the concept of the quiet and the normal that there is nothing left to do but demand more, wait for the next, greater excitement—and don't look back. We are in the middle of a giant drunk, a monumental, dizzying speed trip, and nowhere is there the recognition that it cannot go on indefinitely. Nowhere is there the thought that like all manic binges, this one will end, and that when it does there will most certainly be a price to be paid, a psychic hangover to remind us of exactly what we have all been through.

Of course, the people were disappointed that they had not been able to watch the lightning reach down and touch the boy. Our expectations for a newer, stranger turn-on with each passing day have brought us to that point. The turmoil of the '60s was supposed to be the apex of that kind of thing, but instead of a placid respite from all that, the first years of the '70s have brought us only more of the same, and this time without the saving idealism. Now we can switch on the television and be entertained, live, by the sight of hundreds of policemen firing rifles at a burning house in Los Angeles, and our interest is heightened by the knowledge that there is human flesh inside those walls, and that the flesh is going to fry before this show goes off. We can read all the details of young boys being tortured and chopped apart in Texas, and before dinner we can watch their remains being pulled out of the ground.

The newsmagazines celebrate something called "bisexual chic," as if the erasure of all boundaries is just a natural progression in the sexual revolution. But this is different—this is a desperate reaching for one more forbidden thing to do casually, almost a taunting challenge to the realization that beyond this there is nowhere else to go. In Chicago, a "dirty talk parlor" has recently opened, operated by women who used to work in massage parlors when they were novel. This time around, the women are paid to whisper obscene words to the men who come in off the street; the women in the parlor report that most businessmen ask them to talk about sadism and masochism.

Hard drugs have come to the middle class, and cocaine has been the party drug for so long that it is now almost passé. Keep the pace moving, stay wrecked, and hurry on along the way. Even the old outlets for simulated intemperance have had to adjust: the televised wrestling matches used to draw viewers by showing phony blood, but that was before Palestinian guerrillas were on the other channel, and now some wrestling shows are letting the cameras zoom in and get close-ups of exhausted contestants vomiting in the middle of the ring. Because we have a chief executive who invited it and brought it on himself, politics, too, has found a place in the national frenzy. We are able to enjoy the powerful high of driving a president from his office, slowly hanging him with his own misdeeds; at times the blood lust becomes so pleasurable that we have to stop to remind ourselves that this is all really very noble, and that we are doing it only with the greatest sense of gravity and regret.

And as we lurch along in the throes of this national bender, as the threshold of what it takes to shake us gets prodded ever higher— things still seem to be falling apart out there. Nothing seems to be getting better. We reel and stagger and try to outrun the traumatic realities of life; perhaps, in the end, that is the reason for our frantic, veering drunk. Maybe that is what massive drunks have always been about: a way to give oneself the illusion of moving so fast and being so strong that everything real becomes a blur, a hazy half memory that will always be there, and that does not have to be dealt with right now, flashing by so quickly that it has to be put off until later, when the rush is over, and the new day begins.

If the new day never begins easily, if coming down is always wrenching and brutal—well, no one is exactly shouting for the wild ride to end just yet. Sometimes it even begins to seem like it is leveling off, but then we realize that it is just our perception: we are getting used to it. So crank it up some more, see how much more we can take, and don't talk about the price of the running until later. Right now it's getting dark again, and the urge is to order up anything that's available that promises to keep us ahead of the shadows for a little bit longer. Just put it on the tab.

Where Have All the Young Men Gone?

Ah, nostalgia. Lately my mind has been racing back to the glorious American past, to a simpler time, when men were men and a man did what he had to do and damned the consequences. When the frontier spirit of adventure was in the air, great danger mixed with breathless excitement at every turn and a fellow never knew if he'd live to see the next sunrise. I refer, of course, to the late 1960s.

This reverie has been going on for about two weeks now, and I can't seem to shake it. It began when a local television station showed *Easy Rider* as its Saturday night movie. This was the first time that *Easy Rider* has appeared on television, and the action and dialogue provided historical detail and accuracy of a sort seen previously only in Mathew Brady's famed photographs of the Civil War. Like a ghostly voice crackling hollowly across the ages, there was Peter Fonda saying, "It's not every man can live off the land, you know; do your own thing in your own time." And the thoughtful soliloquy of Dennis Hopper: "Mardi Gras, man, amazing, man, New Orleans, man, we gotta get to New Orleans, man." And Fonda again: "Wow, I think I'm gonna crash." And Hopper: "Hey, man, I was watchin' this object, man, and it went right across the sky, man—I mean yeah, man, I'm stoned, man, but I saw a satellite, man. Really, man, we gotta get to Mardi Gras, man."

Tears came to my eyes. And as days went by and I found myself caught in a time warp, I knew I would have to take dramatic measures. So I made a list of acquaintances I had known during the *Easy Rider* days and determined to hunt them down and see what had happened to them in the years since.

The first person I sought was Ellis Pines. Ellis was the first proponent of "Student Power" at my university, Northwestern. He led massive rallies on the campus; he organized marches on the university president's office; he radicalized and took over the student government. He screamed and shouted and brought SDS-style revolution to the school and was, indeed, our first revolutionary.

I found Ellis living in Chicago. "I went into the advertising business straight out of college," he said. "I have worked as a copywriter for a number of agencies, including Leo Burnett; Weber, Cohn & Riley; and Gardner, Stein & Frank. I have written for Rice Krispies, Kellogg's Corn Flakes, Commonwealth Edison, the National Dairy Council, Rejoice Shampoo, Poppin' Fresh Dough, and Sheraton Hotels, among others.

"At first I thought that my college radicalism might work against me. But the advertising people love it. They thought of it as an asset that they could use. They thought of me as something they could use as a link to the underground. At first they called me 'SDS' around the office, very fondly. I went back to school the other week to apply for an alumni library card, and the person in back of me in line said, 'Wow, there's a name out of the past.' "

Next I looked for John Froines. Froines, a defendant in the Chicago 7 trial, was characterized by the government as the "mad bomber" behind the 1968 Democratic convention protest, the wild-eyed chemist who, among other things, was accused of planning to blow up the Grant Park underground garage.

I found Froines in Vermont. His secretary put me right through to him. "I work for the state government," he said. "I am Vermont's director of occupational health. Most of my concerns are scientific and social. I'm responsible for the health of working people.

"I work with employers in such areas as exposure to toxic substances, noise, radiation, etc. I'm really not into other things too much. I have 14 people working for me, and this takes up almost all of my time. I hear from Tom Hayden and David Dellinger once in a while—Jerry and Abbie and I never were too close, and I don't hear from them."

Next on my list was Milton Gardner, a black activist famous on my campus. Gardner had somewhat of a fearsome reputation at school and was thought of as something of a black revolutionary bent on destroying society and rebuilding it from the ashes. He was involved in a number of hunger strikes, sit-ins, and building take-overs, and was the leading spokesman for the militant blacks on campus.

I contacted Milton in the offices of his LaSalle Street law firm. "I guess most of the people who were involved in activism are now in an institutional setting somewhere," he said. "I still talk to some of the university administrators. They're nice people. I learned a hell of a lot about how things work from them. I worked for the Urban League for a year after graduating from Columbia Law School— that was my year of public service. Now I'm in private practice. In college I suppose a lot of people thought I was a revolutionary of some kind. My public image was far different than my private self. Since law school, I ran for Congress unsuccessfully once, and I'd like to get back into electoral politics someday."

My final call was to a former acquaintance who shall go

unidentified. He was the most famous dope-dealer on my block and operated an awe-inspiring pharmacy out of the glove compartment of his car. He was always certain that his telephone was tapped, and he became physically ill at the sight of a police car. So far I have been unable to talk directly with him; he is a highly regarded $200,000-a-year heart surgeon affiliated with a prestigious New York hospital, and each time I call, I am told that he is in surgery and cannot be disturbed.

As for myself, this has been kind of a puzzling week. My first real contact with Chicago-style politics was at the 1968 Democratic convention, when I stood in the streets and watched in outrage as Mayor Daley's police beat and clubbed innocent demonstrators. There were scenes that week that I knew would stay with me forever. On Tuesday of this week, I stepped into a voting booth. There was this lever with the words "Richard J. Daley" beneath it, and I seem to have pulled the lever. Please don't ask me why. I can't think about it. All I know is that it was there and I pulled it and now it is done. This town makes you crazy. Power to the people.

EPILOGUE

I've been thinking about a way to end this, and I might as well do it with a column. In the introduction to this book I talked about the Johnny Deadline days, and how no one can be sure how long they're going to last.

Well, when they do end, I'm pretty sure that it will be for a combination of reasons that are talked about in this next story. The column was written just before I took a short leave of absence from the paper to do the research for a book called *Billion Dollar Baby*. I had every intention of coming back to the paper after the leave, of course, and I did. But some day . . . well, I think I'll let the column explain it for itself.

Getting Away— Even If It's Fun

A woman has just hung up on me. She called up, with the Doobie Brothers playing on the radio in the background, and she told me that I was responsible for the continuation of the Middle Eastern hostilities because I was "apathetic and irresponsible and without a conscience." I told her that I was sorry that I had disappointed her, and she said "You've done more than disappoint me," and that's when she slammed the receiver down. I am glad that I am going away tomorrow morning. These things have been happening more and more lately.

I am leaving town for a while, and the column will not appear for a month or two. This is the first time in the two and a half years that I have been writing this feature that I will be out of the paper for more than a couple of days in a row, and lately I have been giving some thought to the nature of this kind of work, and why it is so strange, and whether it is ever a good idea to get away from it for large chunks of time.

I think the answer is probably yes. Not that the job isn't fun; it's a kick, and it's exciting, and it's gratifying, and it's honestly the best way I can ever conceive of to make a living—and the one reason I'm sure that I'm not getting too cynical is that there is still not a week when I don't tell myself how implausibly lucky I am to be getting a paycheck for having this good a time.

But even with that, there are moments when you stop to consider the basic paradox: namely, a job that places you on the street with the express purpose of putting your experiences and thoughts and encounters on paper, in front of people who will be entertained or annoyed or bored or angered by the end product, has another inevitable side. And that side is that, before long, you begin to find that the line between the experiences you have, the people you meet as a person living in the world, and the experiences you have, the people you meet as a newspaperman turning out his expected number of columns, is rapidly disappearing.

Everything you do and see and hear is measured as a possible newspaper column; everything is examined for its public value. The idea that something be interesting, and at the same time private, does not occur. You begin to take for granted that it is quite easy for you to enter a person's life, scrape it for whatever you think is useful to you, and then display the scrapings in front of hundreds of thousands of strangers. Since you do this every day, you begin not to give much thought to the fact that most other people do not live this way—and, indeed, would choose not to live this way if they were given the opportunity.

Which is all fine, and it is something that a person who does this kind of work must accept and become comfortable with. Except that there are times when you wonder. Last week, a girl I had known several years ago came back to town. She came in to see me, and she told me that she had returned to Chicago because of a serious, unhappy situation in her family. As we talked, I found myself thinking what an affecting, dramatic column her story would make. As she told me her personal, private, tormenting secrets, I was already writing the story in my head. Now that's pretty sick.

Or the woman who just hung up the phone on me. She wasn't angry about anything I had written; rather, she thought I was being a coward because I had not taken a position on a certain matter in the news. She was quite seriously outraged because I had not expressed an opinion. And as she raised her voice to me, I thought to myself: yeah, you're right, I didn't express an opinion about that. I really didn't have an opinion on that particular slice of the particular story that you are concerned with. There are a lot of things that I just don't have an opinion about, and it is always a little odd to realize again that there are people out there who are offended by that.

So when you begin to think about things like this, when you begin to ponder questions like these, then maybe it's time to just get away from it for a little while, and live a different kind of life, if only for a month or two. That's what I'm doing; starting tomorrow, my temporary world is going to be made up of loud rock-and-roll music, and cities flashing by at the exact rate of one per day, and people who never look at a newspaper.

That world may not be perfect, either, but at least it will be different, which should be enough. And after it's over, I'll be back here, putting pieces of other people's lives in the newspaper again and tossing opinions around just like it was the most natural way on earth to make a living. Don't want to think about that right now, though. Time to get packed. See you.

About The Author

Bob Greene is a columnist for the *Chicago Sun-Times*. His daily reports and commentary are distributed to more than 110 other newspapers in the United States, Canada, Latin America, and Japan. He is the author of three previous books: *Billion Dollar Baby; Running: A Nixon-McGovern Campaign Journal;* and *We Didn't Have None of Them Fat Funky Angels on the Wall of Heartbreak Hotel, and Other Reports from America.* His articles have appeared in *Newsweek, Harper's, Rolling Stone, Sport, New Times,* and the *New York Times,* and his commentary has been featured on the CBS television and radio networks. He is 28 years old.